Praise for

Judith Frank

and

All I Love and Know

"In this wonderfully rich, absorbing novel, Frank sheds light on gender and identity, the anguished politics of the Middle East, the limits of love and one family's struggle to stay intact." —*People*

"The considerable power of Judith Frank's second novel, *All I Love and Know,* comes from two sources not always found in combination: first, the seriousness of the social issues it takes on, and second, its psychological, nearly Jamesian style. . . . Like upmarket Jodi Picoult. . . . Judith Frank even writes her gay characters beautifully—she even writes gay male sex well. . . . From the darkest moments to the lightest, Frank's empathy for her characters transforms front-page news into literary fiction." —*Newsday*

"This beautiful novel is old-fashioned in its approach, taking its sweet time to tell a tender love story between two flawed, good-hearted people, and yet it feels wholly fresh. . . . This is a compassionate, utterly compelling story of how family members, torn apart by tragedy, must reach deep within themselves to meet their greatest challenge." —*Booklist* (starred review)

"*All I Love and Know* is a tender novel that deals with the emotional riptides left by an act of terrorism long after the headlines have faded. It is a brave, moving, and deeply compelling book, written with grace, about the ways even love and family devotion are challenged when the worst occurs. It makes for hugely rewarding reading." —Scott Turow, author of *Identical*

"[A] timeless story . . . beautiful, expansive, and deeply humanistic . . . Frank is a perfect storyteller, creating vivid landscapes and characters and events. . . . We have little choice in how we, or those whom we love, die. But when it comes to life, we can choose. Judith Frank shows us how."
—Huffington Post

"Deeply moving . . . Frank shows profound empathy for her characters, making this book heartbreaking, yet jubilantly hopeful."
—*Publishers Weekly*

"I loved it! Read it non-stop. These people catch you by the heart so powerfully you can hardly believe it is a novel. I've already had to loan it to a friend."   —Dorothy Allison, author of *Bastard Out of Carolina*

"A young couple must deal with both grief and transformation when one of them becomes the guardian of an orphaned infant and a 6-year-old. The fact that the new parents of this instant family are two gay men is a secondary element of this emotional saga and that is part of the brilliance of Judith Frank's *All I Love and Know*. . . . Frank delves into politics, both on the Israeli/Palestinian conflict and on gay rights. The first is handled with a deft hand, the second, with almost a sleight of hand, making the impact of this novel, which is ultimately about the resilience of love, all the more powerful."   —*Boston Globe*

"What a refreshing, impressive novel. That Judith Frank has managed to weave a story about queer partnership and parenting together with an exploration of the moral complexities of the Israeli/Palestinian conflict is rather stunning. This tender, intricate domestic drama both engages and informs what is arguably one of the critical issues of our time. It feels quite revolutionary, not just in the political sense, but in terms of the kind of stories we value."
—Alison Bechdel, author of *Fun Home*

"It seems quite possible the men's relationship will not survive these stresses, which Frank explores in depth and without reassuring sentimentality. . . . [It's] moving to watch them work through to reconciliation. [This is] strong storytelling driven by emotionally complex characters: first-rate commercial fiction."

—*Kirkus Reviews* (starred review)

"This is a big American story, a tapping into the zeitgeist that few other novelists have really traveled—taking the life of gay American couples beyond the struggle for marriage equality and giving a look at the usual challenges of any relationship."   —Bookreporter.com

"A powerful novel about love, loss and the will to endure after inconceivable tragedy."   —*BookPage*

"Frank's deftly balanced tale of grief and redemption simultaneously asks how the American-Jewish left might negotiate religion and identity in the face of Israeli violence toward Palestinians, and how gay parents might raise children in a country still suspicious of them. Frank wraps these big themes around an intimate, fraught family setting; after the funeral in Israel, Daniel and Matthew return to their New England home, a 6-year-old and a baby in tow, and they're forever changed. After reading this book, one of the best of the season, you may be, too."   —*Out* magazine

"Brilliant, thoughtful, [and] unexpectedly funny."

—*Lambda Literary Review*

"The relationship between Daniel and Matt is central to this moving story, which is told with a deep sensitivity. I am not gay, but I never doubted the love between these two young men, or the love and concern that everyone feels for the bereaved children. . . . This is a wonderful book."   —Bookloons.com

"It's so good you won't want it to end. Frank writes with insight and authority. . . . It's both an engaging read and utterly believable. Even minor characters are fully drawn and compelling. With plenty of plot twists and characters you can root for, it is, at its heart, a good old-fashioned page-turner."
—*Jewish Daily Forward*

"An excellent and gripping read." —*Western Massachusetts Jewish Ledger*

"A thoughtful look at how grief isolates survivors and how families may, or may not, come together in crisis." —*Library Journal*

"Judith Frank does a masterful job of letting readers feel what the protagonists feel. . . . It all rings true, from the deeply psychological personal struggles and the ways children mourn, to the question of how to feel and respond to the terrorist act. This issue-packed novel repeatedly moved me." —*Psychology Today*

"Between tackling issues like same-sex marriage, the rights of Palestinians versus those of Israelis and frank depictions of sex between two men, *All I Love and Know* is sure to provide plenty of fodder for book groups." —*Jewish Exponent*

"The best novel I've read in eons. . . . Judith Frank is an exciting new author and *All I Love and Know* is to be treasured."
—David Rothenberg, WBAI

"This is such a riveting book—so vast in its emotional scope, but also very straightforward in its storytelling. . . . It's timely, but it's timeless too . . . in the emotional resonance." —Bill Goldstein, NBC New York

ALL I LOVE AND KNOW

ALL I LOVE AND KNOW

Judith Frank

wm

WILLIAM MORROW
An Imprint of HarperCollins*Publishers*

For my brother and sister,
Tony Frank and Paula Frank-David

And for my mother, Marjorie Frank, 1935–2014
Zichrona l'vracha

But these three cubic feet of bone and
blood and meat are all I love and know.

Loudon Wainwright III, "One Man Guy"

ALL I LOVE AND KNOW

I

CHAPTER 1

H E HAD THOUGHT that watching a movie would agreeably distract him, but the images unspooling on the tiny screen and the tinny sound coming through the headphones were an irritant, like an inexpert touch between a tickle and a scratch. Matt sat back in his seat and took off his headphones, crammed a pillow behind his head and shoulders, closed his eyes. The events of the past day came streaking toward him, and he opened his eyes again quickly. He stole a glance at his partner, Daniel. But there too he had to look away, the sight was so shocking. Daniel's head hung, his chin touching his chest; Matt had called the doctor and gotten some Ativan, and Daniel was far gone on it. His lips were slack, his eyes cratered and bruised. In a single day his dark hair and beard stubble had become streaked with gray, something Matt had always thought was a horror story cliché. Daniel was all of thirty-eight and looked ancient and decrepit, Matt thought, and was immediately ashamed of himself.

Matthew Greene was six years younger than his partner, tall and thin, with a head of thick brown hair that lightened in the summer sun. He had a handsome angular face, and a grin that placed a perfect demonic dimple in his cheek, so that his smile looked more wicked than he intended. Now his eyes were grainy with exhaustion. They were a few hours into their flight to Tel Aviv, and meal carts were starting to be rolled down the aisle, bringing with them the smell of cooked meat. The Ativan was in Daniel's bag in the overhead, and he contemplated getting up and fishing it out. He hadn't till now, because somebody had needed to be on the ball, but now he felt wasted, his mind humming and strung out.

Was it only yesterday that the call had come from Daniel's father? Time seemed bundled and knotted, and when he tried to calculate the hours backward, they evaporated before his eyes. When the call came, he had been sitting at the computer in his study, watching a chickadee make restless, shivery passes at the bird feeder in the bare backyard. After he ended the call, he put the phone back into its charger very carefully. He stood and looked around, then sat down on the floor. The room was thunderously quiet, and he was bewildered to be alone with this information. He wondered, When did an event like this actually *take*? If he sat there very quietly, could he prevent it from coursing out into the wider world, where it would happen to other people instead of just to him and Daniel's father? The dog ambled up and he clutched its big head, trembling, thinking that every moment that passed without his breaking the news to Daniel would remain a happy moment from Daniel's old life.

Twenty minutes passed. He was conscious of his bare feet getting cold, of the dog's sigh, and of the study darkening as clouds passed over the weak March sun. Finally, the image of Daniel working tranquilly in his office, innocent of the knowledge that his world was about to be destroyed, became even more unbearable than the idea of telling him, and he stood. He went into the bedroom and put on a sweatshirt, found his coat and keys, and went out to the car. As he drove, he let his mind deliberate but forbade his heart to register, practicing fiercely how to say it, how to build up to it gradually without torturing Daniel with suspense. He had made Daniel's father promise not to call him at work, to let Matt break the news himself; he was glad he could be the one to tell Daniel but agonized over it too, wondering if Daniel would ever forgive him for being the one to tell him his twin brother, Joel, had died.

He pushed back to recline his plane seat. He remembered getting to Public Affairs and going into the office of the director, Daniel's boss, April, so Daniel could make a quick exit without having to excuse himself. Matt stood before her and made his first attempt at saying the words out loud: *Daniel's brother and sister-in-law were killed in a café bombing in Jerusalem.* April cried out and clutched her heart; he had never uttered words before that had so much sheer physical power. They gave him an embarrassing sense of self-importance, as though he were bragging, or exaggerating, and his body was spastic with apology, even though he knew, as she was telling him, that there was no need.

It was weird, he mused. As a kid, he'd dreamed of being famous, as an artist or an actor. Those dreams had subsided as he'd gotten older. But here all that dream-energy had come rushing back, like a floodlight dazzling him. His mind buzzed unpleasantly around those feelings, knowing that he wasn't really culpable for whatever weird feelings came to him in crisis, but also wondering if they said something definitive about his personality. He stood, took down Daniel's bag from the overhead compartment, found the pill bottle he'd been looking for, and shoved the bag back in. He sat down with a thud and a sigh, and put one of the tiny pills on his tongue.

By the time he'd opened the door to Daniel's office, he'd hardly been able to breathe. Daniel had been sitting at his desk with a manuscript in front of him, scratching his head with a big pensive scowl, and at the sight of Matt his face had broken into a smile whose sweetness Matt was certain he would never recover from. He'd breathed "Dan," and "Honey," and burst into tears. Daniel had rushed around the desk, banging his leg and swearing, and Matt choked out the words as they clutched each other, his head over Daniel's shoulder and his eyes squeezed shut because he couldn't bear to see. He felt Daniel slip through his arms to the floor. Kneeling beside him, his fingers twined through Daniel's dark hair, his throat seizing, Matt had raged against the hard fate of this man who so didn't deserve it, and wondered whether

Daniel's face would ever light up again at the sight of him. Certainly it hadn't since.

He remembered the minutes passing, and he remembered growing drowsy, and his mind beginning to drift. He'd listened to the sounds of office life outside the door, made out a phone conversation between one of the secretaries and what seemed to be her daughter complaining about her husband. They spent so much of that day down on the floor— not only because it was hard to stand, it seemed to him, but also because they were trying to cringe low to the ground to make themselves as inconspicuous as possible, like terrified animals. Finally, Daniel lifted his head and whispered, "Take me home." He let Matt help him to his feet. "Easy, baby," Matt murmured as Daniel stood unsteadily, looking at him with wide, shocked eyes.

After he'd gotten Daniel home, he'd been on the phone nonstop. First with Daniel's father, who was channeling all of his horror into obsessing over whether they should fly El Al or Continental. And then with Continental, trying to get a bereavement rate for a next-day flight. Trying to figure out, without bothering Daniel about it, how they'd get a death certificate in Israel. Finding the passports and ascertaining with relief that they hadn't expired. Logging onto Weather.com to see what the weather would be like in Jerusalem this time of year, and, seeing that it fluctuated wildly, overpacking. Calling their friend Cam to take the dog. Interrupting that conversation when a call came in on call-waiting from the president of the college, offering his condolences and his services. Matt thanked him repeatedly, burdened by his windy solicitude; Cam was crying on the other line and he wanted to get back to her.

All the while, Daniel had been lying on the bed, shaking, his knees drawn up and his arms thrown over his head; his jacket and tie and shoes were strewn on the bedroom floor, and he ran periodically to the bathroom to vomit. Matt kept approaching the edge of the bed, and then, overwhelmed by a sense of his own irrelevance, turning away. He picked up Daniel's jacket from the floor, brushed it off, and hung it in the closet. Finally, he lay down carefully beside Daniel, enveloping him with his arms and drawing the stockinged soles of his feet up his calves, trying to still his shaking with his own bigness, his warm body. Daniel's shirt was cold and damp from sweat, and his teeth were chattering. "Honey, you're chilled," Matt had murmured, "let me get you into the shower." But Daniel had let out a moan and blindly thrown an elbow that struck Matt in the cheek, and Matt had stumbled off the bed and ran out of the room. In his study, he stared out the window at the yard, which was blurred and somber in the fading light, and fought back tears of fury. He touched his smarting cheek, which hurt all the way to his teeth, and told himself not to be such a big pussy. There was a pack of Camel Lights stuffed in a drawer; he took one out and lit it, blowing smoke forcefully out the open window. He knew he was being stupid and childish. And yet, fury coursed through him, and on its heels, a terrifying intimation of the suffering to come.

MATT REACHED FOR THE in-flight magazine, flipped through it looking for the crossword and saw that someone had already done it. He studied the map of Continental's flights, and then the floor plans of various European airports, and then he read an article on how to respect and handle the customs of foreign businessmen. He hoped Daniel's father, up in business class, saw it, because he knew he'd like it. He was a corporate executive, and from the time they were teenagers, Daniel and Joel had bought him, as birthday and Father's Day and Chanukah presents, books on how to be effective, how to motivate others, how to think outside the box. Sam's total immersion in the corporate mind-set was something Matt found both alienating and adorable, and he related to Sam like a fascinated anthropologist, getting him to talk about company retreats where they did relay races based on army training exercises, or used their teamwork to build a jet engine out of matches and cardboard and nail polish. It was Rosen family lore that Sam once read a book about how to utilize humor to defuse difficult interpersonal relations. When his wife, Lydia, saw it, she'd smacked her forehead with her palm. She called him the only Jew in America without a sense of humor.

Matt stuffed the magazine back into the seat pocket and opened his tray table. Around him were the shuffle of newspapers, the drone of the engines, the metallic sound coming through people's earphones, the murmur of *beef or chicken?* Across the aisle from them, in the three middle seats, sat a religious family with a fat baby and a toddler in a frilly dress who was peeling stickers off a sheet and laying them carefully on her armrest. Exploded all over their seats and the floor were wet crumbs in smashed Baggies, crayons, plastic pieces from games, empty yogurt containers, Goldfish crackers. The mother was kerchiefed and red-cheeked, joggling the baby with an expression of hassled professionalism, and the father pale, with blond ringlets down the sides of his face, reading a small prayer book. There was something a little hot about the guy's detachment, his look of being above it all.

Matt needed to pee, but he'd waited too long; the food cart was blocking the aisle behind him. He wondered what Daniel's parents were eating up in business class—probably not something called "beef" or "chicken." They were probably drinking heavily, too. The four of them had found one another in the security line in Newark, where Daniel's parents, looking like ghosts in expensive travel coats, had pulled Daniel toward them with a cry and clung to him while Matt dragged their bags and gently herded the huddled group forward, ignoring the curious glances of other passengers. He was sweating and winded by the time they settled in at the gate. It pained him to see how shock had blunted the normally ingenuous features of Daniel's father; Matt could see the tiny webs of capillaries around his nose, and when Sam put his and Lydia's passports and boarding passes into the inside pocket of his jacket, his hands shook. Lydia had sat huddled in the crook of Daniel's arm, from time to time grasping his sleeve and whimpering, "Those poor babies," and "Why didn't God take me instead?" Her dramatic dark eyes were bloodshot, her face dusted over with recently reapplied face powder. Matt felt terrible for her, but her behavior made him think that she had seen one too many Anna Magnani movies. Since when did she even believe in God? He had gladly gone off to perform helpful tasks, buying a neck pillow and some Tylenol for her, and two new luggage tags for his and Daniel's bags, and *Time* and *Entertainment Weekly* for himself.

Now, as a tray was set in front of him, he had the sudden thought: Maybe Lydia's response was a Jewish form of expression? Maybe the Jews were one of those howling or keening peoples, their mourning a residue of the customs of their often-bereaved peasant ancestors? Matt's fingers grew still over the silverware packet he was trying to open. He was destined to be ashamed of himself, he was learning; since yesterday's call, there was virtually no thought that came without recoil. So, believing it was always better to face his demons, he made a mental list of all the thoughts he was ashamed of:

1. Was grief going to make Daniel look old and shriveled?
2. And if so, would they ever have halfway decent sex again?
3. He clearly wasn't going to make the Rufus Wainwright concert on the twenty-sixth: Could he just let that go?
4. Would his, Matt's, needs and aspirations ever be considered important again?
5. Would he ever get to just be a normal, young, shallow queen again, or would tragedy dog him for the rest of his born days?

But Matt knew these questions were bullshit, that he was evading the real issue: If Joel and Ilana had really done what they said they were going to do, he and Daniel would be returning home with their kids, and the life he knew would open up into dark seas he couldn't even begin to chart.

· · · · ·

THREE MORNINGS AGO, MATT had awakened singing Gershwin:

> *They laughed at me wanting you—*
> *Said it would be Hello! Goodbye!*
> *But oh, you came through—*
> *Now they're eating humble pie.*

He lay smiling next to Daniel in bed, with his hands folded behind his head, singing to the ceiling in a husky morning voice. It was their fourth anniversary; four years before, Matt had come up to Northampton to visit the shy Jewish cutie he'd met at a party in New York. He knew Daniel had never imagined being with him for so long; he'd thought of Matt as an amazing sexual windfall, and continued insisting that it was just an affair even after Matt moved permanently to Northampton, even after Daniel's friends began to tease him that his "affair" had begun wearing Birkenstocks with socks, a virtual guarantee that he'd never be allowed back in the city. Daniel just couldn't believe—and sometimes Matt couldn't believe it himself—that a young gay man would choose to leave New York to live in Northampton, which the *Enquirer* had once called, in an effort to shock, Lesbianville, USA.

That morning he turned to Daniel, stuffing a pillow under his neck. "Remember how you thought I was just some shallow hottie, but then you couldn't help falling in love with me?" he asked.

The memory of that morning made Matt clench his teeth, and as he picked at meat in gravy with peas and carrots, his partner still unconscious beside him, his mind cautiously turned over the question of what the terrain was like in Daniel's head. Like a tornado, he imagined, whipping trees up from their roots and slamming them into cars. He remembered an educational segment he'd recently seen on the Weather Channel, where the quiz question was: *During a tornado, where is the safest place in a mobile home?* After a commercial break they returned with the answer: *NOWHERE; leave immediately.* It had shocked him, the cruelty of the trick question; wasn't it bad enough that these people had to live in mobile homes? They were advised to go outside and find a regular house—*some wealthier person's decent home*, he had acidly glossed to Daniel—and failing that, to find a ditch to lie in. He had been indignant. "'Yeah, you pathetic trailer trash, go lie in a ditch!'—that's basically what they're saying, isn't it?"

He set aside his roll and piece of chocolate cake for Daniel, hoping he'd be able to choke down food that was mild and sweet. He looked at Daniel's sagging head. *NOWHERE*, he thought, *that's where it's safe to be.* Leave immediately, go lie in a ditch.

AFTER DINNER AND A long wait in the bathroom line, Matt read the movie and TV reviews in *Entertainment Weekly* and drifted off with the magazine in his hands. He was awakened by murmuring voices and the jingle of a bracelet. Lydia was standing over them, bringing in the sweet musky smell of her perfume, which Matt always smelled on his ears and collars for a few days after they spent time with her. He looked at Daniel and saw that he'd awakened too, and had a cup of ginger ale on his tray table. He pressed his hand, which lay on the seat between them, against Daniel's knee, in a discreet hello.

"Darling," Lydia was saying to Daniel, with a hollow trace of her old intensity, "for the shiva, I think we should pick up some *bourekas* at that little bakery on Joel's street."

Daniel laid his head back. "Okay, Mom," he said. His voice was hoarse, and he brought his fist to his mouth and cleared his throat. His shirt was open at the neck, the curls in the back of his head flattened.

"It's just that Ilana's parents are utterly useless in this regard."

"Okay," Daniel said. His gray face shifted into something like its usual life as an idea came over it. "Actually, I think the visitors bring the food—the mourners aren't supposed to have to cook. And are we even sure the shiva's going to be at Joel and Ilana's? Maybe the Grossmans will want to have it."

Lydia blinked. "That's out of the question."

"Why?" Daniel asked. "Wouldn't it be better for the kids to have a place to come home to where there aren't a million people sitting around?" Gal and Noam were with their *sabba* and *savta*, Ilana's parents, now, but the plan was to bring them to their own house when their uncles and other grandparents arrived.

Matt could see the struggle break out on Lydia's face, and the stubbornness. "Don't you think the people who loved Joel and Ilana will want to gather one more time at their home?"

Daniel shrugged, and Lydia's eyes welled up. "And don't you think I'm thinking about those children?" she hissed. "I think of nothing else!"

"What are *bourekas*?" Matt asked.

Lydia looked down at him incredulously, and Matt was sorry for the silly question. In front of Lydia, he was a chronic blurter, and he knew that she didn't like him very much. Apparently she'd loved Daniel's first boyfriend, Jonathan. Matt—much younger than Daniel, eye candy, a goy, a lover of television rather than art or opera—was clearly the inferior and less appropriate partner.

"They're small triangular pastries in filo dough," she said.

"Oh."

"They're savory, not sweet. They're filled with cheese or spinach. They're a very popular finger food in Israel."

"I see," Matt said.

"Mom," Daniel said, "why don't we wait till we get there, and maybe this shiva thing will just work itself out." He closed his eyes.

Lydia nodded, drew herself up, and said to Matt with a strange pride, "The place down the street from Joel's house has some of the best *bourekas* in the city."

When she headed back to the front of the airplane, Matt said, "Well, *that* was a surreal little exchange."

Daniel's eyes were still closed. "She's trying not to have to imagine how much of her son's body has been blown to bits."

Matt bit his lip, scalded.

Daniel opened his eyes and looked at him with a weak appeal, laid a hand on top of his. "Forgive me if I'm an asshole, okay?"

"Okay," Matt whispered, squeezing Daniel's cold fingers, unspeakably grateful for the gaze that seemed to recognize him for the first time since the news had come.

"Do we have a piece of paper and a pen?"

"Sure, baby."

Matt fished them out of his travel bag, and Daniel sighed, then bent over the paper and began writing in Hebrew. Matt looked at the round strong veins on Daniel's working hand, which passed rapidly from right to left. "What are you writing?" he asked.

"A eulogy for my brother."

Daniel covered the page and then stopped and gave Matt a stricken look. He set the pen down, took off his glasses, and started to cry. Matt gripped his hand. He had never seen Daniel cry until last night, and he was a little scared he'd cry like that now, in public. He'd seen him well up once or twice, and that was shattering enough to witness. But not really crying, and certainly not crying like that, writhing, screaming his brother's name, his teeth bared and his face sealed off and unseeing so that he seemed like one of those creatures, like otters or monkeys, whose faces lie on the disconcerting boundary between human and animal. Now Daniel was quiet, tears streaming down his face. *Oh,* Matt's heart clamored, *what should I do?* How could he be a comfort to this man who had been such a comfort to him? And those kids! Noam was only a baby! He wasn't up to it, he knew it. He would blow it again, the way he had with Jay, with all of the bad-mouthing and posturing, and his boycotting the memorial service, and the crushing fear that he had failed to be there for his best friend in the right way.

Oh poor poor Joel, Matt thought, and Ilana's face too flashed into his mind, big and raucous, and her sloppy ponytail, and tears rushed, hot and brutal, into his eyes.

·   ·   ·   ·

SEVEN HOURS LATER THEY stood at the airport curb, huddled around a small, curly-haired woman—Yemenite, Daniel would later tell him—holding a walkie-talkie and wearing a neon-green vest marked with bold Hebrew lettering. Her name was Shoshi, and she was the social worker sent by the city of Jerusalem. The Middle Eastern morning sun was bright and penetrating, and they had taken off coats and jackets and put on sunglasses. Around them, cars jostled and honked, and trunks slammed shut. Taxi drivers in open-necked shirts and Ray-Bans jingled keys in their hands as they approached exiting travelers. While Shoshi and Daniel spoke in Hebrew, nodding rapidly, Matt bent over and pulled down his right sock, his heart still thrumming with excitement and indignation at the lunatics in baggage claim. People had bumped into him and shouldered in front of him, and an elderly man on a fanatical push to the conveyor belt had jammed his luggage cart into Matt's heel, knocking his shoe clear off. Matt had wrestled it back on, surprised by the rage surging up his throat, and the rude old prick hadn't even apologized. Now Matt gripped the handle of his own cart with renewed, glowering concentration. He heard a lot of English spoken in American accents with strange glottal emphases. Their language sounded self-important and bullying to him, as though they were talking to children or foreign servants, and thinking that many of them were probably settlers, he felt a strong antipathy for them. Daniel loathed them. Each time they saw one of them interviewed on television, he would shout, "What's the matter, the U.S. isn't fundamentalist enough for you?!"

Matt's heel was chafed, but not bleeding, and he pulled up his sock and straightened. The sun was warming him to the bone, and there was the smell of something sharp in the air, like citrus or guava, mixed with exhaust fumes. This country seemed to him to be a different earthly element than his own, and he found that both exciting and a little frightening. He wasn't well traveled; his only trip outside the U.S. had been to Amsterdam with Jay years ago, right out of college. Here, under a cloudless sky, people were smoking and gesticulating; everyone had a cell phone attached to his or her ear, even the children. Although Matt was shocked by the open display of assault rifles, and officially disapproved of the soldiers in uniform, he found them beautiful. They were short and brown-skinned and very young.

He began to notice that passersby were casting curious and compassionate glances at Daniel's family. He stepped closer to Daniel, laying his hand on the small of his back, and bowed his head into the conversation. The social worker had switched to English, and was telling Daniel's parents that a van would arrive shortly to take them to the morgue. She touched their elbows as she spoke. She projected an aura of gentle authority, and looked into their faces in a way that was somehow both searching and undemanding. Matt had a powerful impulse to sidle up and confide in her. *I'm the gay boyfriend! I'm the goyfriend! I'm in a foreign country where I don't speak the language!*

At that moment Sam frowned and pointed into the distance, where a small group of photographers were snapping pictures of them with zoom lenses. "What are they doing?" Shoshi's face darkened and she took off toward them with her arms outstretched; when she got near them, she wagged her finger in their faces, barking commands. They gave her a short argument, and then walked away, one of them turning to utter a final deprecation.

The family had instinctively turned their faces away, and when Shoshi returned, panting and apologizing, they moved their bodies to gather her within the pack. A white van pulled up to the curb, and a driver wearing a yarmulke got out and put their luggage in the back as they climbed inside, Daniel helping Lydia into the front seat. Daniel sat with the social worker in the middle seat, leaving Matt and Sam in the back. They settled into the air-conditioning, wound up by the unexpected fracas with them at its center.

"What was that all about?" Sam asked.

"Joel was a minor celebrity," Daniel reminded them; he'd been the host of an English-language television interview show.

There was a pause. "How did they know we were . . . ?" Sam trailed off as Shoshi pointed to Daniel's face. "And my emergency gear," she added.

As the van pulled through the guard stations at the airport exit, Shoshi twisted to sit sideways and told them that the ride to Abu Kabir would take about twenty minutes. Her English was proficient but heavily accented, and from time to time she hesitated and said a word in Hebrew to Daniel, who translated it for his family. She told them that Ilana, Joel's wife, had been identified by her parents, but the other body had been held so that, if it was Joel, he could be identified by his immediate family. She pronounced Joel "Yo-*el*," its Hebrew version.

"*If* it is Joel?" Lydia asked sharply.

"If it is," Shoshi said, giving her a steady look.

"Why do you say *if*?" Lydia's voice was rising.

"Mom," Daniel murmured.

"We cannot say for sure until he is identified."

"Are mistakes ever made?" Lydia insisted. She had twisted around in her seat, and was trying to pin Shoshi to the wall with a single flashing look.

Shoshi was quiet.

"My wife is asking you a question," Sam said sharply from the back. Matt started. He had never heard Sam talk like that; his authority was normally genial. Watching Shoshi's sad and patient look, Matt surmised that they did in fact know it was Joel, but that she wasn't allowed to say so until his body was officially identified.

Finally, Shoshi said, "It is very rare."

Lydia's mouth quivered, and she turned stonily toward the front. Matt looked out the window at long fields, a flat and hazy stretch to the horizon, where he imagined the ocean to be. Irrigation pipes sent up a fine glinting spray. Until that moment, as they'd moved busily through passport control and baggage claim and customs, there had been a faint sense of reprieve. There was the unreality of being in a foreign country, the disorientation of a different time zone. And then the weird and unexpected excitement of being the targets of paparazzi. But now, a crushing silence fell over them. Sam exhaled next to Matt, giving off a smell of alcohol, morning breath, dry cleaning.

No one spoke until the van pulled off the highway onto a smaller road and Shoshi turned again. They were there; a sludge of anxiety seeped through Matt and turned him cold. "I want to tell you a little bit about what will happen inside," Shoshi said. "You will be brought into a room where police will ask you questions about Joel's body. I will come with you." She paused, trying, Matt imagined, to give them time to comprehend these barbaric sentences. "They will ask you questions about his body from his toes to the tips of his hair. Then you will be brought into another room to wait. And finally, you will be taken to what is called the separation room, to identify the body there."

The van stopped, and an electric gate was opened. Matt read the English part of the sign, *Institute of Forensic Medicine*, saw photographers bunched outside the gate, getting shots of the van with zoom lenses. They pulled in and parked in a small lot beside another van, and the driver turned off the engine, leaving them sitting there in silence. "I can't move," Lydia whispered. Matt knew the feeling; his legs were numb, and it felt as though the force of energy required to lurch into movement would require a strength way beyond him. It was Daniel who pressed down the latch on the door; it slid open with a roar. "Let's get this over with," he said.

THERE WAS A BRICK path leading to an unobtrusive entrance. There was a hall with white chairs. Around them, people babbled and wailed. The smell was awful—a combination of what? Formaldehyde, for sure, and burnt hair, but other smells too, hideous ones for which Matt had no olfactory memory or vocabulary. They were urged to wash their faces, and to drink some water. Before Matt knew it, Daniel was stuffed in a chair between his parents, his hands thrust helplessly between his knees. Matt slunk around like the loser in musical chairs. Finally, Lydia snapped, "Sit already, would you?" A horrible wave of righteous indignation rose in his throat. But he sat in a chair beside Sam and stuffed it down, his throat cramping with the effort.

He ran his hands over his face. The sound of crying roared in his ears, and his mind worked at the sound until it smoothed out, became an abstract pattern.

They didn't have to wait long to be ushered into the office with the police; Matt learned later that, except for Joel and an Arab dishwasher, the other fourteen victims had been identified already, and that the remaining mourners in the hall were identifying the bodies of victims of a massive pileup that had occurred the previous night, outside of Tel Aviv. He touched the social worker's sleeve. "Should I go with them?" he asked.

Her look was kind, but doubtful. "The room is quite small," she said.

"Oh, okay then," he said in a quick, anxious display of cooperation that he immediately regretted when the door closed behind them.

He thought he could safely leave the building for a little while and be back by the time they emerged, so he wandered outside. He stepped out of the sun into the shadow of pine trees, gravel crunching beneath his shoes, grateful for air that didn't stink of mayhem. His dress pants were damp at the seat and thighs. An old man was sweeping pine needles off the paths that ran between the stuccoed buildings, a lit cigarette in his mouth, and Matt wondered if he dared ask him for one. He felt shy; he didn't know if this dark-skinned fellow was Jewish or Palestinian, and didn't in any case know either language. He slowly walked toward him, and when he met the man's eye, he mimed smoking a cigarette, his eyebrows raised inquiringly. The old man rested the broom handle against his armpit and fished out a rumpled pack from his breast pocket, extended it toward Matt, and Matt drew one out. With a leathery hand, the man gave him his own stub of a lit cigarette to light it with. Matt inhaled deeply and blew two thin streams from his nostrils.

"Thank you," he said, nodding, in this act of bumming a smoke, without social class or nationality, a man among men.

He strolled back to the building, holding the cigarette in graceful fingers. He leaned against the stucco wall, closed his eyes, and rested. Instantly, his peace was shattered by the vision of Joel's body being torn apart, and he opened them again, found himself laboring to breathe. Inside, they were talking about every inch of Joel's body. Matt felt an overwhelming tenderness toward it. Joel looked a lot like Daniel, but with the slight beefiness of the straight man. Matt and Daniel had been together for a year before Matt met him, and he'd refused to believe that Joel was straight. When Daniel said, "He's *married*," Matt asked, "To a woman?" He quizzed him suspiciously. Had Joel gone to Israel to *try* to be straight? Did he think a macho culture would straighten him up? Was Daniel sure they were *identical* twins? Then one summer, Joel came to visit them in Northampton and brought his wife, Ilana, and Matt took one look at the butch with the booming voice and bruising handshake and shot Daniel a look: *Why didn't you tell me?*

Joel was all *ta-da!*—he had a strong sense of entitlement, but mostly in a nice way. He was a child who had madly flourished under the praise he received when he brought home his accomplishments. He acted as though he believed he was handsome, and that *made* him handsome, although in fact, Daniel was much more so. He was the best dancer Matt had ever seen in a straight man. He flirted with Matt, as though Daniel's gayness gave him a delicious permission; he was even a little inappropriate sometimes, maybe coming on too strong as the cool and gay-affirmative straight twin. He pretended that he was dominated by his giant wife.

Matt crushed the cigarette under his shoe, suddenly sickened by it, and went back inside.

Two big, loutish sons were muttering in Russian, bent over their keening mother, who wore a shapeless housedress and a scarf on her head. The sounds she made seemed to come from some hideous marshy place inside her, and the men winced and muttered, patting her shoulder with stiff paws. Matt took a seat and closed his eyes. An hour passed. He opened his eyes to see Daniel's ghastly face; the Rosens had returned. He patted the seat next to him, and when Daniel sat, he took his arm, but Daniel moved it away. Matt looked around at the hall: For Christ's sake, who was capable of crawling out of their own misery to notice they were queers? He told himself: *Daniel can do anything he wants right now, don't get mad.*

They waited. They were taken outside to a different white house, and led into another office, where they waited some more. "Why must we wait so long?" Lydia moaned, and then her eyes fluttered and she fainted. *"Hello!"* they called, and there was noise, and shuffling, and curt instructions. Daniel and Matt knelt, cradling her head; Shoshi ran out and came back with a wet paper towel, with which she patted Lydia's forehead. They brought her staggering to her feet, her dark hair limp around her face, and pressed a water bottle to her lips. Sam paced around her, swatting at the fabric of her suit where it had become dusty from the fall. The door opened, and Shoshi said, "Now we will go into the separation room, to see the body. I'm sorry to say that the body must not be touched, since it has been prepared for Jewish burial."

They stared at her dumbly. Matt felt goose bumps shiver along his forearms. They heaved themselves to their feet and followed the social worker down a hallway. Matt stopped at the door. When it opened, he could see into the bare room where a man in a lab coat stood beside a covered body on a pallet. He had a sudden passionate urge to say good-bye to Joel. Could he go in? But Daniel and his parents glided toward the pallet without looking back, the door swung closed in front of him and Shoshi, and he felt that without an explicit invitation, he couldn't.

His eyes were dry and itchy, red-rimmed; he rubbed them furiously with his fists. He'd been kept from Jay, too. That officious little prick Kendrick had neglected to inform him that Jay was on a respirator, and the following afternoon Matt had heard from a different friend altogether that Jay had died that morning.

He pressed his forehead against the glass of the small window in the door.

Lydia and Sam stepped back, and Matt got a glimpse of Joel. His eyes galloped over the covered body to see if it looked intact, and it did, he thought, except for maybe in the middle; he squinted and blinked hard, until his mind reassured him that the whole body was there. Joel's face was white, his dark hair swept stiffly back off his forehead as if by a sweaty day's work. Daniel looked somberly at him, then bent and murmured something into Joel's ear. The doctor was speaking to Daniel's parents with a serious and patient look, as though he wanted his words to be remembered. He stopped from time to time, waiting for them to nod. Beside him, Shoshi spoke. "He's saying that Joel was killed on the spot, and didn't feel anything."

Part of Matt's mind caught that, and he wondered if the doctor said that to everybody. But mostly he was watching Daniel, and something was coming over him that took his breath away. He squared his shoulders. At that moment he knew the answer to the question with which he'd often secretly tormented himself: whether he would be loving enough, selfless enough, to fling himself into the path of an oncoming car to save Daniel. He would, he suddenly knew he would. He felt stern and important, for all that he was the one left unnoticed outside the door. History had entered their lives with a sonorous call, and it was up to him to shepherd Daniel, and the children too, through this dark flood and onto higher ground. There was no room to ask whether he could do it or not. He had to.

"Good-bye, Joel," he whispered. "I love you."

Shoshi placed a gentle hand on his arm. He was trembling.

BEFORE THEY COULD GO, they had to sign. Shoshi brought them a form in Hebrew and Daniel perused it. "It says that you identified Joel, and that the body is his," she told Lydia and Sam, handing Daniel a pen.

"They wouldn't let me touch my own son," Lydia murmured.

Daniel put the form down on a table and leaned over it with straight arms. He stared at it for a long time. Matt stepped up to him and laid his hand on his back, and felt it heave. Finally, Daniel turned toward his father, his face crumpling like a child's. "Dad," he whispered.

Sam stepped forward and took the pen from him and ran his finger down the page, which was mercifully indecipherable to him, found the blank line, and signed.

And with that, Joel was dead.

CHAPTER 2

I T WAS FOUR years earlier, and Matt was taking the bus from New York to Northampton, his temple pressed against the cold window. He wore a T-shirt and a leather jacket, and a small overnight bag sat on his lap. On the streets of his neighborhood, the late-March wind whipped around corners, making storefront gratings rattle, and pedestrians picked their way around slush and garbage and discarded flyers for clubs. When Matt left the gym in the mornings, showered and dressed for the office, the morning sun gleamed in his face and made him squint. He'd take the train from Chelsea to midtown, and when he got to work he'd go to the men's room and wet a paper towel, then scrub at the dirty splotches on the calves of his pants.

Spring was on its way, and Matt felt it as a ripping sensation in his chest. He was suffering from insomnia for the first time in his life, and had had a few anxiety attacks that made him fear he was having a heart attack. His best friend, Jay, was dying, and he was fighting with Jay's partner Kendrick, who had been with Jay all of a year while Matt had been his best friend since forever. Kendrick, whom he privately referred to as Shmendrick, was bad-mouthing him to all their friends, claiming that when Matt was around Jay, it was like having to take care of *two* patients. Matt knew that wasn't true, knew that when he was with him, a little more of Jay's soul showed.

The night before, at around three, when he'd returned home from the clubs, he had rummaged through his desk looking for the stub of a joint he'd left there, and found the matchbook with Daniel's name and number on it. He took it to bed with him and sat there inhaling smoke, contemplating, until the tiny ragged joint burned his fingers. Once he had the idea that he could leave town, he could hardly wait for morning to come so he could call. He lay in bed imagining a quiet, orderly house in the New England countryside with a guest bedroom that his imagination formed out of a bed-and-breakfast he'd once stayed in: a fluffed-up bed with a dust ruffle and an iron headboard, a painting of English hunters on horseback hanging above. And then, even as he was laughing to himself for being stoned and silly, his mind attached itself to that image with a surprising passion.

Why Daniel, he wondered later, when he had at least three other friends who lived within a few hours on a bus or train, and when he hardly knew the guy? Later, when he told the story at dinner parties, he insisted he'd had some secret intimation. But at that point, it was just a panicked need to flee the drug scene and the whole circus surrounding Jay, who was back in the hospital with pneumonia, and being sick of his friends, whose eyes were starting to glaze over at the whole topic because, he thought savagely, of their own terror at the risks they were exposing themselves to every day. "I gotta get out of here," he told Daniel on the phone the next morning, at ten A.M. sharp, the first moment he felt he could call. He'd reminded him that they'd met at a party, and endured the terrifying moment of pause before Daniel said, "I remember." When Matt asked if he could visit, panic made him lose his breath, and after a long silence that he read as either cold or thoughtful, Daniel said, "Sure, come on up, I have a spare room."

Somewhere in Connecticut, it started to snow, big early-spring flakes spreading over the bus windshield, melting as soon as they hit the asphalt. By the time they crossed into Massachusetts, the trees lining the highway were drooping with snow, and the blinking lights of the salt trucks pierced the blurry dusk. The guy sitting next to him had fallen asleep with his head thrown back and his mouth open. Matt wondered if he would even recognize Daniel, and tried to bring his image into his mind. He didn't remember the conversation they'd had at the party very well—he'd been more than a little drunk—but he remembered feeling drawn to him, and after all, Daniel *had* given him his phone number. He mulled over Daniel's words on the phone, *I have a spare room*, amused and insulted by Daniel's presumption that he was dying to sleep with him. But he knew that he'd have said the exact same thing, just to protect himself.

As the bus pulled slowly into the Springfield station, he looked out the window and recognized Daniel immediately; he was standing under a small overhang, his hands in the pockets of a parka, his face a study in moderate, noncommittal welcome. Matt stood and brought down his backpack from the overhead rack, worried suddenly that his arrival was a chore for Daniel, imagining him complaining to his friends that he had to host some guy he'd met at a party. When he stepped off the bus, he approached awkwardly, smiling. Daniel looked older and more ordinary in the winter dusk than he had in the glow of alcohol and party music, and Matt felt a small pang of disappointment. Daniel proffered his hand, then laughed self-consciously and kissed him on the cheek. That laugh crinkled his eyes and lifted Matt's spirits. They walked out through the station's slush-covered floors. It was snowing hard now, and Daniel brushed the snow off the windshield and back window of his Camry as Matt shivered in the cold front seat, shaking snow out of his hair and wondering what he'd gotten himself into.

It took them forever to get to Daniel's house, visibility was so diminished. "Remind me what you do again?" Daniel asked. He was sitting forward, straining to see the road. When Matt spoke he had to raise his voice over the din of the defroster. "I'm a graphic designer," he said.

"Shit," Daniel said; he had gotten himself stuck behind a snowplow, and clumps of snow and dirt were pelting the car. Matt hugged himself and slouched down into his jacket.

By the time Daniel pulled into the driveway of a small Cape house in Northampton, Matt had lost his bearings and had no idea where Northampton even was. The walk was still unshoveled, and the wind howled in their faces, and when they got inside they stamped their feet, shouting. Matt shook his head, spraying cold drops everywhere; Daniel laughed "Hey!" and took off his glasses and wiped them on the T-shirt under his sweater. A yellow Labrador barged into the mudroom, its tail banging against the walls. "This is Yo-yo," Daniel said, as the dog pressed himself up against Matt's thigh with a crazy, tongue-lolling smile.

The house had pine floors with wide, soft boards. Daniel took him up a creaking flight of stairs to the guest room, where Matt had to stoop under a sloped ceiling. The bed was made up in maroon sheets and a gray comforter, the effect both masculine and warm. Daniel left the room and returned with a sweatshirt and some wool socks. "Thanks," Matt said, peeling off his wet socks and cupping his hands around his cold toes. Daniel said, "Well, we can't go out, so I'm going to see what I have for dinner. Come on down whenever you want."

After he left the room, Matt looked at the dog and said, "Well, my friend, this is quite awkward." Yo-yo pushed his muzzle into Matt's hand, and he scratched the dog's forehead with two fingers, grinning as a faraway expression gathered in Yo-yo's eyes. He lingered shyly up there for a little while, looking at the photos on the dresser. There were yellowing photos, in old-fashioned silver frames, of Jewish-immigrant grandparents. Color photographs of handsome, well-heeled, coiffed parents. And one of Daniel, probably in college, hugging or wrestling with a boy whom Matt surmised was his brother, possibly his twin. Matt smiled. Daniel was delicious in it, his cheeks fuller and smoother, his hair long and wild. He was clearly a little annoyed by his brother's wild grasp. The brother was pretty hot too, even though he looked like a goof with his hammy smile, as if saying "Cheese!" better than anyone had ever said it before.

When Matt came into the kitchen, Daniel was closing the refrigerator with his elbow, his hands full of eggs. "Sorry," he said, "I meant to take you out." On the stove sat a frying pan, of good quality and heavily used, Matt noted. As Daniel cracked eggs and put a slab of butter in the pan, he became quiet, and Matt said, "Listen, thanks for having me. It's nice to get away. I'll probably head back to New York tomorrow." He sat in a kitchen chair and watched as Daniel deftly sliced onions and grated cheese. Snow was gathering silently along the bottoms of the windows. "How do you live out here?" he asked Daniel, with perfect cosmopolitan snobbery. "I gotta be honest, I'm feeling a little like Shelley Duvall in *The Shining*."

Daniel looked at him and raised his eyebrows. "Who does that make me?" he asked. "A dull boy?" Matt laughed; he could tell he was making himself obnoxious. "I like it here," Daniel shrugged. "In the city, everyone's trying to be cooler and more stylish than everyone else. To me, that's a huge waste of time. And I can't handle the crystal thing."

Matt nodded sagely; he couldn't handle the crystal meth thing either—the extent of it scared and horrified him—but he was also taking in the rebuke. He was remembering his initial attraction to Daniel, something he didn't know how to put his finger on. Certainly part of it was the whole Jewish intellectual vibe, the high forehead, curly dark hair, black-rimmed glasses that gave his face a touch of owlish severity. He looked as though he should be chain-smoking in a French café, devising a philosophical system that explained everything in the universe. He was soft-spoken, his voice slightly nasal, with a nelly sibilance to his *s*'s. The blend of masculine and feminine in him was exact, and perfect. His house was well tended without being fussy. Matt watched him stir the frying onions, and, being a restless person himself, was drawn to what seemed like a talent for immersion in the task at hand.

At dinner, Matt noticed that he was feeling self-conscious eating in front of Daniel, which surprised him a little. You could think in your head that you weren't into a guy, but there were certain signs that infallibly told you otherwise, such as being superaware of how you were chewing. He asked Daniel how he'd gotten to that party anyway, and they talked about the couple who had thrown it, their mutual friends

Mitchell and Bruce. Mitchell was an old friend of Daniel's from Oberlin, and Matt knew Bruce from the gym. They dished about their relationship, agreeing with delighted shouts that the two of them were irritatingly symbiotic. "They're all, '*We* like the Chilean sea bass,' '*We're* good friends with the proprietor,'" Matt mimicked, making Daniel laugh, which broke his face into an utterly charming sweetness. "Dude, get a mind of your own!" Matt shifted, leaned a little closer over the table, getting confidential. "Enough about them," he said. "What did you think of me?"

Daniel laughed again, and his eyes shifted in a way that amused Matt; he was clearly rapidly editing his response. "Well, that you were attractive," he said, stiff with shyness.

"Really! Say more," Matt joked. "Wait, did I come out with some big drunken confession? I have the vague memory that I did."

Daniel cleared his throat. "You said that being as good-looking as you are proved to be a curse sometimes."

"Shut up. I said that?"

"Yup. You even choked up a little when you said it."

Matt groaned. "Was there at least some context . . . ?"

"Not really."

"Christ, what an asshole." It was coming back to him. He remembered now that he'd been trying to encourage Daniel, because he recognized on him the diffident look of a man who thought Matt was out of his league. "What did you say?" he asked.

Daniel shrugged, a glint in his eye. "I said that that must be really hard for you."

Matt guffawed. "I'm sorry," he said, shaking his head. "I'm a weepy, and apparently quite conceited, drunk."

He helped Daniel clear the dishes, wanting to tell him that he had thought Daniel was hot too, but not being able to find a way out of their conversation, and not sure what message he wanted to give him. They moved to the living room, where Daniel made a fire in the woodstove. "Do you like hot cider?" he asked. He disappeared into the kitchen

for a while, and Matt picked up the magazine Daniel edited, brows-
ing through stories of Amherst College alumni who were doing DNA
sequencing and building affordable housing for the homeless. Daniel
emerged from the kitchen and handed a tall steaming glass to Matt. It
had a cinnamon stick in it. When Matt told the story in years to come,
he'd say that, between the fire and the hot cider, he was remembering
every sitcom episode he'd ever seen where the wife drags the reluctant
husband to a cozy, romantic weekend in a Vermont inn. But when Daniel settled beside him, and the sweet cider coated his throat, and Daniel
asked him why he'd needed to get out of New York so badly, Matt found
himself choking up. "Oh God," he said, waving his hand in front of his
face, and he told him about Jay, his best friend since high school. "We
started our school's first gay-straight alliance," he said, his eyes gleaming with pride and self-irony. "We spent every Halloween together for
ten years." He took two pictures out of his wallet and showed them to
Daniel: one from their first year of college, when he and Jay had dressed
up for Halloween as the Id and the Superego, and one from their junior
year, when they'd gone as Nature and Nurture. Daniel looked at the
pictures of the boys in preposterous costumes, and Matt was rewarded
by his appreciative laughter. "I was a poli-sci and fine arts major," Matt
said, "so these Halloweens really combined all my interests."

"I see that you managed to be the one who went as Nature and the
Id," Daniel said.

Matt laughed. "Anything to show off bare-chested." He sighed shakily. "Anyway," he said, "last week there was a misunderstanding about
who was going to bring Jay dinner, and Kendrick reamed me out for
not being there when it counted. And then, when Jay tried to intervene,
that little fucker told me I was upsetting Jay and making him sicker. Can
you believe it? *I* was upsetting Jay! This is the guy who made Jay move
out of his apartment after his first hospitalization because Kendrick was
allergic to mold!"

He sat back on the couch cushion and sighed. "It was all very *Angels
in America: The Next Generation*," he said.

Daniel leaned toward him and kissed him, his forehead touching Matt's, his breath sharp, like apples. The dog approached and shoved his muzzle between their knees, and Daniel said, "Yo-yo, don't be rude." He stood and led Matt to his bedroom, where they made out for a while, straining against their clothes like teenagers. Matt kissed him and nibbled him and worried whether this shy and quiet man could give him what he needed. Wind gusted against the windows, and a critter skittered overhead along the attic floor. Then they undressed, and Daniel took Matt's arm and turned him on his side. Matt gasped and tried to make a joke, but Daniel didn't laugh; he leaned over the bed and fumbled for the pants that lay on the floor, reached into the pockets, and pulled out a condom. *You dog,* Matt thought, but then Daniel was gripping his hips with surprising authority. Matt closed his eyes and fell, soaring, into himself, while the world bucked and spun. His orgasm thundered through him, and he passed out. He slept for fourteen hours, and when he awoke the next afternoon, the sun was shining and his body was aglow. He could hear Daniel moving around downstairs and the trickle of water in the gutters. He propped himself up on his elbows and looked outside; the snow had almost entirely melted.

IT WAS LATE AFTERNOON when they began their ascent to Jerusalem. Shoshi had had the driver stop at a roadside pizza and falafel stand and rousted them out of the van, insisting that they try to eat, but the smell of deep-fried and spicy food made everyone indecisive and nauseated. The smell of the morgue clung to them; Matt sniffed Daniel's hair and shuddered. Finally, Shoshi ordered a basket of pitas and some Cokes, which they took into the van. Matt looked out the window, chewing a warm pita, as the highway began to ascend. He was sitting next to Daniel now, his knee pressed against his, wondering what was going to happen next. He thought about seeing Gal, who was almost six years old now; she was a quick, intense child who they all were sure was gifted. Noam he barely knew; the baby had been only a few months old when he had last seen him. He was a cheerful, easy baby with legs that came in fat segments, like dinner rolls. He'd been born after two miscarriages following Gal's birth, and was considered such a gift by his parents that they were, as if amazed out of every expected impulse, completely mellow around him. Matt remembered that last visit, Noam sitting placidly in his bouncy chair in the corner of the dining room as they ate supper; midmeal, Ilana looked over and joked, "Hey, someone should pay attention to that baby over there." The name Noam, Daniel had explained to Matt, came from the word *na'im*, which means "pleasant," or maybe "pleasing"—"nice," but without the banality that word carried in English.

He looked fiercely out the window, deliberately blocking from his mind any thoughts of the future—of those kids living in his house, of himself as the guardian of two children. He thought about playing Uno with Gal, and what a sore loser she was, how she stormed out of the room when she lost and her father had to go speak with her. And almost from the time she learned to talk, if she was in the room, you couldn't tell other adults about the cute thing she'd said or she'd pitch a fit.

She was scathing about American accents, and imitated with withering accuracy the way Matt said her name till he learned to make not just the *ah* sound in the middle, but also the *l* sound at the end, pronounced not with a thick American tongue lazing at the bottom of the mouth but with a sharper tongue tapping the middle of the upper palate. For all that, Matt adored her and couldn't resist pushing the limits with her, making her giggle and howl in protest at the same time. He knew she adored him, too; she greeted him by rocketing into his arms, and he'd make loud strangling noises when she gripped him around the neck. Ilana and Joel had instilled in her a good sense of humor; they were the kind of parents for whom that was a value. Since she was tiny: *Is this my nose?!* they'd ask, pointing to their chin, eyes wide and incredulous. *Naaahhh.* He thought of the look she got on her face when she sensed something was a joke: a hilarious parody of slyness, eyes darting.

They were climbing now; the driver shifted into lower gear and the van paused and then surged. The sky had become both bluer and more cloudy; they drove in and out of the shadow of pine forest. "Look," Daniel said, pointing, leaning toward the window till his face touched Matt's. "Memorials. From the battle for Jerusalem in the '48 war." Matt began noticing the rusty remnants of trucks and tanks scattered among the rocks and pines at the side of the road. "See? There's another one." Matt nodded, impressed by the somber and rustic memorial. They continued to climb; he yawned to pop his ears. In the distance he began to discern, on a series of forested and terraced hills, clustered masses of white stone buildings bathed in late-afternoon light. The van turned and then rose again, and the populous outskirts of Jerusalem began to spread before them. It was called Jerusalem stone, Daniel had told him. Draped over the hills like necklaces made by a primitive hand, the neighborhoods conveyed a sense of inevitability, a rugged majesty. "Wow," Matt breathed, stunned. "Is that occupied territory?"

Daniel raised his eyebrows and turned away. Matt's stomach seized. He hadn't intended the question to be controversial or insensitive. Hadn't Daniel once told him that something like 75 percent of occupied territory was in the area of Jerusalem? His mind scrambled to remember what Daniel had said, and what he'd read, to reassure himself that it hadn't been a stupid question. The van swerved one way and then the other, and a nauseous headache began to gather behind Matt's eyes. They were engulfed by the noise of engines in low gear and the smell of gasoline fumes. They plunged into shadow as they rounded a curve, a towering stone wall on their right. They were rising to Jerusalem, the stench of death on their clothes and hair. His eyes smarted, and he felt profoundly alone, a pebble kicked along by a boot.

They wound around a road on the edge of a hill, then through the twisting narrow streets, all one-way, of Beit Ha-Kerem. Joel and Ilana's apartment building was at the end of a cul-de-sac circled by apartment buildings. Cars were parked everywhere, and every which way; laundry hung from windows, whipped by the wind; when they got out, two cats sprang out of a Dumpster and raced away. The Rosens ran into the dark hallway and up the stairs, while Matt and Shoshi and the driver lugged out the suitcases. The driver held the elevator door open by propping a suitcase against it, and they dragged in the rest of the luggage till the elevator was full, Matt pinned in by suitcases.

He went up the slow, creaky elevator alone. When it stopped, he dragged all the luggage out, and straightened. He grabbed a suitcase and entered an apartment full of crying, huddled adults and a burnt coffee smell. Lydia and the woman he took to be Malka, Ilana's mother, were hugging and rocking with high, keening cries. Daniel had Gal in his arms, her legs swung around his waist and gripping. His eyes were squeezed shut, his mouth pressed against Gal's hair. Matt wondered if he should stand there until introduced; he waited awkwardly for a moment, and then began dragging in the rest of the suitcases. The apartment had tile floors throughout, and windows that slid open to the sun and wind and the dark flapping-crow sound of laundry on the lines. Its furnishings were the cheap hodgepodge of people whose main business is raising children; nothing on the walls but framed family photos, taped-up children's drawings, and a few framed posters from museum exhibits of Impressionist painters. He figured out which was the master bedroom and dragged Lydia's and Sam's suitcases into it, then sat down on the bed. He thought about a novel he'd recently read that depicted an epidemic of blindness, in which only one woman could see. That would be him now, he thought, the one functioning person in a family blinded by grief.

The mattress sat on a low wood frame, and the bed was neatly made. From the little adjacent bathroom he could smell Joel's scent, his aftershave. He ran his hand over a pillow, noticed several long brown hairs. Ilana's. He closed his eyes, thinking about the skin sloughed off all over the bed and floor and windowsills, and the hair on the pillows and in the shower drain. Someday, someone—maybe even him—would clean this apartment, and in doing so they'd eradicate all the earthly remaining traces of Joel's and Ilana's bodies. He stood and opened the door of one of the closets that lined the front wall and thrust his head into Ilana's blouses and skirts and blazers. When he emerged and shut the closet door, he saw a small figure standing in the doorway. Gal's cheeks were a hectic red and she was sucking her thumb. She wore purple leggings and a purple-and-white-striped T-shirt; he remembered Joel saying that purple was apparently young girls' color of choice when they outgrew pink and got snobbish about their previous lack of sophistication. He folded his long legs into a crouch. "Hey there, Boo," he said. "Wanna come give me a hug?"

She came to him and allowed him to hug her, with an obedience that hurt his feelings a little; he picked her up and sat down on the bed with her on his lap. He tucked her hair behind her ear. She pushed him and reared away from him. "*Ichsah,*" she said in the universal guttural expression of disgust of Israeli children. "You smell bad." Then she whispered, "Ema and Abba died."

He thought: *She's seeing if it's true in English, too.* "Yes," he said, squeezing her and kissing the top of her head so she wouldn't see his tears. She wiggled loose and looked searchingly into his face, then put her two hands on his cheeks. Matt tried to return her gaze as honestly as he could. Her features were thinning and becoming more defined as she passed out of her babyhood and into childhood, and her brown eyes were weirdly fierce, as if she were trying to look into his soul. "Has anybody brushed your hair in a while?" he asked, raking his fingers lightly through the tangled mass. "Go get me a brush, and I'll brush it."

She hopped off his lap and went into her parents' bathroom, and emerged with a hairbrush. She stood patiently between his knees with her back to him. He hastily tore Ilana's hair out of the brush and looked at the little nest of hair in his palm, then stuffed it in his pocket.

Her hair was dark, and slightly shorter than shoulder-length. He removed the headband that held it off her face and brushed for a while, bringing out its gloss, thinking that this was as good a place to be as any. Gal was compliant; when he tugged too hard, she let out a quiet whimper that broke his heart because he knew what a shrieky little beast she could be. He wondered if he should be saying something to her, emphasizing how many adults loved her and reassuring her that she'd be taken care of, but he was frightened of saying something that would cause permanent damage. He could hear talking and crying from the other room, and then Lydia's raised, angry voice and the sound of shushing and whispering because the baby was still asleep. Someone turned on the shower. He brushed for what seemed like a long time, until static made the fine hairs crackle around the brush. Then he heard the quick clack of Lydia's footsteps, and she burst in, her lips tight. "Honey," she said to Gal, "go get something to eat, okay? Your *savta* will find you something."

When Gal had gone, Lydia opened her suitcase, releasing a waft of her scent, and began rummaging through the neat piles of knit clothing. "Those religious fanatics are insisting Joel and Ilana be buried tonight," she hissed at Matt. "The funeral is in two hours."

"You're kidding," Matt said.

"No, I'm not," she said, her face livid. "According to Jewish law you're supposed to bury the bodies as soon as possible, and they've already held them so we could get here to identify Joel."

"Wow," Matt said.

He rose and went in search of Daniel, bumping into Ilana's father in the narrow hallway. Yaakov looked at him, bewildered.

"Shalom," Matt said.

"Shalom."

"I'm Matt, I'm Daniel's friend," Matt said, and stuck out his hand, which Yaakov gripped. Yaakov had a strong, broad face, lined from years in the sun. He was wearing a white oxford shirt, the sleeves rolled up to his forearms. His belly strained over his belt. "I'm very sorry about Ilana," Matt said. "I knew her, and she was a wonderful person."

Yaakov nodded with moist, puzzled eyes.

Daniel was in the shower. Matt went up to the bathroom door and hovered there for a moment, then gently tried the handle. The door was unlocked, and after a quick look around, he stepped into the tiny, steamy room, and locked the door behind him. "Hey, baby, it's me," he said, unbuttoning the top two buttons under his open collar and peeling his shirt off over his head. "Can I come in?"

Daniel stuck his wet head out from behind the curtain. He was virtually blind without his glasses, but managed to cast a disapproving look in Matt's general direction. "I don't feel comfortable cavorting naked with you when my in-laws are out there," he said.

Matt looked at him. "*Cavorting?* Honey, believe me, the last thing on my mind is a cavort."

Daniel turned off the water and stepped out, and Matt handed him a towel.

"And I'm worried my parents won't have enough hot water. The boiler's on, but hot water isn't unlimited here."

Matt looked at his foul-smelling shirt. "I'm putting this back on," he said.

Daniel looked nervously at the door and bit his lip.

"Shit," Matt said. He threw the shirt angrily onto the pile of Daniel's soiled clothes and slipped out the door, walking shirtless through the apartment to their room. There was food out on the kitchen table—sliced bread, cold cuts, hummus, olives—and an argument under way between Lydia and her in-laws about whether the baby should be taken to the funeral. It was conducted in English without the benefit of Daniel's mediation, so it was occurring in its crudest form. Lydia was struggling to express the idea that when Noam grew up, he'd regret not being at his parents' funeral. Sam was leaning against a counter, ripping out huge bites of a sandwich, his eyes darting anxiously back and forth, his Adam's apple convulsing as he swallowed.

Matt went into their room, a tiny guest room/office off the kitchen with a sliding door that rumbled when rolled open and shut. He perched on the bed and folded his hands. Maybe he would never get to shower; maybe it was his destiny to reek of death from now on. He sat there for a while, hearing outside the door the noises of raised voices straining to remain polite, staring at his hands till they blurred, trying to recall himself to his life but unable to imagine the details of his friends and his work and the house he lived in. Where had he felt this before, his stomach yawning into an abyss of despair, feeling so implacably plunged into another's dark reality? The closest he'd come was family holidays when he was a child, when he had to dress in a shirt and tie and be ostracized by his cousins because he was a big sissy. One Christmas when he was about ten, he had stolen his cousin Teddy's brand-new toy soldiers, doused them with lighter fluid he found out in the garage, and set them on fire. "Napalm," he explained with a steely look at his cousin as his mother gripped his arm and a big black, rancid fire smoked. Teddy cried "You freak!" and burst into tears, which Matt remembered to this day with satisfaction.

He heard Daniel come out of the bathroom and join the fray, speaking quickly in Hebrew, and then he heard the baby's cry, and silence fell over the apartment.

BY THE TIME IT was his turn to shower, the water was cold. He stood shivering and swearing, turning off the water and furiously rubbing his head with shampoo till the suds ran down his wrists and arms, then rinsed, then soaped himself up again, all over. His nipples were as hard as pebbles, his dick shrunk back like a turtle's head. He scrubbed himself so hard his arm muscles hurt. He got out and toweled off, pushing his dirty pants and underwear into the corner of the bathroom with his toe, and stopped dead when he realized he hadn't brought any clean clothes in with him. He thought for a second, then thought, *Fuck it*, and wrapped the towel securely around his waist. He tiptoed quickly back to his room through the apartment, his toweled-off hair standing straight up and dripping down his neck—passing through the living room where Daniel, dressed in black pants and a white dress shirt, was nuzzling the baby, and his mother was crying. "Don't mind me," Matt waved, with a grimace. As he was closing the bedroom door behind him, he heard Yaakov ask, "Who is that?"

He picked through the open suitcase on the floor, found underwear and his white shirt, only slightly wrinkled. He was pulling on his pants when the bedroom door slid open gently, and Daniel eased in with the freshly diapered baby in his arms, baby clothes clamped under his armpit, and slid the door firmly closed again. "They want to know why you're always half-naked," he said. Matt ignored him and approached the baby. Noam had wispy brown hair, dark eyes in a moon face with multiple chins. "Hey, little baby," Matt said softly, looking at his lover's face and suddenly seeing the handsome dad, which made his heart hurt. "I'm Matt," he told the baby. He took Noam's hand and shook it gently, and the baby's face broke into a smile so crooked and goofy, his little tongue sticking out between his teeth, that Matt laughed out loud.

Daniel laid Noam on the bed and began pulling pants over his fat legs, while Matt leaned over Noam's face and nuzzled him, and Noam grabbed onto his hair. "Ouch," he said, and extricated himself. He looked at the baby's fuzzy tulip skin, the purple shadow of his nipples. "Almost a year, huh. Can he talk?" he asked Daniel.

Daniel straightened and stared at him, his eyes narrowed in thought. "Beats me," he said, shrugging, and they both laughed. Matt pulled Daniel into his arms, and Daniel cried "Don't!" and pulled away. "I can't do this right now," he whispered. "I'm sorry, baby."

"Okay," Matt said. Daniel turned back to Noam, removing his glasses and wiping his eyes with his forearm. As Matt finished dressing, Daniel pulled the waist of the pants over Noam's diaper; he scrunched up the shirt to the collar and pulled it over the baby's head, and stuffed his arms clumsily into the sleeves.

"There," he said, and picked Noam up. "Are you ready?" His lips grazed the baby's cheek.

"Why isn't he crying?" Matt asked. His fingers grew still over the buttons of his shirt as a thought occurred to him. "How do babies mourn, anyway?"

"I have no idea," Daniel said.

Matt considered. "You don't think we'll ruin them, do you?"

Daniel looked at him wearily. "I think somebody has already done that for us."

·   ·   ·   ·   ·

THE FUNERAL WASN'T THE way Matt had feared it would be—not at all like the settler funerals he saw on television, armed and bearded civilians roaring with bombastic song. But dignitaries had arrived in long Mercedeses, and they and their bodyguards stood, their hands clasped before them, at the front of the crowd clustered under the strong lights set up to illuminate the cemetery. There were photographers, too: Matt couldn't see them, but he heard the clicking of camera shutters. The mourners were gathered on an outcrop of rock on a mountainside, huddled in overcoats, hundreds of people crowded around them. The wind was strong and noisy, and the sound of weeping reached up and was taken by it, bobbing on the wind. Gal stood behind her Grampa Sam, wrapped around his leg, while Daniel held the baby, who was crying, joggling him and cupping his head. Headstones stretched out far ahead of them, and Matt could see that there were graves set into the rock wall as well. He had a sudden memory: Ilana at their house in Northampton, packing to go back home, sighing, calling Israel "that sad piece of rock." Ilana hated Jerusalem, the city in which she'd grown up; she hated the religious people, the city's fraught status as a symbol for three religions. She was a teacher, and her work took her close to abused and neglected and hungry children. She had named her daughter Gal, which meant "wave," to evoke her beloved Tel Aviv, which was on the ocean.

They had been taken to the cemetery in the van, and herded first into a large, crowded hall. When they entered, a hush fell over the crowd. Matt walked self-consciously behind the others to the front. He towered above most of the people there, and Daniel had taken a large yarmulke from a box at the door and pinned it to Matt's hair, so he felt like a big beanpole in Jewish drag. The family held their heads high—asserting, he imagined, that they had dignity even though their destinies had turned them into every other person in the room's worst nightmare, to be pitied and avoided, or maybe fetishized in some creepy way, from this point on. They reached the front and sat in seats that had been reserved for them. It was so clear, he thought, who were to be honored and supported here; he had a sudden and unexpected flash of sympathy for Kendrick's loudmouthed partnering of Jay: he was trying to make himself *count*. Before them, the bodies were laid out, wrapped in white sheets draped with cloths with fringes and Stars of David on them.

A man approached Daniel, bent, and murmured something in his ear. Daniel cleared his throat and rose, and removed the folded eulogy from his overcoat pocket. The coat was Joel's; he'd taken it because he hadn't brought a warm enough jacket, and in the van, he kept sniffing at the lapels and fighting back tears.

The paper crackled under the microphone as Daniel smoothed it with shaking fingers. He cleared his throat and neared his face to the microphone and said, "Shalom." He said, "I'm Daniel Rosen, Joel's brother." His voice was hoarse; he cleared his throat. "I have a big strawberry birthmark on my back," he said. "I've always thought that Joel was in such a hurry to get out and take the world by storm, he shoved me aside, right there." There was a wave of low laughter. "But I loved Joel more than anybody in the world."

Matt took in the complicated message and stored it for future rumination, when he was less exhausted and more mature. That was the last thing he understood, because Daniel delivered the rest of his eulogy in Hebrew. Daniel had learned Hebrew in Jewish summer camp and during the year he spent in Israel; he had learned it quickly—he had a facility for languages, spoke French and German as well—and was vain about it. Out of the corner of his eye, Matt saw Lydia whisper in Sam's ear and wring the handkerchief she held in both hands, and he thought it was sad that they weren't able to understand the eulogy. But as Daniel spoke and got into it, Matt found he didn't mind. The actual words might have destroyed him. Instead, he heard a Jewish man speaking the language of Jewish prayer. It was weird: Speaking Hebrew, Daniel seemed somehow more authoritative. More masculine, even—the microphone took his everyday tenor and wove it in rich, colored strands. He gripped the sides of the podium. His mouth moved in ways Matt had never seen before, his lips and tongue making all the consonants juicy. His language was leaving the mundane world of the queer everyday, and elevating itself to the universal. Matt looked on, enthralled, conscious in a tiny part of his mind that he was idealizing his partner's speech, that it was, after all, coming from the same mouth that kissed him and sucked him. But watching Daniel, he felt proud to belong to him.

There were tears, and the honks and sniffles of people blowing their noses. The baby had fallen asleep on his Israeli grandmother's shoulder. He heard Daniel say in Hebrew, "I love you, Joel"—*Ani ohev otcha*, words he had taught Matt long ago, and uttered from time to time when they were in bed, after sex or right before falling asleep. He whispered a few last broken words, and stepped down. He looked over the crowd, blind and disoriented; Matt stood so Daniel could see him, and he stumbled over to his seat.

He sat beside Matt with his face in his hands, sobbing freely. In the swing of crying, he'd picked up the rhythm of marathon crying rather than sprinting, his sobs low and regular and inconsolable. A box of Kleenex was passed their way, and Matt fed tissues to Daniel, and took the used ones off his lap, laying them on the floor between his own feet. The air was chilly, but damp with body heat. Up on the podium, Sam was sighing into the microphone, making a shuddery crackling sound. He was saying that Joel had never hurt anyone, that he had many Arab friends and colleagues, that he didn't deserve to be claimed by this terrible conflict. "What kind of person," he pondered, "blows himself up in order to harm innocent people?"

Matt bit his lip and looked down at the floor. Sam was gripping the podium and looking out into the sea of mourners as though waiting for a reply. He spoke, Matt thought, as if he was the first person to ponder this problem. As if the fact that he—a wealthy and powerful American man—didn't understand was supposed to mean that nobody could, that it was utterly unfathomable. Sam sighed heavily and shook his head. "I just don't get it," he said. "I just don't get it."

Matt shifted. A rancor was rising in him that he wanted to shake off. *Have some respect*, he told himself furiously. The man was mourning his son, talking about his death the best way he knew how; he had no right to criticize him. Matt's ruminations were interrupted by a squeeze of his hand. Daniel was cutting his eyes toward him. His mind tumbled rapidly over the meaning of this communication, and his spirit lifted a little.

It seemed to have been agreed upon in advance that Malka would not speak. And at the last moment, Lydia didn't rise to the podium either; her arm grew rigid against Sam's hand, and a look of terror came over her face. "I can't," she whispered. Yaakov spoke, in a manner so dazed that Matt wished several times that someone would do him a favor and lead him away from the podium. His head and lips sagged like a stroke victim's; it was hard to tell when he'd finished, he trailed off so many times. Finally, he sighed and turned away, walking in the wrong direction; a man jumped to his feet and led him back to his seat. There was a long respectful pause. Then a friend of Joel's named Shmulik, a man with a round droll face and a very slight lisp, got up and told some story in a rapid-fire delivery that sent waves of laughter over the hall. Matt watched Daniel's face break and redden, taken by surprise, and hearing the peal of his laughter made Matt love him so much he could hardly stand it.

There was a brief speech by a fat honcho. And then a bunch of Hasids came and took hold of the pallets the bodies lay upon, and the mourners walked out to the cemetery through the chilly night air, Lydia clutching Daniel's arm, up a long paved incline and onto this hillside. The Hasids swayed and prayed over the bodies, and Matt gazed at their long beards and side curls, thinking that if Ilana was standing beside him, she'd have something sarcastic to say. They laid the bodies straight into the ground without coffins, and each person shoveled dirt over the grave. He looked quickly at Gal, hidden behind her grandfather's leg. She was crying, her eyes darting around, as if trying to alight upon the person who would save her; the wind was whipping at her face, making her hair fly. Matt burst into tears. He cried through the singing of the national anthem. The women's voices rose tearfully at first, tinny and a little shrill, then took strength in numbers and grew in beauty and texture. The sound of voices in unison, men and women an octave apart, in the cold night air, with the stars shining fiercely, pierced him through with grief and something like joy. He looked at Gal and saw that her lips were moving too, even as tears ran down her face. He told himself to remember that singing would bring her solace.

WHEN THEY GOT HOME they were quiet. Ilana's parents had gone to their own house, leaving the children with the Rosens. The baby was fast asleep in his car seat; Daniel reached in and eased him over his shoulder, carried him in. "Should I change him?" he murmured to his mother.

"No," she said. "Never wake a sleeping baby."

Daniel laid him in his crib without waking him. Lydia went into the bathroom to wash up for bed. In the kitchen, Sam was taking a Ziploc bag out of his briefcase. "I just remembered this," he said, and then looked up to see whom he was talking to. His eyes fell on Matt, who sat down with him at the table. Sam sat heavily in one of the kitchen chairs and pondered Joel's effects. He removed Joel's wedding ring and slipped it over his pinkie, where it caught on the second knuckle. Matt saw that his fingers had thickened over the years and his own wedding band was now a tight squeeze. There was a filthy wallet. Sam went through it and took out dirty cash, tiny wrinkled photographs of Ilana and the kids, and laid them on the table. And then Joel's cell phone, still in its holder. Daniel came into the room. "What's that?" he asked.

Sam undid the Velcro fastener and pulled out the phone. Two small black nails clattered onto the table. Sam inhaled sharply. The three of them stared at one another. Daniel reached down and picked them up, brought them to his face, and sniffed them.

"What are you doing?" Sam asked.

"I don't know," Daniel said, stuffing the nails into his pocket.

They fell out later, when he and Matt undressed and folded their pants over the tiny guest room's desk chair. Matt stooped and gathered them off the floor, and suppressing a strong desire to throw them in the trash, set them on the desk. Daniel was taking the pillows off the foldout couch and laying them in a stack in a corner of the room. He slid the bed open and went in search of sheets. At the other end of the apartment, Lydia and Sam were putting Gal to bed.

The window was slid open to the chilly night air, and a lovely smell was wafting in. Matt tried to place it. When Daniel came back into the room, he looked at his still face and closed eyes. "Yeast," he said. "The Angel bread factory is right across the valley."

They were so tired, they crawled into the small double bed without brushing their teeth. Daniel let out a sigh and turned his back to Matt, curling into a ball. Matt gently spooned him, careful to make his touch feel like solace and not a demand. Daniel was hot and sticky from sweat and tears, the air cool and yeasty, and a kind of sensuous peace came over Matt. They fell asleep within minutes.

But two hours later, Matt awoke to find Daniel lying awake beside him. "Hey," he said.

"Hey."

They lay in silence for a while, the only sound the ticking of the desk clock. Matt drifted off for a few minutes, then awoke again, looked over at Daniel and saw his eyelids blinking. "Do you want to tell me what you said about your brother in your eulogy?" he asked.

Daniel continued to stare into space. Matt heard the dry sound of his chapped lips opening. "I said," he whispered, "that Joel and Ilana would not want their deaths to be used as an opportunity for another wave of violence. They would not want people killed in their name. They were people who worked for social justice."

"You said that?"

Daniel nodded.

"That's beautiful, honey. And brave to say."

Daniel shrugged. His face twitched. "A lot of good it'll do," he said.

Matt fell back asleep, and when he awoke two hours later, he found that Gal was in their bed, between them, breathing raucously, one arm flung over his neck. He removed her arm gently and turned toward her and Daniel. Daniel was awake; Matt could see the movement of his eyelids blinking. He fell asleep again and awoke exactly two hours later, grief and jet lag seeming to have planted in him a diabolically precise clock. As the night crawled on, he dreamed ponderous dreams about problems with the designs he was working on back home. He woke again, got up and went into the kitchen, opened the refrigerator and explored the left-overs: pea soup in a pot, some baked chicken in a dish covered with foil, a tiny bit of rice in a Tupperware container. Ilana's food, he thought; the prospect of eating it seemed deeply symbolic of something, but he was too tired to figure out what. He took out some milk, closed the refrig-erator door, and fixed himself a bowl of Honey Nut Cheerios from a box with Hebrew writing on it. He sat down at the table where Joel's wed-ding ring and tattered wallet sat, along with Sam's watch, some worn and folded pieces of paper, the social worker's business card. He picked up the wallet and opened it, and found another two tiny nails caught in the lining. He got up and threw them in the garbage.

The cereal was sweet and comforting; he ate in big mouthfuls, wip-ing milk off his chin. He wondered if he and Daniel would be the kind of parents who gave their kids apples or grapes for dessert instead of chocolate pudding, and sent them to school with horrible *Little House on the Prairie* sandwiches on organic whole wheat bread. He thought that if your parents had been blown up, a Ho Ho probably wasn't the worst thing that would ever happen to you. He went back to bed as dawn was breaking, hearing a donkey's strident bray from down below. In the dim light, Gal was blinking at him, sleepy and solemn. She reached a hand toward his face as he settled in beside her, and he kissed it, and her eyes filled with tears. "I want Ema," she said in a tiny voice. The sound of those words, her wish aloud in the air, made her face crumple. Her grief, Matt thought, already seemed weary and resigned.

"I know, Boo," he whispered. He sat up and pulled her limp body onto his lap, kissed her wet face, and rocked her.

CHAPTER 3

W HEN HE AWOKE in the mornings, there was a moment when
Daniel's spirit felt light. Then a vague unsettled feeling came
over him, and a sense of dread that hardly got its footing before his
awareness broke over him and crushed him with such ruthlessness
he could only cower and whimper before it. The morning after Joel's
funeral, he lay in bed, his arms thrown over his head, whispering the
only word he could think of in any language: *Please.*

He could sense that he was in Jerusalem, and that it was warm. His
undershirt stuck to his back. He tried to bring Joel's face to his mind, but
he couldn't. His throat cramped with the effort not to cry and awaken
the sleeping man and child beside him.

He lay there for a while, his breathing ragged, the sound of sobbing
roaring in his ears. His consciousness began to wash over the sound
Joel; and the idea of Joel, Joel's shining essence, came to him. Joel as he
was, all at once, gorgeous in full, imperfect personhood, and not as
Daniel, swayed by his own ego and needs, had thought of him over the
years, as too this or too that. He imagined himself holding his brother,
their hearts clamoring against each other, and the mayhem in his mind
became something clearer and sweeter, a grief that pierced him through.

He lay there till it subsided, till he felt himself to have been washed ashore, half-dead, panting. He felt the living bodies beside him sigh and stir. His ears made out the rush of traffic on the far side of the valley, and closer, the voices of neighboring women talking over their balconies. And then the baby's sharp wail.

He rose quietly and closed the bedroom door behind him, walked barefoot to the kids' bedroom. His mother was up, walking around the small cluttered room in a housedress with the baby over her shoulder, patting him and murmuring, "I know, I know, honey, I know." Noam was wearing only a diaper, and his red face was covered with tears and snot.

"How long has he been up?" Daniel asked, his voice hoarse. He cleared his throat.

"Since about five. Close the door, will you? The whole house will wake up."

Daniel closed it. "Has he eaten?"

"I tried to give him some Cheerios, but he wouldn't eat. I'm trying to get him to at least take a bottle," Lydia said.

"Did you change him?"

"Of course," she said. "I have some experience at this, in case you've forgotten."

An old skepticism wormed its way up Daniel's throat. He knew that twin babies had been hard for her; she loved the idea of motherhood better than the actuality. He and Joel had always joked that she couldn't relate to them till they were speaking in sentences with subordinate clauses. Her own mother had died suddenly during Lydia's pregnancy—one of those unlucky people who go into a hospital for a simple procedure and never come out again—and by the time he and Joel were born, Lydia was wrung out by months of grief.

"Could you pick up some of this crap on the floor?" she asked. "There seems to be the entire contents of a toy ark. I've already stubbed my toe three times."

Daniel stooped and began collecting Lego pieces and small animal figures fused together in male and female pairs, tossing them into a big plastic toy box in the corner of the room. Above the crib was one of those black-and-white mobiles that were supposed to be good for a baby's development in some way, but whose elemental faces made Daniel shudder. Noam was screaming and arching backward, and Lydia was struggling to hang on to him.

"Do you want me to take him?" Daniel asked.

"No," Lydia said over the baby's crying. "Thank God Ilana weaned him already. That would have been an utter horror." She sat down on the rocking chair in the corner, wrestled him into a reclining position on her lap, and offered him the bottle again. He twisted his face away. "I know, bubbie," Lydia said softly, her eyes becoming shiny with tears.

Daniel straightened, his eyes filling, too. "You're nice with him."

"One is easier than two," she shrugged, laying the bottle's nipple against Noam's lips. "Nothing can prepare you for two." She slipped it in his mouth and he grasped the bottle and began to suck, sighing and shuddering. "There," she crooned. "What a clever boy." She looked evenly at Daniel. "Grandchildren are easier than your own, too," she said.

She was conceding something, Daniel realized. He fixed his eyes on Noam's working cheeks, arms hugging his chest. "Mom," he whispered. "How am I going to survive this?"

Her face broke and sagged, and then composed itself. She spoke to him sharply. "By getting up every morning and putting one foot in front of the other, that's how. By faking it, until it gets real again. That's what we're all going to do."

"Okay," Daniel said in a small voice.

"And by taking care of these children. Listen." Her voice had lowered, become conspiratorial. "We will not let those Grossmans take them. I won't have them raised in that house."

"One step at a time, Mom," Daniel said. "Let's get through the shiva." He was suddenly dying to get away from this conversation before it got too specific. "There's no milk in the house. I'm going to go out and get some."

Lydia nodded. "And while you're out, see if you can find something better than that awful Nescafé, okay?"

"Okay."

"And what about some cookies, at least, for the shiva?"

"I don't think so, Mom," he said. "We have to trust Shoshi on this one." She had told them—as Daniel had assumed—that, according to custom, the family doesn't provide food for the shiva, that the visitors feed them instead.

He found his sandals and wallet, and looked for the key to Joel and Ilana's car for a long time, rummaging through every kitchen drawer, thrumming with the memory of Ilana's periodic tantrums, her bellowing, "I can't go on living in such a shit hole!" It occurred to him that Joel must have had their car keys with him, and there followed a moment in which Daniel tried and failed to ward off the thought that the bomb's impact had driven the keys through Joel's pockets and into the flesh of his thighs, mashing them into his bones. A little starburst of horror went off in his chest, and he had to sit down. A few minutes passed, and he stood again and looked into the open drawer, which was spilling over with lightbulbs, batteries, hair ties, stamps, pens, and paper clips. Suddenly, his eyes lit miraculously upon a single car key, marked with a tag that said *extra car key*. He held it up with two fingers, a smile twitching at the corners of his mouth.

He closed the front door quietly on his way out. He was glad to leave his mother with the baby; she was being a marvel of strength, he thought, but if she didn't have the children to take care of, she'd probably never be able to get out of bed again. She clearly assumed that she and Sam were going to take them, and for a moment Daniel regretted that Joel and Ilana hadn't made that happen. And yet it was hard to imagine that she and Sam would be thrilled to take on two little kids at their age. He considered calling Joel's lawyer, Assaf Schwartz. He, Daniel, sure as hell wasn't going to be the person who broke the news. Let his parents' wrath descend upon a neutral person. He looked at his watch, and then realized he'd see Assaf at the shiva.

. . . .

HE DROVE DOWN THE narrow street toward the center of the neighborhood, flooded by sense memory—sun, stone, squeaking iron gates, narrow streets, little stores like caves crammed with goodies. Last September, he'd spent ten days with Joel and Ilana, having come to Jerusalem to interview and shadow an alumnus who was now a member of the Knesset. At the time, Noam was tiny and Ilana was staying home with him, and Daniel, pulling some of his tastiest recipes out of his hat, cooked for her and Joel and Gal to great applause. It was the best time he'd ever had with his brother. They'd spent much of their lives pulled away from each other in the interest of differentiation, beginning in high school, where being referred to as "one of the Rosen twins" had been a dagger in the heart of teenage boys trying to define themselves. They scoffed at the clichéd schemes people liked to egg them on to do, like switching classes to fool the teacher, or taking each other's exams, and when they co-won the senior prize for best student in English, having to share the prize ruined it for them both. When Joel started getting good at track, Daniel quit sports altogether and began focusing on music, becoming first violinist in the regional youth orchestra and picking up acoustic guitar. They thought of themselves as anti-twins, and during college, where they split up for the first time—Joel to Princeton and Daniel to Oberlin—they invented the semifacetious idea of *twinsism*: the act of stereotyping or fetishizing twins, into which fell such things as Doublemint commercials, fantasizing about having sex with twins, Mengele's experiments on twins, and Diane Arbus photographs.

They spent their junior year in the same overseas program in Jerusalem, deciding, after many negotiations, that after two years apart they could risk venturing into a program that put them in the same place. They lived in the dormitories up on Mount Scopus that looked out over the pale hills all around, which were attached by bus route to the small neighborhood of Givat Tzarfatit and then to the great apartment buildings of Ramat Eshkol. That was Daniel's mental map of the area in which he had lived. It was only much later that his reading brought to his attention that this area was surrounded by Arab villages and a large Palestinian refugee camp. They had been utterly invisible to him.

It was a year of great transformation for them both. They had grown up in a Jewish suburb of Chicago and had spent summers at a Jewish camp they both adored, where they had learned Hebrew and had Israeli counselors, and been steeped in Israeli culture. For Joel, there was a deep feeling of coming home. He lucked out by having a genial and outgoing roommate, and he became friends with his group of friends, thereby winning the unspoken contest in his program for best assimilation into Israeli culture.

For Daniel, the feeling of living in Israel was harder to describe. He had been struggling to accept that he was gay, and when he looked back on it years later, he realized that going to Israel was an attempt to shore up his manhood, which felt compromised among his sexually active college friends. But instead, aroused by sensory Israel—the heady sunshine and cool mountain air of Jerusalem, warm challah and harsh coffee, beautiful men in sandals or in uniform, the language that brought his teeth, palate, throat, and tongue into a new, more vigorous rapport—he was certain for the first time that he was gay. He was also sure that he was the only gay man in his entire acquaintance, and was terrified that anyone would find out.

His own roommate was a neuroscience major who spent most of his time in the lab, and to whom Daniel had nothing to say. During those long, lonely days, he'd sit in his crummy dorm room, listening to Israeli music, learning the chords on his guitar, and then poring over the dictionary to learn the words, many of which came in elevated or archaic constructions. It was how he learned Hebrew, and to this day he loved Israeli folk music: it was hardwired in him as surely as Beatles tunes were, so that when he died and they autopsied his brain, they'd find a marble-sized space for all the information he'd ever learned, and a wrinkly hunk of that matter devoted to the lyrics of Israeli songs. Everybody knew them and who had written them; many of them were poems by the great Israeli poets set to music. They were about beloved places and landscapes—sea, mountain, field—about army life, yearning for peace, clinging to love in the face of craziness. His critique of them became increasingly harsh over the years: he found them baldly nationalistic, staking out biblical and emotional claims to various lands, the songs about longing for peace completely empty and hypocritical. Now when Daniel listened to the playfully simple songs about shoelaces, or thunder, or galoshes, sung by men in childishly flattened nasal voices, he heard them trying to show that they were just boys after all, not part of a highly trained occupying force. But his critique of the songs couldn't prevent them from stirring his heart.

When Daniel came out the following year, back at Oberlin, after he got involved with his first boyfriend, Jonathan, Joel was clumsy and defensive; he wrote Daniel a stiff letter from Princeton in which he said that, while he had some gay friends, he didn't believe any of them were very happy people. Daniel and Jonathan had been scathing about it, imagining him to be threatened by his own sexuality.

Over the ensuing years, though, as he and Joel had moved into their adult lives and inhabited different continents, those conflicts had been forgiven, if not entirely forgotten. Then, last September, Joel had joyfully, and twinfully, stepped toward him. He'd sent him excited emails weeks before Daniel's trip about the things they'd do together if Daniel had time, he'd proudly introduced him to the writers and producers at *Israel Today*, he'd plopped his baby boy in Daniel's arms and marveled at how much Noam and Daniel looked alike. When he took Daniel to the airport to fly back to the States, and the security agent at the entrance to the check-in line asked Daniel how he and Joel were related, Joel grabbed Daniel around the neck and pulled his face close to his, and said, "How do you *think* we're related?!"

It was as though, Daniel thought, they could now finally rest in their twinship, and love and admire each other. It was during that visit that Joel and Ilana told him they were making out their wills, and that they wanted to designate him the guardian of their children if they should die. It was in the morning, on Joel's day off, and Gal was at *gan*; he and Joel were on their third cups of coffee, sitting around the kitchen table, the sink piled with dishes, and Ilana was running a finger across Noam's cheek to keep him from falling asleep at her breast.

"Are you sure?" Daniel asked. Pleasure and surprise and pride had flared up in him, along with a little panic. "We couldn't raise them here, it'd mean taking them to Northampton with us."

Ilana looked down at the sated baby on her lap—his head thrown back, his eyes rolling back in his head, milk dribbling from the side of his mouth—and laughed. She took her giant breast in her two hands and packed it back into her bra, pulled down her shirt. "Look," she said, her face, which was usually tuned toward the comic, becoming brooding. "I grew up in a very, very sad house. I don't want my children to grow up in a house like that. If we will die, take them away from here. Enough is enough." She flicked her wrist, her hand flying out in a gesture of dismissal.

Daniel looked at Joel, who was sitting back in his chair, a hand resting on the table. He switched to English. "And the whole being-raised-by-homos thing? You don't worry that Noam will turn into a big sissy?"

They shook their heads. "In fact," Joel said, his face lighting up with a bright idea, "you're welcome to take them both right now!"

"No, really," Daniel said, laughing.

"No," Joel said, "we're not worried about that."

THE GUY BEHIND THE counter at the *makolet* did a bewildered double take when he saw Daniel, who murmured, "His twin brother." The grocer told him that he participated in his sorrow, the Hebrew way of expressing condolence. Daniel laid milk and bread on the counter, stood pondering the different kinds of coffee on the shelf and hesitantly selected one labeled for a French press. Before paying, he stepped back outside to pick up a paper from the newsstand. The front page of *Ma'ariv* made his heart jump. There was a picture of Matt, handsome and imperious, his face wrapped in dark glasses, his hand on Daniel's back. It had been taken outside the airport; the rest of the family was huddled with the social worker, only the backs of their heads visible. He picked up a copy of the *Jerusalem Post*, which ran the same picture, only beneath the fold, and went back in to pay.

As he got into the car, the driver's seat already hot in the morning sun, he thought about his prickliness, his lack of generosity, around Matt these days. An ethic of rigorous self-examination had made him ask himself over the years whether he had just jumped at the chance of having *any* boyfriend, living as he did in a town that was a mecca for lesbians—a town that posted on the municipal parking garage a sign reading *Northampton: Where the coffee is strong and so are the women*—but something of a wasteland for gay men. Over and over, he had come to the position that while Matt wasn't the man he'd expected to love, life sometimes sent you something wonderful you'd never imagined. Now all he could think was that, given the choice between Joel dying and Matt, he would have chosen Matt to be the one to die. It was a thought that had come to him more than once, and its randomness, its sheer primitiveness, bewildered and horrified him. How could you think that about the man you loved? What did it mean about the quality of his love for Matt?

When he returned home, Matt was up, sitting with Lydia at the kitchen table, eating a piece of toast. Daniel felt his heart hurtle toward him in compensatory love and remorse. "Check this out," he said, tossing the *Ma'ariv* onto the table. Matt looked at it and his eyes widened. "Shit," he breathed.

"What?" Lydia asked. He turned the paper toward her and she studied it for a moment. "You look like a movie star caught by paparazzi," she said.

Matt flushed. "What does the caption say?"

Daniel stooped over the paper. "'Television personality Joel Rosen's family arrived at Ben Gurion Airport from Newark, New Jersey, yesterday, en route to identifying his remains.'" His finger dropped to a headline under the fold. "Wait, there's a little story here about Joel and his show. There's apparently going to be a profile of him in the Friday paper." He looked toward the guest room. "Where's Gal? Still sleeping?" Matt nodded.

"We're going to have to get her up for the shiva," Lydia said.

Sam came in wearing chinos and a white shirt, his eyes bruised and hollow-looking. He peered down at the paper on the table and frowned. "Is that Matt?" he asked. He bent over, squinting, then looked up. "Look, Matt, you made it into the newspaper."

Matt looked at Daniel, who looked up from the paper and gave him a shrug. "I didn't do it on purpose," Matt said lamely. He was thinking how bummed they must be to have his be the face of the Rosen family.

Daniel's fingers were running under the lines of a story in the paper, his lips moving. He tsked, suddenly irritable, and looked up again. "These profiles of the dead," he said. He read, "'Aviva was always smiling, always happy.' Why do they always have to turn the dead into grinning idiots? What if Aviva was really depressed, went around moping all the time? Would she deserve to be blown up? And here's another one," he said, warming to his theme as they all raised their heads in surprise. "A sixteen-year-old survivor of the *shuk* bombing, who's going to have half a kilo of shrapnel remaining in her body. She says, 'My hopes? Everybody wants to get married and have a family—I want to live like everybody else.' Why do they always want to be like everybody else? Why is that the most complimentary thing you can say about someone in this goddamn country?"

They were silent. Then Sam clucked, "They're just traumatized kids, Dan."

Matt, meanwhile, was suppressing a grin, thinking, *That's my boy*. He tried to catch Daniel's eye, but Daniel pushed his chair back and went into the bathroom, closing the door behind him.

And there was Lydia looking at him with her big, probing brown eyes. Matt composed his face and cleared his throat. "You know, honey," she said. "Daniel is going to need a lot of support."

Matt blinked at her, not knowing how to answer, the statement was so insultingly obvious. Support was an understatement: Did she know he was going to be a parent of her grandchildren? "I'm aware of that, Lydia," he finally said.

THE APARTMENT WAS PACKED all day with people who had come to sit shiva. They all recognized Matt from the newspaper. He was introduced over and over as Daniel's "friend." In their mouths, his name was pronounced "Mett." He noted that Israelis seemed to favor the limp handshake over the muscular American one. He continued to find them beautiful, with their blend of Middle Eastern and European looks, the women with stylish hair with henna highlights, the men hunched forward to talk with their cell phones in their fists, sunglasses perched on top of their heads. Many people seemed to be avoiding him, though, and he couldn't tell if they were shy, or rude, or uncomfortable speaking English, or homophobic. One guy, a friend of Ilana's, had "closet case" written all over him. He had turned away just as Daniel introduced Matt, but he kept staring at Matt and looking away, and whenever Matt drifted in his direction, he scurried off under some invisible pretext. It could be amusing, Matt thought, to spend the entire shiva chasing after the poor guy. Instead, he stood against a counter, which was crowded with coffee cakes and casseroles, his palms resting on it, with the aim of looking as though he was in charge of something.

A reporter was making his way around the room, nodding sympathetically to the people he was talking to and taking discreet notes on a little pad without looking down at it. Ilana's parents were seated on the couch, and Matt watched them with a heavy heart. They were Holocaust survivors; their lives had pretty much sucked from beginning to end, he thought. He had heard a lot about Malka, things he wasn't supposed to know. She was one of the few children to survive Auschwitz, and her mother had saved her by hiding her in a pile of corpses, where Malka had remained for several days. She suffered from bouts of severe depression; Ilana had once told Daniel that, in those moments, it seemed as if she was returning to the pile of bodies, pledging her loyalty to them by being dead herself. But she didn't look like the wreck Matt had been led to expect she'd be. In fact, he found her kind of lovely. Her posture, bent forward in courtesy or deference or an inability to hear well, expressed a kind of polite earnestness. Her blue eyes were washed out to their faintest color, and reddish-silver hair hung down to her shoulders, one side held back with a barrette—a girlish effect on a woman in her seventies, but not in a weird Baby Jane kind of way. Matt wondered what she had made of her bruising, loud-mouthed daughter, and imagined many a migraine requiring lying on the couch with a cold compress on her head. She had a way of narrow-ing her eyes that made her look chronically puzzled, or a little dim. Lydia, he knew, thought Malka was stupid. But maybe, he thought, she narrowed her eyes to let everything in more slowly, until her nervous system could stand it.

He knew that taking her grandchildren to the States would be the last straw. Even thinking about it made him have to close his eyes against the awfulness of it. He heaved himself off the counter and went out onto the tiny balcony.

The social worker was there, leaning meditatively over the railing with a lit cigarette in her fingers. "Shalom, Shoshi," he said, glad to see her. "May I bum a cigarette?" He gestured toward the small table her cigarettes and lighter lay upon.

"Sure."

"I'm an ex-smoker," he confided, after lighting up and exhaling.

She shrugged comically. "So am I," she said. "Until there is a *pigua*."

He had heard that word enough times to know that it referred to a terrorist attack. Daniel had explained that it came from the root "to hurt," so that literally it meant something like an injury.

They smoked for a little while, leaning over the railing and looking down at the street, where a cluster of little girls with backpacks was coming home from school, all of them chattering at once. Matt shot a sideways glance at Shoshi. She wore patterned pants and a short-sleeved shell, small gold hoop earrings; she was well put together, if not particularly stylish. He pondered what to say to her, and settled upon, "You must see a lot of horrible things."

She turned and bestowed upon him the gentle, steady gaze he was coming to love. "Yes," she said. "But for me, it's the smell that is the worst."

"Tell me about it," Matt drawled, sniffing his arm and making a face.

"At home, when I call to say there has been a *pigua*, my husband turns on the boiler. But even after many long, long showers, the smell stays with me for about a week."

"How do you keep on going?"

"We don't work all the time. Each unit is on duty for only three months."

He nodded. "How many social workers are there per unit?"

"It's depend," Shoshi said, making a translation error Matt was getting used to. They always went out in pairs, she told him, and had a support team checking in with them. The entire unit met at the very end to assess their performance and to talk through their feelings. "That night, I can't sleep, but I go to work the next morning. I feel sick, weak, nauseated."

She spoke with the openness of the social workers he knew, which to his ear, bordered on the burlesque; if she were American, she'd be mentioning "sharing" a lot. He imagined that there was probably an Israeli equivalent to that language that was a little blunter. He could tell that her frankness came partially, but not only, from her training— and the part that came from her personality felt immensely touching to him. He had been used to feeling outrage that suicide bombings in Israel were widely televised in the U.S. while the bombings upon Palestinian civilians never were. But her struggle to help grieving and traumatized people brought into relief everybody's vulnerable humanity. It pressed upon his worldview and scrambled it a little.

He said gently, "Well, you're very good at what you do. We're lucky we got you."

"Thank you," she said gravely. "I must leave you today. Now it's become the work of the social worker from Bituach Leumi."

They struggled for a while over how to translate that—"national security"?—until Matt understood that it was something like the Israeli version of Social Security. He put his hand on his pained heart. Maybe he was romanticizing her, but she seemed to understand how much he felt like an outsider.

"Won't you check up on us at all?" he asked. "We'll need a lot of checking up on. We're a big mess."

She nodded without smiling. "Sure I will," she said.

IN THE LIVING ROOM, Daniel was listening to talk of revenge. *They just don't want peace! They don't understand peace.* The same old words. Ilana's father and the principal from Ilana's school were huddled together, comparing the moments each had known that Arafat was not a viable bargaining partner. For Yaakov it was Camp David, where Arafat was offered a state on a silver platter and walked away from it—Daniel could have uttered the exact cliché before it came out of Yaakov's mouth. But the principal, an overbearing and pompous man with a knitted *kipa*, whom Yaakov clearly deferred to, clucked and shook his head; naturally, he had known way before that point. Daniel heard from other conversations that the army was already engaged in a retaliation operation called Righteous Sword. It made him miserable.

He looked around for Matt and saw him out on the balcony, talking with the social worker. He knew how to make himself at home; Daniel never had to worry about that, which was a big bonus in a boyfriend. Matt would come home from parties where he'd known no one, and report things to Daniel about his friends that Daniel had no idea about. He watched him now, holding a cigarette away from himself so the smoke wouldn't get into his hair, and nodding as Shoshi spoke earnestly to him. His hair was shaggy—they'd left just before he was due for a haircut—and somehow looked beautiful; he looked most beautiful when careless about his appearance.

The familiar sense of strange marvel that he was with a man like

Matt came over him now. Daniel had always imagined himself with someone more like Jonathan, who was moderately good-looking and with whom he shared a love of George Eliot and John Donne, and who, when they left a movie together, always had a corroborating opinion of it. Matt's judgments were very strong, but always a little weird. He judged the performances of the actors in movies, instead of the narrative or the images.

But for all of Matt's love of crappy movies and reality TV and the same hunky movie stars every other gay man in America had a fetish for, he had excellent instincts about fairness and social justice. Unlike Daniel, he had grown up as a pretty queeny kid, unable to conceal his difference from the other boys, and that had forced him to hone his ability to sniff out piety and hypocrisy, and the violence underlying them. Matt was a political animal. He woke up and read the paper cover to cover; he read political memoirs and contemporary books about politics as avidly and indiscriminately as he did the memoirs of movie stars. His favorite person in the whole world was Bill Clinton, whom he called Shakespearean.

If Matt understood these conversations, he'd rip them apart with indignation and incisiveness. But, Daniel wondered, was that even what he needed? Even thinking about it made his hackles rise.

He looked around the living room at the sober conversations, checked on his parents to see whether they needed any translation help. They were sitting stiffly on the couch, ignored by the other mourners either because of the language barrier or because the guests couldn't face talking to Joel's mother. Lydia had her gracious, attentive social face on—her game face, Daniel thought, and it broke his heart. He went and perched on the edge of the sofa next to her, and she reached up and rubbed his arm. A small group of people from Joel's work was gathered in the corner talking to the reporter, who seemed like a decent enough guy. He had asked Daniel about what Joel was like as a boy growing up, and Daniel had struggled to describe his brother without using cheesy clichés—the last thing he wanted was for Joel to come off as the all-American Jewish boy, likable and popular, a lover of sports and of his adopted country. But whenever he tried to get a little complicated, he found he risked sounding critical. The reporter was very interested in their being twins, and asked him if he felt a part of him was now gone. Daniel had stared at him and said, "Of course. But wouldn't I feel that way if he was just a regular brother?"

Daniel rose when Gal's best friend, Leora, came in with her parents, shyly, edged forward by them, her hair in immaculate braids. Gal came up and seized her hand, pulled her out of the room to her bedroom, and shut the door behind them. Daniel watched them go. He'd be taking Gal away from Leora. He knew and liked her parents; he hugged them, and they murmured in his ear. Leora's mother, Gabrielle, was tearfully saying how much they loved Gal and how happy they'd be to take her anytime, when Daniel's eye caught a man behind them, waiting to get in and looking at him expectantly. Was he supposed to know him? He thanked Gabrielle, and said in Hebrew, "Will you speak to my parents? They're sitting alone." All the while racking his brain to see if he remembered this man.

"I won't stay long," the man said hurriedly, in a confidential half whisper. He was a middle-aged man with disheveled, graying hair and a knitted *kipa* pinned askew on his head. "I just wanted you to have this." He had taken Daniel's hand and was placing something in it. Daniel looked down, and back at the man. It was the nut to a medium-sized bolt, a loosely woven gold chain threaded through it.

"*Ma zeh?*" he asked sternly. What is this?

"My daughter was killed in a *pigua*," the man told him. "Sbarro." He was referring to the pizza place in downtown Jerusalem, which had been destroyed a few years earlier. "The police told us that what ultimately killed her was a nut driven into her neck."

Daniel took a step back, his heart quickening.

"At the funeral, all of her friends from her class wore nuts around their necks, as a tribute to her. And when I heard of your brother's death, I thought you might want to share this tribute with us. To become part of our large family."

"Thank you," Daniel said automatically, his throat constricting.

"I brought some for his children too, in case they wanted to remember their parents by something." He was extending two additional, smaller necklaces.

"No," Daniel said, backing away.

"I understand your feelings," the man said with a look of eager compassion. "May I come in and talk for a moment?"

Just then Daniel felt a touch on his back. It was Matt, standing behind him, big and warm. "Do you need help getting rid of this guy?" he was murmuring.

Daniel turned toward him and nodded helplessly.

"I'm sorry," Matt said to the man, not knowing whether he even understood English. "Family only." He closed the door as the man took an uncertain step backward. "There!" he said brightly. "What did he want?"

Daniel held out the necklace. "His daughter was killed in the Sbarro bombing, apparently by one of these to the neck."

"You're kidding," Matt said. "What a freak."

Daniel gave a surprised huff of a laugh. "How did you know I needed rescuing?"

"You staggered backward and clutched your chest."

"I did not."

Matt looped a finger through the necklace. "Why don't you give that to me."

"No," Daniel said, suddenly uncertain, pulling it back.

Matt raised an eyebrow. "So it's going to join those nails in your pocket?"

Daniel flashed him an angry, self-conscious look. They had pocked his palms and thighs with tiny bloody marks.

"Okay," Matt said gently. "Sorry."

They returned to the living room, and when Daniel noticed that Leora's father was perched on the arm of the couch, talking to his parents, he went over to join them, still a little flushed. His mother had learned that Moti was a builder, and was telling him what a huge impression it always made on her to see an entire city built of stone the color of the hillsides. "Rising to Jerusalem," she was saying, translating the Hebrew verb used to convey the word *going*, when applied to Jerusalem. "It's as though you really are rising, being uplifted—it feels almost spiritual."

"That's the idea of Jerusalem stone," Moti said with a faint smile. He was a big, wide-faced, genial guy; he and Joel had played racquetball together, and Daniel remembered something about his cooking a mean osso buco. "It's supposed to convey a sense of earthiness, but also of holiness." His voice was husky, and he stepped delicately over the English consonants. "The directive to build with Jerusalem stone goes back to the British Mandate. But after the '67 war, when Israel annexed an enormous territory around Jerusalem, the first priority of the city planners was to prevent it from ever being repartitioned. So they used Jerusalem stone to make occupied territory look like an integral part of Jerusalem." He shrugged with a self-deprecating grimace. "Please forgive the lecture. If Gabrielle heard me going on about this she'd be flashing me warning looks."

"No, it's fascinating," Lydia said. "I had no idea."

"The stone mostly comes from quarries in the West Bank now, because stone dust is an environmental hazard."

Daniel had become alert, his sense of Moti shifting and complicating. "So Palestinians produce the stone that's designed to make Jerusalem Jewish forever," he said. "And get sick doing so."

"Exactly."

"That doesn't seem right," Lydia said, and they all laughed uncomfortably at the understatement.

"I'm surprised the supply lasts, there's so much building," Daniel said.

"Oh, they hardly ever use it as a construction material anymore," Moti shrugged. "Now it's usually just used as a facade."

Daniel clutched his chest. "Are you going to destroy *all* our illusions?" he cried.

Lydia sighed and smoothed her dress over her knees, her rings gleaming off creased knuckles. "Of course, I don't know when we'll come back here—that'll depend. Certainly, rising to Jerusalem will never feel the same." She looked up and grimaced apologetically, and Moti took her hand.

WHEN JOEL AND ILANA'S lawyer called at about four thirty, Daniel suddenly felt seized with urgency to open the will. He could continue no longer in this suspended state, with people asking about the kids. His father had cornered him in the guest bedroom, where he'd gone to take a breather, and said, "Your mother is very concerned about the Grossmans. Apparently, Malka told her how glad she was that the children could spend some time with their American family before coming to live with them."

So when Assaf called, Daniel asked him to come over in about an hour. There was a lull in the shiva. Gabrielle had asked if they wanted her to take the kids home with her family for dinner, and after some hesitation, looking at Gal's hopeful face, and at Noam in Gabrielle's arms playing with her necklace, Daniel had asked if she was sure she wanted to take the baby too, and she had said sure, Noam was her favorite cutie-pie.

Assaf Schwartz was a paunchy, middle-aged man with unfashionably large glasses. He shook hands with and offered grave condolences to the whole family, in both English and Hebrew. Daniel remembered that Joel and Ilana had told him about Assaf; they believed that he was a true mensch. Ilana had dealt with him in her work, seen him preside over the divorces and custody fights of her students' parents.

Daniel began to herd them into the master bedroom. Matt headed that way and Daniel caught his arm. "Matt," he said. "I think it's better that you not come in. It'll freak everyone out even more." He lowered his voice. "If they imagine that the kids have been left only to me, instead of to us together, it might prevent a firestorm."

"Oh," Matt said. "Okay." That sounded reasonably strategic to him for all of two seconds, and by the time his outrage surfaced, they were all inside, the door closed behind them. He'd come all this way, he thought, only to have door after door closed in his face. He stood there, his chest heaving. Where could he go? His mind cast around for options. He didn't know where he was, and there wasn't an English-language map in the house as far as he knew, and he didn't know where the car keys were. If he could take the car, he'd just drive and drive along the winding narrow streets till he was good and lost. Or find himself a bar—were there bars in Jerusalem? There must be—and get good and hammered. And pick up some dark-skinned soldier with peach fuzz and traces of acne, and blow him silly.

But he didn't even know what the address was here, to find his way back. He pondered that, his own severe infantilization.

The living room had emptied out, at least for now. He went into the kitchen and started opening cabinets, trying to find a liquor stash. He finally found a bottle of scotch among the vinegar and soy sauce bottles, and poured himself an enormous shot into a coffee mug. He downed it, shuddering. Then he slipped out the front door and stumbled out into the street, squinting from the low, cutting western sun. He walked down the street, stray cats scattering before him. To his left was a nar-row flight of stone stairs, leading up; he began to climb them, walking past little gardens, profusions of flowers falling over stone walls, and shadowed doorways into apartment buildings, some with old, creaky iron gates. At the top, a bus roared by on a wide and busy street. He ran across and turned up another flight of stairs, where again he felt sheltered from the warm and busy city. He could smell some type of wild plant. The loveliness of the neighborhood made him want to cry, and the alcohol hit him then and made him stagger. He found a small raggedy playground where a lone grandma, a scarf on her head, sat near a stroller as a toddler played in the sand. He sat down on a bench and closed his eyes, feeling his head spiral. He would sit there till it got dark. If Daniel needed him, he wouldn't be there.

The conversations he'd had at the shiva bubbled in his mind. What were the names of that couple he'd been stuck in a corner with? The guy was the son of Yaakov and Malka's best friends. Natan Fink, that was his name. And his haughty, elegant wife, whose name Matt couldn't dredge up. Natan had apparently played with Ilana as a kid. When the conversation with Matt faltered, he'd gestured toward the baby gate that normally blocked off the kitchen and now leaned unused against a cabinet, as if to say that he'd just noticed it. "When we were young, they didn't have childproofing, and shmildproofing; they didn't believe that a kid would die if he ate a peanut. Do you understand? These people had survived the biggest catastrophe that could happen, they were trying to begin a new life, they didn't waste their time with nonsense. So we kids ran wild; we played on construction sites, in wadis, we rode bikes—without helmets!" He made a shocked face. "All over Jerusalem, into the Arab parts, where the Arabs all knew us and liked us and gave us rolls with *zatar*." He stopped and laughed. "Not that we weren't a little messed up! If you ever hurt yourself, or felt bad, you looked into your parents' eyes and felt ashamed to think of that as suffering." He looked at his wife and said complacently, "But I turned out okay, right?"

His wife patted his arm. "Sure, sweetie," she said.

Natan's eyes moved over the living room and then rested fondly on Yaakov. "They all helped each other. If one lost a job, the others pitched in. If one had, God forbid, to be hospitalized, or had a nervous breakdown, the others were there to help. And Malka and Yaakov! Well. To this day, my parents say that they wouldn't have made it without them. They got on the same boat to Palestine as Malka. None of them were married yet, of course. They'd all lost their parents, brothers, sisters. So they had to be a family to each other."

They were silent for a while, then Natan heaved a mighty sigh. "He's a hero, Yaakov. A true hero. And now—*ach*."

Sitting on the park bench, Matt wrapped his arms around himself and rubbed. The sun had lowered behind a building and it was suddenly cold. He thought about how he'd tell Daniel this story, about this obnoxious man who worshipped Yaakov. He was sure that by now he knew more about some of these people than Daniel did. Anger rose sullenly in him again. He knew Daniel was grieving, but didn't he, Matt, deserve a little recognition, deserve to be seen as part of the family? As a participant in this drama?

IN THE BEDROOM, THE four parents perched uncomfortably at the edges of Joel and Ilana's bed. Malka, whose feet didn't quite reach the floor, smoothed down the bedspread on either side of her; Lydia had picked up a small framed picture of Joel and Ilana hiking up north before they got married, and was rubbing the dust off the glass with the hem of her blouse. Daniel was crouching at the side of the bed, his pulse racing, ready to get this over with. His mother and Malka kept insisting that he come on up and sit down. "I'm fine," he said, and "There's no room!" till his mother pressed closer to his father, bumping the line of bodies, which moved in a small series of sighs and grunts. Daniel sat, the mattress drooping under half his butt, his mother folding his hand in hers and rubbing it. He pulled it away. "I'm falling off!" he said, and stood.

Assaf stood awkwardly in front of them with a manila envelope in his hand. He twisted and looked behind him at the floor, as though contemplating sitting there, then turned back toward them and cleared his throat. "Is everybody . . . ?" he murmured. He read the opening language of the will, and explained to Daniel's parents that it was just the everyday legal stuff about Joel and Ilana being the parents to Gal and Noam, and being of sound mind. Then Assaf peeked at them over the paper and cleared his throat again. "'It is our wish,'" he read, "'that our children's uncle, Daniel Rosen, be designated the guardian of Gal and Noam, to live with them wherever he wishes.'" He read it once in Hebrew, and then translated it into English.

There was silence. Anxiety gaped in Daniel's chest as he waited for the information to take. Yaakov's face was reddening. Malka looked at him, bewildered, for an explanation. Then she looked at Daniel. "But you'll live with them here, in this house."

Daniel tried to look at her, but it was too hard to meet her stupefied gaze, her sagging mouth. "No, Malka," he said, "I'm going to have to take them to my home, in the States."

"*Lama?*" she asked. Why?

He began to speak, but his parents were staring at him, pulling his attention back. "Have you known this all along?" his mother asked, eyes blazing.

"For a while," Daniel hedged.

"How could you not tell me?" she cried. "I feel like such a fool! I never anticipated this." Her hand was gripping Sam's sleeve hard, and he was murmuring, "Honey."

"I must tell you something important," the lawyer said, raising his voice over the clamor of distress and incomprehension. "In Israeli wills, the disposition of property is always upheld. But not necessarily the disposition of children." He spoke in Hebrew.

Daniel saw understanding slowly dawn over Yaakov's face, and a flash of hope. "What are you talking about?" he demanded.

"The government considers what is the good of the children, in family court."

"What?" Daniel cried. "Their own *parents* wanted this for them. The court would go against the parents' wishes?"

"I'm afraid so," Assaf said gently. He stood with the papers dangling in his hand, and Daniel suddenly hated him, this hypocritical pose of gentle advocacy, his big sorrowful eyes blinking out of those ridiculous glasses. "If they thought it was for the good of the children."

His mother had Daniel by the sleeve; there was the clamor for translation, and he shook it off, he was trying to think. "You can't be serious," he said to Assaf, and then whirled at his parents and spat out an irritated translation. "And I'm sure," he said, his lips curled, "that living with two queers is exactly what the Israeli state thinks of as for the good of the children."

"Daniel," his father said.

"What are my chances?" Daniel demanded in Hebrew, ignoring his father, fixing Assaf with a cold look. He remembered something. "They're American citizens; doesn't that count for something?"

"Not necessarily, Daniel," Assaf said. "You'll still need a court order to take them out of the country." He reached forward and clasped Daniel's shoulder. "But don't assume anything, either good or bad. There are many factors."

His father gripped his elbow. "Don't worry, son," he said softly. "We'll fight this."

Daniel shook his arm free. "I don't understand this," he said. "The *parents* decided what was for the good of the children." He felt he was about to cry and, mortified, covered his face with his hands. "Poor Joel and Ilana," he moaned. "It's what they *wanted*."

"This is crazy," Lydia was saying, looking to Sam for corroboration.

The lawyer crouched and tried to take them all in with his gaze. "Everybody, please be calm," he said, first in English, then in Hebrew. "Look. We are shocked by these terrible deaths. When we recover a little bit, I know that we'll all do our best to make sure that Gal and Noam have lives that are as safe and normal as possible."

Normal? Daniel burst into tears.

Malka was clutching at Yaakov and asking him how Ilana could do this to them, and he was urging her, with increasing impatience, to calm down, to try to understand that the court would surely be on their side.

CHAPTER 4

H E COULDN'T FIND Matt anywhere. Their bedroom was empty, the sofa bed made up, with the bed pillows, in worn pillowcases, stacked upon it. The window was open and the curtain billowing. He checked the bathroom and the balcony, and went back into their room and sat down on the sofa. He unbuttoned the top buttons of his shirt and stared at the desk till his vision blurred. There was a knock on the door frame; Yaakov stood there with his jacket on. "Malka doesn't feel well," he said. "I must take her home."

Daniel nodded numbly.

Yaakov turned away, and Daniel's parents came to the door of his room. His mother's face was tight; she was demanding, "How long have you known about this?"

His father leaned heavily on the desk.

Where the hell was Matt? The thought of not bringing the children home made Daniel sick; the prospect of caring for them was the only thing that had kept him from going off the deep end. He buried his head in his hands.

"Daniel, I want to know how long you've known about this," Lydia said.

"Not long, Mom," he lied, his voice muffled through his fingers, "just for about a month."

"It was Ilana's idea, wasn't it." She had a difficult relationship with Ilana, whom she perceived as constantly policing the boundaries between them; she'd been furious when Ilana had asked her to wait a month before visiting, after Gal was born. They all spent a lot of energy denying that this was true, but Daniel knew that it was. Still, leaving him the kids hadn't been Ilana's idea, not hers alone.

"No," Daniel said firmly, looking up. "It was both of them. We had a conversation about it."

There was silence. Finally, Lydia said, "I have trouble believing that."

"Why?" he demanded. "I find that offensive. You think Joel wouldn't trust me to raise his children?"

"Daniel," his father said. "Please don't escalate this any more than necessary."

Lydia began to cry. "I feel so betrayed," she said. "It's as though Joel were killed all over again."

"Oh, please!" Daniel said. "His having a desire of his own means he was killed all over again?"

"Daniel," his father barked.

"I can't help the way I feel," his mother said. "Do not tell me how I can and cannot feel."

Daniel's hands were sweating on the knees of his pants. This new legal hitch made him feel desperately undermined, as though his bid to be an adult had failed right in front of them. He knew that, to his father, he'd always been the perplexing twin, given every opportunity but lacking in the kind of ambition Sam understood. He'd always suspected that Sam thought of his homosexuality itself as a form of sloth, something that put him in the disappointing category of people without a work ethic. And now—any cachet he'd had, any way he'd been ennobled by the prospect of rescuing the children, had vanished.

His father closed his eyes, and when he opened them again he said, "At least in Massachusetts the kids would be closer to us."

Lydia looked at him sharply, and he shrugged. "Look," he said, "we might have to be realistic about this." He looked steadily at her as her eyes widened with incredulity and outrage, her mascara thickened with tears. "Honey, we're in third place," he said. "For whatever reason, Joel and Ilana clearly wanted Daniel to take the kids, and the state is going to lean toward keeping them here, with their other grandparents."

"That's out of the question," Lydia said. "Malka is mentally disturbed, she can't even keep her house clean. And how old are they? They must be in their seventies!"

Sam shrugged again and gestured toward Daniel, as if to suggest that he was a better option, and Lydia's face, rigid with shock and rage, crumpled. "It's as though he were killed all over again," she cried.

"Mother, would you stop saying that?"

"How are you going to raise these children!" she demanded. "And with whom? With *Matt*?" She gave an ugly laugh.

And then, when Daniel couldn't stand it for one more moment, Matt walked into the room, red-cheeked, bringing in with him the bracing chill of the night wind. "How's it going?" he asked.

Daniel looked up. Matt looked like a miracle, handsome and tousled. Daniel wanted to fling himself into his arms. But instead, he found himself saying accusingly, "We're not going to get the kids."

"What?"

His parents' eyes swiveled heavily toward Matt, and Daniel saw for the first time just how much Lydia disliked him. Sam explained what had happened, with Daniel interrupting to gloss the situation in the bleakest light. "The good of the child," he snapped. "Since when has a religious state considered it the good of the child to be placed in the care of queers?"

His father made an admonishing sound, and Lydia winced. "Don't say that," she said. "I hate that word."

"It's what we are, Mother," he said. "No matter how respectable we are, how well-behaved, to them we're just *queers*."

Matt sat next to him on the couch and put a hand on his arm. Lydia rose frostily and took Sam's hand, and said, "I'm not going to listen to this. We'll let you calm down."

When they'd left, Matt slid the door shut.

"It's true," Daniel insisted.

"You're preaching to the choir, honey," Matt said. He tried to take him into his arms, but Daniel shook him off.

"Where *were* you? I looked all over for you." His face was exhausted and ashy, crusted with layers of dried tears, and Matt's heart went out to his poor, tired spirit.

"I'm sorry, baby," he said gently. "I left the house for a little while and went for a walk." He was proud of himself for not mentioning that Daniel himself had sent him away.

"A little while?! I'm sitting here getting tortured by my parents, who can't believe I'm capable of raising a child, and on top of that facing *losing* the kids . . . Have you been *drinking*?" He paused, letting out a shaky sigh. "It's just that I have to know if I'm going to be able to depend on you."

Matt's face contorted with disbelief. "What are you talking about?" he cried. "That's so unfair!"

"It isn't about fair or not fair, Matt," Daniel said. "It's about being there to help."

Matt's hand was gripped over his heart, wrinkling his shirt. "Hey, I'm a nice, helpful guy, but I'm not a magician," he protested. "I can't be sent away and be there for you at the same time." There was no reply. "You've hardly let me near you in the past couple of days. You've hardly even acknowledged me! Ilana's father asks who I am every time he lays eyes on me. And you know what? This is my life, too; you're not the only one who's going to be raising those kids." He was thinking, *If we even get them*—and he had no idea how he felt about the prospect of not getting them. He remembered Daniel's return from Israel last year, and how, as he unpacked, his hands paused over the opened suitcase on his bed and his face took on a solemnity that Matt had never seen before, and which was so much the cartoon essence of solemnity—his eyes shining and his face drawn long—that Matt thought at first that he was about to joke about something. When Daniel told him that Joel and Ilana wanted their kids to live with them if something happened to them, Matt's heart had tumbled all over itself to join him in the sense that a wonderful honor had been bestowed upon them. And he had felt that all along, on Daniel's behalf, but also on his own. It seemed a sign of tremendous trust and love, and he had a sense of how subversive it was too, how deeply it went against the grain of the Israeli ideology of populating the land with Jewish children. He had never imagined that it would come to fruition; and when it did, he veered madly between excited pride and dread.

"It's my name in the will," Daniel countered, "and I'm the one who will have to go to court."

"And no doubt you'll keep me as far away from those proceedings as possible," Matt said.

Daniel stood and smacked his pants to smooth them. "You know what?" he said, drawing himself up. "I'm not having this conversation."

"Come on, Dan," Matt pleaded, standing between Daniel and the door. In the tiny room he could hear the labored breathing of his partner, could feel stress and sweat radiating off his body. "I don't want to fight."

Daniel refused to meet his eyes. They stood like that for a minute, and then Matt spoke. "This is awful," he said. "This is the most awful time in our entire lives. So let's be friends, okay? Otherwise, we're not going to survive this."

Daniel looked quickly at him, thinking, *We?* He took a shaky breath. "It's just that . . . I looked all over for you," he said, his eyes filling with tears.

Matt leveled him with a stare, knowing he should put his arms around him, even if he got pushed away again and again. But how much could you get blamed for not being there before you decided to just stop being there?

Daniel sat back down and covered his face with his hands. "I just wish I could talk to you," he said. "I come to bed wanting to curl up and talk to you. But I can't. You just don't get it."

Matt sat back down. "What don't I get?" he asked softly.

"The whole thing," Daniel said, waving a hand helplessly.

Matt shut his mind down, like a computer on sleep mode, and waited a few beats, willing himself to be patient. "What whole thing?"

Daniel looked at him. "I know how you feel about Israel, and about Joel and Ilana living here."

"And?" Matt asked, knowing that Daniel was referring to arguments they'd sometimes had, in which Matt had argued that Joel and Ilana should leave the country as long as it was an occupying power. He'd written his senior thesis on South Africa during apartheid, under a South African professor he admired who had gone into exile; and even though Daniel insisted over and over that the comparison didn't hold, South Africa was Matt's model for what the Israelis were doing. "In exile!" Daniel would exclaim. "I'm sorry, but who are you to tell people where to live?" It was the biggest bone of contention between them, and Matt thought it was stupid and a waste, since he and Daniel actually felt pretty much the same way about Israel, and because, when it came down to it, why should he be that invested in it anyway?

"I know you don't really feel this," Daniel said now, "but sometimes I think you might feel they deserved what they got."

Matt inhaled sharply. "Are you kidding me?" he said. *"Are you kidding me?"*

"I know it's not really true," Daniel said.

"You know it's not *really* true, but you think it may be a *little* true? Is that what you're saying?"

"Well, is it?" Daniel asked, looking up with a sudden challenge.

"Stop projecting, dude," Matt said, giving him a cool look. "Stop taking out your fucked-up feelings about this country on me."

Daniel flushed and sank onto the couch. He shot Matt a look of mingled anger and confusion. "I don't know what the hell I'm supposed to be feeling. I mean, I know what I'm *supposed* to be feeling. Righteous indignation at the terrorists for killing innocent people, and all of that." He looked quickly at Matt, then down again. *Aha*, thought Matt, *that's what he's mad about.* If you believed that the Occupation was itself a form of constant terrorism—because what else could you call humiliating Palestinian civilians, subjecting them to a thousand petty and infuriating regulations, stealing their land, depriving them of their livelihood, blowing up their homes? If you believed that, what the hell *were* you supposed to feel at this moment?

But it wasn't fair to take out his anger on him! Matt called it pulling the goy card. Because Matt wasn't Jewish, Daniel always claimed that he couldn't understand the depth of Daniel's misery over it, over the historical irony that his people had overcome oppression by becoming an occupying force. Once, a few years ago, he had made Matt read Leon Uris's *Exodus.* "Every Jewish kid of my generation read it," he'd told Matt. He wanted him to get a sense of Israel's prehistory, however distorted it was by the novel: how it came into being in the wake of the Holocaust, and how Jewish warriors smuggled into Palestine the refugees no other nation would save. He also wanted Matt to feel the romance of Israel, which Daniel had learned to feel in Jewish camp as a teenager, and which he thought the book would evoke in a passionate gay man. The Jewish soldiers were so manly and self-reliant, and there were many scenes of beautiful Jewish teenage warriors dancing the hora around campfires, eyes flashing. Matt gulped the book down, and reported that it gave him a total boner. "But do you get what I mean about what Jews love about Israel?" Daniel insisted as Matt nibbled his neck, whispering, "You be the handsome, emotionally damaged underground fighter, and I'll be the haughty girl in charge of the refugee camp in Cyprus." And then, when Daniel, laughing, pushed him, "Yes, I get it, I get it!"

Now Matt nodded warily. He knew that if Daniel couldn't have this conversation with him, he couldn't have it at all. He reached for Daniel's shoe, removed it, and took his foot into his hands, began massaging it gently over the sock.

"When my dad started talking about how innocent Joel and Ilana were . . . I mean, they *were* innocent. But you know what I mean. . . ."

"Yeah, I've been thinking about it. That whole innocence thing," Matt mused. "It kills me." His lip curled a little. "Your dad—you know, he was just doing his thing, he's devastated. But do you think anyone ever called Jay innocent when he died?"

Daniel snorted.

Matt's hands stopped.

"Don't stop," Daniel said. He opened his eyes. "What?"

Matt's eyes were blinking very rapidly, and his lips were pressed together.

"It's not the same thing," Daniel said.

Anger wormed into Matt's throat. Daniel's tone was so final and derisive. He sat still, fuming, and Daniel propped himself up on his elbow.

"Oh, come on, Matt," he said, incredulous. "It's not."

"Why?" Matt asked. "Because Jay was just fucking without a condom, while your brother was heroically drinking a latte?"

That stunned them both into silence. Then Daniel scrambled back into a sitting position and shouted, "Go to hell!" He glanced in the direction of the kitchen, where his parents were sitting, and lowered his voice to a vicious whisper. "Go to hell! I knew I couldn't talk to you!"

"You *can* talk to me," Matt cried. "Just don't insult my friend! Why do you have to insult him? I know you think he was just a silly queen, but he was a good person, Dan." He sat on the couch, his chest heaving, ashamed that he had insulted his partner's dead brother, and yet so hurt and furious he couldn't help it. For some reason, he remembered going to the movies with Jay, and how Jay always made Matt be absolutely quiet—not even a whisper or a snide comment here and there—even though when they'd watch TV together they could talk as much as they wanted. It was a rule. Jay hadn't had any long-term relationships till Kendrick, and he wasn't a breeder, and he didn't live in a majestic holy city at the center of a world-historical conflict. But did that make him unimportant? And why did Daniel have to be such a huge homophobe?

"This isn't about Jay! This isn't about you!" Daniel hissed.

But it had an impact on him! How could he say that? Just then the door slid open and Gal came in. She was chewing on a piece of bread wadded in her hand, and wore a bead necklace around her neck. The hair around her face had been pulled back and tied with a fancy hair band, clearly Gabrielle's work. She looked at them curiously as they quickly wiped their eyes and tried to compose their faces.

"Hey, Boo," Matt said, his voice hoarse. "Did you play with beads at Leora's?"

"Yeah," she said faintly, being cooperative with an interrogating adult while she eyed Daniel, who had turned his back to them and was wiping his eyes with his forearms. "Why Uncle Dani crying?" she asked.

Matt looked at Daniel. "He's sad," he told her. "He misses your *ema* and *abba*." He hoped it was okay to bring it up when she was having a break from mourning.

She shot Daniel a suspicious look, then backed up till she was standing against the doorjamb. "Why did the bad man hate the Jews?" she asked.

Daniel looked at Matt sharply and sat down beside him. "Who told you that?" he asked.

"Savta."

Matt waited, bitter mirth surfacing in his nose and sinuses; this one was *so* up to Daniel.

"Some Arabs hate the Jews," Daniel said, clearing his throat, "because when the Jews came to Israel, they lived on land that the Arabs say was theirs."

"Was it theirs?"

"Lots of it was," Daniel said. "The Israelis and the Arabs are not good at sharing."

She considered this. Then she asked, without looking at Daniel, "Is that why he killed Ema and Abba? Did they live on his land?"

Daniel and Matt looked at each other, eyes still, minds racing.

"No," Daniel said, "they didn't. He was just a very bad, angry man."

Gal gnawed off another piece of bread. "Leora's scared of taking a shower by herself," she reported to Daniel in Hebrew.

"Really? How come?" he asked, shrugging at Matt when her eyes darted away for a moment.

"She's afraid that water will go up her nose. She doesn't know how to breathe through her mouth," Gal said, and slipped out of the room.

Daniel and Matt sat there, looking at each other stupidly, until Matt rose and slid the door shut. "That was pretty lame," he said. "We better get our story straight."

Daniel laughed a little, and sighed a wide-eyed, shuddery sigh.

"I liked the part about the Jews and the Arabs not being good at sharing," Matt said, and when Daniel looked sharply at him, he protested, "No, really, I'm serious. What did she say there at the end?"

Daniel told him about Leora's fear of the shower, and they shrugged and laughed.

Matt snuck his hand onto Daniel's knee and pressed lightly. When Daniel looked into his face, his eyes were bright and intense. "Dan," he said, "I'm sorry."

Daniel breathed in and then out again, his breath like a small parcel he was picking up and putting down. He wasn't sure what Matt was saying—whether he was apologizing for what he'd said or just expressing general sorrow about the whole sad situation. And he did not forgive him. But it was hard, because Matt looked beautiful as feeling suffused his face and lent radiance to his eyes and mouth, and because, for better or for worse, he was the safest harbor Daniel knew.

Daniel got up to wash his face. Gal had gone into Joel and Ilana's room with his parents; a low TV sound came from behind the closed door. He swallowed a few sleeping pills. When he returned to the bedroom, Matt had opened up the bed. Daniel took off his pants and shirt, crawled under the covers in his underwear, and turned his face to the wall.

LYDIA EMERGED FROM BEHIND that closed bedroom door the next morning with her eyes red and her mouth set, and told Daniel that she was working very hard to accept that Ilana hadn't trusted her to raise the children. When Daniel opened his mouth to protest for the hundredth time that it wasn't just Ilana, she held up her hand and stopped him. "I'm trying to accept it," she said firmly. "She was entitled to her opinion." She heaved a great sigh. "And that's all I want to say."

It rankled, but he decided to let it go. He told himself that she had lost her son and was coping with this renewed injury, trying to be a big person the best way she could.

As it became clear that it would take at least three months for the custody issue to be worked out, Matt began making plans to go home. Daniel would stay for the duration; he'd have to meet with a caseworker and appear in court, probably several times. He had talked at length with his boss, and they'd worked out an arrangement where he could continue doing most of his story meetings and editing by telephone and email, at least through the next issue of the magazine. He found out that he could rent a cell phone on a monthly basis, and miraculously, Matt, who'd initially decided not to haul along Daniel's laptop, changed his mind on an impulse and grabbed it on their way out of the house. "What made you think to do that?" Daniel asked when Matt pulled it— *voilà!*—out of the closet.

"I don't know!" Matt exclaimed, basking for a moment in being the hero. "I just grabbed everything that I thought might help."

Gradually, a semblance of normalcy settled over the family. In private, they would be shaving or brushing their teeth when their knees would buckle, and they would cry out. Each time it shocked them, to be so thoroughly felled. Joel and Ilana came in and out of their dreams, stunned and bleeding and weeping and begging for help, or miraculously alive and wondering what the fuss was all about. In Daniel's dreams he swept past the yellow police tape and the authorities talking into crackling walkie-talkies and the black-coated Chevra Kadisha brushing little scraps of blood and tissue into small plastic bags, into the ruined and burning café, stepping on glass and blood, straining so hard to see his brother through the smoke that he finally did, his enormous

effort making the air crystallize into the shape of his brother. He often
came out of those dreams when Gal stumbled into their room crying
"Ema!"—having dreamed that her mother was angry at her for talking
back, or that she'd appeared in her room and smiled at her. He'd sit up,
stunned by the still-lingering image of his brother, and hold her and
rock her while she sobbed and sobbed, his cheek pressed on her hot,
heaving back, trying to take long, even breaths, to soothe her with his
body warmth and rhythm. They decided that it would be best for
her to get back into her routine as quickly as possible, so Daniel took
her to school, where she marched in like such a resigned and compliant
trouper he almost snatched her back and took her home.

In the late evenings, after both children were in bed, the adults
gathered heavy-eyed in the kitchen, which smelled of soup and dish
soap and clementines. Lydia wiped down the counters while Daniel swept and did a *sponga*—using a mop with a soaking, soapy rag
wrapped around the squeegee end, he soaped up the floors and then
squeegeed the water into a drain in the corner of the kitchen, and then
wiped down the floors with the rinsed-out rag. Matt grew accustomed
to his disquisitions on the superiority of this method of mopping over
the American method of repeatedly dunking the very mop you were
cleaning the floors with into dirtied water. The phone rang incessantly,
but after a certain point they let the machine in the bedroom take it.
They kept the TV and radio, which were reporting the army's incur-
sions into the West Bank, off. They talked about Joel and Ilana's estate,
and the money coming to the children from Bituach Leumi; Sam was
going over the details of their affairs with the lawyer, and research-
ing the most tax-advantageous ways to invest the money in two coun-
tries. And then there was the baby's constipation. They'd done some
consulting among everyone who'd changed a diaper—which was all
of them—and discovered that he hadn't pooped in three days. Daniel
had gone through Ilana's address book until he found the name of the
pediatrician, and called and talked to the nurse, who had told him that
at Noam's age, not pooping for five days or so was normal, but never-

theless recommended lots of fruit in his diet, plus prune juice, prune juice, and more prune juice.

Matt had made a reservation to return on a Continental flight that would leave in four days. One morning, as he was helping Gal get dressed, he said, "You know, Boo, I'm going back to the States for a while." His heart was heavy; a kind of dull depression had settled over him, like asthma settling upon lungs. It was crazy, but part of him missed those first days of crisis. The tears, the rush from experience to experience, the way being a man in charge filled him with an ennobled feeling, as if he were a hero in a tragic film. But there was something else, too. Once the immediate crisis wore off, you had to admit to yourself that Joel and Ilana really weren't coming back. It was so unfair: They were mourning and mourning, shouldn't they get something in return, some alleviation of their pain?

It was morning and Gal was dressing for school. She was choosing between two purple shirts, and from her intensity, Matt thought, you would have imagined that they were even the tiniest bit different from each other. Gal had taken the shirts out of the drawer, which looked as though a tornado had run through it, and laid them both on her bed, tenderly smoothed them out. She was wearing jeans and a white undershirt, and Matt noticed that the kid's belly he'd blown many a raspberry into had flattened as she grew. She still needed to eat breakfast before Daniel took her to school, and she hadn't brushed her teeth yet either. He sat on the bed next to the shirts and folded his hands in his lap, fighting back the urge to hurry her.

Finally, she looked at him, her face darkening, and said, *"Oof!"*

"What's the matter, can't decide?"

She brought one shoulder up to her scowling face in a pretantrum half shrug.

"Do you want me to decide for you?"

"No!" she said, and began to cry.

He reached out his arms. "Come here, Boo," he said, but she stomped her foot and yelled "I not Boo, I *Gal!*" and ran crying out of the room. When Matt rose to go after her, he found her in the living room, in her grandmother's arms, Lydia murmuring to her and wiping her eyes. Matt shrugged. "She can't figure out which shirt to wear."

"Okay, sweetness, let's go take a look," her grandmother said, rising and holding out her hand. Gal went with her back to the bedroom, a thumb in her mouth, turning to shoot Matt a reproachful look. He sighed and went to get some cereal for her. She refused him a kiss good-bye when she left with Daniel for school. "She gives excellent cold shoulder," Matt said.

That evening, Lydia baked the chicken of Daniel's childhood, with Lawry's salt, garlic powder, and paprika. The chicken slid off the bone. The baby was in his high chair with shreds of chicken on his tray, rubbing grease from his knuckles onto his cheek as he crammed his fist into his mouth. A bottle of diluted prune juice stood on the edge of his tray.

Gal sat at the head of the table, smacking her lips over a drumstick like a tiny tsar. She had spent much of the day at school in tears, her teacher had reported to Daniel when he came to pick her up, but her spirits and appetite were rallying. Matt had noticed that she despaired every day, but not for the whole day. They were discussing the logistics of getting Matt to the airport, when Gal turned to Daniel and asked, "When I go to live with Sabba and Savta, will Noam come with me?"

Silence fell over the table. "Who told you you were going to live with your grandparents?" Daniel asked.

She looked at him, and then away, as though she'd been caught doing something wrong. "Sabba," she whispered.

They broadcast to one another grim, significant looks.

"What did he say, sweetheart?" Lydia asked, and when Gal cast a frightened look her way, she said, "You didn't do anything wrong, baby."

"They asked me do I want to come live with them."

They looked at her expectantly. Here was a new twist, Matt thought. He knew right away that she'd said yes; how could anyone as big-hearted as Gal turn down those sad, sad people?

"Did you say yes?" Daniel asked gently.

She nodded, and he pursed his lips and nodded back solemnly.

"Call the lawyer," Lydia said to Sam in a low, deadly voice, without moving her lips.

"Honey," Sam murmured.

Daniel's eyes were fixed on Gal. He reached out his arms and she climbed down off her chair and slid sideways onto his lap. Matt watched him with a lump of love in his throat. "I'm not sure who you're going to live with," Daniel said, gently turning her face toward him with two fingers. "There are lots of grown-ups who love you."

"Like you?" Gal asked.

A teary laugh burbled up from his throat. "Like me," he said. "And Matt, and Grandma and Grampa, and Sabba and Savta. And who else?"

"Gabrielle and Moti."

"*Nachon,*" Daniel sang; in Hebrew you could sing "Right!" in two happy notes. "*V'mi od?*"

Gal listed all the adults they knew, including all of her parents' friends, and a few they didn't know—a girl who was her friend, Leora's older sister's scout leader, and a man who, after much interrogation and clarification, they decided apparently owned a lightbulb store.

"So many people love you!" Daniel said in mock astonishment. She'd warmed to the project, and was bending backward to dangle off his knees upside down. He heaved her up till she was sitting upright again, and became grave. "Matt and I and Grandma and Grampa and Sabba and Savta all love you so much that you'll always be taken care of. But we don't know who you and Noam are going to live with yet. Either with me and Matt, or with Sabba and Savta."

Matt felt a tremor pass through him, and looked straight down at his plate. It was the first time it had been said aloud that the kids wouldn't be living with their American grandparents.

Gal nestled into Daniel's chest and put her thumb in her mouth.

"I hope you boys know what you're getting into," Lydia said quietly. "You know that you're going to have to make some huge adjustments to your lifestyle."

"Duh," Matt muttered, pushing his chair back and going to the cabinet to forage for cookies. He hated everything about those sentences: the sanctimonious parent shit, the condescension, the word *lifestyle*.

"Can I go play in my room?" Gal asked.

"Sure," Daniel said.

Can I go play in mine? Matt wanted to ask. He returned to the table with a handful of chocolate-covered biscuits.

"I'm going to call the Grossmans," Daniel said. "She has so many important questions, and we need to get our stories straight."

Matt tried to imagine them, the ones she'd asked and the ones she hadn't yet. *Why did the bad man kill Ema and Abba? What happens when you die? Am I going to die? Where am I going to live?* He watched as Daniel picked up a little chunk of cantaloupe and put it in Noam's mouth. It seemed to be on the list of things babies could eat, as opposed to nuts or peanut butter or anything with pits. Matt was sure they'd manage to choke or poison him the moment he got to their house. And then their lifestyle would hardly have to change at all!

"Wait," Sam said. "Before you do anything, let's stop and think. You might want to consult a child specialist, so we can learn the most effective thing to tell Gal. Why don't you call the social worker and ask her for a referral."

The baby started to kick and rub his eyes with his greasy fists. Lydia went to the sink and returned with a wet cloth, took each of his hands, and wiped them off.

"You know, Dad, I don't think it's that complicated. I just want to tell them that they can't promise Gal she'll be living with them, when it's unclear where she'll be living."

Daniel called Yaakov that night, and afterward, he came into the bedroom, where Matt was reclining on the bed reading the *Jerusalem Post* and cackling. "I love this food critic," Matt said, holding up the paper. "He described a certain wine as 'Talmudic without being disputatious.'"

"Listen," Daniel said. "I just have to blow off some steam before I report back to my parents."

"What did he say?" Matt asked, dismayed and fascinated.

Daniel told Yaakov he wanted to talk about Gal. He had worked up to it slowly, aware that even hearing his voice on the telephone could send them into a tailspin. He had heard the click of the other line being picked up, and Malka's breathing. "I told him it didn't seem right to tell Gal she was going to live with them," he said. "I said that it was really important to tell her the truth. And then he became a lunatic. He kept yelling, '*Truth? Truth?* Wait until she learns the truth! Wait until the judge hears the truth!'" He sat down on the bed and put his head in his hands.

Matt sat up and smoothed the hair at the back of Daniel's head. How many terrible conversations had they had in this tiny room with the stacked pillows and sheets, the tiny desk scattered with change and watches and wallets and notebooks, the dry wind sifting through? "You mean the truth that we're godless sodomites?" he said lightly.

Daniel craned his head violently away from Matt's caress. "I want to say, 'Okay, the man's in anguish.' He is! 'Okay, the man's from a different culture than we are.' That too! But how many times am I supposed to excuse homophobic insults because the guy is traumatized? Because I know that the homophobic anger is just a cover for his despair?"

Matt knew the answer. The answer was many, many times. He hadn't told Daniel about how Lydia had cornered him that afternoon, sat on the edge of the couch next to him, and put her hand on his and said knowingly, confidingly, "Matt, be honest with me. You can't possibly want to raise two small children."

He'd asked, "Why not, Lydia?"

She gave him a *Don't kid a kidder* look.

He said, "Look, it wouldn't have been my first choice. But I loved Joel and Ilana, and I love their children, and you know how I feel about carrying out their wishes? I feel *fantastic* about it."

She'd stood and crossed her arms and pinned on him the severe look of the prophet. "See how you feel about it when instead of going out dancing at night you're nursing a vomiting child."

Dancing? Did she *know* where they lived?

And now they were going to be in a supplicating position to get custody of the kids, and that meant they'd have to put up with God knows how much bullshit. He could see it already. It would be implied that their gayness was trivial, a luxury, in comparison with the huge issues of terrorism and orphanhood. They'd be told to shut up about being gay already, as though it was they who were constantly hammering that point home, as though they were children clamoring for a Popsicle in the midst of a typhoon.

Suddenly, Matt couldn't wait to go home.

Daniel left the room to talk to his parents, and Matt closed his eyes as quiet settled around him.

WHAT WERE THEY LIABLE to see at the site of the former Peace Train Café? Daniel knew that all signs of blood and broken glass would be mopped up. He imagined that after just ten days there wouldn't be an official memorial there yet, but that there would be an unofficial one. In bed, he imagined himself there, on the site where his brother had said his last words, breathed his last breath. He saw Joel sitting back in his chair, one hand on the table, playing with a book of matches or a packet of sugar. Was he smiling at Ilana, laughing at something she said? Was he smoking the odd forbidden cigarette? Daniel fiercely hoped he'd gotten in a last smoke. It was Windbreaker weather, and the wind ruffled Joel's sleeve. Daniel imagined the soft, hidden parts of him, his armpits and belly and his cock nestled against his leg. He thought of the pictures of the two of them as children, each marked with a D and a J under the corresponding child so they could be told apart, in a kiddie pool in the backyard, their kids' bellies, with their outie belly buttons, jutting over their trunks.

When he imagined the bomber, he saw a sweaty, agitated kid in a big coat.

He and Matt walked downtown, on side streets clustered with stone houses, tall trees that looked like palms, with trunks the texture of pineapple skins, and huge furry-brown firs. Plants tumbled over stone walls and through the bars of ornamental iron gates, narrow verdant walkways with stone steps, the occasional small dog barking shrilly from a balcony lined with planters. It was a dry and sunny morning, and despite himself, despite the dread that seeped over him at the prospect of seeing the spot where Joel and Ilana were killed, Matt felt happiness bound into his limbs from the air, the exercise, the quiet companionship of being with his partner. They passed crowded bus stops, the elderly sitting on benches in hats and overcoats, and teenagers huddled together, laughing. Red Egged buses passed them with huge gasps and exhalations of dark exhaust. Traffic got noisier as they approached downtown, and crossing streets they ran between honking cars.

It was the first time Matt had been downtown. It was crowded and dirty—Israelis were huge litterbugs. Daniel stopped to buy a small bouquet of tulips wrapped in plastic from a street vendor surrounded by buckets of flowers. They turned down the pedestrian walkway, looking at stores crammed with jewelry and tourist Judaica—Star of David necklaces, seder plates, menorahs, mezuzahs—middle-aged proprietors standing outside for a smoke in the sun, the smells of pizza and falafel and grilled lamb heavy in the air. People pushed and elbowed past them without interrupting their conversations. Armed soldiers patrolled the streets, and there were guards posted in front of coffeehouses, most of them Ethiopian, in fluorescent yellow vests. Matt suddenly noticed that he was in a crowd, and also that he wasn't afraid. It had nothing to do with the presence of the soldiers, he thought. It was that they had already been touched, and wouldn't be again. At least by something huge, like a terrorist's bomb. He had already begun worrying about the silly, banal ways of dying, like being killed crossing the street, or slipping in the tub and cracking his head open, or one of the kids choking on something. Because if one of them were to die like that, it would just be too hideously ironic.

The café was down by the bottom of the walkway, and he didn't see it till they were almost upon it. It had been called Peace Train Café, after the Cat Stevens song, not translated, just like that, pronounced "Pees Trrrein." It was boarded up, and in front of it lay heaps of flowers, cards, teddy bears, yarhzeit candles with tiny wavering flames. Tourists were stopping to take pictures, and off to the side, two lanky teenagers stood melancholically, their arms draped around each other.

They stopped and stood with their hands in their pockets. Matt lightly rubbed Daniel's back.

Daniel took a breath. He couldn't tell how big the café had been—it was entirely boarded. Smoke streaks stained the building's upper floors, and its windows were blown out. He carefully laid his bouquet on top of a heap of withered roses. At his feet was a piece of pink construction paper with a snapshot of a smiling family taped to it, and the words *Zichronam l'vracha*—May their memory be blessed—written below it. He knew the names of most of the sixteen dead by now, having encountered them over and over in the newspapers, which had run features on many of them. Five of them, almost a full third, were the Golan family, who had taken their three kids out for ice cream at the end of the Sabbath.

Daniel looked at Matt, who had stooped to peer at some of the pictures. Two women in sunglasses, carrying purses, came up and stood next to him, shaking their heads and making tsking noises. *"Nora,"* one of them said. Terrible.

He stood there, leaden, dumb, like a beast being goaded to haul things. He turned around, and turned back, and scratched his jaw. He'd been building up to see something sublime, and this was so banal, the Hallmark version of his lacerating grief. The sublimity was all in his fantasies and dreams, where his mind soared and blacked out from the enormity of what it imagined, the enormity of his love for Joel, of Joel's body being shattered, his shining life obliterated.

Beside him stood Matt, tears running freely down his face.

Daniel thrust his hands into his jacket pockets. He felt that he should stay there till he'd taken it all in, till the image had imprinted itself upon his mind so that years from now he'd be able to call it up, and to say, *I'll never forget the sight of that bombed-out café.* But it was as if the images before him were fake, the way a child's tinkling keyboard is a fake piano, and he felt cheated by them.

Matt was sniffing and making throat-clearing noises as Daniel steered him away by the elbow. He led him into a tiny alley and past stores with ceramics and handcrafted jewelry, and then they went through a dark passageway, up some stairs, and emerged into a pretty café courtyard set up with tables and umbrellas. "It's still here," Daniel said. Inside, the shop was dark and cool, lined with crammed bookshelves. They ordered espressos and brought outside tiny cups rattling on saucers. Matt hiccupped and asked Daniel if he would bum a cigarette for him from a young man who was reading at another table; Daniel went over and returned with one, whispering, in a faint attempt to amuse him, that the kid was reading Heidegger. Matt lit the cigarette and inhaled deeply, blew the smoke into the sky in a thin stream. He touched Daniel's sneakered foot with his own, and Daniel looked at him.

"Dan," he said, looking into his eyes.

Daniel nodded. He was depressed and didn't know what to do with that, except to be angry at Matt for making him come here in the first place. He felt as though Matt had gone for the facile response to the makeshift memorial, and Daniel was angry at him for that too, but was trying to stuff back that feeling because it was ungenerous and judgmental.

Matt wiped his face with the tiny napkin beside his saucer. "I'm going to leave you all of my underwear and socks and T-shirts," he said. Neither of them had packed many clothes, and Daniel would need them.

Daniel nodded. "I'll buy whatever else I need. They have clothes in Israel." And then, with a half-comic yelp, "Don't leave me alone with them!"

"Oh, honey," Matt murmured, and then with a quick anxious pang: "Do you want me to stay?"

"Don't offer what you can't give," Daniel said with a level look. He knew Matt was dying to go home.

"Okay," Matt said in a small voice.

"Really," Daniel said. "It just makes things worse."

Another surge of emotion rushed over Matt's face. "It's just," he said, his voice breaking, "it's just that it's hard to leave you."

"I'll be okay," Daniel said. Even as he had no idea how he would manage without him, he was longing for Matt to leave, so he wouldn't have to worry about him, so he could handle things in his own way.

They sipped the hot, harsh, grainy coffee and felt the cool wind brush their arms and necks.

THE NEXT MORNING, STANDING at the airport curb with Matt's luggage at their feet, they clung to each other, until Daniel broke away.

"I love you," Matt said, eyes glistening, his fist to his heart. "Me and Yo-yo, we'll be waiting for you and the kids."

"If we get them."

"We'll get them."

"I hope so."

"No, really." His forehead was touching Daniel's. "We will. The house will be a total disaster area. It'll be great."

Daniel laughed.

"Okay, baby?" Matt asked.

Daniel nodded, looking at the ground. Suddenly, he couldn't bear to look at Matt's face. He turned away, got into the car, and drove off without looking in the rearview mirror.

Matt went inside and moved quickly through the line, up to the security woman who took his passport, looked him up and down, and asked him what he was doing in Israel.

Matt's mind tumbled over the answers: *partner* or *friend*, *died* or *killed*? What kind of explanation?

"My friend's brother was killed. I came for the funeral," he said, cursing himself. Later, he wondered why he hadn't just said *partner*. The security guard wasn't screening out queers, just terrorists.

"Killed?" She looked at him, her curiosity breaking through her interrogation technique.

"Yes, in the Peace Train bombing," he said.

She looked at him soberly. "I'm sorry," she said, and put a sticker on his suitcase.

He went through passport control and up to the terminal. He had an hour before boarding, so he cruised the duty-free shop, where determined Israeli men with huge watches on hairy arms and women with lacquered nails were throwing enormous boxes of cigarettes and aftershave into shopping carts. He went back outside and bought treats, a stack of Elite chocolate bars and a bag of sunflower seeds. He sat down by the gate, peeling back the crinkly silver lining of one of the bars. He'd been unprepared for the deliciousness of Israeli chocolate. It was a strange and guilty pleasure to be alone, leaving the Rosen family and their trauma behind. Of course, he told himself, he wasn't really leaving them behind, he was resting up so he could be there for Daniel and the kids when they came home.

He broke off another square of chocolate and sucked on it, and reached into his bag for a magazine and his iPod. He put in the earbuds and turned it to shuffle. A murmuring came into his ears.

I'm so tired, so tired of all this drama.

Oh, God. Too perfect. He closed his eyes as Mary J. Blige's voice—and the voices of her sighing, echoing backup singers—swelled into his ears.

No more pain
No more pain
No more drama in my life
No one's gonna make me hurt again

His music. His music! He closed his eyes, and his big, emotional heart throbbed to the beat of pain and survival.

CHAPTER 5

Daniel got back from the airport to find his parents feeding the kids dinner. Gal and the baby were sitting nicely in their chairs eating spaghetti, Gal trying to twirl it with a fork, the way Matt had taught her, and Noam grabbing it in his fists, his chin glistening with tomato sauce. His father was working on his own enormous plate, a paper napkin tucked into his collar. Daniel tossed his keys onto the counter.

"Spaghetti?" his mother asked, putting her napkin on the table and pushing back her chair.

"No thanks," he said, "I'm not hungry."

The minute the words came out, he wished he hadn't said them, because he was starving. He stood and looked at the placid family, rubbed his temple with his thumb. He'd thought that things would be simpler once Matt left; no more clamor for recognition, no more having to deal, on top of everything else, with the feeling that he was a bad person because he didn't acknowledge their relationship to Matt's satisfaction. But the whole drive back to Jerusalem he'd dreaded coming home alone to his parents, coming home as he had at sixteen, sexless and unpartnered.

"Are you sure?" Lydia was asking. "Maybe just a little plate?" And Gal was asking, "Is Matt on an airplane?"

He sat down at the table. "Okay, maybe just a little," he told his mother, and turning to Gal, "Yes."

She was blinking rapidly. "Matt's plane won't crash," she said in Hebrew.

"That's right." Daniel leaned over and wiped spaghetti sauce from her mouth with his napkin.

Gal's silky hair rose in wisps, and her eyes were dark. "How do you know?" she asked.

His parents were looking at him inquisitively, and he quickly translated.

"I just do," he told Gal, but that made her face fall, and he could tell he was insulting her. "They have very, very good pilots," he said. "Airplanes almost never crash."

He leaned back as his mother placed a steaming plate in front of him. "Don't indulge her," she murmured.

He whirled on her. "*Indulge* her? Are you kidding me?"

Lydia flushed. "The *fears*, I mean. Not the child."

Gal was asking, "But do they *ever* crash?"

"I meant the *fears*," his mother repeated.

"Daniel," his father said.

"Almost never," he said to Gal, speaking in Hebrew, ignoring his parents. "Really, sweetie, I'm just not worried."

"But do they *ever*?"

"Sweetie," he said. He scooted back his chair and patted his lap, frightened, because he'd used up the extent of his repertoire for comforting her. "Come here."

She was crying now, and there was a sudden sweep of her arm and her plate went crashing to the floor, spaghetti and sauce splashing onto the cabinet bottoms and slithering over the tile.

"Hey!" Daniel shouted.

Gal jumped off her chair and ran into her room, and they heard the door slam. Daniel and his mother looked at each other accusatorily.

"I don't know why you have to be so hurtful," his mother said. "You're not the only one suffering."

"I don't like being corrected when I'm trying to manage something difficult," Daniel snapped.

"Your mother was trying to help," his father said.

Daniel rolled his eyes. "Dad, could you just stop?"

"We'll get this mess," Lydia said. "You get your temper under control and go calm her down."

In her room, Gal was sobbing. Daniel got on his knees and gently gripped her shoulders so he could look her in the face and apologize for yelling at her. She wrenched herself away and threw herself onto her bed, sobbing into the pile of the morning's rejected clothes. He stood, irresolute, knowing better than to touch her again, and watched her shoulders quaking, enduring the long moment when she went still and silent before she caught her breath and let out a shattering scream. He murmured her name, whispered, "Shh, shh."

She screamed again, and he winced, dreading the baby hearing and melting down himself. He went over to the open window, glanced out at the geraniums Joel had planted in the window boxes, which none of them had had the wherewithal to keep alive. He wondered if it would be okay to slip out of the room for just a second and find the watering can. But then he reproached himself for really just wanting to escape the screaming. He thought about Ilana, her fierce competence, how she would hold Gal like a big butch mama-warrior when she cried, and the image made him faint with grief and longing. How would Gal ever survive losing that?

He lowered himself onto the floor. Gal's screaming was becoming hoarse and rhythmic. The minutes passed, and then an hour, and still she cried. Lydia opened the door and peeked in, and Daniel waved her away. He said, "*Oof*, Gal-Gal, so many tears." He tried to think of a story to tell her, but it was Matt who was good at that, not he. Finally, he told her a stupid story about how when Yo-yo was a puppy, he chewed all the handles off the cabinets in the kitchen. But that elicited an outraged howl, as though he had mortally insulted her with his frivolity. Hurt clawed up his throat and stung his eyes. It astounded him how badly she could hurt his feelings. And it scared him how long she could cry. He tried to tell himself that his job was simply to be there while she cried, that when she grew up, she would be strong because someone had sat there with her long ago, steadfast, a witness. He remembered her therapist telling him, "Most people think of children's tears as a bad thing, as something they must make go away." They'd been sitting in her toy-strewn office, where he supposed she got children to reenact their traumas with puppets and dolls. "But that's because the tears upset *them*, not because they're bad for the child. Your job is to think of *her* when she cries, not to think about your own distress. She won't cry forever if you don't try to get her to stop."

He clung to that, but Gal cried for longer than he thought a child could cry. Around midnight she began to hyperventilate, and he panicked a little, wondering whether he should rouse his parents, or call the doctor. Before he could do anything, she fell into a coughing fit and vomited all over her bedding. Daniel picked her up and looked for a place to set her down while he stripped the bed; he finally set her in a tiny rocker in the corner of the bedroom. "Oh, it got on your shirt, sweetie," he said, and pulled gently at the arms, shimmying it over her head. He stood and pulled at the sheets, which gave off the acidic reek of half-digested tomatoes, swearing when they caught on a mattress corner. He took them, and all the soiled clothes, out to the laundry porch and threw them in a corner on the floor. Then he walked softly to Joel and Ilana's room. His parents were in bed, watching TV with no sound. "Sorry, I'm looking for fresh sheets," he whispered as they sat up.

"Turn the light on," his father said.

The light made them blink. Noam was in a diaper, curled against his grandfather's side, sleeping with his thumb in his mouth and a massive scowl on his face. Lydia was sitting up, drawing her nightgown to her throat. "Let me take over, honey," she said.

"No," Daniel said. "Let me see it through." He found sheets in the closet and eased himself quickly out of the room again.

In the kids' room, he'd turned off all the lights except for a little lamp on the desk. Gal sat in the chair, hugging herself and rocking and making an unholy keening sound through clenched teeth. Daniel turned on the little boom box to a CD of Israeli songs he knew she liked. He turned it down low and talked to her as he made the bed, making chitchat about how nice the sheets were and what a comfy bed she had and how it was okay to throw up sometimes, even though it was gross. He told her about how once, when he was a kid, he'd thrown up thirteen times, after eating an entire bag of gummy bears. And then he glanced over at her and she was so desolate and so alone on that little chair—her chest naked and skinny, her hair matted around her small face—that his eyes filled with tears.

He lifted her and set her gently on the clean bed, where she crawled weakly onto her pillow. Her chest was still convulsing, the tears still spilling down her face and into the creases of her neck. He lowered himself to the floor again, laid his head back on the wall. He dozed on and off, more or less, a headachy agitation buzzing through his consciousness, and then he awoke. He looked at his watch; it was 1:30 in the morning. Gal was making a racket breathing through her mouth. He got stiffly to his feet. She was curled on her side, her eyes open, shaking and whimpering. He grabbed a box of tissues from near the changing table and crawled clumsily onto the bed, leaning his back against the wall and wrestling her into a seated position between his legs. He wrapped his arms around her, smelling shampoo and vomit. He took a tissue out of the box, held it to her nose, and said, "Blow," and she did. "Again," he said, and mopped her up the best he could. He reached for the extra blanket at the foot of the bed and wrapped it around her, then gathered her in tight again. For a while he just sat there breathing against her back, hoping that the swell of his chest and the beat of his heart would calm her with their warm and steady animal rhythm. She was hiccupping now.

"Gal," he whispered into her ear. "Something terrible happened to us." He was whispering in Hebrew, and his voice broke. She began crying again, but she was tired now, and limp. "Gali, we'll stick together, okay? We will. We have to live in this terrible world." He didn't know whether that was a horribly wrong thing to say to her, whether it would poison her whole idea of the future. But the night had burned him down to ember and ash. "It's going to be very hard. We're going to have to be very brave. But I love you very much and I'm going to take care of you and Noam. Me and Uncle Matt." It occurred to him that Matt would be home soon, and that they could call him to reassure Gal that he was okay. But then he remembered what his mother had said about indulging her fears and suddenly he understood what she'd meant. Why revive Gal's fears about Matt's plane crashing? Maybe it was better to be matter-of-fact about Matt's arrival, to display a casual confidence in the world's predictability. He'd have to move through the world performing that confidence, for her and Noam's sake, from now on.

Gal sighed and shuddered. The desk lamp cast its warm light on the baby's crib with his stuffed bear crammed between the slats, the random toys that always littered the floor no matter how hard they tried to keep them in their box. Gal was moist and warm inside the blanket. He laid his face against her hair.

Gal turned her face up to him. It was swollen and filthy with dried snot and tears. Her dark lashes were stuck together. "I want *choco*," she said.

"*Choco!*" he breathed. It sounded like the best idea anyone had ever had. He rose stiffly and found her a clean pajama top. His left leg was asleep from the butt down, and he stomped his foot on the floor. "Should we get up and see what the house looks like late at night, when everybody else is asleep?"

She nodded and shuddered again, and he slipped the top over her head and stuffed her arms into the long sleeves. They got up and he extended his hand to her, and they walked down the hall to the kitchen, Daniel's leg woolly and tingling, Gal wobbling by his side. "Do you smell that?" he asked, wrinkling his nose. It was fresh cigar smoke.

Gal looked up at him. "Grampa," she said sagely, with a throaty *r*.

In the kitchen, Sam sat at the table in his pajamas with a glass of milk and the plastic sleeve of a box of plain biscuits with scalloped edges, lined neatly up, one toppled into the empty space he created as he made his methodical way through them. A lit cigar was tipped onto a glass plate at his elbow. He looked up at them and cleared his throat, abashed.

"Rough night, huh," he said. Gal clambered up onto the chair opposite her grandfather, reported that the cigar was *fichsah*, and also bad for him.

"I know, honey," he said gently. "I just have one once in a while."

"We're having hot chocolate," Daniel said, finding the box and spooning generous heaps of powder into two mugs. "Do you want some?" His father shook his head. Daniel opened the refrigerator and took out a plastic pitcher with a bag of milk inside it, poured milk into a pot, and set it on the stove. He stood and turned on the burner and stared at the blue flame. He was so tired he could hardly stand. And yet, there was something curious and light in the feeling. As though he'd been scoured until gleaming, as though he were more soul than body.

His father stood and took his cigar out onto the balcony, and when he returned, it had been carefully put out. He sat down and pushed the plastic sleeve of biscuits toward Gal. She leaned onto the table with her elbows and picked one out, and bit off the scalloped pieces with tiny bites of her front teeth.

"I like dunking them into milk," Sam said.

Daniel checked on the milk to make sure it didn't boil, and looked at his niece. What a wild little creature. One look at her, he thought—in her hodgepodge pajamas and bare feet, crumbs on her mouth, her eyes swollen into slits and her nose red and crusted—and social services would whisk her away. She looked just like the dirty-faced Palestinian refugee children they showed on the news. His mind drifted murkily, like weeds on water. He thought of the bulldozers destroying houses somewhere in the West Bank, possibly at this very moment, and the kids out there who were going through the same thing she was. He hoped they had nice relatives to take them in and hold and rock them.

He thought of the news photographs of small coffins swept along on the shoulders of shouting men. It was always men. Sometimes you saw the women. They were always shrieking, which was alienating. They never showed you the quiet daily grief of the Palestinian moms; you never saw a Palestinian adult rocking and cuddling a child. It made you think they weren't a people who rocked and cuddled.

His mind skipped through some association he couldn't follow to Matt, to how much he hated those *Baby on Board* signs on the back windows of American cars. "We don't have a baby," he'd snap, "so go ahead and slam right into us, we deserve it!"

Daniel turned off the stove, and poured the sputtering milk into two mugs.

"You know," Sam said. "I don't sleep anymore. It's very curious."

"Not at all?"

"Not at all. I don't seem to need it anymore."

"Everybody needs sleep, Dad."

"So I would have thought." Sam's hands were crossed in front of him as he watched his granddaughter.

"Are you scared you'll dream of Joel?" Daniel ventured the question shyly. It was a new way to talk to his father.

Sam looked at him and considered. His face was heavy, his nose a blunt bulb studded with pores, as though grief had rubbed his patrician veneer down to its coarse male essence.

"I don't know," he said. "It's hard to know whether dreaming about him is a positive or a negative."

"I know what you mean," Daniel said, bringing the mugs to the table. "You wake up destroyed, but at least you got to see him."

Gal's eyes were moving between them, in a slow drunken version of their usual sharp darting. Her nose was running, her sniffs a deep, crackling rumble. Daniel looked around for a tissue, but all he found was a roll of paper towels, which he worried would be too painful on her tender nose. "Honey," he said, "could you get the box of Kleenex from the bedroom?"

She slipped down to the floor and left the room.

Daniel sat down across from his father. He brought the hot mug to his lips and sipped the scalding chocolate.

"You know," his father said. "When you and Joel started third grade and were separated into different classes for the first time, Joel got massive school anxiety. He woke every morning crying from a stomachache." He paused, and mused. "It wasn't what we'd anticipated. You, meanwhile, sailed off to school every morning without looking back."

He picked up the cigar and ran his fingers along its stem. "It wasn't what we'd anticipated," he said again. "Your mother wanted to let him stay home, but I felt that it wasn't going to get any easier as you boys grew up, and the sooner he got used to it the better. Nowadays, of course, there's probably some new theory about separating twins into different classrooms."

Gal came back into the kitchen with the Kleenex box and one of her model horses, which she set carefully on the table.

Daniel helped her blow her nose, wincing when she flinched at the tissue's rub on the reddened skin around her nostrils. She climbed back onto her chair, dipped her face down to her mug, and stuck her tongue into her hot chocolate. "I a dog," she said.

"I *am* a dog," Sam said, correcting for the millionth time the translation mistake she always made because there was no "to be" verb in Hebrew.

Gal looked at him. "You a dog, too?" she asked her grandfather in a high, comical voice.

"Ha-ha," Sam said, reaching toward her as though he were going to tickle her.

"Drink your *choco* like a little girl, Gal-Gal," Daniel said, "and then we're going to brush our teeth and go to bed." They sat and waited as she drank. Daniel rested his cheek on his propped hand and thought of his poor brother, scared to go to school without him. He was surprised his father remembered something about him and Joel that had happened so long ago; Sam hadn't been particularly involved in the details of raising them. There was a little gleam of pride: his parents had always considered him, Daniel, the fragile one; he'd been smaller at birth, stranger-shy beyond the usual age, prone to hurt feelings. But he'd obviously been hardier than they'd thought.

But then the image came to him of Joel as a little boy in his pajamas, lying about a stomachache and feeling guilty about lying, and it broke his heart. He'd heard somewhere that mourning was like falling in love, and it was, he was—thinking of Joel came with a strange, painful elation. Oh, he loved him.

THE DOG'S TAIL THUMPED madly against Cam's thigh as Matt held his face in his two hands, scratching his chin, and asking him if he'd been a good doggie. "Were you?" he asked, his teeth clenched in play ferocity. "Were you?" He bent his face down and got a slurp right on the mouth. "You *were*? Oh, what a good boy." He scrubbed his mouth with his sleeve and looked at Cam, who stood there with an indulgent look on her face, her own dog, Xena, staring at Yo-yo from between her legs with intense border collie eyes. Xena was an agility champion, and the boss of Yo-yo. "Was he?"

She laughed her grainy guy-laugh. "Except for an incident with a tampon that I won't go into," she said.

"Gross," Matt said, sorry, as he so often was an instant too late, that he'd let Yo-yo kiss him on the lips. It was good to be around dog energy, though; it made him remember walking Yo-yo on the state hospital trails in the late afternoon of September 11, standing around with the other stunned dog owners watching their faithful, goofy dogs wrestling and playing under that gorgeous blue sky.

"You wanna come in?" Cam asked. They were in the tiny hallway of her house, the dog's bed and bowl, and a bag of his food, stacked in the corner.

"I don't think so," Matt said. "I need to unpack and straighten up." He dreaded going back into that bedroom, but what, he wondered, would he even say to Cam? She was looking at him with big, sad eyes. She was still in work clothes, her black striped oxford shirt tucked into belted pants, a man's watch gleaming on her wrist. The prospect of putting into words what he'd been through made him feel like a third-grader tossed an ink pen and ordered to write an epic poem. On the way home, he'd imagined telling their story to his friends, and found himself struggling with something inchoate and hard, that Israelis had become somehow *real* to him; the lawyer, the social worker, Joel and Ilana's friends, the children. The sound of Hebrew had become at home in his ear. He knew these people would be received sympathetically by anyone who heard his story, and he wanted them to be, he supposed, but he wanted his interlocutors to have to move through the whole deadly political judgment first and then cross over to the other side.

"When's Danny coming home?"

Matt shrugged. "We don't know yet. And I'll probably have to go over there at least once for a parental competency exam. You know, to make sure we're not the type of parents who will have homosexual orgies when the kids are home."

Cam laughed. "Bummer," she said. "No more orgies."

"How was your month?"

She shrugged. "Oh, you know," she said. "Same old, same old. I broke up with Diane."

Matt vaguely remembered, but didn't have the energy to figure out, which of Cam's many short-lived relationships she was referring to. "That's too bad," he said.

"Nah, whatever." She shook her head dismissively. "Compared to what you guys have been through, c'mon."

"Well, that's okay, Cam, it's still your life. What happened?"

She paused, then gave him an apologetic grin. "Too much drama. When they throw a clock radio at you and scream that they're sick of your passive-aggressive bullshit after you've been together for just two weeks, you know it's probably not gonna work out."

Matt laughed, and bent to clip on Yo-yo's leash.

"Come over if you get lonesome," Cam said. "We can get takeout or something."

"I will. And thanks so much, Cam. You're the best."

She reached over and clasped his shoulder, and Matt smiled to himself; he and Daniel liked to pantomime being on the receiving end of one of Cam's alarming handshakes or backslaps, writhing in pain with polite smiles frozen on their faces.

It was getting dark as he led Yo-yo across the tiny lawns, stopping to let him sniff and pee, the cold air encasing his forearms under the sweatshirt he wore. The forsythia and azaleas were in bloom; soon his neighborhood would be fragrant with lilac. He'd left the front door unlocked, and they pushed into the house, which had grown dark in the few minutes he'd been with Cam. He turned on every light he could reach. The answering machine in the kitchen blinked with seventeen messages; just looking at it made him tired. He dreaded going back upstairs, into that bedroom. But he'd have to clean it up sometime, and it might as well be now, while he still had all that weird jet-lag energy. He got out a jumbo-sized garbage bag, found a sprinkle of pot in a sandwich bag and his rolling papers in the stamps-and-matches drawer, and rolled a thin joint. He trudged up the stairs with the lit joint at the corner of his mouth, smoke curling up his face, and at the door of the bedroom, turned on the light. He stood looking at it. The garbage can was brimming with used tissues, the bedclothes were thrown back, the pillowcases still furiously rumpled, the closets open, the cap off the Tylenol bottle on the bedside table. Clothes—discards from his frenetic packing—lay in heaps on the dressers. He took a big drag, held it in, set the joint on the edge of one of the dressers. He sat on the bed. His breath was heavy, his throat scorched.

Gently, his buzz began to run over him, as though someone had cracked an egg on the top of his head and the yolk was seeping down. Daniel's pants were crumpled on the bedroom floor, the still-belted seat atop two accordioned legs. Matt rose and picked them up; they were dirty at the seat, where Daniel, his knees buckling as Matt led him out, had sat on the damp asphalt in front of his work building in his jacket and tie. Matt drew out the belt and stuffed them into the dry-cleaning bag. He took the joint off the dresser and, his hand cupped under it, went into the bathroom to tap off the long filament of ash. Then he finished it in two big hits and doused it in the sink. He emptied the trash in the bedroom and bathroom, threw the rest of the strewn clothes into the laundry hamper, stripped the bed and made it up with clean sheets, unpacked his clothes, ran the empty suitcases up to the attic.

And suddenly he was so tired his legs almost buckled.

He stumbled into the bathroom, shedding clothes, and after washing his face for a long time in very hot water and giving his teeth a quick, vigorous brush, fell into bed, where he turned on the TV and watched the last hour of *Stepmom*, sad for the Susan Sarandon character but identifying immediately with poor Julia Roberts, who was so shallow and thoughtless! Oh, but they came to respect her in the end. He blew his nose, grateful to be alone in his quiet bed, just him, deliciously, no one entering the room with a tear-stained face. If that made him a bad person, he thought, so be it.

CHAPTER 6

IT WAS WILD going through the messages. The New York friends had called! Stephen and Scott, guys he hadn't seen for years. Lindsay Price had called to say he'd seen Daniel's family on the news. The local Fox affiliate had dug up an old picture of Joel, and Lindsay said that he'd been horrified thinking at first that it was Daniel who'd been killed, and then relieved when he realized it was just Daniel's brother. There was a long silence on the tape, then it clicked off, and the next message was from Lindsay again, saying, "Not that that's really any better, it's just . . ." Matt rolled his eyes. He played it again, for signs of whether Lindsay was using, but he couldn't tell. He was sitting at the kitchen table with a cup of coffee for which he'd put milk through the steamer, in celebration of drinking good coffee again. Yo-yo was gobbling down his breakfast, his metal tags clattering against the bowl.

"Anyway," the message said, "if you want to call . . ."

Matt snorted and erased the message. He had a lined yellow pad in front of him and was taking careful notes because he remembered his bewilderment in the months following Jay's death, when he'd been mad at the whole world but actually not sure whether this or that friend hadn't called after all. He wanted to keep track now for Daniel. His stomach rumbled. He had slept, on and off, for seven hours, which he thought was pretty good, and he was determined to be on a Northampton schedule today, and to stay up till nine at the earliest. He lit a cigarette he'd brought downstairs from his stash. Smoking was an indulgence of being home alone, like eating cereal for dinner and not making the bed. He rose to open the kitchen windows, and saw that the tulips along the backyard fence were in bloom, nodding and snoozing in the shade.

He wasn't even your boyfriend, Lindsay had said one night when Matt had come down to visit, maybe a year after Jay had died. He implied, with the significant look of someone breaking a hard truth, that he was speaking for all of them, which had infuriated Matt. But in fact, as it turned out, he had been. After that, every time one of his friends asked "How are you?" it became a huge minefield: If he said he was feeling shitty, their silence implied that he was a leech on Kendrick's grief. It was just like now, when you thought about it—Daniel's loss, not his. Him brooding and lurking along the edges of tragedy, trying his damnedest to be appropriate.

He'd dropped them all because they were bad for his mental health, and because half of them were tweekers anyway and he just didn't want to be part of that scene. It was an unprecedented act for Matt, who thrived in the light of friendship. That first year living with Daniel had been a hard and lonely one for him; Daniel had a lot of nice friends, but even as he'd integrated into their circle he'd felt them to be Daniel's friends, not his. And even though it had been he who had cut off his New York friendships, it wounded him that they hadn't tried harder to bring him back—especially Lindsay, whom he'd supported through meth addiction and rehab. The friendship had briefly flared up again after September 11, when Lindsay had been his point person for checking up on everybody, but even then Lindsay acted as though only New Yorkers could possibly understand the profundity and horror of the whole thing, and Matt was sure he was using again, so after many evenings of complaining bitterly to Daniel, he stopped returning Lindsay's calls. Now the messages on his machine gave him a sense of bitter satisfaction. It was irrational, he knew, but he felt that this new tragedy proved that his sadness was legitimate, even his past sadness. He would never call any of them back. Let them just sit with their horrid fascination, and gossip with one another about how horrible it all was, and go get wasted in club bathrooms, and go to hell.

Brent and Derrick, their best couple friends, had called twice. Derrick was Daniel's steadiest, call-every-day friend—a fine, upstanding fellow, as Matt thought of him. Listening, he smiled; Derrick knew his way around a condolence call. He was a psychologist who taught schools how to introduce diversity programs, so he was trained in acknowledging others' feelings. Then Brent took the phone, and there was his voice, a melodious, demonstrative baritone Matt loved, saying in a big rush, "We can't wait for you guys to come home. Come home soon!"

Matt looked at his watch. It was around 8:30, and Derrick would probably be at work, but Brent, who was a professor, might be home. He picked up the phone and dialed them on speed dial, and Brent picked up on the second ring, saying, "Matt?"

"Hi."

"Matt," he breathed, as though hearing Matt's voice was the culmination of all his desires and he could now rest. "When did you guys get back?"

"Just me," Matt said. "Daniel's still there."

"How was it?" Brent asked. "Wow, what a stupid question. How's Daniel doing?"

Matt shrugged. "You know," he said. "He's completely fucked-up. He's dealing with his twin brother being blown to bits, and his parents are there, which doesn't make it any easier, and then there's the kids."

"What's going to happen to them?" Brent asked.

There was a pause. "We never told you?"

"No." And then, before Matt could say anything, he said, "Oh my God, are you guys taking them?"

"We're trying to," Matt said. "Joel and Ilana wanted that; it was in their will."

"Wow," Brent said.

Matt was quiet, parsing that "Wow." Of all Daniel's friends, Brent was the one whom Matt had immediately clicked with; he was hilarious, and a media scholar at Mount Holyoke, and after Matt had stopped being a little intimidated about being friends with an academic, he loved being around someone so smart, someone who made his mind dance. But Matt had also been the laughing audience for many of Brent's scathing performances about moms with kids, and he worried a little that he and Daniel would become the butt of Brent's breeder jokes. Recently, Brent had stopped going to Woodstar Café, down the street from his apartment, since it had become a hangout for moms with kids in strollers, saying that being there made him want to stick a knife in his eye.

"Does that make us uncles?" Brent asked.

"Absolutely," Matt said, smiling.

"You guys will be all 'Do your homework' and 'Clean your room,' and we'll be the place they go when they run away from home. And who takes them to the doctor when they want to transition. Well, *I* will. Derrick will want to make sure the lines of respectful communication remain open between you and them."

"Dude, they're six and one year old," Matt laughed.

"What are their names again?"

"The girl is Gal, and the little boy is Noam." Matt found he was still smiling. "Look, it's not certain. It turns out that the will isn't binding, and the kids' Israeli grandparents are going to go to court to try to keep them there. And they're Holocaust survivors, and Ilana was their only child. So we're basically trying to take away the only thing they have left. Can you imagine?"

"Shit."

"I know."

There was a long pause. Then Brent said, "How are you feeling about it?"

Matt sighed. "I have no idea," he said. "You *know* I've never wanted kids before. I feel awful about taking them away from their grandparents. But Daniel wants them. And it's what Joel and Ilana wanted."

"Sure."

Matt drained his cup of coffee and put it down. "I think maybe I want them just a little bit," he said to Brent, emotion rushing into his voice and surprising him. "Is that weird? Am I just being a competitive asshole?"

"Probably," Brent said, and they both laughed. "What do you think your chances are of getting them?"

"I'm not sure. Fifty-fifty?"

After another pause, Brent said, "Wanna come over? Since after the kids arrive, I'll never see you again?"

"Oh please," Matt said. He opened the back door and looked down at the stoop, which was coated with pollen. "Let me do some cleaning up around here, and go through the bills, and I'll call you later."

"See?" Brent said. "It starts already."

"Shut up," Matt said. "It does not start already."

After he hung up, Matt swept off the stoop and the steps, propped the broom against the house, and sat down, looking out at the garden. His imagination was very gently entwining itself around the idea of being a father. He was ready for something new. He should learn Hebrew! He wanted to be able to understand his daughter—*his daughter*—when she spoke to Daniel, and it would be important for both kids to know their mother's language. It felt a little weird, setting out to learn the language of the oppressor; it felt a little like learning Afrikaans. His mind worried the comparison for a while, as he hosed out the grime from the birdbath and filled it, dragged out a bag of birdseed from the garage, and filled and rehung the feeders. Then he began imagining himself in a classroom with little wood desk chairs and batik wall hangings of Hasidic fiddlers, with all the bar mitzvah boys—the bored kids with braces and chubby cheeks learning their Torah portion from a severe, bearded man.

It was only an idea that caught his fancy; he didn't intend to act on it, at least right now, when there was so much work to catch up on. But the next day, Brent called him to say that a colleague of his knew an Israeli artist named Yossi-something who was married to a physicist at UMass, who was apparently waiting for his green card and taught Hebrew under the table. Matt kept the paper with Yossi's number on it next to the phone for a few days as he caught up on delinquent projects—a poster for a film festival and a boarding school annual report that accounted for about a quarter of his yearly income and that was, miraculously, only a week overdue. He lingered over the number when he came into or left the kitchen, and each time tender fantasies overcame his awareness that, to some people, Hebrew was the language of the set of byzantine, malicious laws that legitimized blowing up their houses or keeping them apart from their farms, their own spouses and children. The idea of learning Hebrew made him think of Gal and Noam as his daughter and son, he didn't know why.

He didn't tell Daniel about it yet because their official attitude on the phone was a guarded neutrality on the subject of the children, as a way of protecting themselves in case they didn't get them. And when he thought about it, he wasn't really sure how Daniel would react. But finally, he put in a call to Yossi. Yossi was unpleasantly abrupt on the phone, asking midway through Matt's spiel, "Who *is* this?" Which made Matt sigh and have to start over: "My name is Matt Greene." Yossi made him tell him exactly how he'd gotten his number, and when Matt couldn't remember Brent's friend's name, there was a stony silence on the other end that made Matt wonder: *Do I need this crap?*

It occurred to him later that Yossi was being extra careful because he wasn't legally allowed to hold a job. But when Yossi arrived at his door a few days later, he thought that he might just be a prick. He was gorgeous—tall and broad, with closely cut hair, a dark beard shadow, and blue eyes that looked a little washed out from gazing into the sun, perhaps, or inward, at his own weighty thoughts. A lovely sprout of chest hair showed above his shirt where it was open at the neck. Matt suddenly remembered that Brent had reported that Yossi had been an air force pilot. If he had extended his hand, Matt would have gripped it with all his might, but he was spared that display because all he got was a curt nod. When Yo-yo barged at him, Yossi quieted him by taking his head into his two large hands. "Don't mind him," Matt said, taking note of his wedding band. "He's a goof."

"I don't," Yossi said.

Matt got him coffee, which he drank black, and as they sat down at the kitchen table, Yossi asked him in a nonplussed way why he wanted to learn Hebrew. "Are you Jewish?" he asked.

Matt felt himself bristle. As happened with some straight men, Yossi made him feel girly and silly. "No, I'm not," he replied. "But my partner is." He cleared his throat and gazed at the man across the table from him as he digested the word *partner*, enjoying for once the anticipation of telling their story, knowing that it would wipe the dismissive look off of Yossi's handsome face. "My partner—his name is Daniel—Daniel's brother and sister-in-law were killed in a *pigua* in Jerusalem, and there's a chance that we are going to raise the children."

Yossi sat back in his chair and placed his hand on his chest. "Ah," he said gently. "How old are they?"

"Gal is six and Noam is eleven months."

Yossi heaved a sigh. "Terrible. It was the *pigua* at Peace Train Café?"

Matt nodded.

"So your first Hebrew word is *pigua*."

It hadn't been, quite, but Matt didn't correct him, Yossi was so obviously touched by the thought, and it felt delightful to have this Israeli warrior feeling bad for him. "Yes, and the word *ptsatsa*," Matt said, bringing out the Hebrew word for "bomb," and then thinking that he was perhaps working the pathos too hard. "But that's about it. Oh— *buba* and *miskena*, things like that."

Yossi smiled faintly. "*Miskena*. Is there a word in English?"

"I don't think so. 'Poor thing'?"

Yossi shrugged. "*Miskena*, that's for a girl. You must also learn the word for a boy poor thing. *Misken*."

"*Misken*," Matt repeated.

"*Miskenim*," Yossi crooned, as though he were actually comforting children. Poor things. "*Im*, that is plural, for masculine."

Matt nodded.

Yossi sighed and got out his books. Then he placed his hands on them and leaned forward. "It's good to learn a language to speak to children."

Matt looked at him, confused, trying to parse the meaning of that sentiment, which seemed either very deep or very cloying, when Yossi added, "Because you will be on a similar level."

"Aha, true."

"I try to think—" Yossi cleared his throat. "What kind of things you might say to children in their situation." He was lost for a moment, lashes fluttering, in tender, brooding thought. "'Try to sleep,'" he said, turning his glance to Matt. "'I love you. I will take care of you.' Shall I teach you those phrases?"

They worked on them for a while, and then Yossi opened a workbook with the Hebrew alphabet and lines for penmanship practice, and taught Matt to read a few basic words. He would break each lesson into two, he said, teaching him simple conversation for the first half hour, and reading and writing for the second. He watched as Matt drew his first Hebrew letters, and he gave him homework for the following week. They smoked a cigarette together on the back steps before he left. Matt asked him if he had kids, and Yossi said he did, three boys, one twelve, one ten, and one Gal's age.

"Oh," Matt said. "Maybe they can play together."

"Rafi is deaf," Yossi said bluntly.

"Okay," Matt said. "Does that mean they can't play together?"

"No," Yossi laughed. "Of course not."

"Do you like it here?"

Yossi opened his palms and shrugged. "It's good for my wife, this job. And it's a very good place for Rafi, because of the school for the deaf. But I miss home. People aren't very friendly here."

"Really, you think?" Matt asked. He thought about this town, where men with gray beards and pedantic demeanors, and willowy ponytailed women, and the million and one psychotherapists and, of course, the stocky lesbians with severe and perfect haircuts engaged with one another with great, inculcated civility; civility he'd initially found, after living for years in New York, phony, almost comical.

"At home, you can jump over to someone's house without calling, and they will pull up another chair for dinner."

"Oh," Matt said. "We don't do that in New England."

On his way out, Yossi instructed Matt to say the sentences he'd learned one more time. He lifted his chin sternly, like a father demanding a recitation from a child. "Try to sleep," Matt said, as Yossi raised his eyebrows and nodded. "I love you. I will take care of you."

Yossi gave him an approving clap on the shoulder and said, *"Yofi! Le'hitraot.* That's mean 'See you later.'"

Closing the door, Matt took a huge breath. Yossi's sternness and scrutiny and praise made him feel a little like a sheepish child, but he had a nice glow from that too, from being praised for being smart. He paced around the kitchen, feeding the dog and washing out the coffeemaker and setting water to boil for pasta. He wasn't used to not being the most handsome man in the room. But he'd found that he gladly deferred to Yossi's alpha hunkiness. A Magnetic Fields song playing and replaying in the back of his mind floated up to his consciousness, and he laughed to himself. He dialed Brent and Derrick's number, and when Brent picked up the phone, he sang, without saying hello, "He's amazing, he's a whole new form of life."

Brent laughed, and finished the couplet: "Blue eyes blazing, and he's going to be your wife."

"Well, not quite," Matt said thoughtfully. "It's more like he's going to be my *ward.*"

He was having to work until pretty late, but now and then he took a little time to practice his Hebrew alphabet. It pleased him to form the letters; it reminded him of design school, where they made them learn to design by hand, painstakingly drawing the alphabet, or cutting out the listed ingredients from some random product and making a composition out of them. He was enjoying being alone, he found; he turned down invitations to dinner and movies from his friends.

ONE MORNING, WHILE CLEANING the bedroom, Lydia cried out; she emerged waving a DVD and crying, "We can see him again!" She clasped first Sam, then Daniel, looking into their faces with a tearful smile. She had come across the DVDs of Joel's show, which were stored, it turned out, neatly labeled and dated, in a flat plastic tub under Joel and Ilana's bed. When she went back into the bedroom to take out the box, Daniel murmured to his father, "She does understand that it's not *really* Joel, just a film of him, right?"

Sam was making plans to go home, to take care of some business and to visit an old friend they were worried about, who was in the hospital with an undiagnosed ailment that had made him collapse several times. He was on the phone with the airlines, on hold; he took off his glasses and massaged the bridge of his nose.

They couldn't stay away—they had to watch them—but they dreaded it, too. After his father hung up, Daniel got in a few whispered moments on the phone with Matt, who told him he didn't have to watch if he didn't want to, which vaguely annoyed Daniel even though he knew it was sensible, and true.

When the kids were down, his parents sat next to each other on the couch. Daniel checked and double-checked on Gal before putting the DVD into the player; he just couldn't face the idea of her waking up and coming into the living room and seeing an image of her living father. He was well into a second beer, and he fiddled with the remote control while perched on the edge of the recliner. The screen turned blue, and then it was on, *Israel Today*. And there was Joel, sitting behind a desk, welcoming the audience to a show about education in the development towns. He was going to be talking to a teacher from one of the towns down south—a new *oleh* from the U.S. who was agitating to get more resources down there—and to someone from the Ministry of Education.

There was a close-up of his face, and Daniel's heart seemed to stop beating, it was so eerie and so piercing to see the brown eyes alive— alive!—and his light skin, textured and mottled, a freckle here and there. Joel's face looked out into the living room. He was in that world and Daniel was in this one; for a moment Daniel had the sense that they were barely separated at all, that the television was a mere technicality. Joel's presence was there in front of him, in its breathing, thinking, sentient animality. What was the difference, really, between that vivid picture and his actual self?

The camera broke away to a short video about the poor conditions in a dilapidated school somewhere in the south.

"It didn't used to be like this," his father said, his voice hoarse. "It used to be that when people died, they were dead, and you just looked at pictures, or imagined them."

"I can't decide if this is better or worse," Lydia said, her hands in her lap, trembling.

They watched Joel interview his guests, clear, incisive, his voice warm, hunching over his crossed arms and leaning toward the guest in the studio. Daniel finished his beer; his father got up to go to the bathroom, and when Lydia asked if they should pause it, he waved his hand no. He stayed away until the show ended, and when he returned, said, "Is it over?"

"That such a lovely man should be killed for this . . . this, I don't know what," Lydia murmured. "It's senseless. Even if he wasn't my son, I'd be devastated by it. He's a wonderful interviewer, isn't he? He manages to be both hard-hitting and likable—you can tell that the interviewees like and trust him."

"If he was hard-hitting," Daniel remarked, "he'd ask how much the Ministry of Education invests in Arab Israeli education."

There was silence as his parents turned to him in surprise. "I really don't think that's appropriate," Sam said.

"Why not?" he said, unable to stop himself from rushing on. "*That's* the big scandal in Israeli education. They're *citizens*, and they're funded at something like one-fifth the rate of Israeli kids. Their schools are a disaster."

"It's a pity you disapproved of your brother so much," Lydia said bitterly.

"He was a good man with a blind spot," Daniel said. He felt that it was a generous assessment. It had always bothered Daniel that Joel hadn't stepped up; he had a responsibility, he felt, as a public figure.

"And I suppose you alone can see clearly," his mother challenged.

"Not me alone, Mother. But I think I saw more clearly on this issue than Joel did."

"That's pretty arrogant, don't you think?" Sam said. "After all, he lived here, and he had an entire research team at his disposal."

Daniel shrugged.

They were quiet. "I had no idea you felt this way about your brother," Lydia said. "Was he aware of that?"

"A little," Daniel said, thinking about the one argument they'd had that had made Joel blow up, when Daniel had told him that Matt saw many analogies between Israel and apartheid South Africa. Joel had turned beet red and tried to pin Daniel to the wall with heated questions about security and self-defense and what specific techniques he was referring to. He'd asked scornfully if Matt was now such a big expert on the subject because he'd written a paper about it in college. Daniel should have known better: The South Africa comparison was like a red flag in front of a bull to most Israelis. And it was shitty of him to use Matt's name instead of just being upfront about his own feelings. Joel was pissed off at Matt for a long time after that.

He sighed. "I could have worked harder at, I don't know, showing him my point of view. But he lives here. *Lived* here." And what? He hadn't thought it was his place to precipitate a whole moral crisis in Joel. Which was sensitive of him, but also, when he stared it in the face, a little cowardly. When it came down to it, he just hadn't wanted to get into it. They'd had such a great time when he'd come last year, and he loved them so much! And maybe it wouldn't have precipitated a moral crisis at all—if it hadn't yet, why would it now?—and he didn't want to see that.

The blue screen was clear and unblinking; he rose to eject the disc, and discovered he was a little buzzed from his two beers. It hurt to be disappointed in Joel; it made his very soul feel sore. And what about himself, what had he done? Just these last weeks, the Israeli army had killed fifteen Palestinians, three of them children. The Israeli authorities denied it. But he'd been reading the Internet reports by human rights organizations and knew about the terrible toll on civilian life. And worse, this violence was supposedly happening on his family's behalf.

His parents rose heavily, and seeing how perturbed they looked made Daniel feel horrible. He'd attacked their beloved dead son—what good did that do anybody? Had he done it to aggrandize himself? If he had, what kind of infantile impulse was that?

Lydia went into the kitchen to load the dishes in the sink into the dishwasher, and Sam shuffled in his slippers to the bedroom and closed the door behind him. Daniel used the bathroom, then murmured a good-night to his mother and went into his room and got into bed. He lay there for about an hour, his mind jangling busily and unpleasantly. Then he sat up and thought about how to make it stop. He rose and pulled on a pair of jeans and a tight T-shirt, and took his leather jacket off the back of the desk chair and slipped it on. Wearing it felt both protective and sensual; he lovingly treated it with lotion twice a year, at the beginning and the end of the leather-jacket season. He'd had the lining replaced once already.

He found his wallet and slipped it into the inside breast pocket, picked up the car keys. He patted his jeans pockets reflexively and turned off the small desk light.

Gal, he hoped, would sleep through the night. He couldn't tell his parents he was going out, and they had gone to bed by now anyway. But he didn't want them to worry if they found he wasn't there. In the end he

left a note on his pillow that said *Be back soon. D.* He looked at it uncertainly, scratching his chin, feeling how very quickly he could regress
when left alone with them. It was only two days since Matt had left, and
already his mother had begun doing things like telling him to clean up
after himself, as though he hadn't cleaned up after himself every day of
his life for twenty years. Without Matt, there was nobody to help signify
that he was an adult. No one to be more immature than he was.

He closed the front door quietly behind him, trotted down the
stairs, and got into the car. He pulled onto the street and nosed his way
out of the quiet neighborhood, making the only turns he could down
the maze of one-way streets. Cars were parked every which way, on
streets and sidewalks. He turned onto Ruppin; the Knesset was yellow
and illuminated on his left, the Israel museum on his right. And then
he was climbing another narrow street, and heading left down Aza. He
turned onto Keren Ha'Yasod and found what he'd hoped he'd find, a
small patch of dirt parking lot still untouched by the crazy development
that had gone up around the park.

He pulled in, closed and locked the door behind him. He walked
silently down the street to Independence Park, his steps quickening as
he saw the high lights of the park ahead and, in their light, the crazy
flitting shadows of bats. It was many years since he'd visited the old gay
cruising ground; he wasn't even sure whether now, in the Internet age,
men still cruised here—in fact, whether regular old face-to-face cruising
still existed at all. The mountain air was cold on his hot face and hands.
He slowed down once he entered the park, put his hands in his pockets.
An occasional person passed on the stone paths, and he could smell a
verdant, spiny aroma—eucalyptus or cypress. The swoon of sensation
and emotion suddenly made his legs watery. He made it to a bench, laid
his arms along the top of it, threw his head back and breathed.

He was overwhelmed because it was Joel he wanted. Not like that, of
course, but his heart strained for Joel. He closed his eyes, and memories
of the summer of Joel's wedding, when he'd come for two months to
visit, came easily to him. Joel was reporting for the *Jerusalem Post* and liv-

ing with Ilana in that apartment on Rehov HaPalmach. There was a ton
of wedding hoo-ha, gifts arriving every day, Joel the bright, exotic center
of their extended family. It was a time when Daniel's critique of com-
pulsory heterosexuality was especially honed, and it galled him that his
brother accepted so comfortably the privilege heaped upon him. Meanwhile, various Rosen relatives were planning tours of the Holy Land,
the kind that took tourists to Masada to climb before dawn and thrill to
the desert sunrise, the story of Jewish fighters choosing death over capture, the motto *Never again*. And his increasingly keen awareness of the
way oppression operated by making certain things invisible to the eye—
things like his own emotional life—began to bleed into distaste and
anger about the things he himself couldn't see because Israel made them
invisible. His relatives' boosterism and romantic idealizing of the Israeli
army and unthinking racism galled him; he read Said's *The Question of
Palestine*, and it blew him away. He thought about summer camp, which
had offered Zionism as a glorious refuge from American suburban life,
and his new knowledge made him have to rethink the whole thing.

His temples pulsed as he thought about that uncomfortable, angry,
transformative time. It was the first time Joel had been in close quarters
with an uncloseted Daniel, and he joked anxiously when Daniel came
home in the dawn hours, just as he and Ilana were getting out of bed.
It was 1990, and Daniel's lack of knowledge of how to find gay men in
Jerusalem was matched only by his determination to find them. He was
shy by nature, and sexually diffident, but he'd experienced gay libera-
tion and love and sex with men in the years since his junior year abroad
in Jerusalem, and he felt almost driven to transpose the experience of
that year into a gay key, as an act of recuperation, of self-assertion. He
cruised Independence Park and answered personal ads in the local city
papers, playing elaborate games of phone tag by pseudonym, sending letters to post-office boxes, and he had a few flings that summer
with men who, it turned out, had felt as clueless as he did about how to
find one another. During the day he read, met Joel for coffee or lunch,
walked the city. But when he stole out of his bed and left Joel's apart-

ment at night, it was with hunger and anger both; it was a way of being separate from his brother, going off to a place Joel couldn't imagine and had no cachet in. A secret Israel in which Joel couldn't succeed brilliantly, where people defied their culture with their stubborn desires.

And here he was again, same place, only better lit, newly abutted by skyscrapers and by the huge crane omnipresent in busy, expanding Jerusalem, and of all those men, it was Joel, perplexed, disapproving, shrugging—*It's your life*—he yearned for. He considered just going home, but a painful lassitude had settled over him, making it hard to move his limbs and rise. A figure was walking toward him, and his mind played a quick speculating game about what he would find when it materialized.

It was a man with a *kipa* pinned onto his curly hair and a wide ingenuous face. He sat down next to Daniel for a while, his knees cast wide, almost but not quite touching Daniel's own. He wore a delicious scent, which Daniel breathed in with pleasure, and his knee jiggled nervously. The agitated presence of an aroused stranger steadied Daniel. Their knees touched. Finally, the guy stood, and Daniel did, too. He led Daniel through bushes into a small clearing, where he grabbed him and spun him around, breathing hard, his beard stubble scouring Daniel's face. He was big and heavy in a way Daniel liked. He knelt and unbuckled Daniel's belt with trembling hands; Daniel saw the glint of a wedding band. He felt the man's hot breath on him and closed his eyes. The guy was more eager than skilled, but Daniel was excited by his nervousness, by the way the desire must have become intolerable for him to sneak out like this. Daniel clasped his hair, his thumb grazing the clip that held the *kipa* on, and that sent another surge of desire through him, getting a religious man on his knees.

His orgasm was bright and high. After he pulled his pants up, he turned the guy till he faced away from him, unzipped and unbuckled him and stroked him, pressing against his naked ass hard enough to give him pause. He would have liked to fuck him, but that wasn't allowed under the terms of his and Matt's monogamy agreement, which they had made one fine Fourth of July they now called "Monogamy

Tuesday." It allowed oral sex and hand jobs only, and sex with any given man one time only; it prohibited bringing anyone home.

The wind cooled his back where his shirt rose above his jeans. Candy wrappers and an empty paper container blew through the patch of hard dirt they stood upon and jammed against a scrubby bush. The man yelped and shuddered in his arms. He staggered away from Daniel for a moment, fumbling to tuck himself back in. Still breathing hard, he kicked dirt and leaves and cigarette butts over the snail's trail of semen he'd left on the ground. *"Tov,"* Daniel said, indicating he was ready to go. He turned, and then suddenly the guy pulled him back and laid a kiss on him, and too shocked to protest, Daniel met his lips and tongue, closed his eyes and felt the blood rush to his head. The man's breath smelled of a hundred cups of coffee. When he pulled away, Daniel staggered, dizzy, clasped his jacket for balance. *"O-pah,"* the man said, steadying him like the nice husband and father he no doubt was.

Daniel drove home quickly through the empty streets, a smile twitching at his lips. He and Matt had debated the question of kissing other men, because they both loved kissing, but it created a dangerous intimacy. In the end they'd allowed it because it almost never happened with guys you picked up. Daniel ran his hand over his chapped mouth and chin, wondering whether his parents would notice that they looked red in the morning. He reached for the lip balm that was always rattling around in one of the coffee holders—Ilana's, he knew—and ran it over his lips, and then he felt as though he'd kissed her too.

He was home in five minutes; he opened the front door as silently as a burglar and eased it shut behind him, crept into his bedroom and closed the sliding door inch by quiet inch, stripped down to his underwear and got in bed. His legs and groin tingled, and he caught and then lost the rumor of the guy's scent. A sense of drowsy well-being gently washed through him. He placed his fingers on his ribs and felt them expand and contract with his breath. Through the open window floated the heavenly smell of the Angel factory. He listened into the silence and heard no rustle or cry.

CHAPTER 7

MATT AND CAM were hunched in front of his computer, reading a smackdown between two mothers on BabyCenter.com. Matt had found the site a few hours ago, and was so riveted he hadn't heard Cam come in until the frantic scrabbling of claws against the wood stairs caught his attention and Yo-yo and Xena burst in, panting, and crashed against his knees. "Ouch!" he yelled. "Cam?"

"Hey," she said, coming in with a squeak of sneakers and looking around his study. "I brought Chinese and a bottle of wine."

"Check this out," Matt said, rolling in his desk chair to grab another chair and pull it up. "You guys, lie down! That means you too, Yo-yo!" He'd read a mother's diary of her child's first year, and the recalls on the car seats—which it seemed nobody used correctly anyway—and the frighteningly intense debates about the family bed, but he'd had no success finding anything about bereaved children, except for those who had lost a grandparent or a pet. Nothing about how to talk to kids whose parents had been killed by a bomb. But then again, he wasn't sure if he was missing some stuff because he was reluctant to register, because that required reporting his children's genders, something he just balked at, fearing they'd start sending him grotesque special articles about how, even in the womb, little boys naturally reach for trucks while little girls reach for dolls.

Now he was reading the milestone chart "What to Expect from Your

Thirteen- to Eighteen-month-old." "Someone seems to have bragged that her two-month-old was already eating solid foods," he told Cam, "and that really ticked the other moms off." He read aloud: "'Well, well, well. In addition to being mother of the year, you are also more educated than a pediatrician. Just because your daughter *can* eat solids, does not mean that she *should* do so. A two-month-old baby's digestive system is not ready for the onslaught of solid foods. You are probably setting your daughter up for an increased risk of allergies, as well as digestive problems later on. I am sorry that your children have a mother who thinks so little of them that she ignores advice given by pediatricians worldwide.'" He looked at Cam, who was squinting at the screen and murmuring, "Dude, lighten up."

"Signed," he said, grinning, "'Sad in Indiana.'" He pouted his lips. "She's sad because those kids have to have such a bad mom."

"It *is* sad, actually," Cam said, and they laughed.

"I'll tell you, it's a cutthroat world out there for the moms," he said. "Those message boards are brutal! But the good news is, they don't expect jack shit from the dads. I swear, if these women's husbands do anything without being hounded into it, they're total heroes. They call them DH, which it took me a long time to figure out meant 'darling husband.'"

"Gross," Cam said.

"I don't know, Cam," he said, rubbing his face, suddenly depressed by all the arguments, the sheer quantity of *information* parents apparently had to be interested in. "Did you ever want kids?"

"Nope. The thing is, I basically raised my mother"—Cam's mother had had some combination of alcoholism and bipolar disorder—"I don't have the energy to be at anyone else's beck and call."

Matt nodded with a small smile; and yet, the women Cam loved were unfailingly troubled and demanding.

"If you get them, it's not like you're going to have a choice or anything," she said. "You'll just raise them. They'll grow up, and be fucked-up like the rest of us."

. . . .

DANIEL WAS RUNNING LATE; he'd gone to the supermarket, where he'd been accosted by a woman who thought he was Joel for a moment, and then he'd had to stay with her as she recovered. And just as he pulled out of the parking garage on his way home, he remembered that he'd forgotten eggs, the thing that had sent him shopping in the first place. He stopped at the *makolet* on his block and bought eggs with his last bit of cash, and wound his way home through twisty, clogged streets. Assaf had agreed to be his lawyer, and he had set up this appointment with the caseworker. She was an American with a New York accent named Dalia Rosenblum, who'd made *aliyah* ten years ago, and he had bet his parents a thousand dollars that she was religious.

"You don't have that kind of money," his father had said with an annoying complacency.

"Okay, I'll bet you *two* thousand dollars," Daniel had shot back.

His father had given him the wise nod of the father humoring the impetuous son.

His phone conversation with Assaf had thrown him into a stew of anxiety and fear. First, Assaf had told him that the social worker assigned to do the parental competency hearing would be interviewing him six times over the course of three months. Daniel had said that he couldn't be away from work that long, and begged him to find out if there was any way to do it more quickly. Assaf also said that the courts tended to want to toss the kids around as little as possible, especially after a trauma like this. When Daniel asked him if he thought it would help or hurt to have Matt present at the parental competency hearings, Assaf was silent for a long time.

"That bad, huh," Daniel said.

"No, no—it's that I honestly don't know. I have never experienced such a situation." He weighed it out loud: On the one hand, it wouldn't help that they were gay, and that Matt wasn't Jewish, but on the other, Daniel couldn't lie about his living situation, and Assaf believed that parental competency assessments explicitly mandated assessing the spouse. "I think you will have to acknowledge him, and that therefore he will need to be present," Assaf had concluded.

When Daniel got home, he saw a strange car parked outside and cursed; he was late for the caseworker. He walked into the house, apologizing, laden with plastic bags of groceries. "Don't worry about it," Dalia said. She was a young woman with a covered head; she wore a dress and hose. Daniel swiveled toward his father, who was hovering over the hissing kettle, as he hefted the bags onto the counter, and rubbed his fingers together to signify the money Sam owed him. He had the sudden memory of Ilana calling the cops on the religious people who'd put up a *succa* by her supermarket and played loud music during evenings of the Succot holiday. They'd told her they couldn't do anything about it, which she'd known before she even called. But it had made her feel better to do something rash and mean toward the religious people she— and most of her friends—lived among in simmering animosity.

He put some biscuits on a plate and brought them out, set them on the big nicked coffee table. His mother emerged from the bedroom in a nice dress, freshly made-up, and introduced herself. They sat. Dalia began by emphasizing that she was the advocate for Gal and Noam, and that the court, to which this case would surely go, would settle it according to its best judgment of the best welfare of the children. "You say that in a way that implies that Daniel doesn't want the best for them, that *he's* not their advocate," Lydia said.

"Not at all," Dalia said. "But the custodianship of the children is contested. I have just come from Ilana's parents, and they are quite determined to raise the children as their own, here in Israel."

"You're aware that Joel and Ilana wanted Daniel to be the guardian, yes?" his father said.

"I have seen the will," Dalia replied, implying, to Daniel's ear, that it was somehow open to interpretation. He wished his parents would shut up; they were making it look as though he couldn't speak for himself. Dalia was probably in her midthirties, with dark eyebrows and straight hair slanting across her forehead. She sat with a pad of paper in her lap and a pen in her hands. Her hands were quiet. "I know this must seem arbitrary and wrong to you," she said. "But evidence shows that the mourning process is best facilitated if the child's physical and social environment remain essentially unchanged."

Daniel's heart sank. So not only might he and Matt not get them, but even if they did, they'd be harming their mourning process.

"You live, in the States, with a homosexual partner, is that true?"

"Yes," Daniel said, holding her gaze.

"Will the court have a problem with that?" his mother asked. Daniel leveled a stare at her, and she looked at him, uncomprehending.

Dalia gave an expressive shrug and said she didn't know. "There are two parts to it: the partner and living in the States. How does your partner feel about raising two children who are not his own?"

Daniel made a quick, strategic decision to read her as simply direct, as many Israelis were, rather than as homophobic. He paused; he wanted to get this right. "Matt hardly knows the baby. But he and Gal have always been close. He's devastated by what has happened and wants to take these children in, to help them heal in a loving home." It sounded wretchedly platitudinous when it came out of his mouth, but it wasn't untrue.

"It will certainly be a big change in his lifestyle," his mother said. *Yes,* Daniel thought, *those are the words coming out of her mouth.* Dalia looked at Lydia and then back at him, then at Lydia again. He saw that she was registering that Lydia didn't like Matt. "What do you mean?" Dalia asked.

Seeing all eyes on her, Lydia backtracked. "Oh, nothing dramatic," she said. "I only mean that he's a young man."

"Mom, he's thirty-two. A lot of men have children at that age, and they adjust just fine."

"That's all I meant," Lydia protested.

There was a pause in which the air seemed motorized, whizzing with brainpower, as everybody made a quick decision about how to proceed. Then Dalia asked a series of questions—about their jobs, their income, their house—and the hum dispersed and settled. She asked

Daniel what his town was like, and where the kids would sleep in his house. He gave her the names of references, Derrick and his boss April; and he had the idea of giving her the name of Joel's best friend, Josh Levinson, who'd come over with them in the junior-year program and had made *aliyah* around the same time as Joel. He'd seen Josh and his wife at the shiva, and they'd tearfully urged him to stay in their lives. Dalia wrote the names and numbers on her pad without looking down at it. She asked if he and Matt knew how to take care of a baby, and he said they hadn't before now, but that they'd had a crash course in the past weeks. As if on cue, they heard Noam begin to cry in his bedroom. Daniel and Lydia stood at the same time. "I'll get him," Daniel said, his desire to display parental competence only slightly stronger than his desire to get his mother out of Dalia's earshot before she said anything else that might sabotage his cause.

He went into the kids' room, sighing in a big release of tension, saying, "Hi, mister!" He stopped in his tracks. In his crib, Noam was red and crying and covered in poop. "Holy shit, Noam, you exploded!" Daniel cried, and hoisted him up, holding him at arm's length. "Mazel tov, sweetie!" He planted a big kiss on the baby's red face, and then pulled away in disgust from the smell. It was even in Noam's hair. He laid him on the changing table and peeled off the filthy diaper with his fingertips, fastidious at first, and then realized that if he just accepted the fact that he was going to get covered in shit, things would go a lot more quickly. He dropped the diaper in the pail. There were streaks of shit on Noam's thighs and on the hands he was grabbing his pacifier with. The stench made Daniel gag.

There was a shadow at the doorway and Dalia came in. "I let the baby get covered in feces!" Daniel exclaimed. "Choose me, I'm a fantastic parent!"

Dalia approached with a faint smile. "Sha-*lom*," she cooed, caressing the second syllable. "Did you make a big kaki?"

"He's been constipated since we got here," Daniel said. "This is an event, his first bowel movement in two and a half weeks."

Dalia nodded, reaching to smooth Noam's hair off his forehead, then clearly thinking better of it. "It's very common in grieving babies."

Daniel stared at her. "Constipation? You're kidding."

"No, why would I be kidding?" she asked.

"That makes so much sense! It didn't occur to me . . ."

She shrugged. "How does a baby mourn? He doesn't have a language for what he's lost."

They looked at Noam, who had picked up the wipes box and was turning it around in his hands with great interest.

"I'm sorry about your brother," Dalia said, moving forward quickly to ease the box out of the baby's hands before he could put it in his mouth. "I have a brother too, in New York. He's homosexual, too."

Daniel nodded warily. She said it without looking at him, without any kind of emotional fanfare. She wasn't a particularly warm person, he thought, except maybe to the baby, but all Israelis loved babies and talked to them with warm expressiveness. He wished she had said "gay" instead of "homosexual," which always made him flinch because it made it sound like a medical condition. But she seemed smart to him, and observant, and not unkind.

After dinner, on the phone with Matt, he told him how, in front of the caseworker, he gave the baby the longest, most disastrous bath in modern history. "It had everything," he said, a grin saturating his weary voice. "We ran out of hot water and I'd forgotten to turn on the boiler. The baby conked his head on the faucet and actually bled." He laughed. "Matt, I actually made him bleed. And those scalps, they're still a little soft, it turns out, so he'll probably have a bruise that his maternal grandparents will show to every social service official in the country. But wait. Then he had a second bowel movement—a much much looser one, I'm here to tell you—right in the tub. Which made me vomit. Yes, literally." He held the phone away from his ear a little and waited for Matt's laughter to subside. "We must have used at least twelve towels. Okay, four. By the end, I was soaking wet." He paused. "We *so* shouldn't be allowed to raise children."

"It probably at least broke the ice with the caseworker," Matt said.

"I guess you could call it that. And the baby's pretty happy tonight. We played a rousing game of Napkin on the Head."

"What's that?"

"A game where you put a napkin on your head," Daniel said.

"Aha," Matt said.

"It was hilarious."

"I'll bet it was," Matt said, smiling. "Hey, listen, I've been wanting to tell you something." He paused. "I've started taking Hebrew lessons."

Daniel blinked. "You have?" he asked softly.

"I know that you'll want Gal to continue speaking Hebrew when she grows up, and teach Noam, too," Matt said in a rush. "So I thought I should get in on it. Is that okay?"

"Honey," Daniel said. He knew what a stretch it was for Matt, what a gesture.

They hung together on the phone for a while, not speaking. "I love you," Daniel finally said.

"Me too, babe."

When he got off the phone he went into the kids' room, where Noam was asleep in a clean diaper and shirt, and his mother was supervising Gal as she got into her pajamas. "I just got off the phone with Uncle Matt," he said. "Guess what? He's started taking Hebrew lessons!"

Gal looked at him and considered. "Really?"

"Really! We can help him, right?"

"Yeah!" she said in the fake chipper voice she used when prompted by an adult to be enthusiastic.

He looked at his mother, who wasn't very enthusiastic at all; in fact, she was tight-lipped.

"What?" he demanded.

Her eyes darted toward Gal. *Later*, she mouthed.

A few hours later, after Gal had had two books read to her, a meltdown, and a cup of water, and had finally fallen asleep, they repaired to the kitchen. Daniel asked, "Do you have a problem you want to discuss?"

"I don't have a problem," his mother said.

"Then what was that back there in the bedroom? And what was that with the caseworker earlier, about Matt having to change his entire lifestyle?"

"I didn't say that!" his mother said.

Daniel was quiet. He didn't often fight with his mother, because when he did she grabbed the opportunity to crowd up too close to him with her tears and her drama. Joel had done better with her, their whole lives, exploding easily and making up easily, too; her drama didn't bother him. Daniel preferred to stay away from that. But he had dealt with her undermining of Matt all day long.

"Just say you have a problem with Matt, Mother. Just say it!"

"I have a problem with Matt! There, are you happy?"

Daniel gave her a look, a challenge.

"He's frivolous! He's pretty and shallow! He cares more about the latest styles than he does about these children. I've visited you; I've seen him have a hissy fit because he got a bad haircut, or couldn't find the right shoes."

Daniel snorted in disbelief. Sam came in, asking if anyone was making coffee, but stopped when he saw the looks on their faces. "What's going on?" he asked.

"Mom's busy getting all the homophobia out of her system."

"Daniel!" his father said. "Your mother is not a homophobe." She had been an avid PFLAG member when Daniel came out, so that was the official position.

"I have no problem with you, Daniel," Lydia said, crying now. "I've come to terms with your brother choosing to leave his children with you. It's Matt I have trouble with. The idea that *Matt* is going to raise my grandchildren—Matt! and not me—I can't get over that, I'm sorry."

"Well, you're going to have to get used to it," Daniel said.

"Don't you think I know that?" she cried.

They stood in stricken positions around the kitchen, and then Sam said quietly, "My only problem is that the kids have already been through so much. Being in a gay family, which is so much tougher, seems like a lot to ask of them."

"Oh God," Daniel said, turning to leave the room. Then he stopped and whirled around. "You know, Dad," he said heatedly. "People always say that about being gay. When their kids come out, they say, 'I'm just worried that your life is going to be harder.' But it's *they* who make their kids' lives hard! It's people like them, who don't support their kids because their lives are supposedly going to be harder. It's totally circular, can't you see?"

"Tell me something," his mother was saying, pointing at him. "What happens when Gal needs her first bra, when she gets her period? Can you imagine Matt dealing with that in a sensitive way?"

"Our friend Peter is a very talented drag queen," Daniel said. "I thought I'd let him take care of it."

There was silence. "Is that supposed to be funny?" Sam asked.

"Do *you* think Matt will make a good, committed father?" his mother demanded with a look that challenged Daniel to be honest, that tried to bore into his soul.

"Yes I do," Daniel said. He said it fiercely, thinking about what a goof Matt was, how imaginative and affectionate and funny. If the kids had any shot at having a fun home with them, it would be because of Matt, not him, who couldn't really be called a fun guy under even the best of circumstances.

She leaned back on the counter. "I don't believe you. I don't believe you think that."

It was this kind of shot, Daniel thought, that made him hate fighting with her. A feeling of shame stole over him, and he flushed. She thought that because she had seen him treat Matt like shit over the past couple of weeks.

"I'm through with this conversation, Mom. He's my *partner*. If I get these kids, he will raise them with me. And I'm just hoping—I'm *hoping*—that you're going to help me get them, and not sabotage me."

"Of course I am!" his mother cried. "I'm just being honest with you. Would you prefer I lied about my feelings?"

Daniel groaned. They always asked you this, and you always had to say no, of course you wanted them to be totally honest about how disgusting and inferior they thought you were.

"Enough," Sam said.

Daniel opened his mouth to speak.

"I mean it," Sam said, his voice breaking and his face red. "Enough! Isn't it hard enough? These kids—their lives are *over*! That bastard—"

Lydia stepped up to him and laid her hand on his back. "Shh," she murmured.

"It's okay, Dad," Daniel whispered. It was hard to look at him: emotion was grabbing and contorting Sam's normally equable face and making it grotesque. Daniel stepped up to his father and touched his forehead with his, eyes shut, gripping his shoulder. "Their lives aren't over. Just very challenging."

Sam clutched the back of Daniel's neck and squeezed, nodding, his chest shuddering.

A FEW DAYS LATER, he drove to Yaakov and Malka's to pick up the kids. He'd had a blessedly quiet two and a half days, and had finally caught up with some work, emailing the various writers for progress reports, and having a long phone conversation with April about the various news stories that needed to go in the College Notes section in the front of the magazine. The president of the college had given a speech on the importance of area studies in the wake of 9/11—along with a blistering attack on the reduced grant monies for scholars in those fields—that had been covered in the *New York Times*, and they sat over it for a while, deciding whether to print the whole thing or just portions of it; after they decided to write a story about it instead of simply printing the speech, they went through and chose the quotations they thought most important to preserve and to highlight. When he hung up the phone, Daniel stayed at the kitchen table for a little while, the yellow legal pad beside him covered with notes, basking in that hour or so of quiet concentration and small problem solving, the knowledge of how very good he was at his work.

He had gotten a call scheduling the first parental competency visit for the following week, and had spent some time haggling with various social service administrators about bunching the visits so that Matt wouldn't have to come more than once. Now they had four bunched within a two-week period, and Matt had bought a round-trip ticket for that length of time. The back-and-forth was starting to be a financial strain, and Sam had offered to pay for this flight.

He parked with two wheels on the tiny sidewalk in front of Yaakov and Malka's apartment. He loved Rehavia: it was one of the oldest European neighborhoods in Jerusalem, stone buildings cast into lovely shade by a profusion of plants and trees, climbing plants shooting up the buildings' sides, the occasional professional building—of doctors or small Europe-based companies—marked by modest gold plaques in Hebrew and English. He walked up the walkway and into the cool dark hall, and up the half-flight to their apartment, where he knocked softly on the door.

Malka opened the door and stepped backward in surprise.

"Shalom," he said.

"Shalom. Are you early? The children are at the park with Yaakov." The apartment was dim behind her, and he could smell the sweet mustiness of an old people's house.

Daniel looked at his watch. "No, I'm on time," he said. "But I can wait. Would you like me to wait outside?" The lawyer had forbidden them to discuss the custody case with anyone, especially the opposing parties, and he dreaded the idea of making small talk with Malka.

She blinked nervously, smoothed down her dress. "No, come in," she said.

She led him into the living room; the blinds were half-closed. Over the couch, which had a tasseled cover on it, hung a fanciful painting of a Hasidic violinist, in the style of Chagall. On the side wall hung a batik of the Dome of the Rock and the Western Wall at sunset. He sat on the couch. A huge oak display cabinet that held decorative eggs and birds, spun-glass clowns, and china plates on stands darkened the other side of the room. On the side table next to him stood some black-and-white photos in heavy silver frames. His eye ran along a few faded photos of Yaakov in groups of khaki-clad pioneers with caps and rifles. One had fallen over, and Daniel reached to stand it up again. It showed a young Malka wearing a white blouse and black skirt, her hair pulled back, holding a violin to her chin with a faraway look in her eyes. He looked up; she was hovering at the doorway.

"Did I hear once that you played in the Jerusalem Symphony?"

"Yes," she said, "first violin," with a touch of pride.

"I play violin, too," he said. "*Played*. It's been a long time. I was in the Chicago youth orchestra."

She nodded. "I used to play a lot when Ilana was a baby, because the music soothed her," she said, perching on the arm of a chair.

They talked violin concerti. He felt as though he needed to be very, very gentle around her. He was remembering a conversation he'd once had with Ilana, in which she told him that her mother carried the burden of the Holocaust for all of them—as though if she only carried enough despair, she could spare them. Yaakov, meanwhile, had suffered the same inconceivable losses—of his entire family, his very sense of personhood—but he had remained moving, surviving labor camps and death marches. It was striking, she told him, what a psychological difference it made to be able to move, even if under the constant threat of machine-gun fire, should you falter and slow.

He sat there for a while longer. Malka went into the kitchen, and he heard shuffling, a cabinet opening, a clink of silverware on a plate. He looked around and tried to imagine a teenage Gal in this apartment with her friends. Where would they sprawl around and talk smack in this silent, stuffy place where dust motes turned silently in the few glimmers of light let in from the blinds? He knew the answer immediately: She would never bring her friends here—she would spend her afternoons and evenings at their houses, while Malka made Yaakov call their parents to check up on her, and Noam played endless computer games behind a closed bedroom door.

Malka emerged with a piece of poppy seed cake, the kind sold in grocery stores in long plastic bags. He wasn't a big fan of poppy seed cake, but he ate it politely. She fussed about what might be keeping Yaakov. When they heard voices sound from the hallway, they stood up with relief.

TWO DAYS LATER, MATT was giving Daniel's guitar to a flight attendant to stash and trying not to think about the last time he'd been on this flight to Tel Aviv. The flight was full, and, already feeling greasy from the stale air, he fought his way to the back of the plane, past people aggressively claiming baggage space, blankets, and pillows. Was it anti-Semitic to think of them as aggressive? he wondered.

Flattening himself to pass a Hasidic family, he found his row and stowed his bag overhead after removing his book, a magazine, and a bottle of water. The memory of taking down Ativan for Daniel flashed through his mind and made him feel faint; he steadied himself and tip-toed past the two children seated in his row, who swiveled their knees to the side, and collapsed into his window seat. He sat there with his eyes closed for a few moments, feeling his heart gallop, pulling the plastic bag–covered headphones out from under him and letting them drop onto his lap. His skin was clammy; he wondered whether he was going to have a full-blown panic attack. He began to take con-certed deep breaths, and after a few minutes, aside from the sweat that coated his face, he was able to compose himself.

The plane took off by imperceptible, jumbo jet degrees. Next to him, a little girl was writing in Hebrew, in a Hello Kitty diary with a tiny lock on it. She saw him look at her and ever so slightly slanted the cover so he couldn't spy on what she was writing. The idea that he would want to see how she felt about her best friend's betrayal, or her mother's new boyfriend, cheered him a little. Beside her sat her brother, his eyes narrowed, his thumbs madly mashing a Game Boy.

Matt got up and washed his face. He drank a soda; he napped.

When he awoke he reached for the book in his seat pocket, a book Brent and Derrick had bought him. He had gone over to their house the previous evening. They were in the kitchen, making a late dinner— one of their fancy homemade pizzas—when he arrived; Derrick was slicing pears into slivers while Brent, wearing an apron over his bare torso, rolled out the dough. Matt helped himself to a beer and perched on a bar stool. Brent and Derrick exchanged a significant look, and then Derrick wiped his hands on a towel and said, "We wanted to give you something." He disappeared into the living room and returned with a book. It was called *Gay Dads*.

Matt colored and laughed. "Thanks, guys."

"It's okay if you're ambivalent," Derrick said, standing before him and looking into his face, kind and forthright.

"I know," Matt said, flipping through, looking at the handsome photographs of men and their kids.

"We know one of the guys in the book," Derrick said, "which is how we heard about it."

Now Matt opened the book and leafed through again, and then began to read. It was kind of moving, but kind of horrifying, too. Many of the guys had moved to the suburbs, many had turned into stay-at-home dads, many said that most of their best friends now were straight. Many said that parenthood offered them a connection to their extended families. "We're just a boring normal family," more than one of them said. It horrified him. He *came* from a boring normal family; he wanted something else. If that made him selfish, he couldn't help it.

When he'd read it through, he closed the book, a little pissed at Derrick and Brent for giving it to him. Derrick seemed so invested in him and Daniel being parents. He felt like saying to him, *If you're so into having kids,* you *have them!* And from Brent, it just felt like a setup. He ran his fingers along the spine. The guys in the book went to such lengths to have children. It wasn't at all like his and Daniel's situation, where the children had fallen into their laps. He wondered how his parents would take it, old John and Shirley Greene from Naperville, Illinois. They'd probably say "Gosh" or "Dear Lord" when he told them about these Jewish children whose parents were blown to kingdom come. They already had four grandchildren whom they doted on: his brother and sister were five and seven years older than he was.

They were fine; he just didn't have that much to say to them. It was something Daniel, whose family was so close and intense, had trouble understanding, even after he'd been home with Matt for several Christmases, and noticed that there were no books in the house, and played every game known to creation—from Hearts to checkers to Monopoly to Matt and Daniel's personal favorite, Taboo—and heard the kids tease Matt's dad about the plastic tree he'd bought because he didn't like having to clean up the needles. Each time Daniel was there, Matt's brother, Craig, came into the house and said, "Oh, the scent of fresh pine, nothing like it!" Same joke every time.

DANIEL WAS WAITING FOR him; he picked him out from among the crowd clustered at the exit. He was wearing sunglasses, and hadn't shaved, and looked like the handsomest Jewish man ever. Matt clasped him to him, but they didn't, as was their custom, kiss each other till they were in the car, and even then Matt saw Daniel's eyes darting around to make sure nobody walking by could see.

It had grown hotter, and there was a wavy haze down on the plains; the pale ocean appeared and disappeared between the dunes. "Thanks for bringing my guitar," Daniel said.

"No problem. I stopped off at your office and picked up some stuff, too."

"Did you pay the bills?"

"Yeah, we're good to go till the end of next month. Your salary went in, and I finally got paid for the reunion brochure."

"It's about time," Daniel said, closing the window now that the air conditioner had taken hold.

They didn't speak much as they climbed to Jerusalem, other than Daniel briefing him on what he knew about the parental competency exams that were going to start the next day. They would undergo a battery of tests he'd never heard of, except for the Rorschach. "Yay, tests," Matt joked faintly. Daniel nodded, getting the joke but worrying just a little about how Matt would perform on them. He felt the disconcerting alienation he always felt when they got together after being apart, as though this large man would make demands of him and thwart him from doing what he'd been doing, which was handling things on his own, his own way. On the other hand, it was thrilling to be seated next to a handsome man giving off delicious male smells; they'd been together for four years, and he never got over it.

"They still do the Rorschach?" Matt asked.

"Apparently."

"Wouldn't you think they had something more electronic, or digitized, now? It seems so, I don't know, I'm thinking Elizabeth Taylor in *Suddenly, Last Summer.*"

A smile softened Daniel's face, and he reached over to touch Matt's hair. "Hey there," he said.

"Hey there," Matt smiled, taking Daniel's hand in his two hands and kissing the palm. He had a thought. "What do you wear to a Rorschach, I wonder?"

Daniel thought about it. "A solid color, not a pattern."

"Ah, yes," Matt said, stroking an invisible beard.

CHAPTER 8

M ATT DRESSED FOR the tests in khakis, a white polo shirt, and loaf-
ers, and gelled his hair so that it lay close to his head from a side part.
It was his idea of conservative, and it made Daniel laugh because it made
him look like the new boy at boarding school, ripe for hazing. The tests
were held in one of the labyrinthine municipality buildings, new buildings
set around a stone plaza right on the very edge of the Old City. An elderly
guard sat at a table inside the shadowed hallway, and made them wait till
he called up to verify that they were expected. Dalia met them as they
stepped inside a vast room with smoky-blue carpets and dozens of cubicles
where city employees did their work. She greeted them in a businesslike
manner and told them that she would separate them for the day as the staff
interviewed them and did a few diagnostic tests. She introduced them to
Dr. Mickey Schweig, the psychologist on their case, a small, elderly man
with a morose aspect. He would interview Daniel, and administer both
of their tests. As she took Matt's elbow to steer him toward his room, he
looked back at Daniel in mock alarm, feeling as though they were suspects
who were going to be interrogated separately to discover the discrepancy
in their story. He wondered: What *was* their story?

Dalia sat him down at a small round table and offered him coffee,
and he said, "That'd be great. With milk?"

She boiled water in a small electric kettle and made him a small glass of Nescafé with milk, and then sat opposite him. She asked him to tell her about himself; she asked if it was okay to take notes. She wanted to know about his parents and siblings, where he grew up, his childhood activities and conflicts. He told her about his parents, friendly midwesterners: how his father glad-handed waitresses, calling them by name and asking them what they'd recommend; how his mother made succulent roasts, meat loaf, Jell-O molds, and ambrosia.

"As for conflicts," he said, looking directly at her, "of course the main one was being a queeny kid."

"Tell me about that," she said.

"I guess I'd like some reassurance that it won't be used against me and Daniel," he said, surprising himself with his ferocity.

Dalia set down her pen, looking mildly surprised herself, and he wondered whether she was just that instant discovering that she should take him seriously. "I can't speak for every actor in this custody process," she said. "But as far as I'm concerned, in my own personal evaluation, I'm less interested in your being homosexual than in the way you handle the conflicts that arise around it."

That made so much sense he thought it quite possibly might be true, and disarmed, he relaxed. "I caught a lot of flak in school. You know, they call it bullying, but let's face it, what goes on in schools is actually child abuse. When kids beat you up and then adults deny your reality, or blame you, that's child abuse. It didn't just happen to me; I saw it happen all the time."

"What do you mean by adults denying your reality?"

"I mean, saying things like, 'Oh, that's just the way boys are,' or 'You must have done something to provoke it.' Yeah," he sneered, "it's my fault I walked the way I walk."

"You feel strongly about this."

"Would you talk to a battered woman that way?" he challenged. "Would you ask her what she did to provoke it?"

"No," she said, and paused. "Would you describe yourself as at peace with your homosexuality?"

"I always have been—it's others who haven't been at peace with it." He said that quickly and belligerently, and then apologized. "I feel strongly about it," he said. "It's about supporting kids when they need support."

"Okay," Dalia said.

"When my best friend, Jay, and I started the gay-straight alliance in high school, things got better. We were still harassed, but there was comfort in numbers. The best day of high school was a demonstration we held—there were maybe twelve of us, and probably half were girls who were 'allies'—against homophobic harassment. These students we'd contacted from the U of I—that's the University of Illinois—came up on a bus to support us. It was covered for eighteen seconds on ABC News in a segment on the new gay activism."

He paused, considered. "Jay died four years ago," he said.

Dalia looked up. "AIDS?"

He narrowed his eyes. Was she stereotyping gay men, or just knowledgeable? "Yes."

"Do you know your HIV status?"

"Yes."

They gazed contemplatively at each other for a few moments.

Dalia looked away first, and cleared her throat. She invited him to talk more about his parents, whom, he hastened to assure her, he was now on good terms with. She asked about his work, his move to Northampton, how he met Daniel. It was close to one o'clock by the time she set down her pen again and pushed back her chair. "Okay, let's break for lunch, and when you come back, Dr. Schweig will administer some personality tests."

Matt stood, wondering if Daniel would be done, too. He opened the door, then turned back.

"Negative," he said.

"Okay," she said. "Thank you for telling me."

Daniel was standing by the elevator. They went downstairs and emerged onto the hot, bright plaza, the sun making them blink and sneeze, and stood uncertainly while people surged around them and buses roared past them with grinding gears. In the near distance rose the craggy walls and golden domes of the Old City. Daniel took Matt's sleeve and steered him toward a falafel stand on the adjoining street that they'd passed on their way in. The street was dingy and shaded. "What did you guys talk about?" Daniel asked.

"Oh, this and that," Matt said lightly.

"Really?" Daniel said. "Us too!"

The falafel stand was manned by a large bearded man in a *kipa*, who was intimidatingly quick and efficient. His spoon flew over pitas, slathering on tahini and eggplant; he turned from the fixings to behind him, where falafel was cooking in baskets dunked into boiling oil, and back to the front. They carried the beautiful warm sandwiches and two bottles of Coke back to the plaza, and found a bench in the shade, where they ate bent forward, so that tahini and hot sauce wouldn't dribble onto their pants. "Wow," Matt said through a burning palate. "Heaven." When he was done, Daniel handed him a napkin and he wiped his hands finger by finger, then took a long swig of Coke.

"I've been thinking," Daniel said, wiping his own face, casting a look at Matt. "You're not going to like this."

"I'm already crazy about it," Matt said. "Go ahead."

"I'm just thinking aloud, okay? Don't jump all over me."

"Dan, just say it."

Daniel reached behind his glasses with a finger and rubbed his eye. He cleared his throat and spoke. "Why shouldn't we just stay here?"

Matt blinked. *You have got to be kidding*: That was his thought.

"I'm not talking forever, just a few years. Think about it. It would make everything so much easier! It wouldn't tear Gal away from her friends, and both kids from their grandparents. We could live here, in the apartment. We could get work here; we both have skills that would make us a good living. For design work, you don't even really need Hebrew."

"Dan," Matt sighed.

Daniel's face was reddening with emotion. "I just can't stand the idea of tearing Gal away from here. It's wrong! It's the wrong thing to do!"

Matt rubbed his face. Maybe if he just let Daniel talk it out, he would work it out of his system.

"What do you think? Don't just have a knee-jerk response."

That was irritating. "We don't live here," Matt said. "Our life is in the States. *My* life is in the States."

"That's not a reason," Daniel said.

"Should I give more?" Matt asked, beginning to heat up. "I thought you were just thinking aloud. Have you decided this?"

"No!" Daniel said.

"It sounds as though you have. You have all the reasons down."

"It's not a decision I can make without you," Daniel said. He was saying the right thing, but Matt, looking at him with narrowed eyes, didn't believe him, and that scared him. Suddenly he had a premonition that Daniel was using this to leverage himself out of their relationship, a premonition that came with such dark fury, he knew it must be true.

"Are you breaking up with me?" he asked.

"No! Jesus!"

"Don't lie to me."

"I'm asking you to do this *with* me!"

"But you know I can't!"

"Why not?" Daniel demanded.

"Do I have to say it?" There was no answer. "Do I? Okay. *Because it goes against everything I believe in to live here*," Matt said, leaning toward Daniel and giving him a gentle piercing look, trying to bring him back to himself. "And everything you believe in too, by the way."

Daniel shook his head. "This isn't about politics," he said. "It's about these children."

"Oh please!" Matt cried. "I don't even know where to start! You're doing just what they do to us all the time, dismissing our politics as though they have nothing to do with real life. You *know* that's not true."

"It's just that, I've been thinking, parenthood means sacrifice, living for someone other than yourself."

Matt looked at him. "Wow, you thought that up all by yourself?" he asked with wide-eyed mockery. "Who *are* you?"

Daniel sat back, resolute. "Maybe I'm not the same man anymore."

Maybe that was it, Matt thought, his heart flailing in his chest. He'd always thought, when wondering whether they'd stay together forever, that no one could be one hundred percent confident. Sure, he'd stay with Daniel through many changes—although, admittedly, some of them might be especially challenging, like quadriplegia, a possibility he'd spent many an hour pondering in some torment. But what if circumstances made Daniel unrecognizable to him?

"You're the same man, Daniel," he said softly, with a silent prayer.

Daniel passed a hand over his face. "It's not as though the U.S. is such great shakes from a moral perspective."

Matt took heart from the weakness of that salvo.

"I just can't stand the thought of tearing Gal away from here," Daniel said, his mouth twisting. "I can't."

"She'll be okay. . . ."

"No she won't!" Daniel cried. "She's going to lose everything she knows! She's such a little trouper, it *kills* me to watch her get up and soldier through her day."

Matt looked at his watch. They had to be back inside in ten minutes. "I can't believe you sprung that on me right now," he said. "We have to go in there now and take personality tests, for Christ's sake. If you've decided you're staying, what's even the point?"

An old Arab woman rolled by, her heavy, lined hand on the shoulder of a young boy, and catching the boy's eye, Matt wondered what he was seeing when he looked at the two flushed, angry American men.

"I haven't decided," Daniel insisted.

"Whatever," Matt said, standing.

They went back in and spent the afternoon associating to Rorschach blots and telling stories about TAT pictures. Matt found the TAT pictures profoundly depressing, not only in their content, but in their style as well. The figures seemed utterly isolated, the cloud formations menacing. The portrayal of gender was taken straight from the 1950s. He kept looking at the psychologist, wondering if this was a joke test, but when he met his eyes he saw no glimmer of connection or humor, just the patient waiting of the diagnostician. He wondered how the hell he'd gotten into this mess, how it came to be that he was sitting in a dingy office in the middle of this hot, teeming, smelly, violent, godforsaken city, being forced to make up stories like a mental patient. For every picture, he wanted to make up a story about deviant gender or sexuality.

When Dr. Schweig finally released him, he was exhausted. He had to wait for Daniel to take his tests, and he didn't want to have to pass through security again, so he sat on a chair by the elevator for an hour, cursing the fact that he hadn't brought something to read, until Daniel came out of a room and closed the door softly behind him. They looked at each other; Daniel crossed his eyes. Then, as Matt raised his eyebrows, Daniel put a finger to his lips and walked quickly to the elevator, his mouth twitching. Only when they burst out onto the plaza did he begin to laugh.

"Were those cards messed-up, or what!" Daniel said. "They were a disgrace!" He started giggling. "Did you get the blank card?" he asked.

Matt began laughing, too. "There was a blank card?"

"Oh yeah," Daniel said. "I said to the psychologist, 'That represents the blankness of God's intent to Man's scrutiny.' I mean, what the fuck?" His mirth was broken through with confused indignation, and that set them off again. People on official business were walking past the giggling men, avoiding them with varying degrees of curiosity and irritation.

"You did not!" It was exhilarating: Daniel had misbehaved, and not him! There was a little bit of hardness to the feeling, for wasn't Daniel a hypocrite for treating him as a fuckup, and then cutting loose himself? Still, it was lovely to watch him seized by the giggles. They went down the steps to the parking garage, Daniel's back shaking in front of him, his shirt damp from sweat. Maybe, Matt thought, the idea of staying in Jerusalem was just a momentary faintness of heart, a streak of crippling empathy for Gal. They passed together into the dark, cool underground, their shoes making soft, clean noises on the concrete floor. "Do you think we could get away with not going straight home?" Daniel asked. He flung his arm around Matt. "Let's ditch the grieving children and stop somewhere for a beer."

"Absolutely," Matt said. Daniel feeling frisky was a treat under any circumstance. "But if you just lost the kids for us because you failed to take this test with the proper seriousness, you're in big trouble."

TWO WEEKS OF FURTHER tests passed. Daniel didn't bring up wanting to stay in Israel again, but a low current of anxiety buzzed through Matt as he waited for the moment he'd have to fight it out again. After they were interviewed and tested separately, Dalia and the psychologist met with them together to discuss their relationship, and then came over to the apartment twice to see them with the kids. It hurt Lydia's feelings that she was asked not to be there for those interviews. "Won't I be a big part of these kids' lives if they go to you?" she importuned Daniel privately, and he knew that it killed her that Matt was being tested as a parent and she wasn't. For his part, Matt noticed that Daniel wore to both interviews shirts that had belonged to Joel, and he wondered if he was trying to channel Joel, or to look like a respectable and upstanding straight man, or maybe enacting some creepy version of those twins who dressed alike well into their adulthood and then married twins, a phenomenon Daniel had spent a lifetime loathing. But it was funny to see how the straightest-looking of clothes—a polo shirt tucked into chinos—got a gay twist when the marvelously delicate Daniel wore them. The interviews themselves—the two of them sitting on the floor, stiff and smiling, among the playing children—were, to his mind, a bit of a charade, although when the psychologist asked Gal what she liked most about Uncle Matt and she said, with a decisiveness that made them all smile, "He's really funny," he felt inordinately proud, both of her response itself and of the fact that he understood the Hebrew.

In Gal, Matt found an even more exacting Hebrew teacher than Yossi—although he didn't have quite the same drive to impress her as he did Yossi—and, as an added bonus, one who was learning to read and write herself. They sat next to each other at the kitchen table, drawing letters and writing simple words onto lined sheets of paper, Gal's eyes darting back and forth from her own paper to Matt's. "You know, Mordechai," she said one day—she had inexplicably begun calling him Mordechai. Why? When he asked, she just shrugged, but when Daniel asked her, she said she thought he needed a Hebrew name. "Your letters are better than mine."

"That's because I'm an artist," he said, "and also, I already know how to write in one language. But often I can't understand what I'm writing, and you can understand everything you write."

She studied her own letters and said, "*Oof!* Let's do a vocabulary test instead." She never tired of testing his vocabulary. She'd call out words she thought of off the top of her head, in English, and he'd have to translate. If he got the word right, she'd ask him to modify it with an adjective like *good* or *bad*, or *big* or *small*, so he could learn its gender. When he got that right, her eyes would widen and she'd give him an indulgent pat on the hand. "*Col ha'cavod*," she'd say. Good job! or, as the literal translation went, All honor to you!

Lydia came into the room, got out a loaf of bread that Daniel had bought that morning, and set it on the cutting board. "Time to set the table, kidlets," she said.

Matt knew that they wouldn't be eating for another half an hour; this was Lydia's way of making it hard for him to have a relationship with Gal. She'd told Daniel that she felt *horrible* about Matt's learning Hebrew with Gal, because there was no way for her to participate since he'd thought of it first. Daniel had told her that that was silly, that it was a good idea for all of them to know Hebrew. And then she made him facilitate it: He had to ask Matt and Gal if Grandma and Grampa could join them, even though Sam had no intention of doing so. She participated from time to time, and when she did, they always had to say how smart Grandma was, and how good her memory was. "Who got 'window'?" she'd demand.

"You did, Grandma," Gal would say.

Since Matt's return, Sam was busying himself with what he called Joel and Ilana's "effects." He and Daniel went through Joel's clothes, a ravaging experience for both of them; halfway through, Sam sat hard on the bed, his face stricken and drooped, and said, "I can't believe I'm doing this." Daniel kept a lot of them. As for Ilana's clothes, Sam insisted upon calling in Malka to help. He'd become the emissary to the Grossmans; he had a calming effect on them—probably, Daniel imagined, because of the quiet, benign quality of his attention, one of Daniel's own favorite things about his father. He and Malka spent an afternoon in the bedroom with the door closed, and Malka left with an armful of clothes, her face pale and set against the indignity of seeming to slink off with the dregs the victor left behind, as hyenas do. They saved Ilana's jewelry for Gal, except for one necklace that had particular sentimental value for Malka that Sam hadn't quite understood.

Sam made two duplicates of the wedding video, and additional prints of all the negatives he found stuffed into the pockets and between the pages of the photo albums. Then he bought photo albums and compiled them. One set for him and Lydia, one for Malka and Yaakov, one for Daniel and Matt and the kids. He set himself up at the kitchen table, wearing khaki pants and sandals, and an untucked, short-sleeved button-down shirt, reading glasses perched on the end of his nose. He was solitary, focused, in his element. He had dealt the photos into three piles, like cards, and now he was trying to manage one of the large piles, putting it into chronological order, using Joel and Ilana's album as the key.

When she got home from school, Gal climbed on a chair next to him and studied the piles. "What are you doing?" she asked.

"I'm making three different albums, so we can all have pictures of your parents, and of you and Noam when you were babies," Sam said. "Careful, honey, that belongs here."

Daniel was on the floor, playing with blocks with the baby. He stood and came over; he could tell that Sam was worried Gal would disrupt his piles and his concentration. The photo Sam had taken from her was a wedding picture in which Joel and Ilana were disarranged, drunk, grinning. "They didn't have me yet," Gal said experimentally, craning her neck up at Daniel. Just checking. She picked up a picture of herself as a newborn, held by Ilana, who was touching her nose to hers. Ilana's hair in a ponytail, eyes half-closed. Content, drowsy.

"That's me," Gal said.

"That's you," Daniel said, putting his hand on her head. "You and Ema. Look how much she loved you."

Gal studied it, then placed it carefully on the correct pile.

"Thanks, honey," Sam said.

"Was I a good baby?" Gal asked in a small voice.

"Yes, you were," Daniel said somberly, turning her face to his. "And a good girl, too."

Did she take it in? Who knew? She looked at him with enormous eyes, then got up and opened the snack drawer. The baby squawked and Daniel picked him up and jiggled him.

Matt flew back home to return to work, and another few weeks passed, in which Daniel had to appear in family court twice. The judge seemed taken by the fact that he and Joel were identical twins, which Daniel hoped meant that he was considering that, genetically speaking, the kids could actually be his.

Then one day Daniel got a call from Assaf, who had gotten a call from Yaakov and Malka's lawyer. "They want to settle, Daniel," Assaf said. "They agree to have you and Matt take the children, under the condition that they can visit them once a year, and that you bring them here once a year. That's fantastic news. Of course, the court has to approve."

Daniel sank onto the couch with the cordless phone. "What happened?"

"There was a car accident," Assaf said. "A minor one, but it looks as if Malka blacked out for a second behind the wheel, and that frightened them. The attorney said they simply want the best for the kids. But I have a feeling that they also didn't do too well with the parental competency visits."

Poor, poor Malka, Daniel thought.

Assaf said that he most likely wouldn't be allowed to adopt the children, at least not yet. Adoption, he reminded him, was the most binding form of custody a court could award to a nonbiological parent. But there were other gradations of custody, ones that were more temporary and contingent upon follow-up visits and testing.

Daniel nodded. They had been over this before.

His mother came into the room and saw the expression on his face, and was hovering around him whispering "What? What?" as he flapped his hands at her to shush her so he could hear Assaf.

"I'll call back when I know more about what comes next," Assaf said. "Daniel. I'm glad."

Daniel hung up, told his mother what had happened, hugged her and his father.

"Thank God," Lydia said, clutching her chest. "Thank God."

"I have to call Matt," he said, taking the phone into the bedroom and closing the door. He sat down, placed the phone on the desk, and buried his face in his hands. Then he placed his hands on the desk and took a deep breath. He dialed, and the phone was picked up immediately by a breathless Matt.

"Hey, it's me," Daniel said. "Who were you expecting?"

"Hey!" Matt said. "The woman from the Forbes Library, who might have some design work for me."

"Not your new lover?"

"You mean the young one without the crying children?"

Daniel laughed with a tiny wounded pang. "Speaking of the crying children, Assaf called today to say that Malka and Yaakov have decided not to contest custody."

Matt shrieked.

"It still has to go through the courts," Daniel said. "But who else can they give custody to?" He was listening very hard for Matt's response, but all he could hear was the sound of his breathing on the other end. "Are you hyperventilating?"

"Kind of."

"Do you need to put your head between your knees?"

"Let me just lie down." Daniel heard a grunt and a sigh. "Okay," Matt said. "Phew. How long do you think before we can bring them home?"

"I don't know."

They were quiet for a few minutes. Daniel took off his glasses and covered his eyes with his hand. *Here it is, bucko,* he thought: the moment your bluff is called. "Do you think we can do this?" he asked.

"You're asking if I think *I* can do it, right?" Matt said.

"No, both of us."

"Oh my God, you're such a liar," Matt said. "Absolutely."

MATT LAY ON THE bed for a while after they hung up. It was still morning in Massachusetts, and the bed was unmade; he hadn't had coffee yet. He would have to move his study up to the guest room, an attic refinished by the previous owners. His current study, a big, boxy, sunny room across the hall from their own bedroom, would be perfect for the kids' bedroom. The guest room was smaller, and the roofline slanted down to cut off some of the usable space.

He thought that all in a rush, then felt a pang: No more guest room! Guests would have to sleep in the living room or in his study. And what, he wondered, would they do with the beautiful guest bed? Was it appropriate to put a six-year-old in a double bed, and would it even fit in the room with a crib? Not if they put a little desk in there, for Gal to do her homework. And when Gal got older and needed her own room, she'd want the attic one, a funkier and more private space than the bedroom she'd be sharing with Noam, so he'd have to move his study again. He supposed he'd rent office space in town. Would they have to buy a bigger house? He sat up and placed the phone back on the night table.

He got up and washed his face, then went up the creaky, bowing stairs and stood in the guest room doorway, running his hand through his hair and trying to imagine where he'd put his computer, his printer, his bulletin board. He sighed. When he moved in, he'd poured his energy into trying to put his own stamp on Daniel's house, becoming a regular at the local antique shops, stripping and refinishing tables and benches, repainting the drab conventional white walls in a palette of boysenberry, deep olive, and lemon. He'd put mismatching chairs, of a variety of materials, around the dining room table. Daniel had put up a fight about the changes, arguing that Matt's sleek tastes didn't suit a farmhouse, but Matt convinced him that Daniel needed to expand his *idea* of the farmhouse, and besides, he needed to feel as if the house were his, too. Daniel had come to love the warm colors of the rooms. And now they'd have to remake the house again, only this time, making it uglier. He'd do something nice with these walls, though, which he'd never gotten to. And get a small air-conditioning unit. He looked glumly at the antique two-pronged electrical outlet under the window. And call an electrician.

He went downstairs and made himself coffee, fed the dog. He opened the door onto a sunny day, and late-spring cold surged into the kitchen through the screen door. He got Yo-yo's leash and snapped it onto his collar, a lingering heaviness at his heart over what was about to happen to his house, thinking, *Let it go, it's okay, let it go.*

DANIEL WENT TO COURT the next week, and Judge Fuchs, a man with a flat bowl of black hair and enormous wire-rimmed glasses, awarded him custody of the children, and permission to take them to the U.S. Daniel had come with his father and Assaf, and the whole thing felt a little anticlimactic. What had he expected? he wondered later. For the judge to rehearse the course of this tragic case, sum it up in sonorous Hebrew? To exchange a hearty, moved look with him? After all, he'd been ruling on their case from the beginning, and Daniel had developed a transference attachment. But the judge's eye contact was sporadic and impersonal. There were certain conditions, which he switched to English for the first time to say. Daniel looked at his father. "Excuse me, Judge. May my father come up and listen?" he asked.

"Of course," the judge said.

His father approached and put his hand on Daniel's shoulder. Daniel, the judge said, was to bring the children to Israel once a year to visit their grandparents for a minimum of two weeks, and allow their maternal grandparents to visit in the U.S. at least once a year, also for a minimum of two weeks. They were to be followed by a social worker in the U.S. They were to return to this court after two years, so that it could follow their progress.

"Do you understand?" he asked Daniel.

"Yes."

"The court expresses its hope that you will give the children every opportunity to express and cultivate their Israeli heritage, and will foster in them love of Israel. Do you understand?"

"Yes, Judge," Daniel said. He did understand, but he'd have to think about how to do that later.

And that was that. Nothing about Matt, about the fact that he was awarding custody to two gay men. No comment about how well they'd done on their parental competency exams, and how great the tests showed their personalities were, and how they had confounded the court's expectations. He didn't even give a knock of the gavel. They filed out of the court and Daniel and his father embraced, Sam clutching the back of Daniel's head with his hand. When they let go, they were flushed. Daniel turned to Assaf and took his hand in both of his. "Thank you," he said.

Assaf took them to lunch in the courtyard of the American Colony Hotel, where they sat at an elegant iron table on a flagstone floor, surrounded by a burbling Turkish fountain and olive trees and flower beds. Daniel brought up the fact that there had been no mention of Matt, and Assaf pointed out that the actual custody, after all, was to Daniel alone. "But you're right," he added. "I think he probably left that out so there won't be any gay rights implications to the case."

Sam ordered a bottle of expensive champagne, and when the waiter had ceremoniously poured it, held up his glass. When they'd raised theirs, he said, "To my grandchildren, Gal and Noam. May their lives, which have gotten off to such a terrible start, get brighter by the day."

"L'chaim," Assaf said.

"And to Daniel," Sam said, turning toward his son and contemplating him with a smile bright with love and pain. "Raise them well, son. I know you will."

Daniel bit his lip and tried not to be a total girl in front of his father. "That means a lot to me, Dad," he said.

THEY DECIDED THAT THEY wanted to tell the children that they were going to move to the U.S. in the presence of their other grandparents, to indicate that it was a decision that the family as a whole was making, for their benefit. It was Daniel who called, and he spoke with Yaakov.

"Yaakov, I want you to know how much I appreciate this."

There was a long silence, so he soldiered on, in stiff Hebrew. "I will take very good care of the children, I promise, and we'll work it so you can see them as often as possible. You're very welcome to stay with us when you come to visit them in the States. Have you ever been to the U.S.?"

"No," Yaakov said. "Only to Europe. And Istanbul."

"I think you'll like where we live," Daniel said, resolutely conjuring in his mind the gentle verdant mountains and rippling streams instead of the tattooed lesbians who lounged and smoked and made out on the streets of his town. He proposed to Yaakov that he and Malka come over that evening for dinner, and to talk to Gal. "It'll be good," he said, quietly calculating how to convey that Matt wasn't there, "if all the adults—you and Malka, my parents, me—could tell her together that we've made a collective decision."

There was a long pause on the other end. Then Yaakov said, "I don't know what there is to talk about. You are taking the children. How hard can that be to tell Gal? It doesn't require an international convention."

Daniel bit his lip. "Don't you want to tell her that you and Malka love her, and that we all agreed that this is how we'd take care of her and Noam?"

"She knows we love her," Yaakov said. "There's no need for a formal declaration."

When Daniel hung up, he had a tremendous headache. It was much harder to talk to Yaakov from the position of the victor than from the position of antagonist, because even though Yaakov was being a big prick and not thinking of what Gal needed, he felt horrible for him. He went into the kitchen to report dejectedly to his mother, who said, "You can't expect them to be happy about it, honey. Just to behave well in front of the children."

But the bad feeling persisted through a trip to the supermarket, through picking up Gal from school. Gal had been irritable all afternoon; her teacher took Daniel aside and told him that she had hit another kid pretty hard, and that she'd had to put her in a time-out. On their way home, carrying her backpack and an art project with macaroni glued onto construction paper, Daniel had tried to ask her about what had happened, but she refused to talk, giving him a lot of the shrug/tsk combination that played such a big part in Israeli children's bad moods. "Are you feeling sad?" he asked as they approached the tiny *makolet* near her school for her traditional after-school Popsicle.

"Are you feeling sad?" she said in a mocking voice, her face twisted into grotesque concern.

"Hey," he admonished, and she ran inside, mingling with the other little kids gathered around the square white freezer. He watched her wait obediently in line, then give her coins to the elderly man in a *kipa*, who handed her an orange Popsicle. She brought it outside, struggling to peel off the wrapper without getting her fingers sticky, and then dropped the whole thing onto the grimy sidewalk. Daniel's heart sank. She looked at it and up at him, and he said quickly, *"Ain davar,* we'll get another one."

"I don't want!" she said, and marched toward home, and he followed her the whole way, watching her stalwart, angry back.

At home, Daniel snapped at his mother, and he picked a fight with Matt on the phone when Matt asked if he should come help them pack and fly back with them, by saying, "It's not necessary, we can really manage on our own," and finally, after Matt persisted with further questions, saying, "You're going to have to decide this one for yourself, Matt, I already have two children to deal with."

"Whoa," Matt said.

"Look, I can't talk right now, okay?" Daniel waited. "Let's talk later."

"Sure," Matt said, hanging up the phone before the word was even out.

MATT COOKED DINNER FOR Cam later that evening, and he told her about his dilemma as he cleared the dishes and put them into the dishwasher, spooned the leftovers into Tupperware containers. He wanted to be part of their coming home. He was wondering if he could just show up a few days before they left, or whether that would be unpleasant or unhelpful in any way. But even if it seemed unhelpful, he still wanted to do it! "We really can't afford it," he said. "Already, two round-trips to Israel for me, and one for Daniel, have been about thirty-six hundred dollars, although I think Daniel's father's going to pay for one of those. This would bring it up to almost five grand, and we'd have to float it on a credit card." He paused. "But I just don't think that money should be the issue here."

"Oh, go!" Cam said.

Matt laughed. "Of course you'd say that." Cam was an impetuous girlfriend, a lover of the grand gesture. She loved to do things like spring a weekend trip to Miami Beach on a girlfriend, secretly canceling all the girlfriend's appointments and packing her suitcase, and then, when she showed up for a supposed coffee date, whisking her away in her car to the airport without telling her where they were going. Matt and Daniel privately thought that that wasn't romantic, it was controlling.

"So I should just show up, even though Daniel said not to?"

"Did he say not to, or did he say he doesn't *need* you to?"

Cam was arguing exactly what he wanted to argue, and that made him doubt himself. He wet a sponge and wiped down the counters. It really wasn't a good idea. It would be far more sensible to wait for them at home, to pick them up from the airport, and have everything lovely and welcoming when they arrived. But the impulse to go was persistent, and he believed in listening to your instincts, too.

CHAPTER 9

DANIEL DREAMED THAT he was in the café. It wasn't the Peace Train Café, it was one he'd never seen before, a café with a huge mirror on one wall that made it seem as though there was a whole duplicate café on the other side. A man entered, bulky, his face sweaty, and Daniel knew he was the bomber. He tried to get someone's attention, but the waitress was talking to a group at another table, with her back turned to him. An enormous cappuccino stood steaming on the table before him, crisp brown grains of sugar speckling and staining the foam. Sunshine slashed across one knee, and he scooted his chair over into the shade. Then Ilana was sitting across from him—she must have been there all along—and he felt embarrassed that he was so baldly standing in for Joel. Someone laughed and shouted in Hebrew, "I told you so! Didn't I tell you so?" His chest was knotted, and he was sweating. The bomber had disappeared, but Daniel knew with terrible dream-certainty that the man's fingers were reaching for the cord that hung under his coat. In the spinning chaos of his thoughts, Daniel pictured his flesh blown from his bones, wondered murkily if his brain would register the agony even if his head was blown clear off.

He woke up screaming, and sat up, stunned, his voice echoing in his ears. He'd never produced such a sound, and for a second he thought someone else was screaming. When he realized where he was, he leapt out of bed as though it were on fire, and burst from his room. The house was quiet in the early dawn light: Incredibly, no one had heard him. He sank to his knees on the living room rug, then sat on his heels and bowed his head and breathed, waiting for the panic to stop.

His headache didn't go away; it persisted through the packing, the visits to various government offices to arrange papers and passports, the accelerated pace of bringing the children back and forth from their house to their grandparents'. A *hamsin* moved into Jerusalem, the sky turning white, hot wind whipping up sand and garbage and twisting laundry on the line. His eyes became swollen, the skin under them chafed and tender. They pulled down all the blinds in the apartment, making it into a dark cave, and congregated whenever possible in the master bedroom, which had the apartment's only air-conditioning unit, as the wind rattled the blinds. They ate cold foods, yogurt and salads and spreads on bread. Lydia complained about crumbs in the bed, where Gal was eating her snacks in front of the TV. "Use a plate, honey!" she said, swiping at the crinkled bottom sheet. Even Noam was cranky, shrieking when they took anything sharp, or a choking hazard, away from him. Daniel took him into the bathroom to splash cold water on his pink, sweaty face, and laughed when he saw Noam's thrust-out lower lip in the mirror, it was the very picture of infantile indignation.

Sam had spent the morning at the kitchen table, writing numbers on a pad of paper, with quick punches at the calculator. He called Daniel into the kitchen in the tone he used for important matters, usually financial, and pulled out a chair for him. "Listen, Daniel," he said, "I'd like you to be able to keep the apartment for the next few years, so you'll have a place to be when you bring the children to visit their grandparents. So I'm going to pick up the mortgage and taxes, to make that possible. Maybe we can find someone to manage it and rent it out for the periods when you're not here."

"Really, Dad, are you sure?" Daniel asked, and when his father nodded, he said, "Thank you so much. I can't tell you how nice that is of you." In the past, he'd turned down all of his father's attempts to help him out financially, except for this most recent gift of Matt's plane ticket, because those offers made him feel that his father thought he couldn't make it on his own. But this gift didn't feel like that at all. It felt like an amazing act of understanding and empathy. The apartment felt to him like a living thing, its light and smells, its tiled floors and thick, strong blinds, the sheets they put on the beds, the gas stove that clicked noisily four times before lighting, the nicked and pocked coffee table, the broom closet stuffed with pails and plastic bags, the mop handle falling down every time someone opened the door. Living in it was like loving a middle-aged person who'd been around the block a few times.

And then their departure was only a week away. Gal's class threw her a going-away party, and when Daniel came to pick her up he stood for a few minutes at the edge of the classroom, watching kids say good-bye with varying degrees of social competence and drama, their faces bearing the traces of chocolate frosting. Gal was flushed and wearing a crown, and when she saw him, she came over to him. "Look," she said, thrusting a small, leather-bound book at him. They had taken pictures of themselves, individually and in groups, and had composed a photo album. Daniel flipped through it, trying not to bawl. There were also cards with crazy first-grade writing all over them, and a bag of candy— candy Daniel was sure he'd be finding in corners of his house a year from now. Gal's teacher, Sari, stooped to give her a tearful hug, and Gal, with a pained look on her face, allowed herself to be squeezed. "You'd better come see me when you come visit," she said huskily. "Or else, *oy vey!*"

They walked home quietly. Daniel didn't dare speak. The wind whipped at them and Gal winced as her hair lashed her face. They descended to the cool dark underground walkway that crossed under-neath Herzl Street, their sneakers making cupped muffled sounds on the sidewalk. Daniel's hand sweated onto the photo album. How could he survive all this tiny girl was losing, when he felt her pain so sharply it made him gasp?

When they got home, Gal said she had a headache. Lydia got her to undress and gave her a cool sponge bath, and when Daniel passed by, he saw his mother murmuring to her and running a washcloth over her back as Gal stood, hands limp, turning obediently. Her face and lips had lost their color. After she was dried off, she crawled into bed and faced the wall, and she didn't stir for the next twelve hours.

MATT PAINTED THE KIDS' room, ordered a bed, a crib, a changing table, and a dresser for it. When the furniture arrived, he and Derrick and Brent sat on the bedroom floor holding Allen wrenches and scratching their chins over large unfolded instructions. When they took a break they went out to the backyard and wiped the accumulated dirt and pollen off of the plastic lawn chairs and sprawled in the shade of the big oak, drinking beer. Matt had a heavy feeling about all the grief about to enter his house, and Derrick gave him a pep talk. Derrick was a tall, forthright man with coffee-colored skin, a shaved head, and a neat goatee—not exactly handsome, but a treat to look at, his face was so open and lively. Derrick told him, emotion catching his throat, that he was about to find himself capable of things he'd never imagined he could do.

"I want them to feel safe," Matt said. "How do you make kids feel safe?"

Derrick looked at him gently. "Is that what you're worried about?"

"I don't know, I've been thinking about it. How can you promise a kid she'll be safe when she already knows, better than you do, how dangerous the world is?"

Derrick sat up straighter, narrowed his eyes in thought. "I'm remembering a study done by Winnicott—he was this big English psychoanalyst—with I think it was English children after World War Two, who were evacuated from London, away from their parents, during the blitzkrieg. The ones who were assured that they and their parents and their houses were going to be safe, even though there was no evidence for that—on the contrary, the evidence pointed in the opposite direction—those kids fared better emotionally in the long term than the ones who were told by adults that they honestly didn't know what was going to happen. Which goes against everything we're normally taught, that the most important thing when dealing with children going through trauma is telling them the truth."

Brent got up and set his bottle on the small brick patio, then roamed the borders of the yard, doing miscellaneous weeding. They were quiet for a while, watching him stoop and grip and wiggle gently, bringing up small balls of dirt and root. They commiserated over the political situation, Israel's ravaging of West Bank towns; as a black man, Derrick thought of Israel as a colonial power, but as a social worker he tried to conscientiously examine his own potential anti-Semitism.

"When you're there," Matt said, "it seems really complicated. There are all these Israelis with their funny personalities, kind of assholes but also really human and likable, and no contact whatsoever with the Palestinians who are living through hell just a few miles away. And then you come home and see from here what Israel's doing, and suddenly it seems very simple: it's a nation committing terrible crimes against another people."

They sat for a while longer, directing Brent here and there as though he were their sexy lawn boy.

"I'm going to fly back with them," Matt said. "I bought a ticket."

Derrick looked at him quickly. "Does Daniel know?"

"No. I can't bring myself to tell him; I'm afraid he'll be mad, or tell me not to come. So I'm just showing up. It'll be kind of like a sitcom!" he said brightly, and Derrick laughed.

THREE DAYS BEFORE THEIR departure, Lydia took Gal to the mall to look for a good-bye present for Leora, and they returned with a necklace that said *Friends forever.*

"Good job, guys!" Daniel said as he and his father bent over, looking at it together, Gal nervously holding open the box close to her body, as though the whole thing might be ruined if they disturbed it. He shot his mother an impressed look, and she said, "It's perfect, isn't it."

It fell upon Daniel to help Gal with the card. He sat with her on the living room rug, legs open over construction paper, scissors, and markers. "What do you want to write?" he asked.

Normal summer weather had returned to Jerusalem, and a soft, warm breeze came in through the open windows, ruffling Gal's hair. She was barefoot, sitting between her heels, in shorts and a hideous T-shirt she loved that said *Princess* in curly script studded with rhinestones. "I don't know," she said. "What should I say?"

"Do you want to tell her that you love her and will miss her?"

"Yes," she said gravely. "And also that she should come visit me in Massachusetts." It had taken her a while to be able to pronounce the name of the state, which they still sometimes playfully called "Massachoochay."

"Okay," Daniel said.

"And I want to draw a picture," she said, her energy gathering.

"Good idea."

She bent forward till she was lying on her stomach supported by her elbows, selected a brown marker, and began to draw. Daniel was pretty sure it would be a horse. He sat facing her with his legs crossed, in a posture of watching and supporting as he brushed the newspaper off the coffee table and snuck looks at it.

"*Oof!*" she cried, and violently crumbled the paper.

"Wait," he protested, "let me see!" He unfolded it. "What's wrong with this?"

She gave him a withering look. "The head is all . . . it's disgusting!"

"Okay," he said mildly, taking a new piece of construction paper from the pile, which she carefully folded in half.

She completed the next horse before deciding that it was a failure too, and this time her small fierce face darkened into tears. Daniel snatched at the paper before she could destroy it.

"Sweetie, tell me what you want to do that you're failing at. Because I think this one's really nice."

"You always say that!" she cried. "Even if it's shit! Where will I put the writing?" She sat up and swiped at the markers, which went flying off the carpet and clattering over the linoleum floor.

Daniel looked soberly at the drawing, turned it every which way in his hands. "Can't we put the writing on the back? I think that'd look really nice. And then you could draw even more around the horse, like grass and the sky."

"No! It's a card, so it's supposed to be inside!"

"Not always, people write in all kinds of places," he said. He patted his lap. "Come sit here for a second."

"No! I have to do this!"

"Just to calm down for a second, and then we'll take another look at it."

She stood and he took her wrist to pull her down, and she smacked his arm and ran into her room and slammed the door so loudly the baby started crying.

Lydia and Sam came out of their room.

"Let her stay there for a little while and calm down," Daniel said, meeting them in the hallway. His face was red, and he was trying to calm down himself, to stop being furious at Gal for refusing his help and comfort.

"What happened?"

"Just a fit of anxious perfectionism," he said.

"Do you want me to talk to her?" Lydia asked.

"No, please, Mom, let me, just let her be alone for a little while."

"Let me at least get Noam," she said, venturing into the room. She emerged with the crying baby a few minutes later, her lips pursed. Daniel looked at her, knowing Gal had snapped at her. She caught his eye. "Brat," she said.

He laughed. They went into the kitchen to start dinner. Sam sat the baby at his high chair and, instructed by Lydia, brought out the little containers of shredded chicken and rice. She handed him an apple and a paring knife and he peeled and cut it into careful slices. Lydia glanced from time to time toward Gal's room, and then at Daniel, until he impatiently said, "Mom, stop, I'll get her in a few minutes."

He sat slumped in his chair, and his anger slowly wound its way through glumness and on into sadness so acute he had to rise again. He went into Gal's room. She was on her bed, folded into a rocking ball, murmuring to herself. He picked up some toys and some Noah's Ark pieces and sat on the floor quietly until he almost dozed off. He started awake and reached for his guitar, which stood propped against the wall. From the open window came the sound of a honking car, and of children shouting. "Gal," he said quietly. "It must be so hard to leave your best friend."

She quieted and lay still, alert.

"If I had to leave *my* best friend. *Oysh.* I'd be so mad." *Offer her something positive to hang on to*, he told himself. But he couldn't think of anything. What was there to offer? The promise of new friends?

How could they do this to her?

He sat and tuned the guitar, then softly strummed the mellowest chord progressions he could manage. He found himself humming the words to a Hebrew folk song called "Shores Are Sometimes" that he and Joel had learned together, in Joel's dorm room on Mount Scopus, the Hebrew-English dictionary between them on the floor.

> *Shores are sometimes longings for a stream*
> *Once I saw a shore*
> *deserted by its stream*
> *left with a broken heart of sand and stone.*
> *So may a man*
> *be left abandoned spent and worn*
> *just like the shore.*

He remembered the sound of their voices rising in unison—he could hear it so clearly! Joel had a heartier voice than Daniel's, while Daniel's was richer and more textured. He closed his eyes and tried to press the memory into his mind so he'd never forget it.

Matt sang with him sometimes too, and he had the best voice of all, a lovely tuneful tenor. When they first started living together, he had been embarrassed to join in with Daniel, joking that his irony forbade him to encourage the corny Kumbaya action. But he was drawn irresistibly to the clean, resonant sound of Daniel's guitar, and before long, Daniel had him sitting with him as night fell, softly singing.

"That's a sad song," Gal said around the thumb still in her mouth, and Daniel said, "It sure is." She sat up on her bed and slapped at her eyes the way she wiped them, a gesture that always made him wince, it looked so punishing. She rose and went to the Noah's Ark box, reached in and took out some animal pairs in her fist. "Why don't any of these have a boy and a boy together?" she asked.

He looked up at her, laughing with surprise, and pulled her into his lap for a rough nuzzle.

THAT EVENING, HE TRIED to reach Matt but kept getting the machine. Where the hell was he? It was early morning in Northampton. *He'd better not be having an affair*, he thought—not while his own days were composed of one mind-numbing task after another, among either bureaucrats or children. He thought of calling Derrick's, but it was too early. The need to talk to Matt brimmed and swelled in him, and Daniel cursed him for being absent when he needed him most. He despaired of its success, but he had to run it by him anyway, had to propose again that they stay in Israel, at least for a few years. The reasoning seemed so unanswerable to him. And even if Matt couldn't live here, maybe they could spend a year apart.

When the kids were asleep, he told his parents he had something he had to talk to them about, and told them his idea. They looked at him, stunned.

"We've made all these preparations for leaving, we have unrefundable plane tickets," his father said. "Are you sure you've thought this through?"

His mother's face was pale and taut. "Honey," she said. "I know it's hard to take Gal away from her home—"

"We really don't need to," Daniel interrupted.

"What about your job?" his father asked.

"I'd resign. But I'm sure I could find freelance editing work here." Daniel was eager and rational.

His mother's voice trembled. "I don't think I could lose two sons."

"Mom, please don't be melodramatic. You could come here all the time."

"Daniel," his father said. "We have a plan, a plan that we've made together after a lot of thought, and I think we should stick to it."

They went to sleep troubled, his mother in tears, and in the morning they carried on a coded conversation with the two children nearby. "Let's ask her," Daniel said in a low voice, gesturing toward Gal.

"Don't you dare!" his mother said, steering him out of the room with a pincer's grip on his elbow. When they were in his room, and he'd yanked his arm away, she hissed, "Do not make that child decide. This is an adult's decision. You cannot put the burden on her."

Daniel slumped onto the desk chair and averted his gaze, unable to look at her, she was thrumming with such anger and resolve. He was aware that he had been stupid to suggest they ask Gal, and rankled that he'd lost ground in their argument by doing so. "I thought you didn't want her raised by Matt," he said, sending out his last-resort salvo.

"I don't," she said. And then there was a rustle at the front door and they heard a delighted shout from Gal. Lydia turned; Daniel stood and emerged from the room, stopped in surprise.

It was Matt himself, disheveled and smiling, a small bag slung over his shoulder, which he dropped as Gal ran up and flung her arms around his hips, crying, "Mordechai, you came back!"

He bent and squeezed her, kissed her hair; the baby let out a squeak and banged his spoon on his tray. Daniel and his parents stared at Matt, amazed. "Surprise," he said, with a sheepish shrug.

Daniel was still in the shorts and T-shirt he'd slept in, morning stubble dotting his chin. "I couldn't reach you on the phone," he said idiotically.

"Well, that must be because I was in the air coming to be with you, honey," Matt said, stepping forward. His shirt was damp at the armpits, and he leaned in, his lips approaching Daniel's, then turning to kiss his cheek.

"I really . . ." Daniel said, and then could go no further.

His parents were standing with their arms crossed.

"Hi, Lydia. Hi, Sam," Matt said.

"We were just going to take the kids to the park," Lydia said, and started whisking everyone together as Gal hopped around and yelled, "No! No! Mordechai is here!"

"Was it something I said?" Matt asked comically. His stomach was sinking. He'd clearly walked into something bad; this had been a mistake after all.

"Of course not," Lydia said, her eyes resolutely fixed on Gal, who was being steered by Sam to where her sandals lay on the floor.

"I was just kidding."

And then they were gone. Matt looked at Daniel, whose face was tense and who wasn't meeting his eyes. *Great*, he thought. He walked into the living room and set down his bag, then went into the kitchen to put on some water for coffee. His face was greasy from travel; he ran cold water in the sink, stooped and washed his face. He rose dripping and ripped a sizable piece of paper towel off the roll to blot himself dry with.

"Matt, I can't," Daniel was saying. "I tried to call."

"Can't what?" He turned, his heart pounding. This was it, Daniel was going to break up with him.

"I can't take them back, I can't do that to Gal."

Matt sat on a kitchen chair, letting the words buzz around him without landing. Because once they landed, catastrophe would ensue.

"Matt." Daniel kneeled at his feet and grasped his hands. "Please understand." His face was stricken, his brown eyes huge.

Matt was nodding reflexively.

"That would mean living without me," he said, feeling the words come out of his automaton's mouth, saying the words that logically followed the thing Daniel had said. "Is that what you want?"

"No," Daniel said, tears spilling over his face.

Matt nodded. *Nod, nod, nod*: That was the way you were supposed to respond to somebody's words.

But then he could hold them off no longer; the words landed, and adrenaline surged through him, making him gasp, making him feel like one of those people who could lift cars off of children. "Daniel," he said. He remembered something—see? Adrenaline!—"Ilana asked you to take them away from here if anything happened to them."

"No she didn't," Daniel said.

"She did! You've told me the story dozens of times, and in every version she asks you to! She says, 'Daniel, take them away from here!'"

Daniel sat back on his heels, then crumpled till he was sitting on the floor. "I can't stand it," Daniel cried. "I can't."

Matt stood and carefully turned off the kettle, then sat in the chair above Daniel, bent over him, so that their foreheads touched. "Honey," he breathed.

"How can I leave him behind?"

"What?" Matt whispered. "Who?"

And then he slid to the floor and wrapped Daniel in his arms. He stroked and rocked him for a long time, thinking about Daniel walking around in Joel's clothes, about the two of them in the womb together, how they'd been together since before they were even human. They'd started out breathing that strange element together, their tiny astronaut bodies floating, bumping against each other in silent salutation, and then they came out with their wrinkly, scaly human flesh, and then they grew and filled out. And then their lives and desires drew them apart, and now those two bodies were going to be buried on different continents. The thought gave him chills, and he gripped Daniel tightly, feeling like the slimmest and most inadequate of lifelines.

"It's like . . ." Daniel's voice caught. "It's like, okay, I won. I won, and he lost."

"What do you mean?"

"It's like, Joel was always barging ahead, making all the noise. Now he's dead, and all that's left is me." He closed his eyes as tears overwhelmed him again. The tiny sound with which he said the word *me* made Matt grip his hands.

"That's a lot! A lot that's left!"

Daniel shook his head, his shoulders deflated.

Matt asked, "Do you feel like he abandoned you?"

"No, I feel like I'm abandoning *him*," he said. "I feel like he got punished, and I . . . I could have been like him, I just pulled back and let him step into the limelight so I could have"—his lip curled—"so I could have my precious quiet space by myself."

Matt didn't get it. It sounded as though he were saying that he'd tricked Joel, let him walk into the path of the bomb. He stroked Daniel's hands with his thumbs and tried to sit quietly and just listen, not to say that that sounded crazy to him, not to try to make Daniel think the right thing. Meanwhile, a hope was racing through him, a hope that, whatever Daniel was thinking, realizing it and facing it would help him let go of this craziness about staying in Israel, would help him come home.

"Do you know what I mean?" Daniel said, looking at him with heartbreaking hopefulness, those killer Rosen eyelashes stuck together by tears into dark spikes.

"Not really, baby," Matt said gently. "But I get how hard it must be to leave him here." In fact, once he said that, Matt also felt a searing sadness about leaving Joel and Ilana.

Daniel sighed a long tremulous sigh and staggered to his feet. He told Matt he had to go out, alone, and left the house without telling anyone where he was going, so that Matt had to eat an awkward dinner alone with Sam and Lydia and the kids, in which Lydia fretted over whether, now that he was there, they'd all fit into the cab to the airport.

Daniel came back three hours later, calmer, sunburned. He'd been sitting at Joel's grave, Matt knew, and had forgotten to put on sunscreen. He didn't want to eat anything, and he had a terrible headache. "You're dehydrated, honey," his mother said. "See?"—touching his arm—"Dried salt."

Gal peered at it. "*Och*, Dani, you must drink," she admonished with a grave look, the experienced veteran of many a sun-drenched Middle Eastern field trip.

"Here, Gal," Lydia said, holding a glass of water toward her. "Bring this to your uncle, and make sure he drinks it."

The two of them forced glasses of water on him until there were three glasses sitting in front of him at a time, which made them laugh.

"Is everybody ready to go home?" Daniel asked.

They turned to look at him sprawled in the chair, his eyes swollen by tears and sun but bright and steady. Daniel's eyes.

"Yes," they whispered.

THEY LEFT ON A late-night flight. The Grossmans came over a few hours before, with small, fragile smiles on their faces. Malka was wearing a pretty dress, and makeup to hide the dark circles around her storm cloud–colored eyes. They sat on the couch, holding Noam and talking nonsense to him, as Matt and Daniel and Sam zipped up suitcases and Gal ran manically around the house. Daniel caught her as she ran from one room to another and said, "Gal, come say good-bye to your grandparents."

"Good-bye!" she bellowed.

Daniel laughed, and brought her over to the small hushed space of the couch. "My father gave her a brownie," he told them, "and now she has a sugar high."

"Gal-Gal," Malka said. "I have something for you." She reached into her purse and pulled out a small box.

"Thank you!" Gal said, the gracious gift recipient. "Oh, Savta, this is pretty!" It was a small silver necklace, a *chai*, from the Hebrew word for "life." She turned around so her grandmother could clasp it behind her neck and then fell on Malka and grasped her around the neck. Malka's face was bright over her shoulder. Then, leaning over Noam, Gal gave her grandfather a big noisy kiss on his cheek.

"We have something for you, too," Daniel said, and Gal pulled away saying "Right!" and ran into her bedroom. She emerged shyly, holding in front of her with two hands a gift that Sam had made and Lydia had beautifully wrapped.

"What could this be?" Yaakov asked, while Malka murmured, "You really didn't have to." The baby reached for the shiny ribbon, his eyes glittering.

"No, Noam!" Gal instructed.

"You open it," Malka told Yaakov, and he handed the baby to her and worked delicately at the paper with his big stubby fingers.

Sam had found a picture of the whole family—Joel, Ilana, and the kids—in a pile of pictures that hadn't yet been put into an album. It had been taken at the beach, and they were all in bathing suits, sprawled together on a towel, Noam in a diaper, the kids both caked with sand, Gal chewing a peach that was dripping over her fingers. They all looked windswept and relaxed, but the eye was drawn primarily to Ilana, who was sitting with her legs stretched out, leaning back on her hands, her eyes closed, raising her face to the sun.

Sam had had it enlarged and framed in a gorgeous, simple wood frame.

Gal hovered over them as they took it in. "Doesn't Ema look like a movie star?" she asked.

"Yes, she does," Malka whispered.

"So now you can remember us," Gal said.

"Oh, *motek*, it doesn't take a picture to remember you," Yaakov said, his voice husky.

Daniel was sitting on the edge of the armchair. "We're hoping you'll come visit us for Chanukah," he said. "And we'll be back for Purim."

They nodded, unhearing, looking at the picture.

Leora and her parents arrived, and the Grossmans said good-bye, clutching the children with ashen faces, Gal chirping, "We'll see you soon! Very soon!" Lydia had packed the perishables from the refrigerator and freezer into a box, and she pressed it upon them to take it home, so they left the house bearing leftovers. Excruciating symbolism, Daniel thought.

Gal and Leora disappeared into her room, and Gabrielle hovered around tearfully asking what she could do, until Matt finally dumped the baby into her arms. They'd sent the toys and baby stuff ahead, and they were essentially packed. Finally, after a cup of Nescafé that they drank quietly while standing, Gabrielle holding and nuzzling the baby, Daniel looked at his watch and they decided it was time to roust out the children. When the girls came out, Gal was clutching a small stuffed horse Leora had given her, and she wore the passive, polite expression on her face Daniel was becoming accustomed to—the look of someone accepting a slightly embarrassing prize. "Look, Ema!" Leora demanded, holding up the necklace she had clasped around her neck.

"Wow, that's beautiful, Gal-Gal," Gabrielle said. "What a fantastic sentiment, too."

They stood, nodding, smiling. "Well," Moti finally said. He hugged Daniel's parents, reaching for the easy ones first, and Gabrielle followed. Then he bent and lifted Gal into his arms. "You're a very special girl, Gali. Very special in our hearts."

She nodded solemnly, and he buried his bearded face into her face, looked over her shoulder at his wife with stricken eyes. Gabrielle was standing with an arm around Daniel, crying. She reached for Gal and squeezed hard, then set her down before Leora.

"Bye," Leora said.

"Bye," Gal said. "But it's not really good-bye, not *totally*, because we'll see each other again."

"C'mon, guys," Daniel said, "let me walk you to your car."

Afterward, he came up and checked the kids' room to make sure they hadn't forgotten anything. He picked up a pillow on Gal's bed to fluff it a little, and noticed a scrap of folded paper underneath it. Unfolding it, he saw that it was written in Gal's wavering and uneven print:

> *Dear Ema and Abba,*
> *I and Noam are at Uncle Dani's and Uncle Matt's.*
> *Love, Gal*

He laid it carefully back under the pillow, tears stinging his eyes. She'd learned only recently to write those letters, and some of them were still backward, and the spelling experimental. She'd learned how to address and sign off on a letter. Maybe the words would be magical, Daniel thought, thinking of the surprise that lit up Gal's face when any of them read aloud a word she'd written. Letters were already magical, the way they conjured actual words, which in turn conjured actual things. Maybe if she wrote them very correctly, very neatly, they could conjure her parents.

THEY SAT IN A *sherut* minibus with other families who had been picked up before them. Within minutes they'd skirted their neighborhood and were on the road to Tel Aviv. The sun had disappeared past any lingering glow behind the hills, giving the city an ashy look. Matt sat squeezed between Daniel and his father, Noam on his lap grabbing at this and that, and finally shoving the strap of Matt's carry-on bag into his mouth. *Here we go,* Matt thought, *here we go.* His heart was in his throat, but he thought that, for twenty hours or so, all he had to do was help move everyone from one place to another. He couldn't wait to get rid of Daniel's parents and start whatever life lay ahead for himself and Daniel and the kids.

Daniel closed his eyes until he was sure they'd passed the cemetery; he couldn't bear the idea of passing it in this direction and watching it fade away in the distance. He was surviving, he felt, by warding off, by stiff-arming at least half of what he felt at any given moment. It wasn't something you could afford to feel all at once. He was following Joel and Ilana's wishes: that was the part he let himself feel right now. He looked across at Gal, who sat staring solemnly at the other passengers, and then at his mother, her eyes closed and head held high, her arms wrapped around the purse on her lap.

They drove down and down some more, ears popping. The air on the bus grew warm, and the odors of the passengers—body odor, perfume, the cinnamon of someone's chewing gum—seemed to thaw and spread in the humid air. Noam whimpered, probably carsick, and Matt touched his face with the backs of his fingers. When they pulled up at the terminal, Matt forced his way out first and held the baby away from him, and Noam vomited, looked at what he'd done, and began to cry.

"Well, this is an auspicious start!" Matt said brightly, looking up from where he was squatting with the crying baby.

"I'm not going to throw up," Gal announced.

"Good girl," Sam said.

When they thought Noam was finished, they went into the terminal and got in the security line. It took about fifteen minutes to get to the agent, who asked for their tickets and passports.

They looked around and patted their pockets. "Matt?" Daniel asked. Matt had been carrying the bag with the passports and court papers.

Matt looked frantically at the bags piled onto the cart, and then looked up, eyes wide. He could barely bring himself to say it, contemplated lying for a moment and claiming that Lydia had been in charge of it. Then he said, "I left the bag on the *sherut*."

They looked at him, shocked. "How do I call the *sherut* company?" Daniel asked the agent.

"The taxi companies are over there," she said, pointing beyond the very end of their rapidly growing line.

Matt took off in that direction as she was telling them they'd have to step aside till they had their papers, and as Gal was crying, "My horse from Leora's in that bag!"

Shit shit shit, Matt thought, sprinting past Hasidim with monstrous suitcases, the stout Arab woman handing out fruit slices to her kids, the thousand baby strollers, and the men calling out orders to their families. He vaulted over baggage carts jutting out into his path. He arrived panting at the line for Shemesh cabs and broke to the front over loud protests. "My bag is on a *sherut*, I left it there!" he shouted to the woman in Hebrew.

"Wait a second, sir," she said with firm white-collar authority, giving him the Israeli hand signal for waiting, which he had thought was an obscene gesture before he'd learned what it meant.

"I can't! I can't! My passport, and the papers for the children—" He'd reached the limits of his Hebrew and switched into English, and then reached the limit of his breath altogether, and burst into tears.

"Okay, don't cry!" the woman said in alarm as people started falling back and staring. Someone patted him on the back, and an elderly gentleman in a white shirt came forward, offering to translate. "I can speak English," the clerk said irritably, tossing her long hair back as she put the phone receiver to her ear. "Everybody, please stand back." She looked at Matt. "What was the name on the reservation and what address did you leave from?"

He told her, and she made a call, and someone radioed out, and Matt heard her say, "Is it there?" and the tinny voice respond through the static, "Yes, here it is," and he clutched his hand to his chest and the people in line applauded and asked him teasingly if they needed to call an ambulance for him.

Meanwhile, Daniel had run over. "They found it, they found it," Matt said. "The driver's on his way."

Daniel doubled over in relief. "Jesus, Matt," he said. "Our papers are in there! What were you thinking?"

"I'm sorry," Matt said, steering Daniel off to the side so that this crowd of upstanding Israeli Samaritans wouldn't witness a fight between two hysterical queens. The adrenaline was just burning off; he could feel it prickle his fingers. "I was trying to get the baby out before he barfed all over us and the cab. I'm really sorry. They found it, it's okay now."

Daniel just shook his head. He was still shaking it and muttering to himself when the driver came up with the bag and they wrung his hand in thanks and headed back to Daniel's parents and the kids, who now stood anxiously at the back of a long, winding line. Matt had taken out the colorful patchwork stuffed horse Leora had given Gal, and was waving it in the air grinning, singing, "Ta-da!"

II

O N A HOT day in July, in a Northampton backyard, Gal was hiding. She was being quiet quiet quiet: *"Shhh,"* she whispered, like Dani did when she was crying; the sound reminded her of her mother too, in a part of her mind balanced somewhere against the very back of her palate, rising sometimes like a taste, or like fumes, into her head. She had closed the shed door behind her; a line of fuzzy gray light marked its edge. She reached out her hands, feeling her way forward in the dark; she hit the handle of a lawn mower, and stubbed her sandaled foot on the edge of something else, and when the pain came, tears sprang to her eyes. In the back of the shed was a pile of cardboard boxes, some flattened, some thrown whole onto a sagging tower. She stepped behind it, and lowered herself onto the floor.

She rubbed a spiderweb off her face, once, twice, then a third time, hard. Her toe still smarted, and her arm glowed with the itch of mosquito bites. She pressed a fingernail into a bite on her elbow till the pain was as intense as the itch. *Try not to scratch*, Matt had instructed her as he rubbed ointment on them, squirted a slug of ointment on her finger so she could rub, too. In the yard, the boy, Yossi's son Rafi, crept, looking for her. He was deaf and had a machine in his ears; he spoke Hebrew with a flurry of hands and a muffled foghorn voice, and at first she'd had to try not to stare, knowing it was rude. They said he was her age, but he was littler, with flyaway curly hair almost as big again as his face. Matt said she had to play with him, so she was, even though she couldn't tell if he understood her when she spoke.

It was quiet here, and that felt good. In the daytime there were always people in the house, and Noam was crying because he was fussy or bumped his head, and someone would wave the others off, saying, "I'll get him." Dani and Matt's friends waggled their fingers ruefully at her, and she said, "Hi," and they asked her how she liked her purple room, and told her how excited Matt had been when he was painting it, and how much he couldn't wait for her and Noam to arrive. Most of them were homos—*gay*, Matt told her to say. Like Derrick, who was the first brown person she'd ever talked to, with his shaved head and big kind eyes, earrings that twinkled on both ears, like a girl's. And Cam, who Gal thought was a man until she heard her uncles talking about her; her mistake mortified her, and she kept it to herself. Agility obstacles were arranged throughout Cam's backyard, and Gal liked running through them, jumping over the jumps, weaving through the poles, crawling on all fours through the long cloth tunnel that she had to barge through face-first. Sometimes Cam let Xena out, and the dog would give Gal a scare by running at her heels and nipping; sometimes Gal had to stop because she didn't like it, although when Cam asked if she was scared, she always said no.

There was something draped over her, as though the sky was a different shade. The air was hot and heavy and damp, and she would forever associate humidity, and the infuriating whine of mosquitoes, with grief. The town she lived in now seemed to her like a circus. She walked with her uncles down the streets of Northampton: the square, honest New England brick buildings with their rippling slate roofs and steeples and clock towers ringed with strange and fascinating looming faces, girls with shaved heads and rings in their noses, fat women holding hands, teenagers crouching in doorways smoking and holding puppies with bandannas around their necks by the leash, men with beards and tattered green coats asking for a quarter. And whenever Daniel or Matt introduced her to a new person, that person beamed at her with a lacerating benevolence, and she had to turn her face away.

When she went back inside, Matt's mother would give her lemonade. Gal liked her plump hands and pillowy stomach, and the food she cooked, pancakes and bacon. The skin of her upper chest was blotchy and freckled, and Noam was quiet on her capable shoulder. In the colors Gal's mind formed, these new grandparents didn't stand out with the stark light of her other grandparents; they were paler, plumper, slower. Being around their stolid, warm shapes was like settling back in a beanbag chair. She didn't have to show them that she loved them because otherwise they'd be sad. They didn't pin her down with laser-beam looks and pepper her with questions to make her demonstrate her knowledge or show that she was okay, because even though Matt told them she spoke English, they didn't really believe she spoke it well. Instead, they patted her and said, "There, there." Matt laughed when she asked about this, said that it means "Everything is okay, don't worry."

She heard the clink of Yo-yo's collar and his big snuffling nose at the door of the shed. Fear blossomed in her heart; she hadn't thought of the dog, who would find her, and then the boy would follow him. He would find her and shout *"Boo!"* in his scary foghorn voice, and the prospect of that made her tremble. But what if he didn't, what if he came to the door and then walked away, leaving her alone in this dirty heap of crushed boxes? A gnawing mix of foreboding and shame filled her up till she sighed and closed her eyes. It was stupid, this hiding place, stupid. When he saw her there, he would know that she was just like the boxes, dirty and crushed.

She heard the clank of the latch as Rafi opened it, felt light arch over her, and then a shadow. She peeked up, heart pounding. He was standing over her, grinning, tapping his chest with two fingers. *"Matzati otach,"* he said. I found you.

·   ·   ·   ·   ·

HE HAD A FEW hours to work while his mother tended to the kids and his father was at the hardware store investigating childproofing gadgets, so Matt was sitting at his computer in shorts and an undershirt, a fan stirring the papers beside him each time it rotated in that direction. To his surprise, his bid had won the design work for the new engineering school at Smith College, and he was both grateful for the regular income and panicky about whether he'd have the time to do the work well. He was trying to design a logo that would convey the idea of empowered women engaged in scientific pursuit, but, as he did whenever he had a moment to himself, he was thinking about Daniel, who, since they'd gotten home, had lost it, slowly but surely, like a tire with a tack in it. It was as though he'd realized that after expending a superhuman effort to get the kids in the first place, it wasn't going to stop, he had to continue working even harder to actually *raise* them.

Daniel's arms were thin and bony, and he was letting his beard grow; together with the weight he'd lost, it made him look older and more ascetic, a touch too rabbinical for even a matzo queen like Matt. Once, there had been a lusciousness about him, an offering of lips and belly and nipples, but it had burned off, leaving pure wire. He could hardly stand to be cared for or even looked at; where he used to lower his lashes shyly under Matt's gaze, he now turned away, evasive. When Matt reached out to touch him, he pulled away with a look of being vaguely put-upon.

In the mornings, Matt had to pull him out of bed and lead him to the shower while the kids dug into their heavy morning sleep. He had to keep him going for the family health care benefits; he knew that after a long absence, Daniel had to show up for work in a big way, and sometimes he was frightened because Daniel was forgetful and carried himself a little like a drunk.

His own emotions were in abeyance; he was just moving forward, helping Daniel function. When you were with someone for a long time, he reasoned, you didn't feel in love all the time; your love waxed and waned. He'd been attracted to other guys before, but their monogamy agreement was meant to deal with that, to provide an outlet and to acknowledge that, hey, it was likely to happen and it was okay. On days when Daniel was away and he was alone in the brisk air of his friendships and his work, enjoying the quiet in the house, Matt could imagine that if Daniel were to stay this way, it wouldn't be such a terrible thing.

And still, he tried to remember, to conjure out of thin air, the things he'd loved about Daniel in the first place. He remembered being with Daniel at a Northampton bar a few years ago, for their friend Mark's birthday, and being introduced to Mark's neighbor, a young guy, a kid, really, named Toby. Shy, long-haired, and husky-voiced, he worked with homeless people in Holyoke and was involved in the recent fracas over their tent shantytown. Mark, by way of introduction, had told them that Toby was a "sneaker freaker" and was working on a documentary about sneaker freakers. They had nodded sagely when he told them that, but when Toby turned away for a second, Daniel had leaned in and whispered, his lips touching Matt's ear, "We'll Google it later," making Matt quake with silent laughter. There were about twenty people at a long table littered with bar appetizers, drinking margaritas and beer and gin and tonics, leather jackets and Windbreakers flung on the backs of their chairs. Matt and Daniel had talked to Toby for a while, and found him not only smart and sweet but so beautiful he gave Matt a headache. Toby slipped out early, saying he had to get to another birthday party, and they left shortly afterward. Out on the warmly lit downtown street, Daniel had turned to Matt and said, "Oh my God. Oh my God! Was that the yummiest boy you've ever seen, or what?!" And Matt had hopped up and down and yelled, "I know!"

In bed that night they were having sex in their tried-and-true mode, using the shorthand of lovers who have been together for years, and whose bag of tricks no longer has the capacity to shock and awe. Then Matt had sung "Hello, Toby!" which made Daniel laugh. "Toby's on top of you," Matt whispered, fondling Daniel lazily and feeling his hard-on become urgent, "and I'm there, touching his ass—"

"Too fast!" Daniel panted, swatting away his hand.

"Oh." Matt backed up, and his mind moved quickly over the narrative requirements of this fantasy. Getting them seated in an advantageous arrangement at the bar. Getting everyone else who had been there out of the way. "Mark's gone off to the bathroom," he said. "Toby's feet are up on a chair. Dan, you're admiring his sneakers. 'What great sneakers these are!'" *Or whatever the hell way you're supposed to admire a sneaker freaker's sneakers*, he thought. "You're pulling gently on the laces—"

"Too slow!" Daniel yelped. "Enough with the sneakers!"

An indignant look came over Matt's face. "But it's his fetish!"

Daniel's head popped up from the pillow, his face no longer rapt, just red. "Yeah, but it's not *mine!*"

They had giggled till they were weak, and made love with the remnants of excitement combined with affectionate goofiness. That's what Matt had thought would carry them into the future when the initial passion settled and waned: their affection and gameness, their ingenuity at making fire out of the sparks created by other people. He'd been proud of his willingness to be that way, proud of his own maturity.

From the window he caught a flash of Yossi's kid darting around, peering behind the trellis and looking up into the trees. He wondered whether it was okay in the year 2003 to let the kids out by themselves to roam the neighborhood backyards, but knew that if he called them in, the house would be louder. Plus, it had to be good that they weren't sitting glassy-eyed in front of a PlayStation. He himself had spent entire summers outside. He supposed that if he'd had a different kind of mother, he might have spent his time at her dressing table, in a room where the shades had been drawn against the heat, smelling her various potions, maybe daring to draw her rouge brush lightly across his cheeks. But his mother didn't even possess a dressing table, so instead he'd meandered on his bike around the neighborhood, past the driveways where groups of small boys debated the rules of their games in shrill voices. He remembered the heat shimmering off of the blacktop, feeling superior to them and left out, with equal keenness.

. . . . .

THE FIRST WEEKS HOME, it seemed he went daily to Target with the kids to solve some urgent child-gear need while Daniel was at work. Noam whimpered in the shopping cart basket and Gal staggered alongside them, ashen, red-eyed, lips and nose chapped, blinking against the assaultive lights. The other shoppers looked sharply at them and asked if they were okay, and considered him doubtfully—a blond man with two dark-haired children—when he said that they were. Gal asked him anxiously if he'd brought money with him. He thought he should probably buy them clothes, but he was shocked at what he found: the pitiless rigor with which they were divided into girls' clothes, which were all pink and covered with flowers and butterflies and sparkles, and boys' clothes, which were all camouflage or said things like *Future MVP* or *Born to Build*. And the toys too, every one of them sporting a logo or design of a Disney character. He went in wanting to buy the kids something and leaving without one single toy.

And then at home, whirling with chores. He'd known that once the kids came, the house would be chaotic, but somehow that hadn't prepared him for the crap all over the floor, the clothes strewn on beds and over chairs, dishes piled up in the sink. Lydia and Sam had come only a week after their arrival, against both his and Daniel's wishes; they simply hadn't been able to keep them away. And while they meant to help, and were thoughtful enough to stay in a hotel, Matt's experience was constant grocery shopping, making dinners for six people, fleeing into his study to escape the many forms—irritability, exhaustion, compulsiveness—taken by long-term grief, feeling as if he and Daniel were still waiting to begin their real lives with the kids.

Quickly, pausing only briefly for regret, he and Daniel had decided to transform the dining room into a playroom, and moved the long pine table and its mix of chairs into the basement, bought a large area rug from Home Depot, a futon couch, and a wicker toy box, from which random tinkling music emanated at night when they walked by, making them stop in their tracks and put their hands on their lurching hearts. Everywhere he walked, Matt picked something up or washed something. He turned to pick up some shoes, and while he was in the front hall, he charged the cell phones and picked up a cup that'd been left on the hall table. He brought the cup into the kitchen and while he was there, whirled around, emptying the dishwasher and getting the dog water, and finding a piece of a toy Gal had been looking for. He took that into her room and plugged it into the toy, then turned in circles in her room, hanging her pajamas on a hook, making her bed. He took the garbage into the garage, where he noticed a dead mouse in one of the traps; opened up the trash, gloved his hand with a plastic bag, and lifted the trap with the rigid mouse inside it, dumped it into the garbage, wondering, *What the hell will we tell the kids when they start discovering all the dead mice?* And tied up the trash again.

At night, the upstairs hallway was lit up like an airport runway with night-lights. They brought Noam to their bed because it was easier than getting up several times a night and going to him when he awoke to find that his pacifier had dropped from his mouth. In bed they could watch TV and just stick it back in. By morning, everybody was in his and Daniel's bed, including the dog. Their sleep was strenuous, cutting from one demanding dream to another to the rhythm of the air-conditioning unit, which hitched on and off from the whir of the fan to the rumbling vibration of the cooler. The sheets were pulled and wrung into rope. When his eyes opened to the early morning, the first thing Matt took in was a clutter of empty cups and bottles and balls of used tissues on the bedside table, left from the middle of the night when the kids awoke in tears and he fetched them things to drink, set Gal up on a bunch of pillows, and had her relate her complicated and nonsensical dreams to him and Daniel while they sleepily stroked her hair and vowed their undying protection during the scary parts, the parts with the witch or the monster. Matt would get out of bed and lower himself to the floor, his bony knees aching as they pressed on the hard wood, peer underneath the bed with a flashlight for her, and come back up with an all-clear, wiping dust off his feet before getting back under the covers.

Now, looking out the window down to the street, Matt saw two women walking slowly with a toddler swinging between them, and turning up their front path. The house was always full of people come to help—their friends, and now his parents, and the congregation of Beit Ahavah! Their neighbor Val, who lived three doors down on the other side from Cam, and whom they hadn't known at all till now, came over most days of the week with her four-year-old Lev in tow, and brought what seemed like half the Reform shul with her. He wasn't sure which ones these were. The lesbians from the shul all had dark hair, dramatic eyebrows, children adopted from China and Vietnam and Guatemala, or hard-won through various fertility techniques. They brought over coffee cakes, clothes their kids had outgrown, parenting guides as thick as metropolitan phone books. Twice now the house had grown so full it was like an impromptu lesbian party, women on the couch and floor with toys between their hairy legs, Noam catching their eyes and holding out toys to them in a quest for their bewitching *Thank yous*! They dispensed advice to Matt and joked self-deprecatingly about their own initial forays into parenthood, when their own nice houses had become pigsties and they'd become incapable of conducting the most rudimentary adult conversation, so busy were they being locked into power struggles with their two-year-olds, who threw screaming fits because their moms had cut their toast into rectangular halves instead of on the diagonal.

Matt heard the doorbell, a swell of voices downstairs, his mother's polite greeting voice. He should go down and mediate, he thought, but then changed his mind: his mother would just shoo him back upstairs. She'd developed a kind of flair for being around Jewish lesbians, whom she called "the gals." She'd tell him and Daniel about so-and-so's struggle to get pregnant and the strain it had placed on her relationship, and explain the intricacies of in vitro fertilization, which she familiarly called IVF, an explanation that necessitated an air drawing of the cervix and ovaries, which made Daniel and Matt and Matt's father exchange alarmed glances.

He was stunned by this new life, the mess of it, the people—some of whom he knew, some of whom were complete strangers—letting themselves in and out of the house, the front door wide open all day long, people swiping mosquitoes off the open margarine tub in the kitchen, his bare feet sticky from dirt and humidity on the wood floors. Stunned. Home had always been where he went to get *away* from his family. Now his house was blown apart, the wind and the grief blowing through it. But a small part of him felt like a flower. He reveled in the sensuality of the kids' baby skin and their hair and the breath sifting raggedly from their mouths. He wasn't getting laid, but he was finding in himself a new kind of desire, milder and wider and sweeter than libido, that spread out onto all the living creatures under his care.

IT WAS RAFI'S TURN to hide. Gal rested her forehead on her arms, which rested against a tree, shut her eyes, and began counting to forty in Hebrew. The air was still and the shrill buzz of crickets elicited a semiconscious memory of the electric station down the street from her apartment in Jerusalem. Her mind glanced off of this and that till she lost count. An impulse of strict conscientiousness made her decide that the rule was, if you lost count, you had to go back to the beginning. She began again.

When she was done, she stood back and surveyed the yard with a raised head and narrowed eyes. She felt as if she were in a movie about a little girl searching for a hiding little boy.

It wasn't a good yard for hide-and-seek; it was small and neat, the grass trimmed yesterday by Matt's father, who said she could call him Grampa or Grampa John or just John. Its only ornaments were the flowers that grew along the fence and the feeders and stone birdbath that Matt let her fill with the hose, showing her how to hold her finger over the nozzle to direct and intensify the stream. You had to go into the neighbors' yards, the ones that drew closer to the woods, to find the sheds and dense bushes and raised decks you could shimmy under on your stomach, startling the cats sleeping under them. And of course the agility obstacles in Cam's yard, which was the first place Gal headed, ducking into the small opening in the shrubs that divided the two lawns.

There was a lump in the middle of the cloth tunnel. Where was his head? She thought her parents may have been buried without heads. That was a secret thought she had, something that nobody was telling her.

She walked up to Rafi and stopped, her heart pounding. He was lying down, trying to make himself as flat as possible in the space between the round opening of the tunnel and where it trailed on the ground. She knew he couldn't hear her approach. She wondered whether if she tapped him, she could make him jump. She stuck out her finger and held it hovering over his body. Would the little girl be mean and scare the little boy? Then she withdrew it, and instead tugged a little at the cloth, to warn him of her approach. The lump stirred, and she laughed as he thrashed his way out, red-faced.

STARING AT THE COMPUTER screen, his mind going through the motions, Matt heard his father come home and the exchange of voices with his mother. He felt a surge of guilty gratitude for their unhurried, unflappable presences in the house. When he'd called to say the kids had arrived, Shirley made him repeat the foreign names several times ("Let me put your father on. How do you spell that? Wait, let me write it down"). She'd said, "Those poor babies," and "Well, I know you have a lot of tenderness in you, Matt, for all you don't always want people to see it." This shocked him, that she'd seen something about him. And they'd immediately made plans to come out to meet the "little Jewish grandbabies," as his mother referred to them. They slept on an air mattress on the living room floor, and the kids lounged on it during the day, watching *Oprah* or *Judge Judy* with Matt's mother, and dragged the blankets around. He had to acknowledge that his parents were helpful with the kids, but their presence made something catch and strain in his throat. Did this mean that they could now come anytime they wanted to? Did it mean that they were a genuine part of one another's lives now?

He went downstairs when Yossi came to pick up Rafi, and Daniel got home from a late meeting as Matt and Shirley were cleaning up from dinner. They ate dinner at five now, which Matt called "gracious living chez Rosen-Greene." The baby sat on the kitchen floor, and Matt's father was placing Noam's favorite toy just out of his reach to encourage him to walk toward him. It was a plastic playhouse where, when you pressed down one of the buttons, a woman's voice cooed "Hello, Daddy" in a voice so licentious and inappropriate Matt insisted on playing it for everybody who came to visit. John stooped and held Noam's hands with his own thick freckled ones, their arms extended in a bow, and he was chanting, "C'mon, buddy. That's the stuff!" while the toy coquetted, "When Daddy comes home, it's a happy sound. Everyone smiles when Daddy's around. Daddy!"

"Hello, Daddy," Matt said suggestively, sidling up and giving Daniel a kiss on the cheek.

"Honey, not in front of the children," Daniel said with a faint smile. Matt turned away and returned to the sink, where he'd been scraping spaghetti off of plates into the garbage. To him, that comment wasn't funny, it just sounded like another way to brush him off. "Crap," he said, noticing a small splash of spaghetti sauce spots on his white T-shirt.

Daniel set his briefcase down on the floor at the doorway to the hall. "Where's Gal?"

"Off watching TV," Matt said.

Daniel went to the refrigerator and got a beer. He sat down at a kitchen chair pulled askew from the table.

"Let me heat you up a plate," Matt's mother said.

"Thanks, Shirley," he said. "That's nice of you."

"Matt," Daniel said, "Val called me at work today. Apparently, we've been discussed at the Reform shul."

Matt turned. "You're kidding." He wasn't sure he liked that, although he'd warmed to Val pretty quickly, and God knows she was a big help. She and her husband, Adam, were true children of Northampton: Adam was an acupuncturist, and Val a massage therapist and yoga instructor. They were active members of the synagogue and of the local chapter of MoveOn, and Adam was on the board of the Men's Resource Center. They were involved in prayer circles and various rituals for life passages. They were both athletic, and took their kids on a lot of camping and cycling trips; you walked into their house, and the mudroom was crammed with hiking shoes caked with dried mud, hiking poles, snowshoes, cross-country skis, soccer balls, baseball gloves, lacrosse sticks, bike helmets. They were so hooked into nature and community they made Matt and Daniel feel like schmucks who hadn't really made an effort.

"No," Daniel said. "Val and Adam talked to the rabbi and 'informally mentioned'—that's what she said—that we were new friends of theirs, and then the rabbi talked about us in her sermon, or speech . . . what do they call it?"

"Don't ask me," Matt said. He was irritated and intrigued by this news. "What did she say about us? She doesn't even know us."

Daniel took a swig of beer. "It was just a brief mention, young children from a war-torn nation, something like that. I think the message was that Northampton is a peaceful town people can take refuge in, but that it's important to have a greater global consciousness. Anyway, it turns out that the features editor from the *Daily Hampshire Gazette* goes to that shul, and he called shortly after I spoke to Val to ask if he could write a story about us."

"What did you say?" Matt asked, weighing the prospect in his mind, thinking about the candid shot of him on the front page of *Ma'ariv*, which had inadvertently placed him in the center of the family while all the articles erased him completely.

"I said I had to think about it," Daniel said. "Don't you think it'll make everybody in this town feel sorry for us?"

Matt's mother murmured, "No. It's just compassion, that's all, there's nothing wrong with that."

Daniel considered. "Also," he added, "isn't it a little annoying the way everybody applauds fathers for simply raising children? If we were women, women raising children, it'd never be regarded as news-worthy."

"That's so true," Matt said. He and Daniel had both been on the receiving end of many a dazzling smile when they were out in pub-lic with the kids, and sometimes it pleased them while sometimes it grossed them out a little. People who'd never given them the time of day suddenly had a lot to say to them.

"I think you're reading too much into it," Shirley said, looking up from where she was bent over the dishwasher, trying to find space for one more sippy cup.

"Mom," Matt said, sounding even to his own ear like a whiny ado-lescent, the old trapped feeling worming its way into his throat.

"Hello, Daddy," Noam's toy cooed, and they laughed, and through his pacifier Noam laughed too, a big, phony social laugh, as he practiced how to be in a group laughing.

THEY LET GAL GO to bed in underpants and a T-shirt because all her pajamas were in the laundry, and they let her begin the night in their bed because even though it set a bad precedent, she was exhausted and looked as if she were on the brink of a tantrum. She was stretching out on the sheets of the big bed, cooled by the air conditioner, while Daniel closed the blinds against the summer twilight. She watched him as he tended to her, bringing a glass of water to the night table, switching on the bathroom night-light, fishing the book they'd been reading from under the covers at the foot of the bed, and, reacting to the sweetness and intimacy of being alone with him, the way that if she closed her eyes just a little, or just listened to his voice, she could imagine he was her father, said, "You're not my *abba*."

Daniel crawled onto the bed beside her, a little stung, even though he knew she was just experimenting—with the names for their relation-ship, with how bad or mean she was allowed to be.

"I don't think I'll ever call you Abba," she said speculatively, glancing sideways at him. In the vivid, shadowy landscape of her mind, something had happened to Daniel since they'd come to America; he'd caved in, like the mouth of an old man she'd once seen who had no teeth. When they came toward each other, she had to go soft, nervously avert her gaze, not knowing whether she'd bump into the solid man or walk right through him as if in a dream. Matt was big and spindly and light, and she could fling herself against him, even though his anger was sometimes blistering, and she might be tickled or stung. Daniel, though, was fringed in darkness. He'd sit with a book, staring vacantly into space; sometimes he walked by her without seeming to see her at all. There were moments when, at rest or at play, a strange fearful pressure built in her chest that made her feel as though there was a balloon trapped in there, bumping against her lungs, trying to break loose and take flight—and she had to struggle not to run, or howl.

"What will you call me?" he asked.

"Dani," she said.

"Okay."

The book was *Abba Oseh Bushot, My Father Always Embarrasses Me.* In Israel, it was a special book that Ema read to her, loudly, so Abba could overhear all the embarrassing things the *abba* in the book did to his little boy, Ephraim: singing loudly on the way to school, warning that if he didn't get a kiss when he left Ephraim at school, he'd have to kiss one of the other children, wearing shorts to Aunt Batya's wedding, sliding down in his seat and hiding behind his fingers at the scary parts in movies. They liked to pretend that her *abba* was as embarrassing as Ephraim's dad was.

Daniel read a page, lingered over the last line with his finger under it for Gal to read herself. The witty Hebrew prose pushed a smile behind his eyes and forehead. He loved the portrayal of the dad as a lazy and slovenly writer, the illustrations in which there was always someone looking at him askance, the way the mother was a cool customer, a newspaper reporter in heels and makeup who gave her son a quick kiss on her way out the door and who laughed at the father's eccentricities.

Partly, it was a book about how embarrassing it was to have a stay-at-home dad.

"Good job," he said to her, and turned the page.

It wasn't really a good job, Gal thought, because she knew the book by heart already. But Dani didn't know that because he wasn't there when her mother read it to her. His oblivion to that made her despair, which converted into peevishness. She snuggled more deeply into her pillows, sliding down from Daniel's armpit till his elbow hovered awkwardly around her face. She pushed it away with a put-upon sigh.

Daniel looked down at her slouchy demon self. "Gal, don't push, please; ask if I could please move my arm."

"You smell bad," she muttered.

Daniel closed his eyes. It was a refrain, one with curious power, and he and Matt had consulted about it. Breath? Body odor? Matt would sniff him all over and shrug. "You smell good to me." Recently they'd wondered if she meant simply that he smelled different from Joel.

"Okay, *buba*, I'm going to give you a kiss good-night, and I'll see you in the morning."

"I want to see my album," she said quickly.

Daniel rose and brought over the album her class had made for her before she left. It made a sticky sound as she opened it. She went through it and pointed to every child in every picture, naming him or her ritualistically in a mechanical voice, without lingering or musing. When she was finished, she thrust the book at Daniel and pulled the covers up to her chin.

He remembered the advice of her grief counselor, that he should offer words to her, words she could use to name the different shades of her grief. "You must really miss your friends," he said, aware that this was not his best effort. She'd been wearing on him since they'd gotten home to Northampton, and he was tired, and helping her find words for her feelings was starting to feel overrated. If she'd only let him hold her, as she had in the early days of their loss, he felt sure things would be better. These days when she got upset, her body stiffened and her voice got shrill. "Tell me what you're feeling," he'd say, and she'd shriek in his face or stomp out of the room.

When she didn't respond, he bent down, kissed her cheek, told her he loved her. He left the door ajar. Gal watched his hand slip along the door frame and out of sight, until he'd left her in the cool dark. She swallowed her desire to call after him. She looked toward the bathroom, where the night-light glimmered. Let's say she had to get there without touching her feet to the bedroom floor. Let's say that if she didn't, a terrorist would kill *her*, too. Could she do it? She could certainly climb onto the bottom slats of the bedside table. But how would she get onto the low dresser next to the bathroom door? Her mind worried it; she gazed at the drawers, which had little bits of clothing sticking out of the cracks, like tongues from the mouths of people concentrating hard. She knew that when Daniel and Matt went to bed, Daniel would go around and tuck all those clothes back into his dresser drawers, because he couldn't sleep unless all the closet doors and drawers were nicely shut, which made Matt laugh and call him OCD.

Her eyes scanned the floor. Matt's sandals were lying there, splayed, their buckles open. She could stand on them to get to the dresser; she imagined stepping down on the straps, the ball of her bare foot pressed by the buckle, pulling them out till she stood on the shiny-worn leather soles. She could do that, and then shuffle with them to the dresser, move everything—the coffee mug with spare change in it, the little wood box that held Matt's bracelets and rings, the bibs and rattles and half-full cups of water—carefully to the side, and get onto the dresser, knee-first. And from there, slide down onto the bathroom's tile floor, to safety.

CHAPTER 11

THEY CALL IT vanishing twin syndrome. The vanishing twin begins as a twin to another fetus, but disappears during the pregnancy, spontaneously aborting and absorbing into the other twin, the placenta, or the mother. It is believed that a significant number of singletons start out as twins.

Metaphorically speaking, he had always thought of himself as the vanishing twin. He knew that when he and Joel were infants, Joel cried for milk while he was a good baby who waited quietly in his crib to be fed. That, in high school, when Joel ran for president of the student council, he ran for treasurer because Joel wanted to be president so badly.

He was so self-sufficient and contained. He always chose the smaller piece—of cake, or of attention. And somewhere, in some tiny, proud place of his consciousness, he'd imagined that he'd be rewarded for it.

But instead there was this grotesque, vindictive punishment of Joel, a punishment straight out of ancient tragedy meted out by a tantrum-throwing god, in which Joel's children would be taken from him and given to Daniel to raise. In which Joel would die and Daniel would be featured in the newspaper, raising Joel's children.

He was in his office with the door ajar, his jacket hung over the back of his chair, his desk a mess of galleys. Looking at the picture of himself and Matt with Gal and Noam on the front of the features section, Yo-yo's big head resting on Matt's knee, he had an uneasy feeling that the article was unseemly, almost gloating. The article's headline read "Children Find Shelter from Terror's Grip." In the picture, Gal was on his lap, and his chin rested on her head. Matt sat back with one arm behind him along the back of the couch, his T-shirt riding up; the baby was on his lap and pressed against his other forearm with both hands outstretched, trying to grab something—a rattle, Daniel remembered, a rattle that the photographer, a hassled and stylish woman who had described herself as "running catastrophically behind" that day, had grabbed and shaken to get the kids' attention. The gesture had mortally offended Gal, who was giving her famous petulant shrug.

Why had he let them write the article at all, if not to gloat just a little? To gloat about how the kids were his responsibility now, and to show what a great and thoughtful job he was doing with them, what a loving home they'd come into? He studied the picture, the intense, propriety expression on his face. He looked like a patriarch in a yellowing photograph with scalloped edges. He had to admit to himself that a secret feeling of exultation came over him whenever he called Gal and Noam "my kids." At home he walked around in shorts and undershirts, his chest hair curling up through the V of the neck, his upper arms, hairless with long, light muscles, exposed. When he looked at himself in the mirror he saw an image of manhood—strong and sweet—that thrilled him. For a boy who was good at music but bad at sports, a teenager who felt there was a big hole where his sexual cachet should be, this was a tremendous transformation.

How did the idea of *dad* carry so much marvelous emotional pull? He'd always envied the natural masculine authority Joel accrued simply by virtue of holding his children. So now he had it, too.

His stomach growled from a mix of hunger and nausea. Matt had made him eat two soft-boiled eggs before he left the house. In the days before Matt's parents had left, Shirley had taken to making him a mash of graham crackers and milk after dinner, into which she slipped a splash of half-

and-half. His pants were belted to the last buckle hole now, and his shirts
sagged under the armpits. At night, in bed, he ran his fingertips over the
prominent jut of his ribs, feeling them rise and fall with his breath, imagining how easily they could be smashed, shards driven into the soft, moist,
pulsing organs underneath. He remembered one of the clichés of twinship
that people used to pester him with, asking whether when his brother was
hurt, he felt his pain. *No,* he'd scowl; to him, it was a stupid question. But
now he could feel his body being ripped out of the world. What happened
in your consciousness at that moment? Somehow he imagined it crying out
Whoa!—bewildered over this thing that had never happened to it before,
managing only the most banal and inadequate of responses.

He turned to the opening of the article:

> *Daniel Rosen and Matt Greene never expected their elegant*
> *Northampton home to be the refuge of two small, grieving children.*
> *The life partners of four years were thrown into turmoil four months*
> *ago when Rosen's brother, Joel, and sister-in-law, Ilana, were killed*
> *by a terrorist's bomb in a Jerusalem coffee shop. In their will, they*
> *had designated Rosen the guardian of their children—Gal, six, and*
> *Noam, one—should they predecease them.*
>
> *Rosen admits that he was surprised by that decision, and his*
> *eyes fill with tears when he talks about it. "There's such a powerful*
> *stigma against gay men raising children, especially in Israel, where*
> *it's unheard of. So my brother and Ilana were demonstrating an*
> *unusual degree of love and trust. That's how I see it."*
>
> *It took the couple three months to get the children to the U.S.,*
> *because the custody arrangement had to be approved by the Israeli*
> *courts. Rosen is grateful to be home, and to live in a community*
> *like Northampton, where people are accepting of two men raising*
> *children together.*

There was a passage about Matt; there was a section about Joel being
an English-language talk-show host, and about his and Daniel's history

at Jewish summer camp, and how that got them initially interested in
Israel. "When asked about summer camp, the normally reserved Rosen
lights up, and he says, 'I *lived* for camp!' It was there that the boys first
learned Hebrew, and their love for Israel was cultivated." The rest of the
paragraph covered Daniel's education at Oberlin, and his gradual transformation on the topic of the Israel-Palestine conflict. It got several details
wrong, such as his major and the year he graduated. He paused for a minute, irritated, then decided it didn't matter. His eyes skipped ahead:

> *Rosen admits to having complicated feelings about the suicide bomber*
> *who killed his twin. "Look," he says, "the safety and prosperity of an*
> *entire society is based upon shutting the Palestinians up where they*
> *can't be seen. So I can understand trying to violently place yourself*
> *within the Israelis' field of vision, in a way they can't ignore. I don't*
> *condone it, but I do understand it."*

Reading that, he remembered the reporter sitting back in her chair
and contemplating him. "You're a very understanding man," she'd said.
"A forgiving one. If someone blew my brother up, I wouldn't be making
these fine distinctions, I can tell you that."

Were the distinctions really so fine?

He folded the paper neatly and put it in his briefcase, and turned to
the email messages waiting for him in his inbox.

AT HOME, MATT HAD the features section spread out on the kitchen
counter, and he and Brent were reading, elbows resting on the counter, pricked by cracker crumbs, shoulder muscles pulsing through
their T-shirts. The sun flooded through the kitchen's screen door, and
at Matt's elbow, crackers lay cascaded out of a ripped sleeve, beside a
container of hummus with its plastic top off. His parents had left the
previous morning, and an airy, expansive feeling of being in charge
of his own domain was mingling with irritation at Brent, who, before

Matt had brought in the paper, had been telling him a long story about something one of his colleagues had said that had made him anxious about his tenure case, which was coming up in the fall. Brent's book manuscript had been accepted by a great press, and as far as Matt could make out, he was a total rising star in his field. Now that his materials were all in, he had the summer to wait till his case came up. "There's nothing more you can do, right?" Matt had said. "So you might as well try to relax this summer."

Brent had been quiet for a moment, and Matt could tell that he was brooding about how little Matt understood about the complexity and direness of his situation. But he didn't have the energy to draw him out. He knew that made him a bad friend, but honestly, after what he'd been through in the past few months, it was a little hard to listen to Brent obsess over what was clearly a nonproblem.

Gal was upstairs in their bedroom watching *The Parent Trap* for the gajillionth time, and Matt had put Noam in the playpen with every single toy he had. He studied his own face in the picture. It was a good picture; he looked handsome; his gaze into the camera was self-assured and masculine, his hair flawlessly messy. It was a picture he wouldn't mind his old New York friends seeing, which weirdly seemed to be his criterion for what was acceptable and what wasn't, even though he didn't even care about them anymore. The dog sniffed around his ankles for crumbs. "Hey, Yo-yo," he said, "once you're in the public domain, there's no telling what can happen. Next thing you know we'll be seeing your head on a naked Labrador's body."

He scanned down the article to find his name.

Sitting on the floor, his partner, Matthew Greene, looks on with a small smile, his blond hair long and disheveled, and his long legs stretched out on the carpet as he leans back on his hands. He projects the aura of a man who belongs in a West Village nightclub rather than in a New England farmhouse, sitting on a crumb-strewn carpet remnant surrounded by toys and stuffed animals.

Matt tsked, irritated at how the writer was hammering at the urban gay male angle; his sensitive ear heard something smug in it. He put his finger on the paragraph. "She's all, 'Look at the shallow gay man brought down by a dose of the real world.' "

"Oh," Brent said, peering at it and wrinkling his nose. "I hate that."

They grunted, settled down, and read some more. The writer described Noam as "a genial butterball of a toddler," and wrote of Gal:

> It was hardest to move the six-year-old, Gal (pronounced "Gahl"), who had the rich social life of the kindergartener in Israel, and who, while raised in a bilingual family, is now living in a new linguistic universe. Gal is full of penetrating questions, the thirty-eight-year-old magazine editor says, about what happened to her parents and about the dangers that she or her new guardians might face as well. "There's nothing you can say to her," Rosen admits, "that can really reassure her. If this happened to her parents, how can I convince her it won't happen to me or Matt? How can I convince her that it won't happen to her?"

THAT WAS AN EXCELLENT quote, Matt thought. Glancing at Brent, who was reading, his face sharp and intent, he had a small feeling of excitement over being in the paper; it brought back those urgent days when he had felt himself to be a rocky pier against which dark and stormy waters pitched. Certainly the storm was still there, somewhere, but it was buried now, somewhere in Daniel's strange disappearance, and indistinguishable from mind-numbing tedium—sitting on the floor, playing endless games of Spit, Chicken Cha Cha Cha, Gulo Gulo, Zooloretto, Tsuro (which Daniel called "Tsuris"), keeping Noam from putting Gal's Legos in his mouth, trying to retrieve the piece that had skittered under the couch without having to heave his whole long body off the floor and then sit down again, so slithering onto his stomach and reaching, fingers outstretched, grunting, spitting dust off his lips, a twinge shooting through his shoulder, while Noam said—mildly, regretfully—"Uh-oh."

There was a loud thump at the bottom of the stairs, then a flurry of pounding feet on the wood floors, and Gal came in, saying in Hebrew with affectionate condescension, "Mordechai, how are you, little uncle?"

"I'm fine, my diminutive niece," he replied. He tilted up her chin to examine the gap where her bottom front tooth had fallen out that morning. Her upper teeth were pushed a bit forward from thumb-sucking, and he wondered whether the adult ones would come in that way as well; he remembered someone once telling him that his kid's braces came with a little payment book, like a mortgage. "Where did you put it?" he asked, and she dug into her shorts pocket and pulled it out, held it out in her palm.

"Can I see?" Brent asked, and she held it out in front of him for a second, then closed her fist protectively. "How much does the tooth fairy give these days?"

"We don't know yet," Matt said. "She's probably off consulting her conversion charts from shekels to dollars right now. Hey, Gal, your picture is in the newspaper."

"Where?" She raised her arms so that Matt could lift her onto the counter beside him, and as he hoisted her he was glad his mother wasn't there to see her bare feet on a kitchen surface, which would put him in the category of people unfit to live in a nice home. "That's me!" Gal looked at him and at Brent with such astonishment they laughed.

"What does it say about me?" she demanded.

"Let's see," Matt murmured. "Try not to scratch." He grabbed her hand gently; her legs and ankles were studded with mosquito bites, some covered with Band-Aids because she'd scratched them till they bled.

He looked at the passage describing Gal again. What should he tell her? Normally, it was Daniel who was in charge of all the official stories about difficult things: where their parents were, where we went when we died, whether he and Daniel would die too, whether the Arabs were bad, why she had to listen to him and Matt even though they weren't her actual parents, why some of the women who came over looked like men. He let Daniel do it because he worried he'd get it wrong and Daniel would be mad at him for screwing up the kids even more. But it was clearly his turn here; her quick eyes were turned up at him, and there was no Daniel to judge his response. "It says," Matt told her, "that it was sad for you to leave Israel, and that you miss your parents very much, but you're adjusting to life in the U.S."

She nodded. "I'm adjusting," she said.

"Yes you are. You're a very brave girl," Matt said, touching her cheek.

"I could never be as brave as you, Gal," Brent said, shaking his head gravely.

She regarded him, taking his measure. "Your parents are alive?" she asked.

"Yes," Brent said.

"Mine are dead," she informed him.

"Honestly, I don't know how you put one foot in front of the other," he said.

Gal's eyes filled with mirth. "It's called walking!" she cried. "It's not very hard to do that!"

Brent laughed. "You're a funny kid," he said.

"Thank you very much!" Gal drawled, with scathing kid sarcasm, a recent acquisition she was enjoying taking out for a spin.

"She hates me," Brent mouthed to Matt.

ONCE THE PARENTS HAD all gone, the summer seemed to ripen and slow and warm. Noam was an urchin in a diaper, his skin warm and damp, dirt and crumbs stuck to the heels of his hands; Gal's tongue was stained purple and red from Popsicles. They enrolled her in swimming lessons with Rafi at the Y, and while a teenager worked with them on the different strokes for forty-five minutes, Matt plopped himself and Noam in the baby pool, holding the baby under the armpits and swirling him in the water to show him what floating felt like. At night they all huddled in Daniel and Matt's bed, the air crisp and cold, where they watched movies selected for their strong images of girls.

Matt enjoyed this, being on the big bed with Daniel, the kids, and the dog—enjoyed it despite the crumbs, despite the fact that before he went to sleep, he lay there thinking over and over, *Don't be a huge princess, it's just a crumb*, till he had to get up and brush off the sheet with long swipes. Just them, no parents, Noam and Daniel falling asleep mid-movie, Daniel's light snore, Noam's cheeks working the pacifier, the clicking sound of his sucks, Gal's fierce, silent attentiveness. He'd lie back on the pillows and watch her face in profile, those crazy beautiful lashes of hers, wondering what kind of intense thoughts were churning away in there. One night they watched *Fly Away Home*, which, if Matt and Daniel had known it opened with a car crash that kills a girl's mother, they never would have brought home. Matt grabbed the DVD box and examined the back, where the summary began, "When a young girl loses her mother in a car crash . . . ," and passed it to Daniel, who'd chosen it, an acerbic little feeling brewing inside that it was ironic that *he* was considered the fuckup. Gal froze watching it, and they held their breath; she turned and looked each of them in the face. It was only when the father comes to fetch the little girl in New Zealand to take her to Canada that she spoke. She turned to them and said, "But he was her *real* father."

"Yes," Matt said. "Her biological father."

She blinked sadly at him. "That's really different," she said. She got up a few minutes later and went to bed, and he and Daniel argued briefly, in tight, insistent whispers, about whether to go talk to her, each implying that the other was dealing with her grief irresponsibly. Finally, Daniel got off the bed with a put-upon sigh and went to Gal's room. He came back a few minutes later, shrugging. "She doesn't want to talk about it," he said.

Later, as he brushed his teeth in his boxers, Noam sacked out in the middle of their bed, Matt inspected the small bulge at his stomach in the bathroom mirror. "You're gorgeous, Matt, relax," Daniel said.

"If you say it automatically like that, you lose all credibility," Matt said.

"Has the dog been out?" Daniel asked. They used passive voice to ask each other whether any one of their thousand daily tasks had been done, to avoid sounding accusatory even while they were in fact accusing each other.

"No," Matt said. "I made coffee and emptied the dishwasher."

They looked at each other steadily, with poorly suppressed challenge and irritation.

"Crap," Daniel said, pulling his T-shirt on and going back downstairs.

Noam was wearing only a diaper, his thumb in his mouth. Matt quietly pulled back the covers, punched and arranged pillows, and got into bed. When Daniel came back up, he got in bed on the other side of the baby, facing Matt.

"Are those thighs the juiciest things you've ever seen?" Matt whispered naughtily.

"Oh God, I know," Daniel said with a playful groan. He ran his finger gently across Noam's forehead, his eyes half-closed and soft. "You're all right, right, buddy?" he whispered.

They were a little worried about him; they'd read up on his developmental stage, and learned that at seventeen months, Noam was late walking. He could stand if they lifted him up by the hands and held on to him, but the moment they moved backward to encourage him to take a few steps, he lowered his bottom to the floor, straining at their hands. Nor was he speaking, any words at all save the syllables *da* and *na*, and while his demeanor was uniformly placid during the day, his eyes were evasive and he didn't respond readily to the sounds of his name when they called him. It hadn't occurred to either of them to worry about that—they just appreciated how easy he was, how you could set him in his playpen in the kitchen or Matt's study and he'd play happily with his toys without bothering you. But then, at Val's urging, and galvanized too by the way Noam loved going over to the stereo and turning it up to blasting, they'd taken him to the doctor for a hearing test. His hearing was normal, but the pediatrician had said that they couldn't rule out autism, at the mildest end of the spectrum. Daniel had been furious, and wanted to fire the pediatrician. "That's the most irresponsible thing to say!" he raged. "Noam's a sweet, beautiful boy who's been through unimaginable upheaval, and this jerk jumps to autism!" But they obsessively read everything they could find on autism on the Web anyway, and argued about whether Noam's passy, or growing up in a bilingual household, was responsible for delaying his speech. Matt knew that autism was unlikely. He saw the way Noam got engrossed with a toy and then brought it over to Gal so she'd admire it with him or show him what to do with it; he noticed his drowsy gaze when you rocked him, the way he reached up to hook his fingers over your lips or grasp onto your ear. He thought about the grief held by that little body, wondering whether by now it was anything more than an inchoate, restless drift of the organs, a confusion he'd moved past because it couldn't be settled. To his friends, Matt joked that Noam was "slow," dramatically mouthing the word.

Matt turned off the light and for a few moments the only sound was the lap of the dog's tongue as he washed himself. Then Daniel's voice came through the darkness. "I was talking to my dad tonight, telling him about the businesses on Green Street being uprooted for the new engineering school," he said. "He's certain they're being abundantly compensated."

Matt smiled. "Oh, well that's a relief," he said. It was a running joke between them, Sam's reflexive trust of powerful institutions. They lay with their fists tucked under their chests and chins. Desire stirred in Matt, and for the next hour, thoughts about their sexual future and the cluelessness of the privileged classes rankled him, until the air conditioner finally hummed him to sleep.

AS THE DAYS PASSED, Matt progressed on the engineering school project with decent speed, got his aesthetic groove back for a stretch of five glorious days in mid-August, fortified by patched-together babysitting and Daniel doing extra kids duty at night. A teenager named Michelle from a few streets away had left a flyer in their mailbox, offering babysitting services, and they went over to her house to meet her and her parents; they used her in the mornings when Matt was upstairs working. Val or Adam took the kids for playdate afternoons, above and beyond the call of duty, sending them home with painted faces, or fancy paper hats, beaded necklaces, bracelets, crowns made of flowers—always one especially extravagant item they were instructed to give to Matt.

It was corn season in the valley, and the kids were crazy about corn. Daniel bought half a dozen ears from a farm stand every day on his way home, and they boiled them for no more than three minutes and ate them with salt, because as Gal, quick study that she was, learned to say, "They're so sweet you don't *need* butter." It was her job to shuck, and she picked every single silk strand off and held it in the air to scrutinize it before depositing it in the garbage, or more likely, draping it onto the outside of the trash bag. "A little lesson in Zen mindfulness," Daniel commented to the fidgeting Matt.

The tobacco harvest began, farmers hanging the large, glossy leaves used for fine cigars in weathered and slatted tobacco barns. And the sunflowers were up, like crowds of periscopes sent up by inquisitive aliens, craning this way and that. Daniel and Matt let the machine take most of the calls, unless it was Val calling to offer them some new kind of fabulous favor. Most of the time, they didn't even pick up for Derrick and Brent, which made Matt feel deeply guilty; his friends had once been everything to him, and deserting them because he now had children seemed like an enormous violation of a queer ethical standard. While Daniel cooked dinner, they let Noam pull all the pots and pans out of the cabinet and play with spatulas and wooden spoons, and Matt lay on the floor with a colander on his head and the tea strainers over his eyes, croaking, "Take me to your leader." Then he took up a wooden spoon and, using it as a microphone, sidled up to Daniel as Daniel skewered vegetables for the grill, and sang:

'Cuz I'm a one man guy in the morning,
Same in the afternoon.
One man guy when the sun goes down,
I whistle me a one man tune.
One man guy, one man guy,
Only kind of guy to be,
I'm a one man guy, I'm a one man guy,
I'm a one man guy
Is me.

Daniel shimmied a chunk of purple onion onto a skewer and gave him a quizzical look. "Doesn't it end up that the guy is, like, himself?"

"That's if you keep that last stanza in there," Matt said, in the voice of a teacher energized by a smart student. "Which I don't."

"Aha," Daniel smiled. "I see."

YOSSI LEANED OVER GAL and showed her a mistake she'd made. They were working on writing down the months; they'd taken down the calendar from the kitchen wall and placed it on the table. She swung her bare feet and twirled her hair, feeling the edges of his body ruffle the edges of hers.

He was coming over twice a week to work with Gal; Matt's lessons with Yossi had become her lessons too as she worked on writing in Hebrew. There was something about Yossi's presence, Matt mused as he watched him focus on the child, one arm on the back of her chair, that made the family a little cuckoo. Although it made him feel like a jerk and he tried very hard not to, sometimes Matt found himself subtly competing with Gal for Yossi's affection and approval. And Daniel too changed imperceptibly around him, his body language more purposeful, less soft, his voice a note lower, Matt could swear, acting with him like a man among Israeli men, speaking in rapid Hebrew that elbowed the others out of the conversation. And Daniel always handled the money. They paid in cash, since Yossi's immigration status forbade him to work, and it somehow always worked out that it was Daniel who peeled off bills from his wallet, the way it was Matt who always brought the coffee or emptied and refilled the ice trays. It felt weird to Matt, as though Daniel were his father paying for his piano lessons, or as though he, Matt, were a housewife on a strict allowance.

Matt's own paper sat in front of him with neatly printed letters. Gal leaned over to look at it and said, "*Yofi*, Matt." Nice.

"Thanks." He and Yossi were working on the names for familial relationships, and starting to get esoteric as they pushed their way into the varieties of queer kinship. Matt had told him a story one of their friends from the shul, Rebecca, had told him about the nurse who'd checked her partner Jen into the hospital the night their son was about to be born. The nurse was visibly peeved about having to do the paperwork five minutes before her shift was supposed to end, and said to Rebecca as she was setting up Jen in bed, "So what will you be called? *Mee*-maw? *Moo*-maw?" honking the names with gleeful scorn.

"How do I say 'I'm your guardian,' although not legally, in kind of a pretend way?" he asked Yossi.

"Pretend is *c'ilu*," Gal said.

Yossi tapped his pen on Gal's paper in a command for her to do her own work. His hand was speckled with tiny flecks of paint.

"When are you going to let me see your studio?" Matt asked.

Gal looked up. Yossi had a trying-to-be-patient expression on his face, the way he looked when Rafi rejected a food before he'd even tasted it. "The law, it's *ha-chok*," he said. "Against the law: *neged ha-chok*. According to the law: *l'fee ha-chok*."

"*Ha-chok*," Matt said, with a juicy guttural *chet*. "Do you, like, incorporate political themes or violence in your work?"

"Why," Yossi said sharply, "because I'm Israeli I must incorporate politics?"

"Sheesh," Matt said. "I was just expressing an interest."

Gal wrote down, in Hebrew, *April May June*. She thought about

Judge Judy, who yelled at people who were too stupid to get a written contract or talked when it wasn't their turn, and she gazed at the calendar with narrowed eyes. Something had been working away at the edges of her memory since they'd sat down, and that, together with the combative tone coming from Yossi and Matt, set her on edge. It was a warm and cloudy afternoon, the kitchen almost dark enough to turn on the lights; a bee batted noisily against the screen door. "You know," Matt was saying, "some people would say that *not* incorporating politics is actually a political act."

Yossi gave him a cool look.

"I'm just saying," Matt said.

"Don't grip the pencil so hard, Gal," she heard Yossi say. "See, your knuckles are white!"

It worked at the edges of her memory and then moved away. She looked down at her hand and let go of the pencil; it rolled off the table and dropped to the floor.

THE STORY ABOUT THEIR family in the local paper was picked up by the AP wires and published by a Springfield paper, and soon after in the *Boston Globe*, as part of a larger story about gay and lesbian foster families; they found out about it from April, who scanned the papers daily. They got a call from a Boston TV station that wanted to feature them on a news program, but they turned it down, agreeing that a local story was one thing, but being a news sensation—and putting the kids in front of television cameras—was another. Gal was about to start school, and they didn't need her to be the object of this kind of attention as she was trying to integrate herself into a class of American first-graders.

At work, Daniel had gotten to a phase where sitting in his office concentrating on editing a story was the only thing that honed and quieted his mind. He reveled in his own expertise as he cut, rearranged, smoothed, corrected emphases, feeling like a carpenter doing fine finish work. They were increasing the magazine's Web presence, and he found that having lived with a graphic designer for four years had rubbed off on him and given him a broad sense of design possibility, so that together with his office's own Web person, he was helping create a fresher and hipper look for the magazine. He felt as though he had answered in the affirmative the unspoken question of whether he would return—really return—to the job they had held for him. Then one day in late August, April called him into her office and handed him a printed email, addressed to her and cc'd to the president. The first paragraph read:

> My deepest condolences to Daniel Rosen on the tragic loss of his brother and sister-in-law. I commend him for taking into his home the youngest victims of a terrorist's bomb, and for raising them in what appears to be a sensitive and caring way. But he appears not to understand that while he has the same right as any citizen to free speech, he holds a high-profile position at the College, and therefore has an obligation to represent it in a way befitting the enlightened values of the liberal arts. To say that he "understands" an act of terror is to defy those values absolutely. His position as College Editor cannot, must not, be used as a platform for what I can only call extremism.

HE LOOKED UP AT April, his heart sinking. "They read the story in the *Globe*," she said, handing it to him with the pages folded back to the article. Terrifyingly prepared, she had highlighted in yellow the paragraph where he talked about the terrorist.

"I wasn't speaking as college editor," he said, scanning it again for signs of extremism, or of having misspoken.

"That's what I told the president."

The president: he absorbed the fact that they had discussed him. "Am I in trouble?" he asked.

"No," she said. "I just wanted to let you know that this is happening. This isn't the only letter; it's the most judicious of the lot." She pulled out another letter. "This one basically says the same thing, but it adds, 'I pity Mr. Rosen, who will realize soon enough that when one has children, one cannot always afford the politically correct position.'" She looked up at him and he wondered why she'd felt compelled to read that to him. "And then there's the one that says, 'What's next? Inviting terrorists to speak on campus?'" The corners of her mouth rose in a wan attempt at wryness.

"What do you want me to do, April?" he asked.

"What's done is done," she said. "I just wanted to alert you to it."

"I didn't go to the *Boston Globe*," he said, provoked by the long-suffering quality he heard in her voice. "It was a local human interest story, for God's sake. I never imagined it would get picked up by the wires." He felt his throat catching with righteous intensity. "I turned down a request to be on a Boston TV news program, did you know that?"

"I didn't know that," April said.

"Are these people who wrote in important donors?" he asked.

She paused, then answered, "Not important ones."

How, he wondered, had he become this person—a needy liability at work, blamed for the bad things that happened to him? He was good at what he did, great at it even, he knew that. But now he felt like one of those single moms who's chronically late for her shitty, low-paying job because she has to take two buses to get there, and one is always late or packed to the gills with passengers and sailing past her as she frantically tries to wave it down.

"They weren't even big donors!" he raged to Matt when he got home. "So why did she feel it necessary to call me out? Did it hurt the college in any way? No. Did it affect my ability to do my job in any way? No. Did it have anything whatsoever to do with the fucking alumni magazine? No."

He was getting into the tight, hyperlogical argumentative mode he got in when he was truly furious. Matt, sitting at his desk, trying to get a little more work done before Michelle brought the kids home, knew that at any moment he might need to duck for cover. "She's an asshole," he said.

"I didn't do anything wrong," Daniel said. "I didn't have any control over it getting picked up by the AP wires—it didn't occur to me for one second that that would happen."

"No, you didn't."

Daniel glared at him. "Don't just say that because you think it's what you're supposed to say. Listen to what I'm saying," he said.

"I am listening! You didn't do anything wrong, Dan. I truly believe that, and I truly believe that April was just taking out some shit on you. She probably got called in by the president or something."

Daniel looked at him, scrutinized him down to his soul, to see if there was any part of him that worried about his competence, because that, truly, would be the last straw. But Matt mostly looked eager to return to his work. Daniel sighed with the petulance of a man who's tried to project his shame out into the world, but failed.

"Baby, I got to finish this," Matt said.

AND THEN IT WAS the end of the summer; Val sang Dar Williams: "It's the end of the summer, when you send your children to the moon." On the recommendation of a friend of Adam and Val's, they'd found a home day care for Noam, run by a woman with a three-year-old, who was only going to take in Noam and one other kid. Her name was Colleen, and Matt and Daniel were immediately taken by her sweet, watchful daughter and by Colleen's gentle energy, and by how, as they sat cross-legged on her living room floor talking to her about Noam's special circumstances, she listened quietly and thoughtfully, without any big reactions, and stroked his hair softly when he came and climbed in her lap.

But after all this time of being a trouper above and beyond what anyone could have expected with his new parents, Noam found day care to be the last straw. In the first week, when they left him for just an hour or two at a time, he cried inconsolably, almost the entire time. Once or twice, gone rigid in the grip of a meltdown, he actually foamed at the mouth, which, when they talked about it, made them laugh uncomfortably. It was the first time he'd been even remotely difficult. Daniel tried to project a sense of calm when he dropped him off in the mornings, and he couldn't have asked more from Colleen, who crooned to Noam as he writhed in her arms and never lost her cool or her compassion, but he had to pry Noam's hands off of his legs; and when he picked him up during his lunch break to bring him home where Matt would take over, Noam fell asleep almost the moment he was in Daniel's arms, which made Daniel want to die thinking of the effort he must have put out to hang in there alone. He lugged the baby's deadweight out to the car seat, where his head lolled as Daniel worked the buckles, and as he drove him home his mind buzzed unpleasantly with possible alternatives; he calculated what the family income would be if he quit his job and stayed home with Noam, and had to keep telling himself that Noam would have been in full-time day care in Israel, too.

They had enrolled Gal in Jackson Street School, where almost a quarter of the kids who attended were being raised by queer couples, and which was adored by everyone they talked to for its sense of community. Daniel had brought Gal in to meet her new teacher, Ms. Wheeler, and to see the classroom Gal would be spending the day in. There were five tables around the room, each with a plastic container full of markers and scissors set in the middle, surrounded by chairs with tennis balls stuck onto the bottom of their legs. At one end of the room there was an alcove with a colorful rug on the floor, for morning meeting. Paper chains and cardboard birds and butterflies hung from the ceiling, and the walls were covered with signs, pictures, charts, and a list of playground rules: *You can't say, you can't play, Go* down *the slide, Kissing is for your family.* Ms. Wheeler bent down to Gal when she spoke to her, and had her say her name several times so she could get the pronunciation just right.

The next day, Matt took her to buy school supplies at Target, where she stared irritably at the ugly Hello Kitty and Dora the Explorer and Pretty Pony lunch boxes. "These ones must be for babies," she said.

"I don't think they are. Babies don't really use lunch boxes," Matt said tactfully. "But I get your point."

"Everything is ugly!" she said, kicking at the display and storming away from Matt, who clearly didn't know where the nice things were, who was going to make her go to her first day of school carrying a Hello Kitty lunch box. He watched her run around the corner, and sighed, bent to pick up the lunch boxes that had clattered onto the floor. The truth was, he didn't know the first thing about what kind of lunch box first-grade girls brought to school, and neither did she, which he knew must feel awful. He went after her and caught up to her, laid his hand on her shoulder to turn her around and talk it through, but she whirled, her face twisted, and dug her fingernails into his arm.

"Ow!" he yelped as she ran off again.

He followed her; each time he approached her she screamed "No!" and struck out at him. He walked out past the cashiers and sat in a chair at the Pizza Hut near the front doors, breathing hard, figuring that she'd be safe as long as she didn't leave the store. A few minutes passed, and then ten, and then he felt that he should look for her. But he was afraid to let the front doors out of his sight.

The pizza and popcorn smell was so intense he felt it must have been concocted in a laboratory somewhere. People were emerging from the cashiers, dazed and stately behind baskets full of bags, diaper boxes, lamps, tall boxes set on the diagonal. He ventured into the long aisle on the store side of the cashiers and began to walk it, his eyes raking over each aisle. He walked all the way to the electronics section, whipping around from time to time to make sure Gal wasn't behind him, then turned and walked back.

He found her standing near the front, gazing into a cooler of sodas and drawing a swirl on the door with her finger. He laid his palm gently on her head. "We'll find you something nice," he said. "I won't make you bring something ugly or babyish to school."

A tremor went through her. She was dreading starting school, where you couldn't kiss people or go up the slide. It seemed to her that once she started, it would mean she was never going back to Israel. And yet the sense of waiting was intolerable, too.

She let Matt lead her into the shimmering parking lot and take her home. They hadn't bought anything, and she hoped, fervently and futilely, that without supplies, there was no way she could go to school.

CHAPTER 12

D ANIEL DROVE GAL to school the first few days and walked her into her classroom, but he soon realized that she was becoming anxious waiting for him to go, and he put her on the bus on the third day. The evening after her fourth day, during dinner, Matt and Daniel got a call from Ms. Wheeler. "Do you have a moment?" she asked Daniel.

"Sure," he said, and took the phone into the other room.

During yesterday's morning meeting, Ms. Wheeler told him, Gal had told the child she was partnered with that her parents were killed when a terrorist put a bomb in a café, and it blew off their heads. So when they were buried in the ground, she said, they didn't have heads. Then, apparently, the boy reported that to the class when it was his turn to show how well he'd listened. "It's not so much that the other children were disconcerted," Ms. Wheeler said, "although I did get a call from a few parents. I'm calling for Gal, to make sure that *she's* all right. And, actually, to find out if she was fabricating. Just so we can know what we're dealing with."

"Whew," Daniel said, his mind blank. "I don't know what to tell you. I am so in over my head here," he said, wincing at the inadvertent pun. "Can I talk to Gal and get back to you?"

He hung up, numb, and went back into the kitchen.

"What?" Matt asked.

Later, he mouthed.

Honestly, he didn't even have it in him to say; he felt dragged down by a lead weight. When, after Gal left the table, Matt finally got him to speak, what came out was sludgy.

"Wow," Matt said. "Why would Gal say that?"

Daniel shrugged. "To get attention? To aggress the other kids?"

They went up to her bedroom and knocked. "Don't be mad at her," Matt said.

"I'm not!" Daniel said, insulted.

She was sitting on her bed with a book, surrounded by all her horses and stuffed animals, which formed a neat ring around her. "Hey, Boo," Matt said.

"Hey," she said.

"Gal," Daniel said, easing himself down onto the corner of the bed. "Your teacher called. She said you told the other kids that your parents were buried without heads?"

Gal blushed furiously.

"Why would you say that?" Daniel asked, sitting on the bed.

"We're not angry, just curious," Matt said.

She looked at him, drawn into his curiosity. She could see Daniel's face in her peripheral vision, and even that glance made her grow hot, made her feel as if there were something wrong with her. She didn't know how to say why. Kids were sharing, and she had had this sudden powerful impulse to take her place among them. It had come from a glistening place in her, the cold water in a lake's deepest spot. Now, though, it seemed so wrong she could hardly look at them. "I wanted to share, too," she said, her voice wavering.

They exchanged glances.

"Gal," Daniel said gently, "your parents did have heads when they were buried."

She looked at him, and her expression was so full of shock and yearning and doubt that tears sprang to his eyes. "I'm not just saying that to make you feel better. You just misremembered. They were buried with heads."

She threw herself facedown onto her pillow. Daniel stroked her back; Matt, who'd been crouching by the bed, sat down heavily on the floor, remembering with a sickening feeling his own avid, terrified scans of their bodies under the sheets they were buried in. She cried something unintelligible into the pillow.

"What?" Daniel asked, lifting her by the shoulders. "I can't hear you, *buba*."

"I told everybody that they didn't!" she cried, her face scarlet and wet with tears.

"But isn't it good that they had heads?" Matt offered. "It must have been terrible to think they didn't."

"Yeah," Gal said, gulping and hiccupping.

She cried some more, and begged them not to make her go back to school, where she'd have to tell the class that what she had said was wrong, and then they would think she didn't even know how her parents were buried. "Please," she said over and over, her teeth chattering, while Daniel and Matt exchanged fierce and meaningful and appalled glances. The memory of her parents was slipping away from her; at night in bed she called to them, but the only images she could conjure were paltry and insubstantial. You couldn't try really hard to imagine them, you couldn't strain; they either came or they didn't.

"Okay," Daniel finally said. "You can stay home tomorrow. For one day only. And you have to let Matt work and not disturb him."

Later, as she and her brother slept in their bed and Daniel and Matt were brushing their teeth, Daniel said, "She's been carrying that image with her this whole time, and we didn't know. What other horrible ideas and images does she carry with her that we don't know about?"

"I know," Matt said through a mouthful of toothpaste. He spat. "I was thinking the same thing. She has this whole secret life in her head, so we can't even comfort her about it because we don't even know how to ask her about it."

"Do you think it's okay to let her stay home from school tomorrow? I don't want to set a precedent where every time she's upset she gets to stay home."

"I think it's okay this once," Matt said.

"Don't make it a huge treat, okay?"

"Okay," Matt said. "I'll make her sit in a corner, and only feed her cabbage."

Daniel realized that he had a pounding headache. Poor Gal, he thought, called on the carpet, for being—what? Inappropriate. Socially inept. A blurter. He knew exactly how she felt, confronted with words that had come from her heart, but which didn't mesh with her environment. The words came back at her blazing and crazy, revealing something deep and frightening about her that couldn't be unsaid. He knew exactly how she felt.

He rubbed the big muscle on the side of his neck. Matt came up behind him and massaged it gently, his other arm clasping Daniel's torso vertically, over his shoulder. He clasped Matt's massaging hand and squeezed it, then eased himself away and into the bedroom.

Early the next morning, Daniel called Gal's teacher and explained that she hadn't been trying to shock or scare the other kids in the class—that she actually believed that her parents were buried without heads, and felt that she was honestly sharing. As Ms. Wheeler murmured, "Oh boy" and "Man oh man," he told her that they'd be keeping her home for the day because she didn't know how to face the other students, now that she realized she'd told them something that wasn't true. "I think it's important to collaborate on a strategy for her, a way to tell the truth without her losing face, or feeling mortified," he said.

She told him she'd talk to the school psychologist for advice on how to help Gal do that.

He hung up and sat down at the table. "Maybe when I get home I can talk with Gal about how to make it comfortable for her to return to school."

"I can do that this afternoon, too," Matt said.

"You don't have to," Daniel said.

Matt closed his eyes, trying not to snap at him. The baby was slumped back on his lap, sucking loudly on a bottle of milk, stopping every once in a while to catch his breath with a big gulping sigh.

"What would you say?"

"I don't know what I'd say, Daniel. From your standpoint, I'd no doubt recommend she do something highly inappropriate." He didn't want to say it because it would sound mean and competitive, but he kind of felt that if Daniel would just leave the house already, he and Gal could work it out. Because he *got* her.

Half an hour later, having sent Daniel off with Noam, he made pancakes, against the small voice in his mind that was reminding him not to make the day a fun one. Gal came into the kitchen as he was spooning a ladle of batter into the pan, a small stack of finished pancakes sitting beside him on a plate on the counter, draped with paper towels.

"Pancakes!" she sighed dreamily, sitting on a kitchen chair in her monkey pajamas and plopping her elbows on the table.

He brought her the finished stack, and set butter and syrup on the table. "Do you want me to pour the syrup for you?" he asked.

"No, I can," she said, with mild indignation. As he returned to the pancakes in the pan, she wrestled the top off the syrup bottle and tipped it carefully, her hand trembling with concentration.

When Matt's pancakes were cooked, he brought them to the table and sat. He pushed the side of his fork into the stack and glanced up at Gal. "So. No heads, huh."

She shook her head through a thick mouthful.

"That must have been a crazy thing to imagine."

She nodded, and crammed another forkful into her mouth.

"Why didn't you say anything to us?"

Her eyes met his as she chewed, cheeks bulging. Yo-yo groaned from his station at Gal's feet and lay back; a lawn mower several doors down sputtered and roared. Gal swallowed. "I thought you already knew about it, and you didn't want to talk about it anymore. Especially Dani."

Matt nodded gently.

"Because if you knew your twin brother didn't have a head . . ." She trailed off and gave him a solemn look.

Sometimes, Matt couldn't believe the conversations he was having, couldn't believe the sequence of words and thoughts uttered in his presence. Had anybody on earth ever uttered that sequence of words, and what were the odds that anybody on earth ever would in the future?

"But *you* had to think that your mother and father didn't have heads! That's even worse!"

Gal considered this, shrugged. "But I knew that in heaven they have their heads."

"Okay." *In heaven,* Matt thought, *everybody will be reunited with his or her head.* "So when you said this in your class, how did the other kids react?"

"They just looked at me."

"Do you think they were freaked out?"

She laughed. "Maybe." She'd finished eating and was dragging the side of her fork into the pool of syrup that remained on her plate, then lifting it toward her outstretched tongue and licking it clean.

He watched her, a faint smile on his lips.

"I don't want to go back there," she said.

"Why?"

She gave him a miserable shrug. "Lots of those kids already know each other. I'm the only one who doesn't know anybody." There were other reasons too, reasons that didn't find their way into her conscious mind. Her accent, which made her the weird kid. The fact that many of them read better than she did in English, when she was used to being the smartest kid in the room.

"You'll make friends, Gal. It's only the first week of school!"

"I don't think I will make friends," she told him.

"Why not? You're a cute and fun kid. You know how to make friends—you had a lot of them in Israel."

She craned her head toward him and lowered her voice. "I don't think I'm so fun anymore." She was thinking about the small groups of kids who milled together talking about things, and how she sat by herself at a table, her stomach churning unpleasantly, trying to look busy with paper or markers or scissors, because she didn't know what to say, and couldn't bring herself to just stand among them silently.

His eyes stung when she said that. "Gal-Gal," he said, then cleared his throat and looked hard at her. "You've had a life unlike any other kid in your school. The hardest thing most of them have had to face is losing their favorite teddy bear, or falling down on the playground and getting a boo-boo."

She cracked a reluctant smile.

"Honestly," he insisted. "Not one of them has had to be as brave as you have to be every day. So if you're not the funnest kid in the class, so be it. You don't have to be like everybody else. Not everybody has to like you. Lots of people didn't like me when I was a kid. Hell—heck—a lot of people don't like me now."

"I know," she said, deadpan.

"Oh, that's hilarious," he said.

That evening he and Daniel snared Cam for an hour of babysitting, tossing at her a bag of Goldfish and vanishing out the door, grabbing the rare chance to take Yo-yo for a walk in the woods behind the abandoned state mental hospital, just the two of them. Yo-yo plunged into the river, wading and slurping, and Daniel threw sticks for him to wear him out in the current. "Drop it," he'd command as Yo-yo emerged from the river, circling with the stick and shaking furiously, until setting it down. Then Daniel would snatch it up and throw it high over the river.

It was a late-summer evening, thick, with a warm wind that seemed to coat their faces and arms. Dogs and their humans walked the paths that ran between the river and the harvested cornfields that looked as if they'd been trampled by a wanton giant. Matt told Daniel about his conversation with Gal, which he was pretty proud of: he felt he'd brought the topic into the light of day and maintained a light touch that encouraged her to confide in him.

Yo-yo emerged from the river, shook himself, then flung himself on his back on a patch of grass, where he writhed ecstatically while they uttered a mild, sad "Oh, Yo-yo," anticipating the dirt he'd be bringing into the house.

"Did you talk to her at all about how to make friends," Daniel asked, "or did you just tell her it was okay for people not to like her?"

Matt paused, said humorously, "I'm not sure I like your tone."

"Well, come on, Matt," Daniel said. "If she doesn't know how to conduct herself, she'll be hurt by people."

"Really?" Matt said, recoiling. "*Conduct* herself? How about being encouraged to *be* herself?" He was physically repulsed; how priggish could you get? He looked at Daniel and saw a thin, bearded man in sneakers and socks, and wondered if he'd look at him twice if he didn't already know him. A small well of panic bubbled in his chest. He was used to wanting sex wanting sex wanting sex. Could it be, he wondered, that he was no longer attracted to Daniel, rather than the other way around? He stopped to fish a pebble out of his sandal, and his eyes blurred as his mind shrank from that possibility.

"I'm calling her therapist," Daniel said. "This is ridiculous."

When they got home, he went up to Matt's study, closed the door, and called Gal's grief counselor, Peggy Sheridan, at home. "Do you have a moment?" he asked, knowing she'd say yes, because having a child whose parents had been killed by terrorists made therapists cut you a lot of slack.

"Sure," she said.

"I just wanted to check in," he said, "because Gal's been pretty volatile at home. And yesterday, she told the kids at school something kind of inappropriate. That her parents were buried without heads."

"Oh dear," Peggy said.

He sat down on the love seat and put his feet up on Matt's Lucite coffee table. "I guess I wanted to ask how you think she's doing."

Peggy was quiet for a moment, and he could hear the clink of dishes in the background, a dishwasher being loaded, or maybe emptied. He conjured her red hair with strands of silver, her freckled skin and clear gray eyes, the Eileen Fisher clothes in earth tones, and wondered if she was in sweats and a T-shirt now, barefoot maybe. Derrick had referred them to her, and Daniel had chosen her without interviewing anyone else based solely on the way she'd first greeted Gal, with a warm seriousness that made Gal visibly relax and open.

"She's struggling," she said. "There's a lot of anger there. She was dreading starting school."

"Do you think there's been any progress?" he asked, careful to keep his tone neutral.

Peggy paused again, and then asked him if he minded holding on for a second while she went someplace quieter. When she returned, she asked, "Are you concerned that the therapy isn't working?"

"No," he lied. "I just thought it might be good to check in."

"I'm glad you did," she said. "You must be having a helluva time yourself. I mean, your twin brother!"

Why was it always the simplest statements that filled your eyes with tears? During that first session, he'd told her what had happened to Gal and she'd said softly, "That's so sad." Just that, and Gal had started to cry. He was quiet for a moment now, knowing his voice would catch if he tried to answer.

"Who's helping you get through this?" she asked gently.

"Well, my partner," Daniel said. "My friends." He paused. "You probably mean I should be in therapy."

"Well," she said, "if it were my twin sister, I'd be running to therapy as fast as my legs could carry me."

Daniel closed his eyes to absorb this. It felt as if she were crossing a line. Was she suggesting that *he* was the problem? His left leg had fallen asleep, crossed under his right up on the coffee table. He uncrossed them and stood and stomped. "We're trying to do right by Gal," he said.

"Of course you are."

"We're trying to be stable and loving, and to help her remember, and put her feelings into language. We've read the books about helping a grieving child. Not to mention consulting with you."

"And you're doing a terrific job," Peggy said. "I guess what I want to say is that she's very attuned to you, Daniel; she's watching, and she takes her cues from you."

That surprised him. Gal was so difficult these days, flinging herself from him, stomping around the house and putting them all on edge—it didn't feel as if she were attached to him at all. He wanted to ask Peggy what she was trying to tell him, but didn't want to come off as confrontational. He told her that he heard Noam crying, and pulled his way off the phone despite some concerned follow-up questions; she knew she'd pissed him off. Then he sat back down, angry that they hadn't had the conversation he'd hoped for. He kicked off his shoes and lay down on the couch with his elbow crooked over his face. Let Matt handle baths and bedtime, thinking he was still on the phone. He knew Matt cheated sometimes in just this way, retreating to the bathroom and sitting there longer than necessary, reading a magazine on the toilet while Daniel was getting the kids into pajamas or reading them stories.

It was starting to get dark in the study now, the sky outside drained of color. He squinted at his watch; it was only six o'clock. The long days of summer would soon come to an end, and his heart was heavy with the thought of coming home from work in the dark. He thought of Gal again and a little starburst of anxiety went off in his chest.

He thought about Peggy saying that Gal was taking her cues from him. What was she trying to tell him? He heard a message there, one that implied that he was sending bad cues. He tried to push aside his defensiveness and to examine himself honestly. He was a mess, he knew that. He was heavy-limbed these days, a little zombielike. But this is what he couldn't get past: How could he not be? Was he supposed to set an example for Gal by being as normal as possible?

He loved her and his heart ached for her, but above all, he wanted to do right by her. He wanted to be a parent she felt safe with, with whom she felt at home. If she didn't, it wasn't fair to get angry at her, he knew that. He closed his eyes and prepared himself to get up and help with bedtime, to enter the fray.

Later that night the principal of Gal's school called. Daniel had never talked to her before, but he'd heard she played trombone in the school band and was known to join in a soccer game when patrolling at recess. At the sound of her voice, Daniel relaxed; she had that ability. When he told her that Gal had actually believed her parents were buried headless, there was silence followed by the sound of nose-blowing. "Poor kid," she said. She said that she wanted the record to be set straight, not just so that the other kids didn't have to imagine something that horrific, but to spare Gal any teasing that might occur. "Because otherwise she's going to be the girl with the headless parents." She said that she'd do it herself the next morning.

"What will you say to them?" Daniel asked.

She paused. "Who the hell knows? Okay. That Gal went through a terrible experience, losing both of her parents when a bomb exploded in a café in Israel. That the experience upset her so much, it's hard for her to remember those days when they were buried. That they actually did have heads, although Gal thought they didn't. And that I'm sure they all want to help Gal, and support her. And I'll ask them if they have any ideas about what might be the most supportive."

"Great," Daniel said.

"May I speak to Gal?" she asked.

Matt went to get her and brought her back, shrinking and shy. "Hello?" she said. "Hi." She listened for a little while, fingering the *chai* necklace her *savta* had given her. "Okay," she said. "Okay. Yes. Okay. Bye."

She hung up and sighed with relief. "Okay, I can go back to school now," she said.

SHE WENT TO SCHOOL the next day, and Daniel called from work to say that Colleen had taken to wearing Noam around in a carrier on her back, which he seemed to like. Matt worked hard all morning, steeling himself against the impulse to clean the house instead. After lunch, he put on the kettle, took out the dog, and got the mail. There were two letters in regular envelopes, addressed to Daniel in handwriting. When he talked to Daniel at lunchtime, he mentioned them, and Daniel told him to go ahead and open them. Matt opened the first.

> Dear Daniel,
> 2 Jews are being marched before the Nazi firing squad, and the executioner asks them, "Do you want to wear a hood?" The first Jew defiantly says, "No, I want them to see my disgust and anger," to which the second Jew whispers, "Shoosh, you might upset them."
> You are the second Jew.

The other was typed on a manual typewriter, and the keys had unevenly pressed the letter imprints on the paper.

> Dear Daniel Rosen,
> I read the newspaper article in which you expressed your understanding of the terrorist who killed your brother and sister-in-law. Please do not talk about things you don't understand. Compassion is a noble impulse but it must always be balanced with WISDOM. If it is not, the result is always foolish stupidity.

MATT LAID THEM CAREFULLY on the kitchen counter, smoothed them with his hand. "Christ," Daniel was saying, and Matt said, "What are the odds that after not receiving any mail at all, you'd get two letters in one morning? And who even sends hate mail via snail mail these days?" Then he thought: *These people know where we live, and they want us to know that.* The thought came gulping up and swallowed him. His eyes scanned the windows. Would he and Daniel be like those abortion doctors, shot in their living rooms by deranged snipers? If one of the kids got hurt . . . At the very thought of that happening, his chest swelled and his blood seemed to roar through his heart.

The whistle of the kettle broke into his consciousness, and he went and turned off the burner. "I gotta go," Daniel was saying. "Let's talk about this when I get home."

Matt opened the letters once more and reread them, and calmed himself with the observation that they didn't seem threatening, just officious, condescending, obnoxious as hell.

CHAPTER 13

HE TRIED TO cultivate a sense of superiority—they didn't deserve to be even considered—but the letters got to Daniel; a reflexive feeling that he'd done something terribly wrong nagged at him, and made it hard to fall asleep.

"That's just what they want you to feel," Matt said hotly. "They want you to think that *you're* the crazy person."

Daniel knew that. Still, sometimes, just sometimes, he had the heart-stopping thought that he'd missed something, or breached an important code of conduct, or failed at some response crucial to the common human enterprise. Wasn't there, just possibly, something strange—even disturbed—about the fact that he couldn't muster any anger at the man who had killed his brother?

Now he looked at Matt, who was sitting cross-legged on the playroom floor and taking apart the foam puzzle alphabet floor. He thought about how irritated Matt was that people who hadn't given him the time of day before suddenly fell all over him in camaraderie once he had kids. Yes, he got why Matt was irritated, but it wasn't entirely sinister, was it? Wasn't having and raising children simply part of the common human enterprise?

"Sometimes," he said, "I wonder, are we so perverse, so used to thinking against the grain that we can't even recognize a normal human sentiment when we stumble upon it? Like, for example, that it's bad to kill people?"

Matt tsked. "We know it's bad to kill people, Daniel. We know that."

"But understandable," Daniel said, feeling the ugliness press at his eyes and face.

Matt looked at him and sighed, stood and put the stack of alphabet floor pieces in the corner. "Is that it?" he asked, looking around the play-room. "Kitchen clean?"

"Yes," Daniel said.

In the living room Daniel threw himself on the couch, covering his face with his crooked arm, while Matt found the newspaper and sank into the armchair. Legs crossed at the knee, swinging a bare foot, he read. The news was all horrendous, the depredations of the Bush administration terrifying; but Matt felt it was his duty to witness it all. So he read and groaned, and his heart sank and swelled.

"What if," Daniel said, sitting up. "What if you said—in print!— that you understood Matthew Shepard's killers? And then the whole gay community turned on you? Would you call *them* lunatics?"

Don't bite, don't bite, Matt told himself, and then he said, "It's *so* not the same thing! When did gay people ever do anything to straight people to warrant being killed?"

"So you think Israelis deserve to be killed!"

"Oh God," Matt groaned.

THEY GOT MORE MAIL, some snail mail, most via email. Much of it— laced with the straining, acid language of political extremism, words like *brutal, mockery, hypocrisy, bloodthirsty, fanatics, agenda*—gave them a headache. *Nothing worse than a Semite who is anti-Semitic. Do your home-work before speaking. You're the same type of so-called intelligentsia that propa-gated Hitler's Holocaust.* A few letters came in the form of long treatises so strenuously argued—one of them was even footnoted—they sounded like the ironclad cases the insane make about their persecution. Then Adam called to tell Daniel that his name was up on a website by a group called TheCancerWithin.com. Matt and Daniel logged on and scrolled down the luridly fonted home page. "Islam, a religion of peace? Or is it preparing to sodomize the world?"

"Lovely," Matt muttered. He pointed to a link titled "His Ugliness Yasser AraFART: decades of stinking lies." "AraFART. Clever!"

"Here," Daniel said, clicking on a link called "Israel-hating Judenrats."

"Oh," Matt said, scanning. "It's everybody who ever signed a petition."

Daniel clicked on the *R*s, and scrolled down to his name. There was a tiny picture of him, a cutout of his face from the *Daily Hampshire Gazette* article. " 'This Judenrat believes that the terrorist was *right* to kill his brother and sister-in-law. He's a rabid homo—why are we not surprised that he likes to bend over for terrorist cock?' "

"Close it," Matt said.

"Jesus," Daniel said.

"Close it!"

But there were other kinds of letters, too. One was from someone who'd lost a son in 9/11, and wanted to direct Daniel to the group of bereaved family members who'd gone to Afghanistan on a peace mission before the war broke out. One was from a man who ran a workshop called Men Healing From Violence at the Kripalu yoga center; he sent his flyer, on the bottom of which he had written, *I wish your spirit peace, friend.* Daniel read it, feeling, as he always did in the face of the New Age, touched through layers of irony.

There was a letter from a gay man who'd lost his partner in Tower Two and had not received a penny of his estate, or a word of acknowledgment at his funeral, because they hadn't made any legal arrangements, and his partner's bio-family had elbowed him out. *I'm trying not to hate them,* he wrote, *because I want to remember Robert without hatred attached to it. Can you tell me what your secret is for avoiding hatred?*

I don't really have a secret, Daniel wrote back. *I think I'd hate your partner's family, too.*

THE READING ROOM OF the Smith College library was dim, lit by lamps with ornate shades; there was an antique fireplace, and the worn dark leather furniture was pushed against the walls to make room for two sections of folding chairs with an aisle in between them. A long table with water pitchers and cups was set at the head of the room, a small huddle of people talking at one end. In the audience were Smith students, some in tattered jeans and tight shirts and others in head scarves, white girls with dreadlocks, young women pierced in tendentious places, women with blunt features and buzz cuts who were transitioning to manhood. That was what they did these days, instead of living as butches, Daniel thought, regretting the loss of the gender deviance in both men and women that always stirred him. There were older people too, from the community—women in corduroys and wool sweaters with thick gray-streaked hair pulled back in ponytails, men with Abraham Lincoln beards.

Daniel sat next to Derrick in a chair near the door, leaving his coat on, picking out the speakers from the hosts. He'd known about this event for a few weeks, since Derrick had forwarded him the announcement posted on one of his social justice Listservs. It was a discussion by two members of The Families Project, a group of Israelis and Palestinians who had lost a family member to the conflict, who met together seeking peace and reconciliation. A Palestinian and an Israeli man, they were touring the States talking about their group and their friendship, and promoting a peace agenda. Daniel picked them out of the huddle of chatting organizers and faculty members, or was pretty sure he had. The Israeli was in his late thirties or early forties, with glasses and sandy-brown hair brushed evenly over his forehead, the kind of man who perhaps in high school, the army, or university was rejected by women because he wasn't good-looking enough, but who goes on to happily marry in his thirties. The Palestinian was a young man in a worn gray leather bomber jacket, thick dark hair cut short. Chubby, heavy in the chin, with beautiful eyes and lips.

Next to him, Derrick sat with his hands folded, his shaved head stately and gleaming, emanating the scent of his aftershave. He had called Daniel a few hours after emailing him about the event, to ask if he planned on going. Daniel had said he'd try to go, that it depended on what was going on at work. "Don't you think you should make this a priority?" Derrick had asked, and then added, after a chilly silence, "No pressure."

"No pressure," Daniel said.

"It's just that these are *your guys*," Derrick said in a burst. "And I'd like to see you get some support for your . . . your way of being. That's all."

"Support for my way of being, huh?" Daniel said. "You say it a lot nicer than Matt. He says I either come to this event or I stop complaining to him about the hate mail." He continued to compulsively open the messages, instead of—as Matt wanted him to do—deleting them from his email without reading them. The loonies were bad; they called him a faggot, a traitor, a guilty liberal asshole. But it was the ones who debated Middle East policy with him who got to him the most, and his mind scuttled about in constant, heated rebuttal; his lips moved in argument as he went about his day.

Daniel was seized by a fit of yawning, tired from work and depressed as always by the early-winter dark, wanting and not wanting the presentation to be perfect. It was unpleasant sitting there, feeling a kind of scathing irony toward the audience, for he knew that if this peace-loving, gender-queering, intellectually high-flying audience wasn't his ideal community, or very close to it, there was nowhere he belonged. A faculty member with a spray of steel-wool hair came to the front of the room to begin his introduction. He projected the aura of someone popular enough with his audience to extemporize, but he wasn't actually good at it; he had to consult a piece of paper for the key facts, and labored over pronouncing the Israeli and Arab names. At the end, though, he grew grave. "They are the people who are supposed to most desire revenge," he said, "and yet they turned in a different direction, a direction more difficult, more exacting, than retribution. They are here to tell us their stories."

The applause was emphatic and encouraging, and the speakers nodded and said "Thank you" till it died down. The Palestinian man spoke first. His name was Ibrahim and he lived in Ramallah. He had lost his brother in the First Intifada, and spent seven years in an Israeli prison. Strangely, he said in very good English, his Arabic accent like water rolling over rocks, it was there that he developed compassion for Israelis, when he learned a little about Jewish history and about the Holocaust. "For six years I attended the Project's meetings, and met Israelis who were grieving their own losses. I learned that our blood was the same color, that their tears were as bitter as mine, and had the same salty taste."

Then his seven-year-old daughter was killed by a settler on her way home from school, and the IDF spokesman told the newspapers that she wouldn't have been killed if she had been looked after properly. There was a collective intake of breath when he said that, and he paused for a minute. "My faith in peaceful coexistence faltered then," he said, "and I left the Project. I thought that the Israelis I had met must be an aberration. I told myself that they were, after all, only a few. Most Israelis were the savages many Arabs thought they were. But I am not a violent man. I did not seek vengeance—instead, I grew weary, and spent most of my time in bed. I lost my job; I had been a photojournalist. I lost twenty kilos. You can see that I've put them all back." He patted his stomach ruefully, to gentle, relieved laughter. "My wife grew desperate; she had lost her beloved daughter, and now her husband was disappearing, too."

Then someone told him about the Israeli man, Eitan Goldberg, who had just joined the Project after his own young daughter died in his arms after a bus explosion. A Palestinian on the board of directors called him and asked him to reach out to this man. He knew, Ibrahim said, that this was a ruse to bring him back to the Project, and his first impulse was to refuse. But the board member was persuasive. He said,

"So what if it's a ruse? A bereaved man needs support, and Ibrahim, so do you."

"We arranged to meet at Eitan's house in Tel Aviv," Ibrahim said. "It took me many weeks to get there. I was afraid, you see. Afraid that I might look in his eyes and see my own broken image. Afraid I would come to be friends with another Israeli, when I now knew for certain that Jews were evil. There is comfort in knowing that, in living without ambiguity. Much easier to live that way." He paused, gazing at the audience with mild eyes, then picked up briskly. "And then, once I grew brave enough, I had to get a permit, which of course took a long time." He paused and took a sip of water. "When the cab left me off at his address, I walked up and down his street. I was nauseated, I was so nervous."

Eitan cut in. "Meanwhile, I was inside, also nauseated."

The audience laughed.

"Remember," Eitan said, "I was a new member of the Project. My sister had convinced me to try it. She is very important to me, and despite everything that occurred, does not have the least trace of hatred or spite in her heart. And I had not yet met any Palestinian members. My whole life, I had met exactly one Palestinian outside of the army, outside of people trying to pass through the checkpoint I was stationed at. What if I hated him, if he confirmed all the bad ideas I had about Palestinians? And there was part of me, a shameful part, that wondered, can a Palestinian love and grieve as I do?" He paused for effect, and Daniel felt Derrick nodding beside him.

"When he opened the door," Ibrahim said, "we looked at each other, and we embraced without words. I went inside, his wife brought us tea, and we talked for over two hours. We found that we disagreed about many things," Ibrahim said. "But to this we agreed: We must stop this vicious circle of violence. It is a never-ending cycle of murder and retaliation, revenge and punishment, with no winners. It is not a decree of fate. This is not our destiny!"

There was uncertain applause, and then it picked up and became full-fledged. Derrick reached over and took Daniel's hand and squeezed it.

"So! Here are a few of the projects we have done." There was a hotline on which bereaved Israelis could find a Palestinian to talk to, and vice versa. Since the two men became friends they'd gone together to Palestinian high schools and talked with classes of Israeli kids who were about to become soldiers. With two other Palestinian members of the Project, Ibrahim had gone to Magen David Adom, the Israeli Red Cross, to donate blood, while Eitan and several other Israelis made their way across the Green Line to a Palestinian hospital to do the same. "At first they had no idea what to do with us!" Eitan said. "We were trying to make blood flow for peace and healing, instead of from warfare. We were affirming that we all have the *same* blood."

Tears prickled in Daniel's eyes, and he bit his lip.

The moderator opened the floor to questions. There was a longish silence, then a man raised his hand and stood. "I'm sitting in my seat listening to your stunning stories, wondering how to respond, wondering what words could possibly be adequate to follow upon them. And I finally found a single word that does justice to you. 'Bravo.'" He stood for a moment, flushed, until someone started to clap and a string of applause smattered around the room.

"Oh sweet Jesus," Derrick muttered. "Give me a break."

Daniel laughed, which felt like such a great release after his clenched and pent-up listening, he struggled to swallow down the giggles.

A young woman with short hair and a bull ring in her nose, wearing a T-shirt whose writing Daniel tried to make out in her half turn toward him—he was pretty sure it said *Bite me*—stood agitatedly and said, "We learn in college about occupation, nationalism, globalization, migration, oppression . . ." She broke into a grin as a few people laughed. "All those intellectualized concepts! What you have said is simpler and truer than anything I've learned in the classroom."

A bespectacled man in his sixties with disheveled hair stood and spoke. "I commend you for your commitment to peace. I too am agonized by the violence on both sides." Daniel recognized him as one of those Jewish men who speak like a rabbi—heavy-consonanted, sorrow-ful, stooped from the weight of all his great thoughts. "I wish I could believe that yours was the right way. Let's hope that it's you who turn out to be right, and not me." He shook his head woefully and sat back down.

A student with a round, light brown face and a head scarf stood. "My cousin was killed in Jenin last April," she said. "How can my aunt and uncle get in touch with you?"

Eitan began to answer, but Daniel didn't hear him. He stared at the back of the woman's head, his mind buzzing, his heart making an unpleasant whir in his chest. Her cousin was probably killed in the name of his brother and sister-in-law. He wanted to stand and say: *I didn't want it that way. I was not comforted by it.*

He wanted to say these things with a blaze of righteous fury. But he couldn't; something seized his tongue. Derrick was directing a steady, gentle gaze at him—a gaze Daniel knew well and normally loved, but which felt unbearable to him now.

When the event ended, they sat with their hands pressed on their thighs, getting ready to stand. Derrick said, "You should go talk to them."

Daniel looked at the men, who had already been approached by several audience members.

"I can't. I can't hang around here."

"You'll hate yourself if you miss this opportunity."

Daniel shot him an aggrieved look, then sighed and stood, approached the men. Eitan was talking intently to the young woman whose cousin was killed in Jenin. An opening presented itself in front of Ibrahim, so Daniel stepped into it and extended his hand.

Ibrahim had the soft handshake of the Middle Easterner.

"Thank you for your work," Daniel said.

Ibrahim nodded and said, "You're very welcome." Daniel looked at him for a sign that this handshake meant anything at all to him, that he was open to being touched by something Daniel might say. But what he saw was the somewhat distracted politeness of a man who has done this presentation a hundred times and shaken many hands, and is perhaps thinking ahead to dinner, or to being able to take his pants off in his hotel room. He held Ibrahim's gaze for a moment, then turned around, somehow humiliated and tearful. When he joined up with Derrick, he was furious at him.

"Okay," he said, shrugging into his coat and heading for the door. "Let's go."

Derrick grabbed his coat and rushed after him. "That didn't take very long."

Daniel was silent as Derrick fell into step beside him and they headed out into the cold darkness toward the parking lot.

"Are you okay?" Derrick asked.

Daniel stopped abruptly. "What do you want from me, Derrick?" he demanded.

"What do you mean?"

"We didn't have a deep, meaningful conversation, if that's what you're wondering."

"Okay," Derrick said. "That's cool."

He held Daniel's gaze as Daniel stared him down.

They walked quickly to Derrick's car, and Derrick let it idle for a few minutes to warm up. Their breath puffed around them. "I just—I just didn't want to be another sanctimonious Jewish jerk talking about his own pain," Daniel said.

"Man, are you crazy? You're nothing like that."

"*Jesus*, I hate those guys!" Daniel burst out. "They're so *sorry* they don't believe in peace, they're *agonized*"—he made scare quotes with a scathing gesture, his mouth twisted—"about the necessary civilian Palestinian losses in any given conflict. Bullshit! It's all a performance of Jewish moral superiority, and I'm sorry, it's *bullshit*."

"Okay," Derrick said with comic care, as though trying to humor a lunatic. "But you realize that . . . that there's no connection between talking to someone about your own losses and what you're talking about. Right?"

"Whatever," Daniel said.

Derrick shifted into reverse and stretched his arm across Daniel's seat as he backed up. They were quiet during the short ride home, and when they got there, Daniel thanked him for the ride. "You're welcome," Derrick said, adding, as Daniel got out of the car, "And honey, give yourself a break."

Matt was in the bright kitchen, which was warm and steamy from boiling pasta water, sitting at the table with Gal, who had a bowl of pasta and a little container of organic applesauce in front of her. His elbow was on the table and his head rested in his hand as he watched her eat, his own plate cleaned. Noam was in his ExerSaucer, spinning wheels, making beads clatter and little bells ring. He had outgrown it several months ago, but it was enjoying a resurgence of his favor, after he had played in one belonging to the six-month-old twins of a lesbian couple from the shul.

"Hey," Matt said.

"Hey. Did he eat?" Daniel asked, coming into the kitchen in his socks but with his coat still on.

"Yes," Matt said. "How was it?"

"Fine," Daniel said. He went into the hall to hang up his coat, and when he came back, Matt said, "I made pasta with chicken and broccoli and lemons."

Daniel went over to the warm bowl sitting on the counter and helped himself to some pasta, put it in the microwave for a minute, and leaned against the counter.

"Remember all those sitcoms," Matt said, "where the wife is furious because the husband came home late from work and his dinner's cold?"

"Not just sitcoms," Daniel said, loosening his tie and his collar. *"Ordinary People."*

"No, that was pancakes for the son's breakfast. I think you're confusing *that* Mary Tyler Moore character with Laura Petrie."

"Oh yeah."

"Well, anyhoo, I think the microwave has made that situation obsolete."

"So it has," Daniel said.

"Lucky for us, huh?"

"Are you saying you're mad at me?" Daniel asked, bringing his plate to the table.

Gal looked up with interest.

"Nope. Just making conversation," Matt said. He watched Daniel hunch over his plate and eat. There was a click and then "Pop Goes the Weasel" played, manically cheerful. "I haven't managed to accidentally break the music on that thing yet," Matt said.

Daniel smiled dutifully. Matt looked at him, at the sharp dusty planes of his face, and wondered, again, if he was still in love with him, and if he wasn't, whether he ever had been—because surely a good, real love could get them through tragedy together. The thought didn't pain him, because he put it in a place in his mind marked *On Hold*—things, like his own death, that he would someday have to make it his business to think about, but that he didn't have to think about right now.

"Are you fighting?" Gal asked.

"No," Daniel said, while Matt brushed her hair out of her eyes and said, "Why do you ask that?"

She shrugged. "It looked like you were fighting. Even though you weren't saying anything like 'I'm mad at you' or 'You hurt my feelings.'"

"How can you tell, then?" Matt asked.

She shrugged again, smiling faintly this time. "I just can," she said complacently.

"You can, can you?" He reached over and gave her a squeeze in the ribs, and she slapped his hand away with an aggravated "Stop it!"

"Oh, are *we* fighting now?" he asked.

"Yes!" she shouted.

"Everybody stop fighting," Daniel said.

A song—"London Bridge Is Falling Down"—began to tinkle, loudly and spontaneously, from a toy in the corner of the kitchen. The three of them looked at one another and laughed. "I swear I switched that thing off!" Matt leapt up and grabbed it. "Ha!" he cried, and thrust the toy under each of their noses so they could see the switch on "off." The thing played again in his hands, and he tossed it in the air as if it had burst into flames, which startled Noam. "Oh, sorry, honey," Matt said, running to the small useful-things drawer and pawing through it in search of the tiny Phillips head screwdriver. He unscrewed furiously—the screwdriver tiny and spinning in his hands—one, two, three, four screws; they each hit the table with a tiny click. Then he dug out the D batteries, set the toy on the table. "I'm taking bets that it's like a smoke detector, and will still play," Matt said. "Anyone care to make it interesting?" They waited in suspense. The toy was silent.

"Dang," Matt said.

THAT NIGHT MATT AND Noam read the color book in Matt and Daniel's bed, and then Matt carried him—marveling that they really did get heavier when they started falling asleep—into his own room, and laid him down on his bed. He turned on the humidifier and Noam's Norah Jones CD, his lullaby music. "Good night, monkey," he whispered, running his hand over Noam's hair and putting his little fleece with the puppet head near his hand, so if he awoke in the night he'd know he was in his own bed.

He was drowsy when he went into the bedroom, where Daniel had spilled the basket of clean laundry onto Matt's side of the bed for folding. The water was running in the bathroom down the hall—Gal running herself a bubble bath, about which she'd become a fanatic; every trip to the drugstore now involved the purchase of a fancy potion for her.

Daniel was pulling out all of the kid pajamas from the pile. "Did you turn on the humidifier?" he asked.

"I did," Matt said. He pulled out all the sheets and towels, the things he liked to fold first, to make the laundry pile quickly smaller. He folded the towels, then turned to put them in the linen closet and to go check on Gal.

"Could you check on her?" Daniel asked.

Matt sighed and flashed him a look. "I'm just going to check on her."

"What? Why do you have to be a prick about it?"

"Because ten times a day I'm *in the very process of* picking up a blanket when you tell me to cover the baby with a blanket," Matt said, "or opening a dresser drawer to get a sweater for Gal as you tell me that it's cold and I should put a sweater on her. It's maddening! I know you're the Boss Man, but I'm an adult, too! Jesus."

Daniel stared at him. "Can't you cut me some slack?" he asked. "Think of it as a great-minds-think-alike moment? It's not about you."

Matt took in the semi-hostile apology, unplaced. He sighed. "You didn't used to treat me this way. Now . . ." He shook his head.

"'Now' what? Do you really want to start a fight right now?"

"Remember yesterday when I came back from the supermarket and was stacking apples in the bowl, and the top one rolled off and hit the floor? What's your response? You laughed! You said, 'I knew it! I could see that one coming.'"

"So what?"

"That's so mean! And you do it all the time."

"You're mad at me because I could see that one coming?"

"I'm mad at you because you treat me like a fuckup." Matt pulled out a pair of jeans and gave them a shake and a snap before laying them on the bed to fold. He knew he was the clown in their family dynamic, the tackler, the tickler, the one who pretended he couldn't find his hat when it was sitting on his head. Most of the time he relished that, and thought it was important to be that way, especially since Daniel was so—what? Deadened. But maybe, he was thinking, it was a mistake, too. One day, he'd reached up to pull the light cord on the kitchen ceiling fan and it had come clear out in his hand. Daniel had gone out and bought a new fan and installed it himself, and for days, Gal had walked around informing people, "Matt broke the ceiling fan, but Dani fixed it."

"Matt made a big steaming pile of doody," he'd said irritably to Brent, "but Daniel cleaned it up. That's what she's saying."

"But just look what a perfect couple that makes you!" Brent offered optimistically. "What if you were both ceiling fan breakers, and neither of you could fix it? Or if you both could fix ceiling fans, but there was no one to break one?"

"Oh please," Daniel said now. "Admit it. This is about sex."

"It is not!" Matt cried. "And what if it is? Is it so terrible for me to want to have sex with you?"

"I knew it," Daniel said with bitter satisfaction.

"Jesus," Matt said, feeling as though he'd just lost a major point. "You make it seem as if I'm an insensitive, shallow jerk for wanting it, so I have to pretend I don't. But I'm tired of pretending, and I'm not shallow and I'm not insensitive. Okay," he said, with an impulse to joke self-deprecatingly to increase his own credibility, "I'm a little shallow and insensitive. But not because I want to have sex with my boyfriend."

Daniel whirled on him. "Don't you think I would if I could? Don't you?"

Matt looked at him with interest, a pair of sweatpants dangling from his hands. "Why can't you?"

"I . . . I just can't. I feel very strongly that I can't."

"Why not?"

"Maybe because my twin brother was blown to smithereens?" Daniel's tone was ugly with suppressed tears.

He was dropping a bomb on the conversation, Matt thought, to make it stop. But Matt pursued it: "So if that happened to his body, then your body can't get any pleasure?"

Daniel shot him a withering look. "Oh, aren't you clever."

The phone rang, and he reached for it, Matt saying with a warning tone, "Don't!" He knew he'd scored, and he didn't want to give up his advantage.

"Hi," Daniel said into the phone.

"That's not cool," Matt said.

Daniel was casting his eyes up, defeated. "It was fine, Val. Thanks for asking. No, I'm not mad, it's just that a lot of people seem to be very interested in how it went, and I feel— No, of course, there's nothing wrong with that."

Matt watched for a minute as Daniel listened impatiently. "Listen," Daniel said, "I'm in the middle of something, can we talk about it tomorrow? Thanks. Thanks." A pause; he was lowering his head toward the telephone base with the receiver against his ear. "Thanks, Val. Okay."

"See?" he said, turning to Matt. "This is what I mean. You, Derrick, Val—everybody knows about the Families Project event, and everyone's on my case about it. 'How was it, Daniel? Did you talk to them, Daniel? Did they show you the right way to grieve?' She keeps trying to give me the name of this therapist she knows."

"Whoa!" Matt said. "You think people think you're grieving wrong?"

"Peggy Sheridan sure does! Don't you?"

Matt sat on the bed, making the pile of little washcloths Daniel had folded cave onto his thigh. "I don't know what that means." He said that even though he sort of knew what it meant. He'd been thinking about it. It was amazing that Daniel didn't feel rage at the terrorist, at the Palestinians. Mostly he thought that was because Daniel was simply an amazing and compassionate person, wise enough to see the big picture. Because he was. But sometimes Matt wondered—he couldn't help it—if that response was entirely real, entirely human. If Daniel could let himself be angry, would things be different?

"It hasn't even been a year!" Daniel said. "But clearly I haven't learned to do it right yet."

"No," Matt said.

"You're messing up my pile! So why is everyone pressuring me?"

"Then fold the laundry on your own freaking side of the bed!" Matt stood and picked up the empty basket to take into the bathroom. "They're not pressuring you."

"Oh, come off it! Sitting next to Derrick at that event was excruciating. He kept turning and gazing into my eyes with this, this soulful expectancy."

Matt laughed. "He always does that, Dan. He does it when he asks if you like his new recipe for tofu stir-fry with shiitake mushrooms, or whatever the fuck."

"He was just dying for me to have a huge catharsis, right there at Smith College."

Matt put the basket into the linen closet in their bathroom. When he came out, he asked carefully, "Do you think therapy's a terrible idea?"

Daniel was hanging a clean shirt in his closet, shaking and smoothing it, buttoning the second button around the hanger. He threw his head back, his eyes closed, his Adam's apple a shard against his throat. "I'm not going into therapy."

"Why not? It's not like you haven't done it before." Matt felt carefully for the words. "I think . . . It's not that you're grieving. It's that you're . . . frozen. You're different."

"What do you think grieving is?" Daniel cried. "Do you think you can really grieve—and I mean grieve *so hard it takes your breath away, day after day after day*—and not be changed?"

Matt was quiet. Was that true?

"Christ!" Daniel said, his face red and his nostrils flared. "It's not—it's not pretty, or ennobling. And if you think therapy can touch it, well—"

Matt stood gazing at him, leaning against his dresser with his arms crossed. Daniel was acting as though Matt had never grieved himself, but as Matt thought resentfully about that he also felt embarrassed, because he had felt his grief for Jay to be a little bit ennobling.

"So excuse me if I'm not exactly lusting after you," Daniel said, sensing an advantage from Matt's pensiveness.

"Stop it," Matt snapped. "You're like straight people, acting like sex is trivial. I can't stand that! And I'll tell you something, we're setting a crappy example of a healthy couple for these kids. They're going to think we hate each other!"

"I don't hate you," Daniel said, his eyes glistening. "I really don't. You've been a total saint, and I don't know what I'd be doing without you."

"Well, thanks," Matt said, thinking, *A total saint: just kill me.*

They sat down on the bed and slumped against each other. "What now?" Matt asked.

"Let me go make sure Gal hasn't flooded the house," Daniel said.

That night, curled against a sleeping Matt, Daniel's mind continued to churn. Therapy! What were they thinking? Sure, he believed in it— back in college, it had been a lifeline as he struggled to become comfortable with his sexuality. But to make him all better from terrorism, from one of the biggest and most violent losses a person could sustain? It felt so galling, so puny and trivial, in the face of what he was going through, so massively deluded as an enterprise. He couldn't get past that. You might as well tell that guy Ibrahim, or the woman whose cousin was killed in Jenin, to go to therapy.

Thinking of them let in a fresh wave of confusion and self-reproach. He'd felt so victimized, as a gay man, in the face of the Israeli legal system. What a joke that was! It mortified him now to even think about it. What an obscene luxury to have all his friends worrying and whispering about his mental health, while the children the Israeli courts had handed to him slept in a safe house that would never get bulldozed, when he would never be stuffed into a tiny strip of land he couldn't get out of and then bombed, or have one of his kids shot and then, on top of that, have the very people who had committed the murder blame him for being a negligent parent.

He didn't know what to do with all that, except to scorn his friends for their naïveté and privilege. His mind stalled there for a while, clotted and pulsing. Who was this man whom his friends said they missed? It was so hard to remember him! He knew, somewhere in the shadows of his mind, that he was a good and loving person, even a charismatic one—or that he *had* been anyway. In their early days together, Matt had prodded him: "You know that that whole shy and sweet thing you've got going on is irresistible, right? Remember fifth grade—'He's cute but he doesn't know it'? That's you." It had been hard to fully believe that Matt was in love with him. Sometimes he still had trouble believing that he could command the attention of such a smart and beautiful man.

His mind cast about for the sweetest moments in his life, the ones where he felt most himself, and most connected to others. Playing guitar, for sure: girls curled up in beanbag chairs in his dorm room, or on his bunk at camp, to listen to him play and to sing with him. He suspected now, although it hadn't occurred to him back then, that more than one of them had been crushed out on him. He remembered sitting barefoot on his bed in the darkened cabin, practicing a new melody line or picking pattern till the fingers of his left hand became red and tender, then calloused, as the shrill voices of campers rose from the moist New Hampshire heat that blanketed the woods and fields outside.

He grew drowsy, and his mind drifted and played in camp memories. He and Joel had loved Camp Ramah, lived for the chance to be away from their parents for four weeks and be steeped in Jewish *ruach*. Camp confirmed for them their sense of the soullessness of their manicured, suburban upbringing, where their accomplishments were paraded by their parents and even their bar mitzvahs seemed like just another opportunity to perform. He remembered the bliss of being without parents, the bracing feeling of competence that came over him when he was freed to take care of himself. To this very day he could conjure it. He remembered the beautiful grove where Shabbat services were held—a lovely peaceful shrine as dusk fell and the smells of dinner drifted in from the dining hall—and the Israeli counselors, who worked there in the summer before or after their army service. They were fair and curly-haired or dark-skinned with thick hair cut short, small and soft-spoken, their masculinity different from the masculinity he'd been, till then, making it his business to emulate. They were unspeakably glamorous, with their Ray-Bans, their flat leather sandals, and their throaty accents. Well into his young adulthood, they played a big role in his erotic fantasy life. His counselor, Ilan, a quiet and gentle soul who went everywhere barefoot and who had been a member of an elite infantry unit, loved hearing him play, and Daniel had basked in his attention—because for whom did he endlessly practice if not for Ilan, hoping for his attention and praise?

Where was Joel all day as he was practicing? Probably in the lake, or on the softball field. He thought of the long, thrilling games of Capture the Flag, and remembered one fine day when Joel actually captured the flag. Daniel himself was the kind of player who didn't imagine he could actually capture the flag. He'd thought of it as a crude, obvious goal, while the less glamorous roles—busting teammates out of jail, drawing a contingent of the other team toward you so another could advance— held risks that were more subtle and complex. Was that true, he wondered now, or was it just the defense of someone who hadn't wanted to take such a big risk? Or someone stepping back so his brother could shine, because his brother wanted to so very badly?

And then his memory shifted and he opened his eyes. Joel had wanted to be elected something or other—he couldn't dredge the desired thing from his memory now—and campaigned by going from bunk to bunk and introducing himself and bringing cookies that he'd had their mother make. Then one night, some of the older camp- ers did a skit in which one of them played Joel, whose Hebrew name was Yisrael, bursting into bunks, singing—instead of *"Hevenu Shalom Aleichem,"* We've brought peace upon you—*"Hevenu Ugiot Eleichem,"* We've brought cookies upon you. It was silly and harmless enough, but the guy who played Yisrael mimicked Joel's ingratiating eager- ness, and the slight childhood speech impediment that made Joel's *n*'s extra heavy, to a tee. Joel was sitting a few rows ahead of Daniel and to the side, and Daniel could see him laugh and then a cloud of uncer- tainty pass over his face, and that killed Daniel right then and there, stabbed him right in the heart. That pain returned to him over the rest of the camp session whenever he saw Joel going about his enthusiastic business—but he was also furious at him, because vulnerability that accrued to Joel accrued to Daniel as well.

He pressed his cheek to Matt's back. Joel had put himself out there, and Daniel, with a mixture of relief and contempt, had let him be the twin who did that. He stayed on the margins, and told himself it was somehow more noble, more interesting, to stay there. Honestly, when it came down to it, he'd just wanted to be distinguishable from Joel. He wanted people to know which one he was.

So who on earth was this man all his friends seemed to miss? Who did they want him to be? Who was the man whom *Matt* missed? Would Mr. Personality have even looked at Daniel twice if Jay hadn't died, if he hadn't had to flee the New York scene to save his own skin?

He blinked into the dark night, his mind throbbing, his heart choked.

CHAPTER 14

THERE WAS A skeleton hanging from Cam's front porch. Gal caught a glimpse of it swaying, antic and ghoulish, through the backseat window one windy gray Saturday afternoon as they pulled into the driveway. *"Ma zeh?"* she asked, whipping around to follow it from the back window.

But by then Noam was crying and the uncles were arguing, as Daniel wrestled him out of the car seat, about Matt driving too fast. She shouted, "I'm going over to Cam's house!" and crossed their lawns and marched up Cam's porch steps, keeping her distance from the skeleton, suddenly determined not to look at it, but not trusting herself to keep her eyes averted, as if in spite of her best effort, they might swivel in their sockets and look.

By the time she rang the doorbell she was terrified of it, could feel it behind her and hear the clicks of its bones as it moved. She heard Xena's wild bark get louder as the dog rocketed toward the front hall, and she took a step back, although she knew that by the time Cam opened the door, Xena would be at a polite, attentive sit-stay by her side.

The door opened and Cam said, "Hey, buddy, how's it going?" She was barefoot, wearing sweatpants and a T-shirt, and her thick dark hair was smashed in one direction, as though it had been fiercely blown and then frozen. "Okay," she instructed the dog, and Xena came forward with a gently wagging tail, thrust her muzzle into Gal's hand. Gal pulled off the new mittens the uncles had bought her for the coldest weather she'd ever known, so Xena could smell her, and she could feel the dog's fur and wet nose.

"Why do you have bones hanging up on your porch?" she demanded, her mind fumbling for the word even in Hebrew but not finding it.

"What? The skeleton? That's James."

"Who's James?"

"The skeleton, that's his name."

Gal stared at her. Was Cam making fun of her? Sometimes Cam played jokes on her, like knock-knock jokes that made her say, "I eat mop who?"

Behind Cam a woman was coming to the door; she had short frosted-blond hair and held a cup of coffee in two hands. She poked out a friendly freckled face. "Hi, cutie!" she said. "Crikey, it's cold out here."

"Don't treat her like a baby," Cam said gruffly. "This is Gal. She's mature."

"Hi," Gal said.

"You can play with him if you want," Cam said. "It's fun to make him dance." She stepped out onto the porch in her bare feet, and as she approached the skeleton Gal let her eyes drift that way too, let them take in the legs and the long, intricate hand bones and move up to the frozen gape of a face. Cam started moving the skeleton's arms and legs around in a grotesque jig. "I'm freezing, give me some skin!" she piped in a high squeaky voice. "Poor James," she sighed in her normal voice. "His eating disorder got out of hand."

Gal reached out and touched a bone of the hand, but she was too embarrassed and too repulsed to play with it, or even to examine it, in front of Cam. Had it really once been a real person named James? She was dying to ask, but feared risking one of Cam's jokes.

Cam smacked him fondly on the shoulder blade. "I got him on Craigslist, from a former yoga teacher who used him to show her students their pelvic floor."

"Okay," Gal said.

Over the next few days Gal began to see skeletons and witches and bloody faces everywhere—in shop windows, on TV commercials, in the front of people's houses. The people in one house on her block hung a spiderweb made of string between two oak trees, a hairy plastic spider the size of a dishwasher suspended inside it. On the front lawn of a house on her school bus route, a headless scarecrow in faded overalls and a checked flannel shirt held his head—a pumpkin with a very surprised expression—under his arm. She didn't know what to make of the gruesomeness that had burst out all over; she could tell that it was supposed to be fun and make her laugh, but it didn't feel fun to her; instead it cast a shadow over her mind and made her move through her days with a sense of foreboding, as if anything she looked at might be gross and terrible. She studiously avoided looking at those houses as the bus passed by, busying herself with her backpack or her shoelaces, but she couldn't shake the feeling that her eyes might look inadvertently, or—and this fear grew and festered over the span of a single afternoon—that her mind would see them even if she managed to keep her eyes averted. At recess, one of the boys told a story about going into a haunted house and putting his hand in a bowl of squishy eyeballs, and several other kids yelled, "It's just peeled grapes!" The image of a bowl of eyeballs tormented Gal.

The next day, Ms. Wheeler told them to come to school next Friday in a costume for Halloween. Gal mouthed the word, her hands tingling. It was a holiday, like Purim. "I'm going to be a ghost!" someone hollered. "Whoo," he said, waving his fingers in the air to express how spooky he was.

She didn't know what a ghost was, although she reasoned that it must be part of Halloween. She thought of waiting till she got home and asking the uncles, but now that she knew a little bit about what she was dealing with, her curiosity became urgent, and she risked sidling up to Hannah as they were waiting for the bus. Hannah was the smartest girl in the class, and asked the best questions during show-and-tell. While most kids asked, "Where did you get it?" Hannah asked things like, "If you lose it do you think your parents will get you another one?" or, if someone brought in a book, "Do you like it better or worse than *Charlotte's Web*?" She was nice to work next to on a project, although she never went out of her way to make friends with Gal. She was friends with Sophia and Lexi and sometimes Ava.

"Hi," Gal said. Hannah greeted her and they stood for a few minutes before Gal mustered her courage and asked, "What's a ghost?"

Hannah turned to her with interest. She had pulled up her hood, and her nose was pink from the cold. "You don't know what a ghost is?"

Gal shook her head, her face growing hot.

"It's someone who died, and then came back. They can move through doors and walls."

Gal's eyes were moving in quick darts as she furiously thought. "What do they look like?"

Hannah pondered that one, her eyes cast up to the sky and blinking hard. "Well, when people dress up as a ghost for Halloween, they sometimes wear a white sheet, with the eyeholes cut out so they can see."

There was a pause. "But I think that's stupid," Hannah said.

"Me too," Gal said.

"Because that's not scary, and a ghost *haunts* people. A ghost looks like—" She screwed her face in thought, and Gal waited, tense with anticipation. "Well, I don't actually know what a ghost looks like, except that you can see through their body."

Gal had never heard of such a thing.

She tried to tell Matt and Daniel about the bowl of eyeballs during dinner, and they frowned and tried to understand as Daniel picked out for her the red peppers, her favorite part, from the salad. "What on earth is the child talking about?" Matt asked Daniel. He turned to Gal. "What is this 'bowl of eyeballs' of which you speak?"

"He was in a special kind of house," Gal persisted, her temper rising.

Daniel's face lit up. "A haunted house?" he asked.

"Yes!" she cried.

"Oh!" they exclaimed. Then Matt leaned forward urgently over his plate and said to Daniel, "Good God, has no one told her about Halloween?"

They looked at each other. "We are pathetic excuses for parents," Daniel said. "Not to mention for gay men."

"Why?" Gal asked.

"Why are we pathetic excuses for gay men?" Daniel asked. "Because many gay men have a special place in their hearts for Halloween."

"Why?"

Matt scratched his face. Since Jay's death he had stopped celebrating Halloween, cold turkey. It was just too painful. He'd buried Halloween deep in his mind, back in some spot near his spine that thoroughly numbed him. It surprised him every time how even that time of year could make him so very heavy and blank; how the sharper cold and the shrill caw of geese moving south, the early dusk, could strip away all the sustaining illusions that made it possible to do things like, say, move his legs to cross the street.

"Because . . . ," he said, and faltered.

"Gay men like dressing up," Daniel said. "We have a really good sense of humor, and we like to make funny costumes."

"People in Israel make funny costumes, too," Gal said in the argumentative tone that could drive Daniel off the deep end, "and they not gay."

"Okay, first of all, some of them *are* gay," Matt said.

Noam took a piece of the cheese slice he'd been eating and rubbed it in his hair. "Honey, just put it down on the tray when you're finished," Matt said, lifting him out of his chair and carrying him to the sink to wash up. Then he set him down on the kitchen floor, and Yo-yo came to clean up inside and under his high chair. The arrival of the kids had been a windfall for him, and Daniel had already put him on a diet.

"I want to have a costume of a ghost," Gal said. "I'm supposed to wear one for school."

"That's not hard," Daniel said. "We'll just get you a white sheet and cut out holes for your eyes."

"No," Gal said decisively. "That's stupid." She paused. "How you say *ghost* in Hebrew?"

"*Ruach refa'im,*" he said. "And you don't have to call me stupid. But I don't think it's the same thing. I don't think you have ghosts in Israel the way we do here. Do Israelis have ghosts?"

"How could you not have ghosts?" Matt asked.

"I wasn't calling *you* stupid," Gal said.

"Well, how do you want to do it, then?" Daniel asked.

"I supposed to be invisible," she said.

"That's the big problem," Matt said, scratching his head in mock perplexity. "How do we make a visible child invisible?"

"Maybe I won't go to school!" Gal shouted.

"Great idea!" Daniel laughed. "'Dear Ms. Wheeler, Gal couldn't be seen in school today, because she came dressed as a ghost. But I want to assure you that she was present, because Gal is a serious student who takes her attendance very seriously.'"

"I have to look like I died and then came back," Gal said.

Matt and Daniel studiously kept their eyes away from each other. Daniel thought: *What the hell is she supposed to do with that information?* He said carefully, "You know that there's no such thing as a real ghost, right?"

"Okay," Gal said.

Later, Daniel said to Matt, "I don't love this new compliant *okay* of hers. What does it even mean? It sounds as if she's saying that she'll play along with whatever horrible or confusing thing you throw at her."

"God, that's so true!" Matt said. "It's like *you* say, 'There's no hope left, there is no God in heaven or goodness in the world,' and then *she* says"—he made his eyes go blank and slackened his face in a spot-on imitation of her—"*Okay.*"

"So what do you think a ghost would look like?" Daniel asked her now.

She thought of Cam's skeleton and then her mind stalled out and she looked at him, finding angry tears gathering between her eyes. "I don't know!" she cried. "You tell me!" She stood, knocked her chair over, and ran out of the room. Noam looked up, startled, and began to wail.

"Here we go," Daniel said, sitting down heavily and patting his knees for Noam to come over.

Matt rose to clear dishes to hide the tears stinging his eyes. "I don't know if I can do this, Dan," he said.

"Let's think it through," Daniel said, lifting Noam onto his lap and grabbing the long transparent plastic tube with the tiny plastic beads that clattered down through a maze, and turning it vertically so Noam could watch them drop. "She needs a costume for school. That's the very minimum. And we should probably count on trick-or-treating, which means a costume for Noam, too."

"I don't think I can handle this," Matt said.

"I heard you," Daniel said.

"So can you take this one?" Matt asked.

"Sure," Daniel said.

"Thanks, honey," Matt said, his voice thickening as he loaded dishes into the dishwasher.

"Are you crying?" Daniel said. "Don't cry." He turned the toy upside down and inhaled sharply in mock surprise as the beads cascaded down again, making Noam laugh. "It's just such a huge bummer," he burst out. "She's totally weird and unpredictable, and now she's being totally morbid. What are we paying the damned therapist for?"

"It's Halloween," Matt said gently. "She's supposed to be morbid."

They were quiet, aside from the sounds of clattering beads, as Matt filled the dishwasher with soap and turned it on, lifted the tray off the high chair and brought it to the sink to wash off the tomato slime and seeds, and the warm, gunky cheese plastered to it. He wanted to thank Daniel more profusely, Daniel who wasn't good at crafts and preferred to leave that stuff to him, but he didn't want to press the volatile Jay issue. He ran the tray under the water, rubbing off the cheese with his fingernails, then shook it off and wiped it with a towel. He looked at

Daniel and Noam, who were watching the tube toy with lazy eyes and the same faint smile, Daniel barefoot in jeans and his Oberlin sweatshirt, the baby slouched against him. Noam's wispy brown hair was darkening, coming in the color of Daniel's, and his eyes, too; they'd become the chocolaty color that Matt had fallen in love with in Daniel.

"I'm going to encourage her to be something more innocuous," Daniel said, "like a Teenage Mutant Ninja Turtle or something."

"Dude, don't," Matt groaned. "That's so twentieth century."

"Or Pocahontas."

"Please."

"Then what? What's an appropriate and benign cultural figure?"

"SpongeBob," Matt said. "Any Harry Potter character. Batman. He's a classic—he never goes out of style."

"Okay," Daniel said, standing and lifting Noam into Matt's arms. "I'm going up. Wish me luck."

He tapped gently on the bedroom door and waited, but didn't hear anything. He opened it slowly and peered in to see Gal sitting crosslegged on her bed with her horses arranged around her.

"Hi," he said. "I have an idea." He came in and stood against the door frame, his arms crossed. "How about dressing up as one of the Harry Potter characters? You could be Hermione."

She'd been waiting for him to come, hoping he would, and now she was torn by the impulses to draw him in and push him out. If she closed her eyes, she could hear her father's voice, and it pained her to have this strange and difficult shadow-father instead of her real one. "I don't want to be a Harry Potter character," she said, pronouncing it scornfully with chewy American *r*'s, instead of the Israeli way with guttural *r*'s—"Herrie *Poe*-tair"—as if it were the English way that was bastardized. "I want to be a ghost."

She eyed him as he lowered his backside to the floor and sat up against the wall. "Why is that so important?" he asked. "You can be anything you'd like."

"I don't know why, it just is," she said. It was the one costume she knew for sure was appropriate, that was one thing. She feared that if she listened to one of his or Matt's suggestions, she'd be dressed as something that would make grown-ups laugh but kids wouldn't even know what she was supposed to be. And she'd looked forward to it! She had a vague but urgent sense that she'd be scary as a ghost, only scary in a way that was acceptable, even fun. Not scary as the girl with the accent, with no-heads parents. She imagined drifting through her school, Hannah looking at her with admiration for wearing something so much better than a white sheet.

"Can you explain why?" he asked. "If you could explain, I'd understand it better."

A hitch of ire, of defeat. *Takshivi la'milim sheli*—Listen to my words—it was something Sari, her teacher in *gan*, used to say, stooping and turning her face toward hers. Why did she have to explain it to him? Hadn't she already explained? She felt winded; talking to him was like trying to blow into a recorder, where you couldn't get your breath to gather into a note and all you could hear was panting and spit. "You never listen!" she said. "Forget it, I don't want your help!" She threw herself facedown on her pillow.

Daniel rubbed his mouth with two fingers, picked up a barrette from under his thigh, closed his hand over it, and looked at the cluster of totemic objects sitting on her desk among the messy piles of workbooks and the spray of pens and pencils: a tiny framed picture of herself with her parents, various rocks, beads, and small plastic animals, a flashlight powered by a hand crank, a coral bracelet Val had brought her back from a trip to Florida, a Lego helicopter. He wanted to help her, but everything he could think of he knew she'd reject. He proposed to himself that her difficulty was bigger than just one of arts and crafts, that it had to do with the concept of returning from the dead. Maybe it was his job to help release her from her painful fixation on that idea. That thought warmed in him and became pressing.

"You know that people don't come back from the dead, right?" he said gently.

"*Oof!*" Gal shouted. She rose abruptly and kicked over the little stool she used as a side table; her clock and cup shot across the room and the clock burst open as it hit the wall, its batteries clattering to the floor. "Why you keep saying that?" she screamed. "You say you're helping me but you're *not* helping me, you never help me!"

"Fine," Daniel said coldly. He got up and left the room, fuming, closing the door behind him, hearing her angry sobs as he went downstairs.

Matt had risen from the couch at the noise, and come to the bottom of the stairs. "What happened?"

Daniel moved past him and sank into an armchair, his face rigidly set. "Nothing. I'm a terrible person who refuses to help. A ghost? It's not even original."

"Did you say that?"

"No," Daniel said, indignant. "Why does everybody keep treating me like a monster?"

Matt regarded him thoughtfully. "I'll tell you what," he said. "I've been thinking, and I've made a decision." He paused for dramatic effect. "I'm going to pull myself up by my bootstraps about this Halloween thing."

"What?" Daniel said, mouth agape. He pounded himself on the ear. "I hear someone saying something, but it's very faint, very foreign, I don't know what language it's in. *Sprechen sie deutsch?*"

"Are you finished?" Matt asked. "Are you pleased with yourself?"

"Kinda," Daniel said.

"Okay, forget it then."

"No, tell me. Tell me your decision."

"Don't condescend to me," Matt said.

"I'm not. I really want to hear."

Matt's hands were on his hips. "Okay. I've decided to use the kids' presence as an opportunity to get over my Halloween issues."

"Really! Good for you, Matt," Daniel said.

Matt shot him a look, a spot check for condescension, and when he saw none, his voice picked up with eagerness. "Don't you think this is a good moment for it? I can honor Jay by channeling his spirit into the holiday. And what do you think about this? I'm thinking of calling Kendrick."

Daniel's eyes widened; this part took him entirely by surprise. "What for?"

"Just to get some closure on it. I ended things with him on such a bad note, and that bitterness isn't a healthy thing for me to carry around. It taints Jay's memory."

Daniel was quiet. He was remembering Matt's stories about Kendrick's self-important bustle around Jay, the way he instructed visitors on how they should behave at Jay's sickbed. Kendrick once gave Matt a list of topics he was not to raise—pets, parties, and the movie *Terms of Endearment*, to name just a few—and Matt had snorted, thinking he was joking, until Kendrick shot him a withering look. After hearing that, Daniel thought that the lengths Matt went to in order to stay close to Jay were nothing short of heroic.

"I know," Matt said. "Risky, right?"

"I don't know if it's risky," Daniel said. "It's just that I don't know if Kendrick's the kind of guy you can get closure with. He'll always say just a little something that'll piss you off, put a little bit of poison out there."

Matt nodded thoughtfully. "Maybe," he said. "It's just that I don't think Jay would want his partner and his best friend to be estranged."

"You're a generous soul, sweetie pie. I just hope it doesn't bite you in the ass."

The next day Matt and Gal went to the craft store, after Matt made her promise that she would not scream at him even if she thought he was doing something wrong; instead, she would explain her objection in a regular tone of voice. They bought gauze, and washable white and black paints for the as-yet-undetermined way they would paint her face. They decided that she would wear white, but not a sheet, white tights and a white T-shirt, and that whiteness and sheerness together would make her seem invisible. They practiced draping after dinner till they had Gal wrapped in a way that she could make the fabric ripple a little, yet still move and not trip. Then Matt said, "Okay, let me paint your face."

"What are you going to do?" she asked warily.

"Just let me do it." He raised his eyebrows when she hesitated. "I'm a trained professional. Just let me."

She came to him and lifted her beautiful face to him, its normal stormy twists smoothing into an obedient expanse of creamy cheek, her mouth closed over the adult front teeth that had recently come in and that her face had yet to grow into, her eyes hooded by her dark lashes. He rubbed a delicate wash of white paint over it, letting some skin show through, used just a touch of black paint to hollow out her eyes. Then he said, "Okay, go," and pushed her toward the mirror.

She opened her eyes and looked at him. "I scared to look!" she said.

He took her by the shoulders and marched her to the mirror and she opened her eyes and took in a breath. She lifted her gauze-covered arms, turned her whitened face this way and that. Her dark hair fell to her shoulders; she raked her fingers gently through the hair on one side and tucked it behind her ear, the first preening gesture Matt had ever seen her make. She turned and looked at him, nodded approvingly.

"Good, right?" he asked. "You look amazing. So much more sophisticated than your normal sheet-on-the-head ghost. Go show Daniel."

They could barely stop her relieved chattering to get her to bed; she made use of every adjective she knew in both English and Hebrew in an attempt to describe the effect of the costume. "It's spooky but not *scary*," she said, and then repeated that, enjoying the fine distinction. "It's sophisticated, don't you think? How do you say *sophisticated* in Hebrew? Where's Dani? How do you say *sophisticated* in Hebrew?"

MATT DECIDED TO DRESS Noam as Mr. Potato Head. "Did you know," he'd said to Daniel as he boned up on Mr. Potato Head on the Web, using the laptop they kept in the kitchen, "that on Mr. Potato Head's fortieth birthday, they announced that he would no longer be a 'couch potato'"—he made ostentatious air quotes with his fingers—"and he received a special award from the President's Council on Physical Fitness? That's awesome. I wonder if he had to do little pull-ups."

Matt spent the day on Noam's costume, sewing elastic into an old brown sheet to close at Noam's neck and thighs, gluing paper plates on for ears, and colored felt and cotton for the facial features. He went to three different stores looking for blue socks to put over Noam's sneakers. He bought a kid-sized hard hat and spray-painted it black. He worked in a swirl of quiet satisfaction, diligent problem solving, and blistering self-irony. He was spending the day making a little kid's Halloween costume. He was a stay-at-home mom—in the lingo of the blogs and message boards, a SAHM! It blew his mind that his life had led him to this point. Not that he was the most ambitious guy in the world. What was his ambition? For a while, at the New York firm among the design hotshots, he'd entertained the fantasy of becoming the next Carson or Sagmeister. But over time, working among incredibly single-minded and talented people, he was forced to admit to himself that while he was good, *very* good, he wasn't a design genius, and didn't quite have the drive and focus to convincingly fake it. The realization pained him, but it didn't devastate him. He liked his work, a lot, liked the quiet focus of it, the visual pleasure of something falling into place and the pride of submitting work that was clean and stylish and impeccable.

And let's face it, he thought, moving away from New York to live with Daniel, who had the talent to be a great musician and writer but who viewed ambition as frivolous and crass, pretty much put the nail in that coffin.

Still, what would he tell Kendrick about what he was doing these days? He gingerly peeled back one of the paper-plate ears, testing the dryness of the glue, wondering if he should put in a few staples for good measure. When identifying himself, should he say, "It's Matt," or "It's Matt Greene"? Should he just catch up with him, or should he actually say that he'd called to bury the hatchet? He reminded himself to stick to "I" statements, as he had been instructed to do in a brief and irritating couples therapy with a short-lived boyfriend. And if Kendrick was an officious fuck, what would he say? His mind ran over various options, honing their wit and cuttingness. Then he grabbed the phone before he could think anymore and dialed.

Kendrick answered on the second ring with a quick and intimate "Hi."

"Hi," Matt said uncertainly, thinking that Kendrick couldn't have recognized him from the caller ID, because their phone was listed under Daniel's name. "It's Matt. Greene."

There was a long pause.

"Jay's friend."

"I know who you are. I thought you were someone else." The voice was slightly peevish, slightly congested.

"How's it going?"

"It's going well," Kendrick said.

"That's great," Matt said. "I'm glad to hear that."

Kendrick didn't reciprocate, but then again, Matt remembered, he'd never acquired the skill of saying "And how are *you*?" If you wanted to say anything about yourself, you had to put a stick of dynamite in the conversation and blast right through it.

"Are you waiting for another call?" Matt asked.

"Yeah, I'm fighting with my credit card company about a finance charge," Kendrick said, "and we got disconnected."

Matt smiled, remembering how Kendrick made a point of keeping excellent medical and financial records, and making sure he didn't get overcharged or double-charged; he checked his credit rating obsessively for errors, and reported everything. "Because otherwise how will they learn?" Matt and Jay loved to use his mantra in their conversations.

"I wanted to call," Matt said, picking up a pen and starting to doodle on the little pad of paper sitting on the kitchen table, "because it's Halloween, which always makes me think of Jay."

"Oh, right," Kendrick said. "So where are you living again? Elmira?"

Matt smiled at the snobbery of the New Yorker. "Northampton. Massachusetts."

"Oh yeah, where all the lesbians are," Kendrick said.

"Right," Matt said. "I'm basically a lesbian now."

Kendrick laughed.

"Listen," Matt said, warmed by that, always a sucker for anybody who laughed at his jokes, "I just wanted to touch base, maybe bury the hatchet. I think Jay would want that."

Kendrick was quiet for a few moments. "Well, I appreciate that, I do," he finally said. "He wished we could get along better; it was painful to him that we couldn't."

"I know," Matt said, and continued to the line he'd practiced before calling: "It's just that—I think that we both loved him so much, and were in so much pain, that we weren't at our best with each other."

There was another pause, and then Kendrick said, "True."

"So I'm sorry for my part," Matt said, thinking that this was easier than he'd thought it would be.

"Thanks, Matt," Kendrick said. "Me too. It's just that— I don't know if I should even say this. No, never mind."

Matt's head rolled back on his neck and he closed his eyes. *Here we go*, he thought.

"It's just that—this may be a fault of mine, but I just can't pretend to be nice to people who hurt the people I love."

"What are you talking about?" Matt said while Kendrick continued, "And it really bothered me how bitchy you were to him for making money and being successful. It was like the minute he stopped being your sidekick, you couldn't handle it anymore. That really hurt his feelings, Matt."

"What are you talking about?" Matt repeated.

"Calling him a corporate tool . . ."

Matt cast his mind back, stunned. "That was a joke!" Matt said. "Jay called *himself* a corporate tool!" He worked in the finance department of Goldman Sachs, a job he had landed straight from college and been incredibly successful at.

"He didn't think it was funny."

"You're so full of shit," Matt said heatedly, propelled to his feet, pacing. "He never said anything to me about it, and believe me, he was no shrinking violet when it came to telling me my flaws."

"Forget it. I thought you wanted to have a genuine conversation, but apparently I was wrong."

"I sincerely wanted to make amends," Matt said. "I didn't call to get attacked by you. Jay and I handled our relationship just fine."

"He was *dying*, Matt! He wasn't about to start some huge drama with you."

Matt's mind was spinning. "Look, I don't have time for this. I'm living with a family that's been devastated by a terrorist attack, raising two orphaned children." He winced as he uttered the word *orphaned*.

"Whoa," Kendrick said.

In Kendrick style, as though devoid of the slightest bit of curiosity, he failed to follow up, leaving Matt to wonder if he was undignified enough to throw more unsolicited details out there himself. *You probably read about the Peace Train bombing in Jerusalem earlier this year. It was all over the papers.*

He hung up, sickened. The thought of trick-or-treating had been drained of all its energy and color. Once, he'd loved the huddle of citizens at dusk scurrying from house to house. So what if the occasional house got pelted with eggs, its trees draped with toilet paper? It was a day when Americans answered the door for other American strangers, which seemed marvelous to him. But now: he'd wanted to honor Jay this Halloween, but now he didn't feel like honoring him at all; he was furious at him for hanging on to that hurt and not telling him about it. It was so stupid—it felt petty and vindictive for him to play the game of calling himself a corporate tool and then turn around and complain to Kendrick about it. They'd both seen the absurdity of Jay's huge success at Goldman. Both of them had! This was the guy who had to ask his professors for extensions for almost every paper he wrote, who got behind in his bills, whose house was always a total mess. Then he turned around and got this high-paying job, and lived in the West Village in a building with a doorman, while Matt, in his first design job, lived in a studio sublet all the way over on Ninth Avenue, surrounded by someone else's crappy, tasteless things.

He did have to admit that he'd been jealous; he had never cared about money until he found he wasn't making very much, at least by New York standards. But he felt that he and Jay had managed that well, through the high-level aggressive irony in which they told each other truths they couldn't say more straightforwardly. Apparently he was wrong. And Jay had complained to Kendrick, not him. Of everything, that was the thing that sickened him most. He'd always thought of himself as closer in than Kendrick was, even though Kendrick was Jay's partner. They'd seen lovers come and go, and dished about them all, even to Jay's dying day, when they'd rolled their eyes together over some antic or other of Kendrick's. It was unbearable to think that Jay and Kendrick rolled their eyes about *him*. Unbearable. And he couldn't even conjure Jay to be furious at him, because most of his memories were of Jay after he was already sick, emaciated, with Kaposi's lesions on his neck and face.

THE NEXT MORNING WAS gray and cold; Matt, wearing only a sweatshirt over his pajamas, shivered as he yelled at Yo-yo to poop, knowing that if someone was yelling at *him* to poop, he'd never give them the satisfaction. Inside there was a squall of panic, yelling, and frenzied phone calls, because it turned out that Gal didn't know if they were supposed to wear their costumes on the bus to school, or bring them and put them on there. "What if I'm the only one on the school bus wearing a costume?" she'd asked, eyes wide in panic.

He hoped it was solved before he went back inside, and it was—at least the kids whose parents they'd reached would be wearing their costumes on the bus. Matt got busy working on her face. He waited with her in front of the house, said "Look, see?" when the bus pulled up, populated by kids in masks, capes, armored suits. "Just be careful not to step on the gauze," he reminded her for the tenth time. He watched her stomp up the big stairs and felt a pang, knowing he was sending her off to a world with so many land mines, knowing how hard she thought about every step she took, every word she spoke.

Daniel was waiting for him inside. "PHEW!" he bellowed, and they laughed. Matt followed him up the stairs as Daniel went to shave and dress for work.

Gal sat on the bus, adjusting the gauze around her, carefully checking out the other kids' costumes. Emma was dressed as Hermione! And James as Spider-Man. Ava, who brought tofu for lunch, was a kitty cat in a wool striped bodysuit, whiskers painted on her face. What a baby, Gal thought.

Did they know what she was supposed to be? She dreaded someone coming up to her and loudly asking, "What are you supposed to be?" A bigger boy, a third-grader dressed as a knight, stomped up to her row, examined her through his visor, and sat down without a word.

Ms. Wheeler was waiting for the bus, and when Gal stepped off, she said, "Oh, Gal, what a great, scary ghost you are!" and Gal watched carefully to see if she gave similar compliments to the other kids, which would mean she just said that to everybody. She turned at the doors and looked for Hannah but couldn't find her. She noticed that she was the only ghost, which first pleased her, because it might mean she was original, and then scared her, because it might mean that everybody else thought it was stupid. She went in and sat down at her desk, pulling at the gauze where it caught in the chair's joints, listening to the chatter of kids, holding herself in readiness to be addressed.

Ms. Wheeler was clapping her hands to get them to quiet down, and soon her tablemates jostled around. She peered around them, looking for Hannah, but couldn't find her. Hannah was absent today! She knew because Miles and Jake were both on Hannah's bus, and they were there. Maybe, she thought, Hannah had missed the bus, and her mom would come rushing in with her soon, a harried expression on her face.

Jake was a lion with whiskers drawn on his cheeks. "Gali pacholly," he said to her with a look of complacency. "You're the most ghost."

She looked at him with an uncertain smile, trying to figure out if he was teasing her in a nice way or a mean way. A minute later she thought that she should have made up some singsong nonsense, too. She mouthed to herself, *Jakie pachakie*. But by then they were lining up for a parade through the school, and Hannah wasn't there, and Alexis, who was dressed as a princess, was crowding in front of her. Gal felt herself jostled backward, felt a jolt of irritation. Alexis's princess gown trailed on the floor; Gal surreptitiously stepped on the hem. And when they began to walk, there was a rip, and then a howl.

"It was an accident!" Gal said.

Ms. Wheeler came hustling over to examine the ripped and dirty hem. "I'm sure Gal didn't mean to," she said, crouching in front of Alexis like she did when a kid was upset so she could look her in the face.

She hadn't meant to. She told herself that she'd meant just to pull it a little. But seeing Alexis glower tearfully in her direction, Gal decided that it didn't matter, because she was dead anyway, she was invisible, floating through the classroom and through the wall to the hallway, where she drifted, trailing a finger along the bulletin boards and the banks of lockers, looking down on them because they belonged to little kids, while she was so big and so old she was dead.

CHAPTER 15

I N THE DAYS leading up to her grandparents' arrival, Gal grew increasingly excited. Everywhere they went, she wondered aloud whether they'd like it there. A visit to a sushi restaurant gave loose to a torrent of speculation. "Do you think Sabba and Savta have ever eaten sushi?" she asked. She spoke in Hebrew now that Matt could understand most of what she said, although sometimes, when he missed a word but clung to the narrative for dear life, hoping the context would explain it, and then realized he couldn't do without the word after all and was forced to stop her, she heaved a mighty sigh and let out a long-suffering *Oof!* Matt relished the Hebrew he was learning, because it gave him an excuse to be rude. His favorite expression was *"Ma pitom!"*—which meant a combination of "No way!" and "What are you talking about!"—which he loved to exaggerate by uttering it with the loudest, most obnoxious heap of scorn. Or *"Nu?"*—uttered like an elbow to the ribs. He loved that, and he loved the difference in pronunciation between *chet* and *chaf*, the Sephardic *chet* being throatier, gaggier, as *ayin* was to *aleph*.

"I think Savta will love edamame, don't you?" Gal said now. "Because she loves little tasty things like that. Sabba, though, not so much. He likes chicken, and he likes cake. I really can't think of anything else he likes to eat. Oh! Watermelon seeds. I personally"—Matt's and

Daniel's eyebrows rose: *I personally?*—"don't like those as much as sun-flower seeds or pumpkin seeds, and when I eat them I just eat the whole thing, because they're so tiny it's not really worth it to get off the skin."

She paused, stabbed a piece of maki with a chopstick, stirred it in the cloudy soy sauce, and nibbled a tiny piece off the edge. "But to get back to Savta and Sabba," she said. "I thought I wouldn't remember them because I didn't see them for such a long time, but as you can see, I remember a lot! Hoo! Spicy!" She reached for her glass of water, gulped it down. "I like spicy foods even though I'm Ashkenazi, and Ash-kenazim don't usually like spicy food. Sabba and Savta *definitely* don't like spicy food." She cast Matt a warning look.

"Then we shan't cook spicy food," he said, responding as he nor-mally did, in English. "Any other instructions?"

Gal furrowed her brow and pondered. "You have to be nice to them," she said, her voice lowered. "They had a very hard life."

They looked at her and nodded. Daniel said, "We'll be very nice to them and make them feel very welcome, Gal, okay?"

"I really will make them feel as welcome as I can," Matt later said to Daniel. They were sweeping through the house as they did every night after the kids were asleep, tossing toys into the wooden blanket chest that had become a toy chest, picking up stray socks and jackets, putting the plastic keyboard with the mirror and rattle karaoke microphone, and the toy vacuum cleaner with the popping balls, and the musical phone on wheels with the popping eyes—rotary style, bells ringing as the rotary jiggered and the handset clunked along, a weird anachronis-tic appendage—into the corners.

Daniel had dug up his old copy of *Survival in Auschwitz*, and over the past week had been reading, flinching now and then at the marginal comments he'd written as a college freshman. "Here's the thing," he told Matt now, his hands and elbows crammed with toy pieces that had to be distributed to their proper toy. "People who survived didn't survive by putting down their heads and being invisible. They schemed, they bartered, they used—or often faked—certain skills, like metalworking or sewing, in order to get in with the SS. They walked away from the edges of a camp or a death march. They jumped into the latrine and hid in the shit.

"But there are also a ton of split-second decisions, sudden pre-monitions—get into this line, not that line! Or arbitrary events like being marched with a group up to the very door of the gas chamber, and a commander comes in yelling that it's the wrong group. Can you imagine the fucked-up messages you'd take from this? You have control over your own survival, and your survival is totally arbitrary. How are you supposed to go on after that, put one foot in front of the other? No wonder Malka loses her mind." He paused. "So you can imagine," he said, "what Israel meant to them."

"Totally," Matt said. "Israel was awesome because it nurtured the delusion that they had control over their own survival."

Daniel laughed. "I wouldn't have put it that way," he said, "but— yeah."

Matt stood and leaned back groaning, hands at his lower back, as Daniel put the plastic cake pieces onto the plastic cake dish, and two crayons into the big plastic bag of crayons, most of whose wrappers Gal had peeled off, in the art supply basket. "I'll be super nice and welcoming. But Jesus Christ, *more* parents? I'm dying here, Daniel."

"It's written into the custody agreement," Daniel said. He'd danced a tortuous and delicate dance with them over the course of several phone conversations, in which he invited them to stay with him and Matt and the kids, certain they couldn't afford two weeks in a hotel, but trying not to mention that fact, knowing that staying with him and Matt was a deeply unpleasant prospect for them. Because he felt that visiting their grandkids shouldn't be a huge financial drain. But he hadn't told Matt that; he'd told him that staying with them was written into the custody agreement. It was easier that way; he just didn't want to have to negotiate *everything*.

"I know! Stop saying that," Matt said from the playroom doorway. "It doesn't mean I have to be happy about it."

"I'm very aware of your feelings, Matt. I'm not exactly thrilled either, and it doesn't help for you to keep bitching about it."

"I'm not *bitching*, Daniel. I'm trying to say something serious." He stared at Daniel till Daniel turned and looked at him. "You know, I never expected to have kids, and that's turned out to be *fine*. It's having three sets of very present parents that's destroying my soul."

Daniel raised his eyebrows. "Destroying your *soul*?"

"Doesn't it bother *you*?"

Daniel shrugged. "I think the more people around, the less I dwell on things."

His honesty softened and disarmed Matt, who said, "Honey."

"But, hey!" Daniel said with a sudden bright idea. "Your Hebrew has gotten really good, so you can talk to them now."

"What am I supposed to talk to them about?"

They were quiet for a second, then Matt said, his spirits lifted because they seemed not to be fighting anymore, "How 'bout that Holocaust! That sure sucked, didn't it."

Daniel cut his eyes at him.

"Oh, is that one of those things I'm not allowed to joke about because I'm not Jewish?"

"Yeah, this might be one of those things," Daniel said drily. "Ask them about fighting for independence, that makes more sense."

"Hmm. So, how 'bout that *Nakba*!" he said, using the Arabic word for "disaster." "It sure sucked for those Palestinians to be driven from their homes, didn't it!"

Daniel shot him an irritated look. "Do you have to do that?"

"What?"

"You always take it a step too far."

"Please! It's not like you believe they were such cowards they just fled."

Daniel sighed. He had just one thing left in his hands, a plastic spotted dog that went with the Legos, and he tossed it into the plastic bin that held them. "It's one thing not to believe that, and another thing to drive the point home, over and over, all the time."

"You mean like the way gay people have to rub it in the faces of straight people over and over, all the time?"

Daniel groaned. "Oh God. That too! That drives me crazy!"

Matt stared at him. "Remind me why we're together again?"

"I don't know!" Daniel said. "Because you keep a lovely home."

"That's true," Matt said complacently.

"And because you deal with the other parents."

Matt thought about those conversations he had with some of the moms during drop-off or pickup from school, where they shrieked with laughter as though everything that came out of his mouth was a camp classic, and called him *darling* in affected theatrical voices. "Well, I'm their gay pet," he said.

He was finding that the why-are-we-together jokes were helpful, that if it was spoken aloud, the idea didn't frighten him so much. When they went upstairs to look at their closets and figure out how to make space for Malka's and Yaakov's clothes, and Daniel emptied his own closet because it was less full than Matt's, and because he knew how much it pained Matt to have his clothes mashed together in the downstairs hall closet, Matt thought: *Ha! Another reason.* Then he was depressed that he was thinking of reasons at all.

His new strategy was to stop acting as though he wanted sex, to hold himself proudly aloof. Brent had laughed when he told him that. "Aloof?! That's not really your thing."

A SNOWSTORM WAS FORECASTED for that night, but it looked as though Malka and Yaakov's flight would just squeak in before it arrived. Daniel took Gal down to pick them up in Hartford, while Matt stayed home and put Noam to bed. Gal was pensive in the car, and Daniel peeked back at her periodically in the rearview mirror to see her gazing out the window, where she'd wiped a clear circle into the fog. It was late, past her bedtime, and her eyes were puffy. A cold sleet was falling; the dusk traffic was heavy; the wipers left a streak across the center of Daniel's vision. The billboards imparted messages from grocery stores, from jewelers and ophthalmologists, of holiday faith and goodwill, the kind of messages that always made him grateful he was Jewish, and therefore not implicated. Gal was relieved to be on vacation; she continued to find school a strain, which pained him. He suspected that as a bilingual kid whose English was still developing, she wasn't considered one of the smartest kids in the class, which was probably excruciating for a superquick and competitive kid like her. What was happening socially, he didn't know; he just knew that she didn't bring friends home, or ask to go over to kids' houses.

He made the perilous merge into Springfield traffic. An enormous Santa and reindeer in lights lit up the office buildings and parking garage to his left. He glanced back again in the rearview mirror and saw Gal drawing imaginary letters on her pants, spelling something out.

The flight from Newark was half an hour late, and they had to wait in a stretch of airport with two rows of four chairs set against the wall, and no shops or restaurants except for the ancient cafeteria, which was already barred shut. Daniel cursed the fact that he hadn't brought anything for them to read or do. He took a stray section of the *Valley Advocate* from the sole empty seat and sat on the floor, facing a monitor, his back against a wall. Gal scuffed her boots along the airport's carpet and watched the people emerging from the gates. "They're not on this flight," he told her. "They haven't landed yet."

"*Oof!*" She wheeled around and scuffed away, and he watched her take a very long drink from the water fountain. She came and asked if she could ride the escalators, and he said he'd rather she didn't because he wouldn't be able to see her when she was downstairs. "You will if you stand at the top," she said. He sighed and stood, and she rode down and back up, down and back up again, solemnly. The thought of seeing Sabba and Savta made her shiver, as if she were under a billowing silk cloak, dark and dangerous and beautiful, waiting for it to drape over her. She tried to conjure their faces. She remembered the constellation of pocks on Sabba's cheeks, and the way she could see his thick tongue resting behind his bottom teeth when he laughed. She remembered the soft feel of Savta's shoulder under a cardigan and her baby powder smell, and then a very clear memory popped out, Savta looking at her with a strange expression, saying, "You are a miracle, you and your brother both. You were not supposed to be born." That had made Gal uneasy even though she didn't know what it meant exactly, and she'd somehow known that it wasn't something she should ask Ema about, because Ema would be mad. She pondered this for a moment, and then her mind moved deftly away from it, concentrating on stepping on and off the escalator at the right moment.

When the flight from Newark finally landed, it seemed to take ages for the passengers to deboard, and by the time people began trickling through the exits, first one or two and then bigger groups, Gal was grinding her fists into her eyes with peevish exhaustion, and Daniel was suddenly finding things wrong with the way she looked—her face white with exhaustion, her hair ratty, a shoelace untied. He actually had a comb in his coat pocket, but he didn't dare bring it to her hair. He detested himself for his worry about her appearance, but he never forgot that his guardianship of her and Noam was provisional.

Then she squirted out from under his arm and ran toward the elderly couple in enormous coats that was coming through the door. They bent over and caught her in a hug that made the people around them smile, exclaiming, "You came!" and "You're still awake? You must be so tired!" The duty-free shopping bag looped over Malka's arm slipped to the floor, along with her purse, and Yaakov stooped to pick them up, then took his beaming granddaughter into an awkward hug, the bags banging on Gal's back.

Malka was wiping tears from her eyes. Daniel hung back, smiling, pained as he felt the reunion from their perspective. They were wearing new matching parkas, shiny navy blue, bought for a harsher winter than they were accustomed to, and carrying shopping bags and plastic bags that looked as if they contained a hundred tin foil–covered paper plates of mandelbrot and rugelach.

They came up to Daniel and he had a moment of uncertainty: kisses or handshakes or neither? Yaakov extended his hand with a bluff, mirthless "Shalom, shalom," and Daniel shook it, saying, "Welcome." Malka lifted her face, with its delicate web of lines, to kiss his cheek. "I look at you and I see your brother, even though you've grown so skinny," she murmured.

"Oh, not that skinny," he said.

She gave him a keen appraising look, very Israeli, and said, "You're really very skinny."

Their suitcases, which Daniel hauled off the carousel, were ancient paisley canvas, pre-wheels vintage. By the time they got to the car, he was panting and sweating, cursing himself for being too cheap to rent a luggage cart. It had begun to snow.

MALKA AND YAAKOV REFUSED to take the master bedroom, insisting that he and Matt sleep in their own bed. Matt and Daniel brought every argument to bear they could. The only TV in the house was in their room. It was so much more private! It was warmer up there! They wouldn't have to share a bathroom! But they were adamant that they didn't want Daniel and Matt to go to any trouble. So Daniel and Matt carried all the clothes back into their closets and re-set up their toiletries in the master bathroom. "This is making more trouble," Matt said. "They'll be in the middle of the house all day, every day."

"Don't," Daniel said. "I'm trying to keep up my morale."

Malka and Yaakov carefully hung up their clothes in the front hall closet. Then Daniel came down and helped them blow up and put sheets on the air mattress, while Gal sat on the couch, gazing at her grandparents beatifically. "I'm so glad it's snowing outside," she said. "Because that's something you don't see in Israel very much."

It snowed all night, the huge, silent flakes that cluster in a moment on hair and eyelashes, and when Matt and Daniel awoke it was still snowing. "Great," Daniel sighed, his heart sinking at the thought of a day at home with grandparents and children. He called the college weather line, which informed him that nonessential personnel did not need to report to work, and as the children slept, he and Matt turned on a local news station without the sound and watched the school closure tickers. They could hear movement downstairs, the toilet flushing, the ding of the toaster. "There," Matt said. "Closed." There was no sound from the kids' room, so they sank back under the covers, Daniel draping his cold legs over Matt's warm ones, and sank back into a rare morning sleep.

Gal awoke buoyant, taking in the snowstorm and the warm, full house, and ran downstairs, where Malka and Yaakov sat at the kitchen table with toast and coffee. She buried her head in their laps and chests and let them stroke her, and showed them how she knew how to make her own breakfast of cereal and milk, with a banana cut on top. She ate with relish, milk slopping over the spoon, talking with her mouth full about snow days and the kinds of things American kids did in the snow.

AT FIRST MATT AND Daniel enjoyed the new and improved Gal, cheerful and cooperative—the "Sure!" that met her grandparents' suggestions or requests. "I'll get them!" she'd yell when Yaakov patted his shirt pocket for his reading glasses, and off she'd go. She talked to Noam in front of them in a fulsome loving voice, and volunteered to set the table every night.

"What!" Daniel and Matt would jocularly exclaim. "Who are you and what have you done with our Gal!" After a while, though, Matt confessed to Daniel that he was finding it a little creepy. "It's just not her!" he said. "There's something about it that makes me sad."

"Really?" Daniel said with surprise. "I think she's just happy to have them here."

Matt shook his head. There was something about them that made you lurch to take care of them. To the naked eye, they were just old folks who drank tea, had a passion for Sudoku, and watched the American nightly news, translated by Daniel, with clucks of the tongue and shaking heads, invariably asking if this or that public figure was Jewish. Their pills and vitamins lined the windowsill above the kitchen sink, doled out carefully by Yaakov every morning. They had set up a five-hundred-piece jigsaw puzzle of a Swiss chalet surrounded by wildflowers on the dining room table, and Malka and Gal worked on it for half an hour before bed, Malka sitting with her glasses on her nose, patiently trying this piece and that, Gal pacing around the table mumbling to herself: "There!" and "*Yofi*, Savta!"

Maybe, Matt thought, it was the way they never asked a follow-up question—so when Gal told them about getting one hundred on a spelling test, they didn't ask what the hardest word was. The bottom just dropped right out of the conversation. Or maybe it was the way there was never the right amount of food in the refrigerator. When Daniel went grocery shopping with Malka, he came home with twice the amount of food he normally did, and then, when the refrigerator was full to bursting, Malka anxiously exhorted everyone to eat the food before it went to waste. "What did we buy this yogurt for, if nobody's going to eat it?" she'd demand. She peered into the pots as Daniel or Matt cooked, and asked whether they were sure there would be enough, whether they should take a bread out of the freezer to supplement the meal. And then, at the end of every meal, Yaakov groaned, "Why did you let me eat so much?" and spent the next few hours with his belt unbuckled, complaining of gas.

It was hard, when Matt and Daniel fell into bed at the end of the day, not to attribute their behaviors to their childhoods in the Holocaust, even though that felt weirdly hushed, ghoulish, fetishistic. They knew only what they'd heard from Ilana, or heard from Ilana via Joel, who said that the information Ilana had was itself spotty and contradictory. She knew, he told them, that her parents didn't want her to know about their lives in the Holocaust, and she wasn't even sure how she did know; she felt as though she'd learned by osmosis. Then she pretended that she didn't know.

They knew that Yaakov had been a child in the Lodz ghetto; that he'd survived by looking bigger and older than his ten years and being sent to work in a Nazi metalworking factory, and by running with a pack of teenagers who stole and shared food. His parents and his two younger brothers had not survived. The aura he projected around them and around Malka was that he was surrounded by a pack of incompetents—lots of condescending laughter and put-upon sighs at the way they blundered. "Do you think he acts that way because everyone around him died?" Matt asked. "Because they just weren't competent enough to stay alive?"

"Beats me," Daniel said. "But the food thing is definitely about having been a hungry kid."

He and Matt peered up at the ceiling and blinked, their minds working at what profound hunger would be like for a child, imagining against their wills being unable to feed Noam and Gal.

One night after the kids were asleep, Daniel invited Malka and Yaakov into the living room to have a conversation about Noam's developmental delays. He sat with a glass of wine in the wood rocker, while Malka warmed her hands around a mug of tea and Yaakov shifted beside her on the couch in a posture of uncomfortable readiness. He'd never had a serious conversation with them by himself, or a conversation where everyone was on the same side, and he found himself turning toward Malka; it was just impossible to maintain eye contact with Yaakov. "He's twenty-one months old now," he said, "and he isn't walking yet or saying very much."

"He's such a good boy," Malka said. "He seems calm and contented."

Daniel suddenly remembered something Ilana had once told him—that Malka hadn't grown up around other children and had never had a normal childhood herself, so when she had Ilana she was at a loss. Ilana said she remembered quite clearly that when she became a toddler demanding independence and throwing tantrums, it was very frightening to her mother.

"I know. We love him very much," Daniel said, conscious of using the word *we*. "There doesn't seem to be anything wrong with him physically. Our pediatrician wanted him tested for neurological disorders and autism." As he said that, he saw Malka's eyes fill with tears. "But till now, we've refused. We think he has suffered very badly, and because he doesn't have the words for what he lost, this is how we're seeing it. But now, more months have passed, and we might have to reconsider."

"*Misken*," Yaakov said. "Poor little boy. So once again, the Arabs finish what the Nazis started."

"Yaakov," Malka murmured.

"You're very right in what you're doing," Yaakov said. "You must stand strong. The doctors have no idea what they're doing."

"Do you need a new doctor?" Malka asked.

"We don't think so, but honestly, we're not sure."

"Maybe you should take him to a specialist," Malka said. "To a . . . what's it called?" She turned to Yaakov, snapping her fingers to bring on the word. "A neurologist."

"They don't know what they're talking about," Yaakov said bitterly. "They think that if they have a fancy degree, they can take the measure of a child who has suffered—who has suffered beyond what they can imagine."

"But maybe the child—"

"The child is fine!" he snapped.

Malka sat back on the couch with a look of resignation and folded her hands. "Okay," she said, her mouth pursed. "I just thought—"

"You thought, you thought!" Yaakov mockingly smacked his hand against his forehead. "That's the trouble, you thinking!"

Daniel felt the blood rise and burn in his face. "I thought it would help me to have this conversation," he said coldly, standing, "but I see I was wrong."

Yaakov's face worked; he put his fingers to the bridge of his nose.

"He's sorry," Malka said. "This is sad, about the child. And with the birthday coming up." Ilana's birthday was in a few days, and they were all dreading it.

"He's not the only one who's sad, Malka," Daniel said.

"Shh, shh, I know," she murmured.

CHRISTMAS CAME WITHOUT NOTICE by anyone but Matt. He drove to Derrick and Brent's house on Christmas Day, listening to holiday songs on the radio, thinking that he didn't really mind missing Christmas in this household of Jews but that he did kind of mind their not noticing that he was missing it. The day was gray and the streets were empty; clusters of cars were parked askew in people's driveways. Derrick and Brent had gone to Derrick's sister's in North Carolina to visit the nieces and nephews, and he was supposed to stop in and feed their two beautiful and haughty tortoiseshell cats, Miles and Ella, twice a day. He parked on the street and let himself in. Their condo was in downtown Northampton, a small but pristine two-story apartment back by the fire department with a galley kitchen whose space they maximized by hanging their pots and pans from a rod they hung from the ceiling, and a living room with a bay window with a bench along it, which was padded with bright cushions and pillows. They'd left the radio on low, and it was playing classical music. Two champagne flutes stood upside down in the dish dryer; the news of Brent's tenure had come right before they left. At the sound of the can opener, the cats sauntered into the kitchen, chirping, and wound themselves around Matt's legs.

He watched them eat for a few minutes. Then he opened the cabinets and contemplated. Derrick was a vegetarian, and glass jars of pasta and grains, some of which Matt didn't recognize—bulgur? quinoa? farro?—lined the shelves in austere harmony. On the top shelf there was a box of schoolboy biscuits covered with dark chocolate, and although Matt preferred milk chocolate, he took out two and ate them, then opened the fridge and swallowed some milk out of the carton. He looked at the calendar hanging on the wall and saw all the dates Derrick and Brent had made in December with other friends. Steve and Bruce—he'd met them once at a concert—were marked down three times, the third time as *S&B*. They were getting ahead of him and Daniel, he thought with anxious rancor. Were they still Derrick and Brent's best friends? Well, it wasn't Steve and Bruce they'd asked to feed the cats, he thought. Surely that meant something.

THE EVENING BEFORE ILANA'S birthday, Matt and Daniel went through the photo albums with Gal and Noam, Noam making the rhythmic *scritch-scritch* sound of hard pacifier sucking, Gal all interruptions and whipping hair and knees on the page and knocking the wind out of them with hard plops onto their laps.

The birthday fell on a Saturday, and after breakfast Daniel gathered them in the living room, where they sat in their separate spaces with their feet on the ground and hands in their laps, made self-conscious by the aura of solemnity. On the coffee table he'd set the most recent photo album, the one taken after Noam was born. He had set a yarhzeit candle beside it, which Yaakov objected to, since it wasn't the anniversary of Ilana's death. "I know, Yaakov," he said, "but I wanted a memorial candle." Gal was cross-legged on the floor, and next to her, Matt sat with his legs spread, Noam between them, playing with a stacking toy.

Daniel scraped a match against the box and it flamed, and nearly went out as he brought it to the candle's wick; then they both blossomed into a glow. They watched the candle wobble in its small glass. "Can I speak about a memory?" Daniel began in Hebrew, leaning against the wall, his arms crossed. "Well, my brother was always a pretty happy guy—successful, tons of friends. But when he got together with Ilana, it was different. His eyes glowed as if he had a special secret. He looked satisfied, completely comfortable in his skin."

They sat in awkward silence for a few minutes, until he said, "That's all." Then Malka reached over and pulled Gal onto her lap on the couch. "I remember, like it was yesterday, the day you were born. Of course, your *ema* read all these books about childbirth, and had ideas of how she wanted it to go. Very strong ideas, as she always had, you know her.

She had a CD she made of songs celebrating life, and children, and the waves, and new beginnings, and when she got to her room at Shaare Zedek they told her the CD player was broken! I thought she'd be furious! She worked very hard on that CD, and wanted you to come into the world with those songs in your ears. But she gave a big laugh and said, 'My first lesson in having children! It just doesn't always go the way you think it will!' "

"Really? She said that?" Gal said, craning around to look into her grandmother's face.

"Yes, she said that. I was so proud of her. She was such a wonderful mother. She loved you two more than anything in the world."

"Yes, she did," Yaakov said. "But for some reason I remember her most as a little girl herself. I remember teaching her to ride a bike, how she howled and howled till she could do it by herself. She was like that with everything—crawling, tying her shoes, every new thing she had to learn, until she learned it, she made our lives miserable. And then suddenly: sunshine! 'And I love you, Abbaleh, and I love you, Shmabbaleh.' " He said that last in a high-pitched, grateful, obsequious way that made Gal laugh and Daniel narrow his eyes, hearing the derision in it, milder and more comic than the derision he'd aimed at his wife, but there just the same.

Then it was Gal's turn; she saw them look at her. She looked at the picture of her mother, looked at herself in the picture, her hair plastered by drying seawater across her forehead. These days she was having more and more trouble remembering her mother, which she kept secret from everybody, even her grief counselor. What remained were tormenting snatches of sense memory: being lifted under the armpits and rising into the air, the pain of a comb being pulled through her hair, her mother's arms bobbing on the water as she encouraged her to swim to her, ballooning huge in the water's reflection, then contracting, the feeling of dark and thunder when her mother was displeased. But no funny stories. Nothing she could tell.

Matt and Daniel were looking at her with unbearable sweetness;

her grandmother's chin rested on the top of her head. Finally, Matt's eyes narrowed. He turned to them with a bright expression on his face. "I have a story," he said.

They looked at him with surprise.

"I know I came late into Ilana's life," he said, blundering forward in Hebrew, "and didn't know her very well, but wow, she made a big impression on me! I remember the first time Joel and Ilana came to visit us here. I was waking up, and I heard yelling downstairs. So I stayed, cowering, in the bedroom. I thought they were having a big fight. I didn't want to interrupt. *Lo na'im!*" He spoke with élan and many hand gestures, stumbling over this word and that, gripping his upper arms with his fists and shivering to convey his fear, suddenly worrying even as he was telling it that his story might be a little inappropriate. It was the familiar feeling of the blurter: he was into it now, and he'd gone too far to turn back. "Finally, I came downstairs and approached the noise, and when I went into the kitchen I saw that they were just having a conversation!"

It didn't go over very well. Malka and Yaakov were looking at him with amazed puzzlement. He was telling Ilana's parents that their daughter was loud. He was a gentile telling Jews that they were loud.

For her part, Gal was still lost in thought, staring at the framed photograph of her mother till her vision blurred, trying to think of something to say. And then it came to her, descended upon her like an angel's touch, and she looked up brightly. "I want to go back to Israel and live with Savta and Sabba," she said.

In the few seconds before the din of dismay and confusion set in, Matt felt relief: This certainly overshadowed his inappropriateness! Then Yaakov slammed his hand on the table, making them all jump, stood abruptly and walked out of the room. Malka squeezed Gal and rocked her, her chin still on her head, her eyes shut. Daniel slumped in his chair with a stunned expression.

Matt stood and went into the kitchen, which held a big messy pile of syrup-covered plates, coffee mugs, a griddle glistening with the residue of melted butter. There were a few cold pancakes left on a plate, and he picked one up with his fingers and tore it in quarters, dragged a piece through the syrup streaks on the top plate, wadded the sweet mess into his mouth. Then he ate the other three quarters as well. From the other room he could hear Gal talking excitedly, saying "No offense," her favorite new expression. "I love you and Matt and Yo-yo. I just think Noam and I should be in Ema's family. Don't you think Ema would be happy if I was?"

Matt found the screw top to the syrup bottle, set it on top, and twisted it closed over a ring of sludge. Then he sighed and headed back into the living room.

"Actually, I don't, sweetie," Daniel said. "Ema and Abba wanted you to live with us, and we have to honor their wishes. And we went to court, and the judge agreed that you and your brother should live with us."

Matt turned around. Gal said, "But back then, I was still pretty little, and didn't know how to talk to him myself. Maybe we should go back to the judge and this time I'll talk to him." She was still sitting on her grandmother's lap, and Malka was pressing her lips against the side of her head, whispering, "Shh, shh." He saw that Gal didn't look so much defiant as exalted, although uncertainty was beginning to cloud her face. The front door slammed: Yaakov taking Yo-yo out for a walk.

"There aren't any do-overs," Daniel said evenly. "The judge thought very carefully about what's best for you, and once he made his decision, we had to obey him. Otherwise we're breaking the law."

Matt opened his mouth with the urge to say something like, "But we understand how much you love Sabba and Savta and how nice it is to be with them," then closed it. It wasn't really his place. Instead, he asked, in Hebrew, "Malka, would you like another cup of coffee?"

But she was standing. "There's no reason to be cruel," she said to Daniel. " 'Breaking the law'?"

"That's true, Dani!" Gal said. "There's no reason to be cruel!"

Daniel turned to Matt with a shrug of puzzled and angry dismay.

"It's a hard day for everybody," Matt said.

Gal was sitting by herself on the couch now, crying. She'd tried to make a grand gesture, Matt thought, now sitting heavily beside her, and it had given all the grown-ups a heart attack.

"Oh, sweetie," he said.

THE NEXT MORNING THEY couldn't get Malka out of bed. She lay on the air mattress with her hand splayed over her face, emitting an occasional animal whimper. Yaakov was up and dressed in stocking feet, his steely gray hair standing up, hovering over her with a cold washcloth and a mug of warm tea that shook in his hand. "She has a migraine," he told Daniel.

Daniel nodded, studying them for a moment. They were ashen, both of them. From outside, he heard the loud rumble of the garbage can being wheeled to the curb by Matt. "Let's move her into our bedroom," he said. "Don't say no." And he ran upstairs to change the sheets and straighten up, thinking with strange excitement as he pulled down the fitted corners of the clean sheets, which smelled of a long stay in the linen closet, that this was it, one of Malka's famous breakdowns. Not that he wished it upon her—God, no—and not that he wished it upon Gal, either. And yet, if Gal witnessed her grandmother's incapacity, surely his and Matt's guardianship of her would be settled in her mind, once and for all. And then he berated himself for even having that thought, for who wanted her to accept being in their family because all other options were closed off to her? At six years old?

He grabbed their shaving kits and toothbrushes and toothpaste, the hairbrush and hair gel, brought them downstairs and piled them on the bathroom sink. Matt was stomping his boots on the kitchen entry mat to rid them of snow, then bending to take them off, when Daniel hurried into the kitchen. "You went outside without socks?" Daniel said, as a bare foot emerged from the first boot. "You're nuts."

"Tell me about it," Matt said, giving it a rueful rub.

"Hey, listen, it's happening. One of Malka's breakdowns." Matt looked at him sharply. "Yaakov is calling it a migraine. But I'm pretty sure."

"What should we do?" Matt asked.

"I'm clearing out our bedroom and bathroom so we can move her up there."

"Okay. Do you need help?"

They spoke with quiet urgency. Daniel was imagining Matt stepping into the room where one person was disintegrating and the other was trying to hide it, and apparently so was Matt. "I'm going to leave the house," Matt said. "Not because I don't want to help."

"Okay."

"Because I don't want to add stress to them."

"I know."

Matt looked at his watch. "Yo-yo!" He reached for the leash as the dog came into the kitchen with a quizzical wag.

"Get socks!" Daniel said.

"Believe me," Matt said. They looked at their watches again and agreed that Matt would be home in half an hour.

Back in the living room, Yaakov had gotten Malka into a sitting position, and the kids were sitting on the floor on their heels, watching gravely. "Savta has a migraine," Gal announced. "That's a horrible, horrible headache."

"I know," Daniel said. "So we're going to give her mine and Matt's room, because it's darker and quieter."

Malka was in her nightgown, her feet bare; Yaakov had placed her bathrobe over her shoulders. Her eyes were closed, the lids translucent, and the skin on her face sagged, drawing down the corners of her mouth as if gravity had fought energy and brutally pummeled it. Daniel's impulse was to act quickly, to move this frightening, spectral version of her grandmother away from Gal, and yet, even a few feet away from her, he felt the energy draining from his limbs. He sat down beside Malka, and although a feeling of entropy made him wonder how he'd ever get up again, he draped her arm around his shoulders and helped

Yaakov hoist her off the bed. "Stay down here with your brother," he told Gal sternly.

They brought her upstairs and laid her on the bed, and hastened to cover her with the comforter. Daniel pulled down the blinds, and turned to Yaakov. "Tell me what you need," he said.

"Take away your razors and medications, your scissors and clippers," Yaakov said. "And then go. This happens. I'll stay with her."

Daniel looked at him doubtfully. "Lech!" Yaakov barked, flapping his hand toward the bathroom door. Daniel saw that he was ashamed, and angry at Daniel for witnessing his shame.

"Okay," Daniel said gently.

He got a plastic grocery bag from under the sink and gathered all the sharp things and all the medications into it. Then he went downstairs and peeked into the kitchen. Noam had climbed into the Tupperware drawer, and Gal was feeding him Goldfish crackers, placing them onto his orange, gummy tongue, saying, "Don't worry, Noam."

Over the next few days the house was so silent they became aware of the refrigerator hum, the water in the pipes, the infuriating tinny whine of the cable box. They spoke in quiet voices that barely rose from their throats, and leaned toward each other to hear. Everything had to be murmured twice or three times, as though it required a running start before the noise it made could heave itself into something intelligible. They awoke from restless sleep with headaches, blaming the barometric pressure that had brought in unseasonable warmth. Yaakov shuffled in his slippers back and forth from the kitchen to the bedroom, bearing tea and toast Malka didn't touch. Matt and Daniel privately wondered whether she needed to be hospitalized and put on a drip for nutrition. They heard Yaakov moving around at night. In the daytime he fell asleep in the living room rocker, snores blubbering out of his lips. He was both less himself and more himself, Daniel thought. Quieter and more shadowy. But also, the sole, stern sentry, the last competent man on earth.

Gal squatted on the rug and watched him. His chin was squashed double against his neck; his big hands had lost their clasp at his lap, and now the lifeless fingers barely touched. She could see his chest rising and falling above the gut that pushed out his shirt. She had seen Savta sick once, when she'd gone over to their house with Ema. While Ema argued with Sabba in the kitchen, Gal crept into the bedroom. Savta was under the covers, her face as bleached and immobile as stone in sun, and Gal focused fiercely on her chest to see if it was moving. For a second, terror plunged through her. But there—there was the faintest of movements. She imagined Savta in a pile of corpses. She wasn't supposed to know about the pile of corpses, she was pretty sure. Was it cold in there, or warm? She imagined it having this same sick smell. That night, in bed, and for many nights after that, Gal practiced breathing so shallow nobody could see her chest move. She could do it about five or six times before she needed to gulp in air, and felt its clean, beautiful swell inside her. *C'mo gal*, she thought. Like a wave.

DERRICK AND BRENT RETURNED home, and Matt and Daniel planned to spend New Year's with them. But that evening Daniel felt he couldn't leave the kids alone with their grandparents, given Malka's condition, and he didn't want to bring a babysitter into this situation either. He sent Matt over alone, saying, "You have to go, we haven't seen them since Brent got tenure," and promising a thousand times that he didn't really care about New Year's anyway.

When Matt arrived, he could tell Brent was already slightly drunk: his cheeks were flushed and his eyes narrowed and a little watery. Soon he would become cuttingly observant and funny. He also had a tendency, when drunk, to climb onto Matt's lap and kiss him wetly, wondering with sentimental fervor why they'd never gotten together.

They toasted his tenure with tequila shots and beer. "Really, honey," Matt said. "Knowing you can stay here—whew! Because what would I do without you?"

"No kidding," Derrick said. "I was all, 'I can move, my job is portable'—but really, I didn't mean it, I was just trying to be supportive."

Brent laughed. "You talk a good game, Mr. Man, but I saw through that one."

They sat on stools at the kitchen ell, and Matt filled them in on Yaakov and Malka's visit while they winced and sighed. They ordered in pizza, and after they'd eaten, they went into the living room and sprawled out. There was a party Brent had heard about, some rich guy on Pomeroy Terrace, and they'd go in a little while. They watched a *Project Runway* rerun, a challenge in which the designers had to create looks out of salad vegetables, and then another reality show in which contestants apparently made famous from other reality shows were given a series of team challenges on an obstacle course. Matt was deeply relaxed, for the first time in weeks, sunk into an easy chair with a cat on his lap, Derrick and Brent on the couch with their legs draped over each other. They pondered the reality show convention of being challenged to eat disgusting things like insects and maggots, and decided that it was some kind of commentary on Americans consuming such a huge share of the world's resources, although what kind of commentary, they weren't sure. Around eleven thirty, they looked at their watches and at one another. Derrick stretched and groaned, settled more deeply into the couch. "I can't do it," he said. "Too tired. Too old. You guys go. Do you despise me?"

"Yes, we despise you," Brent and Matt said in unison. But Brent wasn't up for going either.

Matt stared at him in exasperation. "Well, as intrigued as I am by the idea of a rich guy on Pomeroy Terrace," Matt said, "if you're not going, I'm not going. I should go kiss Daniel at midnight anyway." He stood and got his jacket. "Thanks for letting me celebrate with you."

He hugged and kissed them both, and stepped out into the Northampton night. Christmas lights from the fire station dotted his peripheral vision and glinted from the puddles; mist rose from the huge piles of melting snow that had been plowed into the meridian, giving the night a billowy movie set feel. He walked through the wet streets of downtown with an unzipped jacket and ungloved hands, stepping around groups of teenagers and families celebrating First Night.

He wasn't in a hurry. He was drunk, and the night was comfortable, and the air cooled his face. Music—bluegrass, swing, zydeco—emerged from various events in the buildings around him. His boots made a pleasing noise as his heels ground the wet, gritty pavement. The house would be quiet by now, Malka and Yaakov huddled under the spare comforter in the dark bedroom, Daniel asleep on the air mattress unless one of the kids was up with nightmares. He thought of the house, the people in it, and it tilted in his mind till he saw it from the perspective of an alien observer. It was a box full of strangers. Strangers: Somehow, out of its billions and billions of people, the universe had hurtled these six from the plots of earth they were born and lived on, across the seas, over the prairie, and into the very same set of rooms. The randomness of it blew his mind. He thought: There wasn't one of them he'd have chosen under normal circumstances. Even Daniel. He was glad he'd chosen him, but he had to be honest about it.

A notion on the very surface of his mind, separate from thought, made him turn toward Pomeroy Terrace instead of toward home. He picked up his pace, his mind nowhere, his will glimmering in twitches of his muscles like the faintest of radio signals, until the sound of dance music and the sight of cars crammed next to each other at the curb indicated which house it was. It was a huge purple Victorian he drove past almost daily, and the party was in a turret.

Inside, a techno baseline thundering in his ears, he nosed his way toward the bar, sidling past clusters of men talking loudly over the music and laughing. The house was broken into several condos, but even still, this one was huge, with lustrous oak floors. He nodded at a colleague of Brent's whose name he'd forgotten; some guys from the gay runner's group he'd run with a few years ago; Jeff Schafer, another designer he knew, who occasionally referred work his way. There were women here and there, spiky-haired, short-skirted, lipsticked—straight, he assessed— but it was mostly men, as though a gay scene had popped up out of nowhere, like those barns and castles and old-woman-who-lived-in-a-shoe shoes that rose, looming and latticed, out of the pages of Noam's storybooks. On the windows, heavy flowered curtains hung from iron rods curiously hammered and curlicued at the ends. Built-in bookcases soared to the ceiling. An enormous flat-screen TV broadcast a New Year's countdown show with the volume off; it was six minutes to midnight.

Who on earth owned this place? Matt found the long table serving as a bar and poured himself a vodka tonic, found a strip of lime next to a wet paring knife and squeezed it in, feeling it bite at a tiny cut on his thumb. He drank it quickly in order to re-kick-start the buzz that had faded. How had he ended up here? He was still wearing his jacket; he would stay for just a few minutes, absorb it as a strange tale he would tell Daniel tomorrow, the story of a gay wonderland that had sprung up in the middle of honest, lesbionic Northampton. The sight of full-speed flirting—bursts of fake laughter, voices brimming with irony, eyes careless and languid and calculating, or darting to gauge the impression a joke had made—made him feel superior, repelled; at the same time, taking in the rich tones of male voices and male scent made him giddy. He quickly finished his drink and poured himself another as people started gathering in front of the TV screen, counting down. At midnight, they gave out a shout and started hugging and kissing.

Happy New Year, Daniel, he thought. *Let's hope it's an improvement on the last one!* He was dying for a cigarette; his eyes sought out and found a pair of elegant French doors leading out to a deck. He went outside with his drink, trying to pick up the smell of cigarette smoke, the glow of an ember. The house was on a fairly busy street, but back here it was quiet except for the occasional celebratory burst of honks from passing cars. On a separate level of the deck a few steps down, a canvas cover wet with melted snow and plastered with dead oak leaves stretched over a hot tub. The bare branches of trees waved gently in the misty sky. There was a couple making out, hands clutching. A man stood smoking at the corner of the wood railing, and as soon as he saw Matt zeroing in on him, he laughed and held out a cigarette pack.

"That obvious, huh?" Matt said. He set his drink on the railing and pulled a cigarette out of the pack, leaned forward as the guy reached toward him with his hand cupped around the flame of his lighter. He was drunk by now, and as he lightly touched the man's hand and drew on the cigarette, he was fully cognizant that he was an utter cliché of a gay man on the prowl, only somehow that very awareness made it unreal, the way a stick figure gestures toward a portrait, or a portrait gestures toward the living, breathing human face.

"Happy New Year," the guy said. "I'm Andrew."

"Matt. Happy New Year." He drew on his cigarette and exhaled with pleasure. Through the dim reflected light coming through the French doors, Matt was taking in this guy's particular brand of beauty. He was bigger and younger than Matt, full in the face; in middle age he'd be cursing what would become a double chin, but now that fullness made him look younger rather than older, at once angelic and sensual. His eyes were clear and wide and he had the expression of someone on the verge of laughter, or amazement.

"Can you believe this place?" Andrew said. "Apparently there are seven bedrooms upstairs."

"You're kidding," Matt said, his heartbeat quickening gleefully.

They drifted back in, languorously, "to explore the house," Matt thought merrily, fingers making big cartoon scare quotes in his mind, and found that people were clustered around the bar, heads thrown back, lips sucking, throats working. Jell-O shots! He slid his way in. They had been set out in trays, artisanal, glistening in layers of fluorescent colors, as gorgeous as tiny pastries, or jewels. He lifted one and Andrew lifted one, and they brought them to their noses first, then their tongues, and then they slurped them down. They looked at each other with narrowed eyes, evaluating: Matt tasted a complicated mix of tequila and lime, and was that something spicy? His tongue and palate tingled on the perfect edge of the pleasant-unpleasant continuum. He ate a pellucid champagne shot with a raspberry suspended in it, and reached for another, this one in the shape of a tiny house. It dawned on him: It was *this* house!—with gables and turrets—the owner must have had them specially made. *Good for you, bucko!* he thought, biting into the house, sucking it in and feeling it slide down his throat. By now he could no longer parse the flavors; they were too layered, too subtle, and his mind was rapidly losing its capacity to make fine distinctions.

He felt fingers touching his own, and a gentle tug; Andrew was leading him away, and upstairs.

The bedrooms were up in the turret, and looking up into the domed ceiling above them, which was whitewashed and crisscrossed by silver braces, Matt grew dizzy. There weren't seven bedrooms, but there were five. Five bedrooms: Matt's mind held on to that as though he might be tested on it later. He stood at the doorways while Andrew went in and handled things: bed ruffles, picture frames, jewelry boxes. Was he going to steal something? Matt wondered vaguely, but it seemed that he was mostly just a toucher. At the doorway of one of the smaller bedrooms he heard a murmur: "Check this out." The clunk of a latch being lifted, then a curve of a tight, patterned shirt as Andrew ducked into a small trapdoor opening in the far wall. Matt looked quickly around the hall, feeling like a cartoon spy, or a cat burglar, then slipped into the room and bent to enter the small space. He expected to be entering a roughed-out storage space, full of suitcases and mouse droppings and milk crates filled with old record albums, but when he heard a tiny click and light warmed the space, he saw that it was somebody's hideaway, with a love seat, a tiny table, and a tiny lamp with birds and butterflies painted on the shade. Even where the roughed-out ceiling peaked highest, it was too cramped to stand. It smelled of wood chips.

"Whoa," they breathed.

They fell onto the couch and kissed the jarring, tooth-clashing kissing of urgent strangers, hands clutching each other's hair. Andrew's lips were full and dry, his breath raucous from cigarettes and alcohol, his tongue a little rude. They pulled down their pants, awkward in the tiny space, seams and belts scraping their thighs, then collapsed back onto the couch, looked at each other nose to nose, eyes crossing, and laughed.

Matt's body absorbed the weight of the man on top of him, the cool scented air, the silence that swathed them after the noise of the party. They kissed and kissed, to the sounds of their own breathing and grunting. Matt's hard-on was warm and rosy. It was exciting to be with someone larger than he was, to watch his face become blind and bloated with need.

Andrew slipped onto the floor and turned Matt away from him, and Matt felt Andrew's fingers slide down his back to his ass. His fingers, and then his tongue. This was a new development; he stiffened with shock and pleasure, feeling himself fondled, tasted, handled like an intriguing object on a dresser. He heard a rip of foil and the snap of a condom. He heard Andrew whisper again, felt the press of his hard-on against him.

"Wait," Matt murmured, his mind arrested, a swamp animal popping its head out of the ooze. Andrew was nuzzling his neck with his lips, stroking him, sliding in by small degrees. He was using lube, thank God; Matt wondered where he had stashed it in those tight pants. He couldn't do this, he knew. One part of him was pulling away; the other was experimenting with just one more moment, one more moment before it really counted. His life outside that tiny room had dimmed and fallen away. Matt breathed and tried to open up, leaned into the pain, leaned into it till it became a glowing ember instead.

He let it happen. He let himself be carried on waves of pleasure, like a sloop, by gentle thrusting. And then it stopped. "Don't stop," he croaked, and then he heard Andrew say, "Shit." And then, fumbling, "Shit. The condom broke."

Matt groaned and rested his head on his forearms, his body tense and hungry. He waited for Andrew to pull out, but he didn't; instead Andrew's arms came around and slid under Matt's shirt, stroked his nipples, his belly. He kissed, and then bit, Matt's shoulder blade. When Matt tried to break away, Andrew's arms tightened around him. He was whispering something, holding Matt down, his breath hot on Matt's neck. Matt made out the word "please," which brought another piercing surge of pleasure. Held by a determined man in this sighing, enfolding space, he felt as if he might fly apart at the seams. He closed his eyes and let his mind swirl, felt a grand, gorgeous submission swell over him. He felt Andrew move inside him again, harder this time, then faster; felt his fingers gripping his hips, and then there was a cry as he came. They rested there for a moment, Andrew's body heaving on top of his. Matt heard the high faint whistle of his own orgasm, approaching and then blasting through him like a blaring bass beat from a teenager's passing car.

He lay wasted and pulsing. When Andrew pulled out of him he was overcome by relief and then a sadness so pungent it made him want to cry. *Daniel, see?* Those were the words that glinted in the dim light of his mind. *This* was a real conversation, *this* was being intimate with someone. He was shattered. It was all he'd ever wanted.

His cheek was pressed into the rough weave of the love seat, his heartbeat swishing in his ear. He was nowhere. *Maybe I'll stay here forever*, he thought.

CHAPTER 16

M ALKA AND YAAKOV left two days after New Year's, in a cloud of shame and regret, Gal clinging to them and weeping as they entered the security line, Noam taking his cue from her and letting loose with a fake melodramatic wail. Daniel held Malka's hand in both of his own. "Thank you for coming," he said, his voice raised over the noise of the crying children. "You are welcome anytime." *No matter how you feel.* He wanted to convey that, but she'd recovered only enough to rise from bed and totter tentatively through the house, as though moving through a new element with precarious footing, and he thought he'd mortify her if he actually said so. Instead, he held her hands for an extra moment, then pulled her toward him into an embrace. He squeezed her before letting her go, and she patted his cheek.

"*Yalla*, let's go," Yaakov said. He shook Daniel's hand with the same hearty evasiveness he'd greeted him with, and let his grandchildren hug him before kissing each on the head, rising, and taking Malka's elbow. "Until Purim," he said, and Gal said, "Until Purim." That was when they planned to go back to Israel for the children's mandated yearly visit, and for a memorial for Joel and Ilana.

They watched them stop in front of the first security guard, and Yaakov handed Malka their passports and tickets. They watched him help her off with her coat, and lay it on the conveyor belt with his own, and then, one at a time, they went through the metal detector and disappeared in the crowd of people on the other side.

"Oh, I'm so sad," Gal said as Daniel shepherded her toward the exit, Noam in the stroller in front of them. "I already miss them so much!"

As they stopped at the elevator and Gal pressed the down button, and he made sure the children's coats were zipped, Daniel imagined Malka boarding the plane, sitting down, closing her eyes, and waiting for takeoff. He could see her prepare—which she did perhaps better than anyone else—to sit quietly, hands in her lap, as they tore loose and roared into the sky.

IT SNOWED AND WARMED, then snowed and warmed again, so that it became treacherous to walk outside, and everybody tracked sand inside the front door, an irritant when they walked barefoot or in socks. Gal went back to school after the Christmas holiday, and without her grandparents to come home to, the household felt smaller and more tenuous. Her birthday was approaching, another event to dread and to get through. Her grandparents were going to come, but she didn't want a party with kids. Dani kept asking her if she was sure, and each time he asked, anxiety and embarrassment crept over her because she didn't have any friends. Except Rafi, who didn't really count because none of the girls in her class had a boy for a best friend, and because he was deaf. Dani said she used to have lots of friends when she was little, but it was hard to conjure that person; when he showed her the album of her kindergarten class, the faces gazed out at her, impassive, patterns of light and shadow, each called something that felt like a label on a picture. Peggy said that she did still know how to make friends, she was just dealing with a lot, and that the first year of all the big events and holidays without her parents was the hardest. Dani said that they could just invite her whole class, but she didn't trust him to throw the right kind of party, whatever that was.

She was pretty sure Grandma and Grampa were going to get her horseback riding lessons, and that was the one thing she looked forward to.

WHAT GOT TO MATT was having done something he couldn't tell a soul about, used as he was to enjoying events in retrospect, in storytelling, almost more than he did at the time itself. If he could tell someone about it, he thought, he could work through its strangeness, the sense of radiant connection it had given him. He could work through what had made him cave the very first moment having sex without a condom had presented itself to him as an option, after so many years of disapproval for those who did it. At times, as he worked, his mind drifted back to the party, and he could hardly believe it had even happened. Then he remembered the sensation of being looked at with such intense desire, of being grasped in a man's arms, and he thought he understood what Jay and all the reckless men he'd known and disavowed were searching for.

When he had come to, Andrew was gone. Matt had risen and pulled on his pants, ducked through the little door and into the dark, silent bedroom and hallway. The party was over, and he felt his way down the stairs on the toes of his boots, his heart hammering when the steps creaked, into the living room, then rushed for the door, certain that he would be confronted by a haughty guy in a dressing gown demanding an explanation. He slipped out and closed it as silently as he could, fled down the front porch steps into the neighborhood. He still felt noodly and stoned, a little nauseated, and the night air coated his hot face. He expected to be stopped by the police at any moment. It wasn't till he was six or seven blocks away that his heart slowed.

At the dark doorway of his house, he'd fumbled with the keys, turning and holding them toward the streetlight a few houses down, till he found the right one. He shushed the dog and went into the living room as quietly as he could; he waited till Daniel stopped shifting at the noise, then slipped quickly into the bathroom. In the shower he soaped copiously between his legs, winced at the sting around his asshole, worried that he was torn. The adrenaline was wearing off, and he could feel the soreness at his chin where Andrew's beard stubble had rubbed him, bruises at his knees where they'd pressed into the floor. He had been keeping his mind intentionally blank, but as he rubbed himself briskly with a towel, his body felt something coming on, and by the time he was beside Daniel in bed, the sheets clinging to his still-damp body, a great cloud of fear swarmed over and deafened him. What had he done?

Now Malka and Yaakov had gone, at least, and the house was beginning to feel like theirs again. Every single day Matt enjoyed being in his own bedroom, enjoyed going downstairs to make breakfast for the kids and not having to make conversation with anybody but the dog. When everybody had gone—to work, day care, school—he took his second cup of coffee up to his study and played computer games for half an hour before getting down to work. He'd bought a new pair of small, high-end speakers for the computer, and he played music turned up loud, the way he'd worked as a young man, singing, embraced and stirred by the clear, powerful sound. Lydia and Sam were coming in a few weeks for Gal's birthday, but they were staying only for a few days this time, and in a hotel, and he thought he could manage that.

The bruises had faded, his chin healed. Most of the time now, the encounter seemed very far away, and his body chaste and contained. Did it have to have happened? Did the reality held in memory have to translate into a raw, physical event at a party somewhere? Wouldn't it exist only if they insisted it had?

A FEW WEEKS LATER, Gal stood with Lydia and Sam inside a drafty paneled room, breathing in the smells of hay, horse sweat, manure. There was an old oak reception desk in the front with an appointment ledger flopped open upon it, its pages a mess of scribbles in pencil and pen. Farther in, a few adults and kids sat at the edges of cracked leather couches, in a sitting area with tack hung on the walls, horse magazines splayed on trunks and tables, a fire going in the fireplace. Gal stuffed her coat in Lydia's arms and looked the kids over. She was in a beginner class with three other girls and one boy. Two were wearing jeans and sneakers, and her confidence wobbled for a second: Were they dressed wrong, or was she? But the others were wearing jodhpurs and boots like she was. She'd gotten them, and a helmet, as presents from Matt and Daniel this morning, her birthday.

Their teachers were Briana and Shannon, Briana a ponytailed teenager with a quick smile, Shannon older, weathered, a little stern. It was Shannon who took her into the stall to meet her horse. It was cold, and their breath mingled in the air. "This is Caesar," Shannon said. She explained how Gal should never stand behind a horse, always by its side or shoulders, and cross to the other side in front of it instead of behind. "Don't even do it once," she said. "Don't think, 'Oh, no one's looking, I can just slip around him this one time.' Horses can be unpredictable, and they can kick you to kingdom come." Caesar bent his face down toward her and snorted, and Gal touched the impossibly soft skin around his nostrils. "We call a brown horse with a black mane and tail a bay," Shannon said. "Now, Caesar here is a bit of a clown, and if you let him get away with it, he'll do all kinds of shenanigans. So I'm assigning him to you, because you look like a girl who doesn't take nonsense from other people. Am I right?"

Gal didn't know what shenanigans were, but she did understand nonsense, and the way Shannon described her set off a little rush of delight and pride.

Shannon set a footstool near Caesar's neck and gestured for Gal to step up on it. She left the stall for a second and returned holding a bridle by the crown. "I'm going to show you how to bridle him. You're a little short, so I'll do the top part. Here's your job: putting the bit in his mouth. It's the hardest and most important part of the process."

She showed Gal how to hold the bit in front of Caesar's mouth, and slip her thumb into the back of his mouth. Gal felt the warm slime of his spit, the spongy tongue. He shifted with a groan. "Slip it in!" Shannon said, and she did, feeling it clonk against his teeth, then settle.

"Nice work." Shannon put the crown over his ears, showed her the correct tightness of the throat latch. Gal wiped her hand on her pants, then surreptitiously gave it a smell. If she had to go home right that moment, she thought, she'd have had a fantastic time.

They saddled Caesar, Shannon inviting Gal to run her hand between the cinch and his gut, to see how tight it should be. Then she led him from the stall and tied him in the barn's big hallway, and boosted Gal up onto him. Dizzied by the unexpected height, Gal gripped his mane, but Shannon showed her how to gather and hold the reins, how to pull back to stop him. There were three already mounted as well, but Gal tuned them out, sat back, and reveled in stable music: the saddle's creak as she shifted on it, horses heaving and snuffling, the *slap slap* of the straps as Shannon adjusted the stirrups, Caesar's munch on the bit.

Five helmeted kids rode in circles in a chilly ring, Shannon and Briana calling out instructions from the middle, stopping them sometimes to demonstrate on one kid the way the foot should sit in the stirrup, the height at which the reins should be held. Shannon said, "Horses are flight animals, not fight animals. Do you know what that means?" Parents lined the sides of the ring behind the barrier; Gal glanced at Sam when she passed him, got a thumbs-up. She nudged along Caesar's immense body with her heels and thighs, swaying with his rhythms, feeling the pull in her calves as she strained to keep her heels down, the jolt of the trot that yanked her forward and made her teeth clatter till she could get into a posting rhythm for a second or two before her tailbone smacked back onto the saddle. She watched the swishing tail of the horse in front of her, which lifted for a moment as its anus turned inside out and released steaming grassy turds. The cold encased her cheeks and fingers; she felt the bones in her butt and the warm rub on her crotch, saw her breath materializing in front of her. And when she'd dismounted and Shannon took Caesar's bridle and saddle off and handed her a curry brush, she brushed his coat where it was dark and wet from the saddle, stroking hard with the grain and grooving fine lines into the hair, then moving to his rear and brushing, dust and dirt motes swirling in the air, till she was sweaty and her arms ached. Briana brought her a carrot and showed her how to offer it to Caesar, and Gal laughed as his big lips scrabbled on her open palm, and he chewed it with a deep meditative grind. When she rejoined her grandparents in the reception area, she was beaming. "Did you like it?" they asked, and she flung her arms around them. "Bye, Shannon!" she yelled as her teacher came up to the desk to look at the schedule, and when Shannon looked up and her scowling face broke into a smile, she thought: *She smiled at me!*

After dinner the grandparents and uncles and Rafi and Yossi sang her the Hebrew happy birthday song, and they had a chocolate birthday cake Daniel had made. Yossi handed Rafi the present they'd brought and nudged him toward Gal; he thrust it toward her with a grin. It was two costumes, a police officer and a pirate. Gal and Rafi dressed Noam in the pirate costume, then took turns arresting him in severe authoritarian voices. It was native Hebrew Gal heard from Rafi, but slightly distorted. When you told him something, your words spooled out there and maybe they clicked into the machinery of his ear and maybe they didn't. He always had a slightly distant look, as if he were trying to remember where he'd put his shoes; she thought he might be a little slow, but Matt told her he wasn't. Sometimes she took his chin in her fingers and turned his face toward her before she spoke.

A package from her Israeli grandparents had arrived a few days ago, and Daniel had hidden it till now: it contained bags of Bamba and Bisli and Israeli chocolate and biscuits. There was quick, intense negotiation: Did she have to share with Rafi and Noam, even though it was her birthday? She got a lecture about how, even though she technically didn't have to, it would be nice of her to share, and she and Daniel reached a compromise: She would split one bag of Bisli with the other kids. She ripped open the bag and counted out four for Noam, and while she kept

a sharp eye on how many Rafi took, they gorged on the primordial flavors of home.

AFTER THE KIDS HAD gone to bed and his parents to their hotel, Daniel
came into the bedroom, where Matt was sprawled on the bed, watching
TV. He lay down next to him, moved into the crook of his arm. "Hi,"
Matt said.

"Hi." Daniel took a deep breath and let it out, closed his eyes and
curled against Matt, his knee sliding over his legs. Matt patted his arm
absently.

It was the laziest feeling, Daniel's head light and tingly, his prick
pressing against his jeans, his legs weightless. He moved his hand onto
Matt's thigh and ran it lightly up to his crotch, touching his jeans very
very lightly. "Phew, what a relief," he murmured.

Matt raised an eyebrow. "What, getting through the birthday?"

Daniel rose and leaned over him, touched his lips with his, then
pressed harder. Matt felt the familiar gentle query of his tongue,
breathed in the familiar smell of his breath, which still—after all this!—
triggered all kinds of pheromonal happiness, and thought about a silly
conversation they'd had when they'd started sleeping together, a conversation that had led through the giddy, winding road of older man/
younger man teasing, to his giving Daniel an A-minus grade as a kisser.
Daniel had reared back in laughing indignation, and asked, his lashes
still lazy from the kiss, "Why, pray tell, the minus?"

"*Pray tell?*" Matt said. "Okay, that just brought you down to a B-plus."

They'd been kneeling on the bed, undressing each other, and Daniel sat back on his haunches with a haughty look. His shirt was unbuttoned, half-revealing the delicate brush of dark hair around his nipples,
the cleft between his breasts, and his surprising, disarming, little-boy
belly button. "You need to modulate better between wet and dry,"
Matt said, with the air of the connoisseur. He himself was a world-class
kisser, thank you very much.

Now Daniel's hands were in Matt's hair, and he felt himself enormously touched and disquieted. The house was quiet, other than the slurp of the dog washing himself on the floor and static from the baby monitor. Matt's mind began to race through all the things he knew about what was safe and what wasn't, wondering if he could limit this to oral sex, thinking about all the nicks and cuts on their dry winter hands. He could do that, and not tell Daniel.

But when Daniel said, making light of it, "Do you still remember how to do it?" he imagined doing it without telling him, with a condom; he imagined—well, all of it, the whole sweaty, teary, exultant thing, up to the point of Daniel curling up and passing out. He swiftly tried on the idea that in not volunteering the information, he wouldn't be exactly lying to Daniel, the kind of lame sophistry that had served him pretty well when he was younger, and a jerk. But he knew he wouldn't be able to live with himself if he didn't tell him. Even though Daniel had pushed him to the last extremity by denying him all this time and making him feel like shit for wanting him in the first place, and even though he, Matt, deserved to be cut a ton of slack for performing sensationally well under the pressure of this new life. He defied anyone to have done a better job as a partner and a parent! But after all they'd been through, it just seemed tawdry to lie.

Crap, after all these months, who knew that Daniel would suddenly be horny?

"Dan," he murmured. "Honey." He closed his eyes, steeling himself, and turned on the light to Daniel's blinking, rosy, hungry face.

Matt struggled to a sitting position. "Daniel," he said.

Daniel murmured, ran his hand up Matt's chest under his T-shirt.

Matt clasped his hand, over his shirt. "Honey." The word came out hoarse, so he cleared his throat and said it again; this time, as he pressed it out of his throat, it came out loud and harsh. It made Daniel sit up and look at him, his face questioning and a little irritated.

"I don't know how to say this," Matt said.

Daniel was quiet, waiting.

Matt swallowed, feeling blood beat against his face. "It's a really hard thing to say," he said.

Daniel's face grew alarmed. "Are you breaking up with me?"

"No!"

"Phew," Daniel said.

"But this might make you want to break up with me."

Daniel sighed. "Then will you just tell me? What, did you bareback or something?"

"Yes," Matt said.

Daniel snorted, then, seeing Matt's face, grew serious. "Seriously?"

Matt nodded, then rushed to add, "Well, it wasn't really barebacking—the condom broke."

Daniel was bewildered. "Where?"

"At a party."

The words were so strange, it took Daniel some minutes to understand what Matt was saying. *At a party*—what on earth?—it still felt theoretical, as if his mind was testing what it would feel like to hear those words and to attach them to an event. Then his face grew hot, as he felt the rejection, the sheer *No, I won't* response to his advance that he heard, primitively, as *No, go away, disgusting, it's not you I want, it's someone else.* Mortified, he pushed himself away and went into the bathroom and closed the door. Matt pulled the covers over his knees, tense and watchful, only half-resigned to the anger he knew he deserved and was trying to get ready to absorb. His bare feet were cold.

Noam gave out a cry, magnified to a yowl by the monitor. Matt got out of bed, grabbed two pacifiers from the dresser, and went down to his bedroom, where he put one in Noam's mouth and one in his hand. These days Noam slept with three pacifiers, two stuffed dogs, and his special blanket, and Matt wondered if he was waking more often because he had trouble hanging on to all of them at once. On the way out, Matt stepped on two of the pacifiers that had made their way out of the crib, and took them back into the bedroom, where he determined to sit and wait for Daniel to emerge and respond.

Daniel was sitting on the toilet with his head in his hands, his mind blank. It seemed as if it would take a tremendous effort to make it produce a thought, and that it just wasn't worth the effort. He'd think about it after his parents left. He knew that it was bad, very bad; he could also sense, if not quite make contact with, the minor-key pleasure of being aggrieved and in the right. Other than that, all he could feel was his left leg getting numb. And his swollen, itchy eyes.

Matt turned on the TV, but without the sound, so Daniel wouldn't accuse him of checking out during a fight. He held the remote with his thumb on the power switch, ready to turn it off the moment he saw the bathroom doorknob turn. Twenty minutes passed, and a new sitcom cycle began, and still Daniel hadn't emerged. "Daniel?" he called, then, when there was no answer, he went to the door and slowly turned the knob.

Daniel was still sitting on the toilet, sleeping.

Matt roused him and led him to the bed, turned back the covers for him. "Don't touch me," Daniel mumbled, getting into bed and curling himself into a ball facing away from Matt's side.

Matt awoke the next morning with the knowledge that he'd have to face Daniel's wrath, not to mention the last morning of Sam and Lydia's visit; he groaned and rose to get the baby's bottle. Daniel got up and got into the shower, and all through breakfast—which was taken up by Lydia's exclamations of "I'm going to miss you so much!" and Gal's "I'm going to miss you even more!"—he gave him the cold shoulder. Matt wanted to talk about it—they needed to—but they couldn't yet, certainly not till Lydia and Sam had left.

After they'd all left the house in a flurry of kisses and "I love you's," Matt went upstairs to work. He sat down and booted up his computer, and instead of opening his design software, opened the word processor and began composing an email message to Daniel. He caught a whiff of Lydia's scent on him from their good-bye hug. Maybe he'd send the message, maybe he wouldn't, he thought; but he had to write it.

"Daniel," he began:

I can't tell you how sorry I am about what I did. I knew
the minute I got back home that I'd done one of the worst
things I've ever done. I feel like a huge hypocrite, and a terrible
partner. I want to explain how it happened, but I don't think
you'd particularly want to hear about it. If I'm wrong about
that, let me know.

It's just, I love and miss you so much, and the less
contact I had with you, the more intense contact it seemed I
needed. Okay, I just explained how it happened, when I said I
wouldn't.

He wiped his eyes with his sleeve.

Anyway, I hope we can talk. I miss that too, it seems like
all we talk about these days is the kids. And I hope you can
find it in your heart to forgive me. Not right away, of course, I
don't expect that.

I love you, honey.

He sent it before he could second-guess himself, and then, exhausted,
took a nap on the couch, his coffee cooling on his desk.

When he awoke he immediately checked his email; there was no
response yet. He went downstairs and got himself a fresh cup of coffee, came back up and checked his email one more time before getting
down to work. Over the course of the day he logged back onto his email
account incessantly. He knew Daniel hadn't responded in the morning
because he had a meeting, but as the hours went by, he realized that
Daniel was going to let him flap in the breeze.

MATT PICKED UP NOAM from day care, arriving home as Gal was getting off the bus. "Take off your shoes," he said as she pushed inside,
backpack sagging on her back.

"I'm starving," she said in Hebrew.

He sat her down at the kitchen table and gave her a granola bar and a glass of milk; hair in her eyes, feet swinging, humming something tuneless, she dunked it and ate the wet parts in tiny rodent gnaws. Matt lifted Noam into his high chair and cut up a banana onto his tray, watched him mouth a piece off his palm. "Use your fingers, honey," Matt said, picking up a piece. Noam had the small-motor coordination to do that, but still ate baby-style a lot of the time, one of the many small things that continued to make them anxious about his development. *You'd better not leave me alone with these kids*, he silently warned Daniel. It was something he said whenever Daniel set out for work, alongside *Drive safely*. But now he caught himself: Daniel was more likely to *take* the kids than to leave them with him. Waiting for a conversation with him was like waiting for a verdict, head spinning, mouth dry. Daniel hadn't called, hadn't let him know when he'd be home, and Matt had decided the only thing to do was to keep moving; if his life wasn't going to be normal, he was going to put his head down and pretend it was.

He was cubing tofu for a stir-fry and working himself into a state when he heard the key at the door, then the clatter of keys on the counter. He was too afraid to look up. But then he heard footsteps recede: Daniel was going upstairs.

Gal drifted into the room. "I hate tofu," she said.

"Actually, you don't," Matt said, his knife gliding through it. He would fry it till it was golden, add garlic and ginger and soy sauce.

At dinner, Daniel was a model of smooth parental dedication and guidance, but his eyes glided over Matt without seeing him, like skis in glassy waters. Did the kids detect the rage under that warm surface? They didn't seem to: Gal was letting Daniel draw her out about her day at school, where one boy had gotten in trouble for calling another boy fat, and a loser.

"He *should* get in trouble," Daniel said, and although Matt agreed, the words sounded ominous.

. . . .

AFTER DINNER DANIEL WENT upstairs while Matt cleared up and put the dishes in the dishwasher, his mind bubbling with bad feeling. Noam had crawled out of the kitchen and into the living room, and by the time Matt had emerged from the kitchen, he found him halfway up the stairs. "Holy moly, Noam!" he cried, poking his face in between two balusters. "Look at you!"

Noam, on hands and knees, looked down at him, then raised a knee to take another step. He placed it on the very edge and it slipped off, and, flattened on his stomach, he slid down a few stairs and bumped his chin on one of the stairs. Matt ran up the steps to pick him up just as he started crying.

Daniel came running down at the sound of thumping and crying. "Jesus Christ," he said. "Can't I leave him with you for a second?"

When Noam started to fall, Matt had been just about to follow him up. "Will you just stop it?" he snapped. "I can take care of him."

"Obviously, you can't! Did you just stand here watching him go higher and higher?"

"I was trying to help him feel competent." He was patting Noam's back and searching for a pacifier.

"Well, he's not competent!"

"And why do you think that is?" Matt said. "Why do you think he's not walking? It's all the fear locked up in his body."

"What kind of New Age crap is that?" Daniel said, taking Noam from him and cradling his head with his hand, examining his face.

"He's fine," Matt said.

"He's bleeding," Daniel said, turning him toward Matt so Matt could see the smudge of blood where Noam had bitten his lip.

Damn it. Matt followed them into the kitchen, where Daniel sat down with Noam on his lap. Matt went to the freezer and got him a frozen teething ring. "Here, honey," he said, touching Noam's hair. "Suck this."

Daniel grabbed it from him before Noam could take it, tossed it in the sink, and got a different one from the freezer. Noam, squeezed on his hip, grunted and squalled.

"C'mon," Matt said, coloring.

"Stop," Daniel said. "I'm not fighting in front of them."

"Who started the fight?" Matt whispered furiously.

"I'm not fighting in front of him," he said again. "Wait till they go to sleep."

Gal came down the stairs. "Are you fighting?" she asked with great interest.

"No," they said.

"Okay, whatever."

Efficiently and with careful cheerfulness, they got the kids bathed and Noam put to bed. As Daniel went into Gal's room to tell her it was time to stop reading and turn off the light, Matt sat on the bed, waiting.

Daniel came into the room, avoiding his eyes.

"Hey," Matt said.

Daniel sat down beside him. "Matt," he said, looking at the hands in his lap. "This isn't working out."

"And by 'this' you mean . . . ?"

"Any of it. You living here. Our being together."

"What? Are you kidding me?"

"I'm not kidding. I can't do this anymore."

Matt sat back on the pillows, stunned. "Why?! Because I let Noam go up the stairs?"

Daniel gave him a look. "You know why."

Matt's face grew hot. "Because I had unprotected sex?"

"That's just part of it," Daniel said. "That's just a symptom of the whole thing. I feel that it's not safe to have you around."

"Oh please," Matt said.

"Oh please?" Daniel said. "You bareback!"

"*Barebacked* once! The condom broke!"

Daniel rolled his eyes. "Do you realize how pathetic you sound? *The condom broke?*" His voice was withering. "You drive like a maniac. When you take them to the playground by yourself, I spend the whole time worrying that they're going to kill themselves because you let them do whatever they want. I can't handle it! If I'm the only one keeping this family safe, I'm better off doing it on my own."

"I didn't just let Noam go up those stairs. I was watching the whole time." When Daniel threw another derisive look his way, he burst out, "You have to make a calculation! You have to balance between safety and his sense of competence, autonomy."

"Don't condescend to me," Daniel said. "I know that. I make those calculations all the time."

"No, you don't," Matt said. "You just grab the kids and pull them back. Gal complains about it all the time! You don't hear it, but I do."

Daniel flushed. "I need you to get out of here."

"We're not even going to talk this through?"

"No," Daniel said.

Matt stared at him. "You want to do a whole get-out-of-my-house scene instead? Can't we do any better than that?"

"This isn't a joke! Do I look like I'm kidding?"

He very much did not look like he was kidding, Matt thought, looking at Daniel's haggard face and cold eyes. But he was not going to let himself panic, and damned if he was going to let Daniel see him break down. "Do you even *get* to kick me out of the house?" he asked.

"Yes, I do!" Daniel cried. "It's my name, not yours, on the mortgage. My name as the kids' guardian. Where's your name, Matt? Where's *your* fucking name?"

He spat the words while Matt looked at him, shocked, thinking that he sounded as if he'd consulted a lawyer, which made this way more serious than he'd imagined. "Dan," Matt said. "I hear that you're furious and very hurt, and also scared."

"I said don't condescend to me," Daniel said. "Look," he said quietly. "I can handle the sexual betrayal. It hurts, a lot, but I know I've turned my back on you for a long time, and I get it, fair is fair. I can get over that." He was looking steadily at Matt. "But I can't get over the sense of danger I feel when you're around. I've been trying, but I can't. I have no choice but to ask you to leave."

"I'm not leaving the house!" Matt shouted, making Daniel shush him furiously and close the door. "Okay? I live here! I'm not going outside and shiver on the front lawn while you throw my clothes out the window like a betrayed wife with mascara running down her face!" He grabbed a pillow and hugged it.

"I don't want you here," Daniel said, his face red and twisted. "I don't want here anymore. Do you know what these kids have been through? I can't believe you! What if you got sick? Do you think they could take another loss like that? Or if you got *me* sick, or *them*?"

Daniel brushed his forearm against his eyes, and Matt sat quietly. *I won't get sick!* is what he wanted to say, but he knew he couldn't, he knew that once you're thunderstruck, you no longer live in a country where the natives can decipher that kind of utterance. How he wished it was six months from now!—and the apologies and drama and penance and feeling like a horrible person were over, and he'd been tested and found negative. "I'm so so sorry, Daniel," he said, his voice hoarse.

"I'm sure you are," Daniel said. "And I accept your apology. I do. But that's the best I can do; it doesn't change how I feel."

Despite his best efforts, Matt felt his eyes begin to prickle. "I *told* you, didn't I? I didn't have to do that!"

"Oh my God!" Daniel said. "You want to be congratulated for that? You want me to throw you a big party because you didn't knowingly give me HIV?!"

Matt flushed angrily. "Of course not!" he said, embarrassed, because he did think he'd behaved decently. "But isn't it proof that I can be trusted to observe precautions?"

"Proof that you can be trusted would be not spreading your ass for strangers!"

Matt flung himself facedown onto the bed, acting as if this was a regular fight, hoping that if he acted that way, it would be.

"Please go, Matt," Daniel said. "I can't have you here. It makes me feel . . ." He put his hand on his chest and tried to continue, but he couldn't find the air. "Panicky," he whispered. For a second, until the breath came, he thought he might be having a heart attack. He was focused like a laser on Matt leaving the house, it was his sole need, it was all he could do not to scream *Go!* a thousand times. He sucked in air with the sound of a screeching engine. "I can't," he panted. "I can't have you here, I can't take the vigilance, I can't be reassuring you night and day that you're still a good person, I can't go back to feeling the way I did when Joel died. . . ."

Dismay flared in Matt's chest, and he thought, *Just for now, just for now.* He forced himself to his feet, got his gym bag from the closet, and threw it at Daniel, who fended it off with his forearm. He'd go to Derrick and Brent's. He got dressed and began packing, just a change of clothes, and then, in the bathroom, his toiletries. He took, without hesitation, the things they shared: toothpaste and shaving cream, the hairbrush. He scanned the bathroom, then took the Ativan and all the vitamins from the cabinet. He left the bedroom without looking at Daniel, the bag slung over his shoulder, and went downstairs. From the kitchen, he took a bag of oranges, the mint Milanos, all the beer in the fridge, and the vodka and scotch from the cabinet. He set the bag down at the back door and went back upstairs.

Daniel was lying facedown on the bed, his face buried in the crook of his arm. "I'm going to say good-bye to the kids," Matt said.

Daniel looked up quickly, his face red. "Don't you dare wake them up! I'll tell them in the morning."

"What will you tell them? That I up and left? Don't you dare blame me."

"I won't," Daniel said. "I promise."

"What are you going to tell them?" Matt demanded. "I want to hear the exact words."

"Please," Daniel said, sitting now cross-legged and slumped. "I'm really tired. Let me sleep on it."

Matt's lips tightened and he got a surge of adrenaline at getting the upper hand for the first time. "I'm not leaving till I hear what you're going to tell them."

Daniel sighed tremulously and rubbed his eye hard with his forefinger. "My mind is drawing a blank," he said.

"Tell them you kicked me out of the family."

"I'm not saying that."

"So you're going to lie? I don't want it sounding even mutual, Daniel. You're so big on taking responsibility—*you* fucking take responsibility."

Daniel rubbed his face hard, exhausted from the energy it had taken to get Matt to agree to leave. "I'll tell them that you didn't want to leave, because you love them—"

"Love *us*. Say 'because he loves us.' And why did I leave, then?"

"Because I decided it wasn't safe for you to live with us."

"No—I don't accept that."

They wrangled for another twenty minutes, for each proposition, Matt posing the difficult follow-up questions he knew Gal would ask. Finally, they decided on "I'm very angry at Matt for something he did, and I told him I don't want to live with him anymore. What he did is between him and me. And he didn't want to go, because he loves us."

Matt nodded tiredly. His mouth was dry, and tasted terrible. He thought he should also demand visitation rights with the kids, but didn't have the energy for it right now.

The dog followed him back down to the kitchen, and he stooped and kissed him on the snout. He called Derrick and Brent from the freezing car as he waited for it to warm, his breath billowing and his fingers aching from the cold. He woke Derrick up, so he told him to go back to sleep, that he was coming over but he'd let himself in. When he got there, Brent emerged sleepily in a bathrobe and said, "Big fight?"

"Big fight," Matt said, taking off his jeans and putting on sweats, which, cold from the car, encased his legs in cold.

"What'd you do?"

"Funny," Matt said. "Can I have a blanket?"

"Sure," Brent said, and went back into the bedroom, from which

Matt heard a quick conference in low voices between him and Derrick.

He took two sleeping pills and went to sleep on their couch, a cat curled behind his knees, thinking of all the smart retorts he'd failed to make—*Haven't you learned by now that nobody can keep anybody safe? Safety isn't the only value in the world!*—and vowing to remember them for later, when he and Daniel spoke again. Noam, he thought, would be up a few times during the night coughing, but that was Daniel's problem. If he, Matt, had no rights—what a shit Daniel was to say that!—at least he would now have the right to a good night's sleep. His mind spun and spun, and finally sleep came over him.

DANIEL OPENED THE CABINET and cursed Matt when he discovered the Ativan was missing. He went back into the bedroom, lay down on the bed, and pulled the covers up to his chin. His heart was hammering in his ears and fingers, and when he thought of Matt, panic tickled inside his chest with intolerably pestering fingers till he shuddered. Just as he'd felt when he'd heard about Joel, as if there were something tormenting inside him that he couldn't get out. To go out and court unnecessary danger—as if they hadn't been blown, like fish hunted with guns, into the bloody welter of those who lived every single grim, aching, horrible day with its consequences!

Crying would have helped ease him out of that free fall, but he couldn't muster more than a humid and itchy tingle around the eyes. He'd cried enough over this past year, he thought bitterly, and he was not going to spill more tears over Matt. He had an urge to call someone, call Derrick, but everyone would think he was crazy for kicking Matt out; they'd think he wasn't considering the kids. But now, honestly, he felt that he should have broken up with him as soon as he brought the kids home. Matt had tried to be there for them, because he needed so badly for people to think he was a good person. And sure, fine, he was good with them, especially with Gal, who didn't have the intense entanglement with him she had with Daniel. But what good did it do to make an ace Halloween costume when he never pulled the harness in the baby's car seat tight enough?

He got up and took a hot bath, lay in the tub reading Matt's *Entertainment Weekly* to still his thoughts, feeling the hot water encase his limbs but not penetrate. When he got out, his skin was red. Yo-yo came in and licked his wet feet. Daniel dried off, put on pajamas, and sat on top of the bed, flipping channels. The heat of his bath hit him belatedly and he broke out into an unpleasant prickle and then a sweat. He closed his eyes. He felt like a mangled crustacean on a hot beach littered with soda cans and cigarette butts. He knew he had no right to complain, since he was the one who'd done the breaking up, but he felt awful, and angry for being forced into it, too.

The TV flashed its disturbing late-night images, the ads for weight loss and call girls, the waxen or battered faces of murdered people being studied by medical examiners. He drifted to sleep and then woke up again, and sometime later he pushed off the bed and left the room, walked softly up the stairs to Matt's study.

It was warmer up on the top floor. He turned on the nearest lamp, habituated from long cohabitation with Matt not to use the overheads. The red walls gave off a muted glow against off-white wainscoting. Matt had moved into the smaller, less comfortable space when Gal and Noam arrived, and cast his magic over it, so that it now looked like an ideal design space—comfortable, modern, lovely. On his desk stood a chunk of engraved Lucite, a Best Young Designer award he'd won long ago, along with framed pictures of Matt with Daniel, with the kids. On the bulletin board was pinned the *Ma'ariv* front page with Matt in the photograph. Daniel gazed at it. His expression in the photograph was inscrutable behind the sunglasses, but you had to hand it to the man, he was gorgeous. Being loved by him had been an awesome treat. There was a hitch at Daniel's heart, and for a second, he felt faint. He sat down on Matt's swivel chair and closed his eyes. In the beginning, Matt was so beautiful to him that Daniel had had to learn to re-see him through a human lens rather than a purely aesthetic one. He had broken down that beauty in his mind and constructed a new one, so that the Matt he saw and loved was fresher and more real than the Matt their culture held up as the beauty standard for men. It was a beauty he believed only he could see.

And now—now Matt had let some other man in, some man who could see only the obvious beauty, and let him in closer than he'd ever invited even Daniel.

Daniel sank into the chair, becoming heavy and inert. After a few minutes he became aware that something was hurting. His jaw; he unclenched his teeth, opened his mouth wide, waggled his jaw from side to side.

Against the back wall stood a file cabinet, where they kept all the information about the mortgage, property taxes, and home repair, as well as their passports, the legal information about Daniel's guardian-ship of the kids, the kids' medical records. Daniel rose and opened the drawer, pulling out those files and stacking them neatly on the floor. He didn't know what he was going to do with them, he was going on instinct, and hadn't meant to look into the file cabinets in the first place. He felt ridiculous, like a character in a heist movie. If Matt forgot some-thing and walked in, he didn't know what he'd say.

He bent and took up his stack of legal documents, removing Matt's passport and tossing it on the floor, and brought them over to the small pearl-colored sofa, sat down with them on his lap, and put his feet up on the coffee table, on which sat some brochures Matt had designed and a coffee cup filled with crayons and markers for Gal's visits up there. These were the things he had: the kids, the house. These were the things he would tend, safeguard, cherish. He fell asleep with the files cradled to his chest.

CHAPTER 17

MATT WAS DAZED. He kept thinking it wasn't possible, that for Daniel to break up with him while he was already destroyed by loss, for him to prefer parenting the kids alone to having him in the house—it seemed insane. For the first few weeks, Matt crashed on Derrick and Brent's couch, protected from utter devastation by his belief that, soon, Daniel would come to his senses. Because what could he possibly tell the kids? Could he really look them in the eye and tell them that yet another parent had vanished from their lives? Could he really be that cruel? Or so furious and implacable that he'd rather take on the burden of dealing with Gal than have Matt in his house? He felt sorry, and guilty, and contrite about what he'd done, but Daniel's reaction was so huge—so outsized and disproportionate, so utterly punitive to the kids, so fucking *crazy*—that he felt that it outweighed even his own crime, and that he and the kids were the ones who had been wronged.

Derrick and Brent were bewildered and appalled by this turn of events. When Matt told him what he'd done, Brent said, "Are you kidding me? You of all people!"

Derrick turned his face away and went into the bedroom. A few minutes later he emerged again into the living room, where Brent and Matt were sitting silently, hands in their laps. "Well, you showed him, didn't you," he said, sarcasm twisting his normally placid face. "You don't have to be responsible if you don't want to. You don't have to put your family first—you're too hot for that."

"Derrick," Brent said.

"For God's sake, Matt," Derrick said, sitting down heavily. "You know better than anyone else how terrible things happen to people in the world. Why would you go out and look for danger?"

They stayed up late, worrying and analyzing, drinking the booze Matt had taken from home. They speculated about his behavior, which he found kind of interesting and pleasurable—who didn't love being the riddle to which his friends' searching analytical attention was tuned?— until it quickly became irritating. "Like Derrick said—only nicer—I can totally imagine rebelling against your new domestic status," Brent said, "that's totally understandable. Or rebelling against Daniel, who, let's face it, can be an arrogant prick at times. But in a way that harms yourself?! That's what I'm struggling with. I mean, I never pegged you as self-destructive or suicidal. . . ."

That word made them all look at one another. "First of all, I told you the condom broke. Second, Christ, it was the *opposite* of that," Matt protested. "It was— It made me feel more alive than I had in months."

"It's not just about you, though," Derrick said. "When you have kids, it's not just about you anymore."

"Oh, for Christ's sake, Derrick, could there be a more self-righteous cliché?" Matt snapped. "Even I wouldn't say that, and I *have* kids!"

"You *had* kids," Derrick said.

Matt's face grew hot. He'd never been talked to that way by Derrick, who was one of the least judgmental people he knew. And he was conscious of deserving it, which made him feel even worse.

"Maybe it was a cry for help," Brent interposed. "A cry for help, to get Daniel to notice you and your own pain."

Matt sighed and sat up, placed his beer bottle on the coffee table. "Okay, let's stop talking about this," he said.

"Well," Derrick said, interlacing his fingers and reaching his palms up in a big stretch, "you wouldn't be the first gay man to fuck without a condom because it made him feel more alive."

"Was it at least good?" Brent asked.

Matt considered what to tell them, and settled upon a simple "Yes."

"Well, at least that," Brent said, while Derrick leveled at him a disapproving stare.

"At least that," Matt said. He was sitting at the edge of their big armchair; it was late at night and they had already said "Okay, time to go to bed" three or four times.

Derrick and Brent were standing now, and collecting bottles and glasses from the living room tables; Matt went into the kitchen to get a damp sponge. Derrick disappeared and came back with a pillow and blanket as he was wiping off the coffee table. "Are you scared?" he asked.

It was one of those moments where Derrick reached out simply and touched your very soul. "Yes," Matt whispered.

"MATT WENT BYE-BYE" WAS the way Daniel told Noam. To Gal he said, "Honey, I have to tell you something. Matt's not going to live here anymore."

"Did you have a fight?" she asked.

"Yes," he said, setting a bowl of cereal in front of her.

"I knew it," she said.

It was a cold January morning, and the radiators were clanging as the heat came on. He sat down opposite her, moving her orange juice away from the edge of the table, and told her the things he'd promised Matt he'd say: that Matt loved them and didn't want to leave, that it was his, Daniel's, decision, because Matt did something that made him very angry. His eyes were dry and grainy and each time he blinked he felt as though his corneas were being scratched. He needed to get some coffee into his body. Still, he was conscious as he spoke of doing a good job using age-appropriate language, and of being conscientious to Matt's demands.

Gal watched him, taking it in. Her lips were smeared past their edges with lip balm—the effort to heal their chronic winter cracks had obviously been an impatient one—and she pressed them together in a blotting motion. "Maybe you could marry a girl now," she said.

"Gal," he sighed. "Is that all you have to say?"

What was she supposed to say, she wondered, gazing at her uncle. His face was worn and dotted with bumps and bristles. Without his glasses she could see the purple under his eyes. Her bare feet were cold; her cereal was puffing up in the milk. Noam's eyes were flitting back and forth from her to Daniel, staticky filaments of his hair stirring gently in the air. "Bye-bye," he whispered.

"I'll take you to school today," Daniel said. "So we don't have to rush for the bus."

Gal put down her spoon, went up to her room, closed the door without slamming it so that Daniel wouldn't follow, and lay down on the unmade bed. With an irritated grunt, she twisted and pulled out the pajamas that were balled under her hip, flung them on the floor. She knew without question that she was never going to see Matt again. Something awful seeped over her, a sludge of panic and helplessness. Hatred of Daniel, for making Matt leave. She told herself that actually it was okay, Matt wasn't really a parent anyway. It wasn't like her parents dying. But who, she wondered, would take her to her riding lessons? If Daniel made her give them up, she would never talk to him again; she would live silently in this house till all the heavy silent air made it burst like a balloon, or a bomb.

About ten minutes later Daniel came up and sat next to her on the bed. Her face was turned away; she was curled up in a ball; his weight plunging down the mattress and the intolerable sound of his breathing made her feel like she was about to scream. *Go away go away go away*, she mouthed to herself. *Go away.*

"Ready to head out?" he said.

She staggered to her feet, avoiding his gaze. Downstairs, she put on her coat and hugged her backpack to her, and climbed into the car without a word. He dropped off Noam, and she waited in the cold silence of the car as he spoke with Colleen. Then he got back in and started the engine and she felt the heat blast back on. At school, she got out of the car and walked by herself to class before he could follow.

Daniel watched her march away from him, wanting to rush and tighten her backpack straps, but turned toward the principal's office instead, to let her know about Gal's changed circumstances.

"Oh, poor Gal," she said, shoulders sagging. "Not again."

"Nobody died," he said.

"Of course not," she hastened to say.

His friends came over to see if they were okay, flooding in again as they had when they'd first come back to the States after Joel's death. It was hard not to feel the parallel, to feel that their solicitude made things a little worse. Hard too to explain that he was feeling kind of good, even a little exhilarated by the clean anger hurtling through him. His days were utterly grueling, a chaos of work, child care, endless cooking and chores; the kids were brittle and God only knew how he was going to keep their financial ship afloat without Matt's income. But when he fell into bed at night, he occupied his light, living body restfully, feeling the tiredness tingle in his arms, his thighs and genitals. His thoughts would drift to Matt, and as rage mounted in him he breathed through it and calmed his own heartbeat.

"Tell me you didn't bring a casserole," he said when he opened the door to Adam and Val; Val swept him into her arms and rocked him back and forth, smashing his cheek against her earring. "Geez, Val," he said, and she released him, took him by the arms and held him at arm's length to look deeply into his sheepish face.

Gal came downstairs and accosted them in the front hall. "Dani decided he didn't want to be partners with Matt anymore," she announced to Adam. "Are you on Dani's side or Matt's side?"

"Nobody's side," Adam said, taking Lev's and Val's coats and reaching into the closet for a hanger. "I'm just sad."

They went into the kitchen while Lev scuttled into the playroom, where the toys were always more scintillating than his own. Gal barged into the kitchen just as they'd huddled around the table to talk, complaining that Lev was touching one of her bead necklaces. "Lev!" Val called, while Daniel said, "Try to be patient, Gal, he's littler than you are." Gal tried to palm off on him a plastic duck instead, but its lameness deeply offended him; his whole idiom and belief system were about bigger/smaller, older/younger, and he cried "That's for babies!" as his mother took him by the shoulders and gave him a little push out of the kitchen. There was a flurry of complaint from the playroom, then the sound of escalating objections. Daniel groaned, and he and Adam rose.

"Guys!" he said. In the playroom, a vaudeville "Yankee Doodle" was tootling merrily from Noam's plastic scooting car; he was sitting on it, gripping the handles hard, as Lev tried to pull him off, while Gal was blithely swinging a collapsible rod from her toy tent, pretending to be a ninja. Daniel caught her wrist and said, "Careful!"

She swung it around again, once, experimentally, her eyes on his face. "Seriously?" he said. "I will take that away from you and put you in your room so fast you won't even know what's happening." Adam was prying Lev's fingers off the car's handles. "Lev, you gotta take it easy, honey," he said. "You want to draw?" He went to the bookcase where the art supplies were stacked, Lev flailing on his hip, found crayons and construction paper.

"Look," Daniel said, "come sit at our new table"—pointing to the bright blue kid-sized plastic table with four chairs—and settled him on one of the chairs.

"I want the green chair," Lev said stoutly, hopping to his feet.

"No problem," said Adam.

"I'ma make a card for Mommy."

"Good thinking," Daniel said.

"Why am I always stuck playing with babies?" Gal was saying as they returned to the kitchen.

Val was eating a banana and leafing through a *New Yorker*, and the coffeepot was gurgling. Daniel sat down and she laid her hand on his wrist. He looked down at the silver rings on her fingers. She had been leaving I-just-wanted-to-see-how-you're-doing messages on his machine for days, and her desire to be there for him and the kids exhausted him. Now she and Adam clearly wanted to feel him out on the juicy details. He'd been avoiding them because he didn't feel he could tell anyone why he and Matt had broken up. Especially straight people, for whom the information would just confirm their stereotypes of gay men, even if they tried not to let it. He looked into their intense empathic eyes and said, "I really can't go into it."

"Whatever it was," Val ventured, "it must have been something pretty terrible. Because—well, because you've been through so much together, and you've done it so beautifully, and seemed so rock-solid as a couple."

Adam was mouthing the patch of beard below his lip and watching Daniel carefully, as if he might at any moment have to apologize for Val.

"Really, Val, I can't," Daniel said. Keeping Matt's secret, being put in that position, was compounding his outrage, he found, and his sense of clarity about having done the right thing. "You know what, though? I'm doing okay. Surprisingly okay."

"I don't think I've ever known someone as strong as you," Val said, and he didn't tell her that it wasn't really a question of strength.

There was a cry from the playroom, a shocked, breath-snatching cry—Noam. They leapt to their feet. He was sitting on the rug, his eyes wide and shocked and his mouth agape in the silence before a scream, his hand clapped to his face. Gal had poked him in the face with the tent pole, and put a gash under his eye. The scream came. Daniel lifted him and sat him on his knees on the couch while Adam ran for the first-aid kit in the upstairs linen closet. "Jesus, Gal," Daniel fumed. "I told you again and again. Do you know how close you came to poking him in the eye?"

Adam returned with sterile pads, and Daniel ripped one open and pressed it gently to Noam's cheek. The gash was about an inch long, and beading with blood; the skin underneath was starting to turn bruise colors. Gal stood on the stand of the floor lamp with her legs and arms twisted around the pole, frozen, watching.

Lev had run into the kitchen and come back with an ice pack, which he was trying to administer to Noam's face. "Lev, honey, step back a little; you're crowding them," Adam said, reaching out and taking him by the elbows.

"But he needs ice!" Lev cried. "And Band-Aids!"

"It's really nice and helpful for you to bring it, honey," Adam said as his son struggled in his grasp. Lev started to cry too, big half-fake sobs. "I know, buddy," Adam said. "It's hard to see your friend hurt."

The extra drama was not helping, Daniel thought. He peeled back the gauze to see if it was still bleeding, and when Noam saw his blood on it, he broke into fresh tears. "You could have blinded him, Gal!" Daniel said. "And you would have felt bad about that your whole life!"

"No I wouldn't," she shouted. "I wouldn't care at all!"

"Gal, sweetie, come here," Val said from the futon couch, patting her lap.

"Why don't you just mind your own business?" Gal said. "You're not in our family, we didn't ask you to come over."

"Gal!" Daniel barked while Val looked at her, hurt, and said, "I'm sorry you feel that way. Because I think of you as family."

"It's a stupid *defective* family," Gal said.

"Gal," Daniel said, his voice deadly. "Get into your room *now*. Damn," he said, "this thing is still bleeding. I'm going to take him to the emergency room."

Gal was on her way up the stairs; she turned and looked down. "We'll stay here with her," Val said, while Adam stroked her arm and said, "You know she's crazy about you."

Up in her room, the knowledge that she'd done something very bad was clawing at Gal, making her quiver between abjection and defiance. She threw herself on the bed, electric with anticipation for Daniel to come storming in, trying to summon him with the force of her hatred. *Oh, he was mad!* The thought brought a painful, agitated laugh. She imagined his grip on her arm, the glare of fully awakened eyes into hers.

She heard stomping downstairs, but nothing approaching her bedroom door. She stood and took down one of her two favorite horses, Cochav, whom she sometimes called by his English name, Star. She sat on the edge of her bed and pressed his plastic hoof into her arm, where it made a small, precise indented square. She carefully fit the hoof inside the square and pressed again, till the plastic mashed her skin up against the bone. Then she made another, till there was a satisfying pattern of squares on her throbbing forearm. She'd known even as she said those words to Val that she was being stupid, a baby nobody would listen to.

She put her arm to her nose and smelled but it didn't smell like anything. She stood and crept into her bed, pulling everything around her: Star, her stuffed dog, her comforter. Her arm still ached from the press of plastic.

Lying there with the covers pulled over her head, her face warmed and moistened by her own breath, she felt something work away at the edges of her memory. She twitched with irritation, as if she were being poked by an obnoxious kid. When the memory broke through, her breath stilled. She was shoulder to shoulder with Abba, kneeling on a chair at the kitchen table, the big calendar before them. Ema was in France, staying for a week with her friend whose mother had died. Gal was drawing a big X with a red marker into the square of the day that had passed, as she did each evening Ema was gone. The memory stunned her. The triumph of drawing that last X, and then Ema picking her up from school the next day, how her shirt smelled and the feel of her hair falling around Gal's face. Waking up the next morning and the sweet jolt of remembering that Ema was there. *Don't go away again!* she'd said, and Ema said, *I won't.* But it was just one morning. When she woke up the next day, Ema was gone, and Abba too, and everyone was crying. *Did Ema go back to France?* she'd asked.

The memory slopped against her; she had to make a conscious

effort to draw air into her lungs. The one night when they were all together after Ema returned, she'd melted down and ruined their Shabbat dinner. She didn't know why—she remembered the sensation of even then not knowing why, just tearing loose in the wind and there being nothing to catch onto as she shuddered and howled, knowing she was ruining everything.

Now, a metallic taste leached into her mouth; she put her finger inside her lip and when she removed it, it had blood on it. When Sabba told her, he'd tried to pull her into his arms, but she'd stiffened, bringing up her elbows to steel herself against the ugly wailing sounds he was making, the explosion of wetness and slime on her face and neck. She'd sensed that she needed to remain very still and dignified in the face of this degrading display of agony. Something of that old sense unfurled over her now. She imagined herself on horseback, sitting tall and stern next to her teacher Shannon, who wanted to go riding with her. She imagined Daniel watching her as she did something amazing. She heard the front door open and then shut hard, then the sound of the car's reluctant winter sputter before it broke into a roar.

AT THE EMERGENCY ROOM, sitting in an orange plastic chair with Noam on his lap, the irony wasn't lost on Daniel. He'd kicked Matt out for being impervious to the family's need for safety, and here he was in the ER for the first time since they'd brought the kids home. He felt stupid and careless for not having taken the pole away from Gal, because she was fragile, and he was feeling bad for her. He just hoped Matt never found out about it. And what would the social worker say? Maybe, he thought, he should have kicked out Gal instead of Matt. If she just mourned like other people—crying, maybe, or moping—it'd be easier to help her. But she was so mean and provocative and obnoxious. A headache pressed at his temples. Telling Val to mind her own business: He knew that if Matt were here, they'd be admiring the perfection of that insult even as they were deploring it.

The nurse called in the only other people in the waiting room, a mom with frazzled hair and a large teenager with patches of acne on his face and neck, who was pressing his elbow and upper arm against his chest and whimpering. It took forty-five minutes for Daniel's name to be called, and after a nurse finally examined Noam's cheek and eye, she said, "That'll need a stitch or two. We'll need to call down a plastic surgeon, because it's right there on the face." She put a Band-Aid on it and escorted them into an interior waiting room, and Daniel sat down with a sigh. He took out his cell phone and called Adam on speed dial, and Adam said they'd made quesadillas with the leftover chicken and cheese in the fridge, and were just sitting down to eat lunch. Gal was fine, he reported; she'd settled down and come out of her room. "I think she feels really bad about what she did," Adam said.

"Good," said Daniel.

They waited for another hour before the plastic surgeon showed up. By then Daniel had bought them a lunch of Pop-Tarts, pretzels, and lemonade from the vending machine, and relented and set Noam down on the floor, where he shredded a magazine and the arts section of the free local paper. He had to accost another nurse when the blood started seeping through Noam's Band-Aid. When they were called back in, the plastic surgeon said it was almost too late to put in stitches, and Daniel refrained from complaining that they'd been waiting forever for *him*, because there was no reason to anger someone working on his baby's face. The surgeon put some numbing gel on Noam's face. After a few minutes, he had Daniel hold Noam on his lap with his arms wrapped around his body, pinning down his arms, and washed it, then gave him a little shot in the cheek that made Noam cry out and Daniel blanch. As he leaned to put in the stitches, Daniel could smell his breath and the latex gloves on his hands, and he turned away, leaning his cheek on Noam's head.

When he was done, and Daniel, wild with his own relief, was nuzzling Noam and praising him for being a brave boy, the surgeon said, "There. Nobody will ever notice." He snapped off his gloves and tossed

them into the garbage, ruffled Noam's hair. "You're good as new, Noah,"
he said. "Stay away from your sister."

"Noam," Daniel said.

"It will leave a small scar, but it should become imperceptible over
time."

They waited again, this time for the nurse to return with a prescrip-
tion for antibiotics. Another nurse came and leaned against the doorway, chirped, "Hi, honey! I heard you were super brave!"

Noam was crawling toward the wheels on a stretcher; he turned
and sat down, cast her a friendly look. "Not walking yet, huh," she said
in a loud, falsely reassuring voice, like a colonial administrator. "How
old is he?"

"Twenty-two months," Daniel said.

She looked surprised. "Well, you wait till you're good and ready,"
she said to Noam, which sounded in Daniel's ears like saying that Noam
was a spoiled brat just killing time.

"He's been through a lot," Daniel said, staunch in the face of this
irritant but newly anxious about the baby. "He lost both his parents in
a terrorist attack."

"Goodness!" she said, flinching in a way that was highly gratifying
to him. "I'm so sorry to hear that!"

ON SUNDAY, YOSSI CAME over for Gal's and Matt's lesson, unaware that
Matt wasn't there anymore. "Oh shoot!" Daniel said, staring at him as
he stood on the stoop.

"Dani and Matt broke apart!" Gal announced. "And Dani won't let
Matt live here anymore!" Yossi looked at Daniel in surprise, and then,
as Daniel opened his mouth to explain, he cut him off with pieties about
his own impartiality, as if fearing to be drawn into a catfight. "It's none
of my business," he said, waving his hand to stop Daniel's imaginary
insistence on spilling all the juicy and inappropriate details. "The main
thing is taking good care of the kids, helping them feel safe."

Daniel sighed, half wishing at that moment that Matt was there to walk into the idiotic slight and throw open the blinds by saying something like "Geez, Yossi, it's not like I'm about to start talking about the mechanics of sodomy." He was worried about paying for these lessons now, feeling strapped without Matt's salary, but he knew he couldn't cut Yossi's regular lessons out of Gal's routine. One day he mentioned to Yossi that he was thinking that he might have to cancel the cleaning lady, and the next time Yossi came, he proposed a barter arrangement: He'd give Gal an hour lesson around noon on Sundays, and then he'd go out for a few hours to paint, leaving Rafi there to play with Gal.

For her part, Gal relished getting Yossi to herself. She sat next to this man whose language felt like home—sure, Daniel could speak Hebrew and even Matt could speak a little, but they didn't sound *Israeli*—feeling her sleeves brush against his, smelling his special Yossi-smell, soapy with an undercurrent of body smell. At his house, where they met once in a while, they had little glasses for coffee, an electric *kumkum*, clementines in a bowl and chocolate spread in the refrigerator, and Yossi's wife, Anat, and the two older boys came in and out in a burst of Hebrew and a flurry of signing hands. Yossi pressed Gal's small hand in his large, warm one to encourage the curve or veer of a Hebrew letter, or encouraged her to watch his own hand as he drew, and sometimes she'd reach out with her finger and touch the little sprigs of hair coming from his knuckles and chuckle, "Hairy!" He asked her what happened this week, and she was supposed to tell him in Hebrew. So she told him about a classmate whose mother had died—"of *cancer*," she whispered. "Everyone feels terrible for her," she said. Where she faltered, he wrote down a word, until each week he had five new Hebrew words for her to learn. He called her a *yalda chachama*, a smart girl, held out his palm so she could give him five, beseeching her for a gentle one, and then howled with mock betrayal when she gave it a hard smack instead.

Rafi had become like another brother; she took his presence for granted without seeking it. He was the only kid around who lived in a more complicated linguistic ecosystem than she did, and her official position on him was pity. Once, she had asked Yossi if he was sad Rafi was deaf, and he'd said, "I've only ever known Rafi deaf. If he wasn't deaf, he wouldn't be Rafi." That was an intriguing philosophical revelation to her, and she mulled and mulled it. Rafi could be wild—he could plow through a house with maniacal energy, leaping off of furniture and landing with an explosion of noise you didn't think his small body could create, grabbing cherished or fragile objects and making the grown-ups have to chase him to snatch them out of his hands. Gal sometimes suspected he was just pretending he couldn't hear so that he wouldn't have to listen to anybody. But his blithe oblivion, which had been off-putting at first, had come to feel relaxing to her. When they were bored, he taught her signs in Israeli Sign Language, and in those few moments where they sat, moving only their fingers, palms, wrists, there was a strange pleasure in the silence, in pretending she was deaf.

MATT STOPPED CALLING, RESPECTED Daniel's wishes not to be in touch. Derrick, who went over to pick up his computer and printer, told Matt that he'd tried to talk to Daniel, only to be told that he welcomed Derrick's support and friendship as long as they didn't involve his agitating on Matt's behalf. Matt knew there were things Derrick wasn't telling him, too: When he asked about seeing Gal and Noam, Derrick was evasive, and said, "Just give it a little time."

After a few weeks, Matt found a house in Derrick and Brent's neighborhood to sublet. It was owned by an anthropologist couple from Smith who were going into the field for a semester, and they were charging him next to nothing in exchange for his taking care of their deaf elderly springer spaniel, Molly. They worked in Japan, so the house was filled with Japanese prints and paintings and sacred objects that made him feel loud and hairy and big-footed, and at times, under the tranquil eye of the Buddha, pleasantly reverent. In the big sunny study the owners shared, the dog slumbering at his feet, Matt threw himself into his work, finishing a few projects that he had procrastinated over.

Cam came over at night to visit, as did Brent, and they shook their heads woefully and recalled their own traumatic breakups. He made movie dates with a few people he liked but whose friendship he'd never had time, or was too complacent in his couple-hood, to pursue. He had dinner at Val and Adam's, and endured a wearying meal of watery vegetarian lasagna, during which the older kids answered questions about school in monosyllables, hair flopped over their faces, and Lev, tired and irritable, baited his parents by throwing food on the floor. After Lev finally went to bed, Matt discovered that Daniel hadn't told Adam and Val what he had done to make Daniel kick him out, and had to tell them himself, knowing even as he spoke that they wouldn't have invited him over to dinner if they'd known. They tried to be cosmopolitan about the mysteries of queer desire and behavior, but they were clearly shocked. For the rest of the evening, Val couldn't keep exasperation out of her voice. He suspected that she had planned to get them back together, but was sensing now that this breakup confounded even her abilities. He couldn't wait to get out of there, and excused himself wearily as soon as he could without being rude.

He called Yossi, whose company he missed, and left a message, but Yossi didn't call him back. He wondered if he'd gotten the message; it was a chaotic household and someone could have deleted it. He wondered if Yossi knew what he'd done, in which case, okay, he deserved to be dumped. But if Val and Adam didn't know, he didn't think Yossi would either. After a week had passed, he figured that Yossi just didn't want to be friends. He tried to be a grown-up about it; if he didn't want to be friends, Matt couldn't force him. But he'd thought they had a genuine connection, and as the days went on, the thought that he was so easily dispensable made him increasingly bitter.

He put one foot in front of the other, functioning on the very edge of believing the breakup was final. He just didn't believe that it could be, although he also vowed not to be one of those boyfriends who sent obsessive emails and left phone messages dark with meaning— beginning with a low, terse "It's me"—one of those guys who refused to see the evidence staring him in the face, the evidence all of his creeped-out friends could see. One day, he fell over the edge, and then the agony of his loss shocked him. He'd lost his family because he'd failed them. He'd tried and tried to rise to the occasion of their loss, and he'd done a great job until the effort had become just too great. And then what? The most ignominious of failures, he simply couldn't keep it in his pants. Was that the true Matt? The thought that there might be something fundamentally selfish and childish about him distressed him. And it made him rethink his whole relation to Jay's illness, too. Had Kendrick been right, and he'd just been a big handful the whole time? He spent that day stunned and immobilized in bed, while the stiff old spaniel snored and twitched on the floor beside him.

Other days, though, there was a glimmer of chilly optimism, a little piece of him that felt freed. In a few years, he thought, surely this whole awful, demented interlude would seem like a dream. In the quiet, scholarly rental house, it was sometimes hard to believe it had happened. Terrorism! The Occupation! The Holocaust! The grieving grandparents and stricken children! His house teeming with toys, diapers, strewn bedding, strange people washing dishes or cooking food. *Jesus Christ,* he thought at those moments, *what a freaking melodrama!* And what a stupid, deluded, paltry role he'd played in it. He *so* didn't belong with those people: Hadn't they made that abundantly clear?

He thought about being in Israel, about every door that had slammed in his face, and every time, back home, that Daniel acted surprised when Matt did something that hinted of being an actual parent. Anger would worm into his throat then: they'd exploited him, and he'd let them. Had Daniel been waiting the whole time to pull out that legal crap that he alone was the legal guardian and the sole owner of the house? Throughout this whole nightmare, Matt had reassured himself that Daniel still loved him, but that his love was like a tiny sacred object buried under layers of grief and confusion, so he couldn't find it. Now he thought that Daniel hadn't loved him after all, and just kept him around because it was too hard to parent on his own. Maybe he even did it consciously; he could just imagine the cold calculus of need, affection, dissimulation, self-justification.

And he—he'd reveled in the poignancy of being there to soothe the brokenhearted, the glamour of being a handsome man riding to their rescue. It made his face burn now to recall all that welling up of deep, tender feeling, as if he'd just come across and read his adolescent journal.

Released, he could do as he pleased. He could break through this whole carapace of grief and horror and emerge, gleaming and tender, into a new life. Would he go back to New York, where any respectable gay man would choose to live? He knew he could be picked up by a design firm and make a fair living there, even though rents in Manhattan had gone through the roof in the years he'd been gone. There would be more than three excellent restaurants in walking distance, and things to do after dark; the thought of hanging out and drinking with more than two gay men made his lips twitch with a smile. And art! He missed art so much.

He went through a few weeks of purification, cutting out smoking and eating meat, running in a pattern of two days on, one day off. He joined the gym so he could do weights. He circled the date of his sexual encounter on his calendar, counted six months and circled the date in June he'd get himself tested. He slept late in the mornings, enjoying not having a toddler who awoke at six, and kept the house super tidy, washing strange dishes and using up the laundry detergent in their laundry room, which made him experience a new, not unpleasant smell in his life that it took a few days to identify with his newly washed clothing.

WHEN IT HAD BECOME clear that they would become a couple, Daniel and Matt had made a half-joking pact never to tell Daniel's parents if they broke up, because they knew how gratified they'd be. Even these years later, with all the water under the bridge, Daniel couldn't bring himself to tell his parents right away. He did, though, call the social worker, Christine, thinking it wisest to be up-front about his change in status. She came for a visit late one afternoon, files jutting out of the big purse beside her on the couch, her feet puffing against the strictures of her pumps. "I won't lie to you, Daniel," she said. "I was happier when you and Matt were together."

He shrugged.

"I don't like these kids experiencing another loss so soon, and I don't like seeing them so dark and quiet."

"Do you think *I* do?" he asked, stung that she thought that. He'd actually been feeling pretty good with them, feeling that, as a parent, he was on his game. Last night at supper they'd both been on edge, Noam whining in his booster—he had a stuffed nose, and had been up a lot during the night because he couldn't suck his passy and breathe at the same time—while Gal complained bitterly that she hated every single bit of food in front of her; and Daniel had sat down with them, his mind chugging about how to salvage dinner. "Remember the time we went to the fair and that llama spat on Cam?" he finally asked. "Wow, was she ever covered in llama spit!" Their scowling faces turned toward him. He imitated Cam touching her hair and bringing her hand away, looking at it with revulsion. Simultaneously, they laughed, disarmed, and dinner was saved.

"Of course not." Christine's composed professional face relaxed for a moment, and the expression was kind and weary. "Look, it's none of my business why you fellas broke up. Or to encourage an unhappy relationship. But if you can find your way back to each other, that would be the optimal situation for these kids."

Daniel was silent. Wasn't it a commonplace that staying together for the sake of the kids was a bad idea, because it modeled a bad marriage for them?

"And if you can't, I sure hope you're figuring out some arrangement where the kids can see him. He was an involved parent. They're close to him."

"I will," he said. "Just not yet."

"When?" she asked, waiting him out as he groaned and rolled his head on his neck.

"Do I even have to, from a legal standpoint?" he challenged. "I'm the one who has full custody."

"Legally? No," she said. "But I think you know this isn't only about the letter of the law."

"Gal hasn't even asked to see Matt."

Christine was quiet for a moment. Then she said, "That's for a reason you don't have access to, Daniel. For all you know, she's just used to the world taking parents away, and can't imagine that she has any control over it."

That surprised him, and wounded him too, her thinking of him as some pitiless force crushing his child; and it was still rankling when he opened the door to let her out. He was the one betrayed—how had he become the bad guy? He jammed his leg in front of Yo-yo, who was trying to barrel out into the cold, and watched as, with a jangle of a massive key chain, Christine got into her dinky Prizm.

That night Derrick called, and they were barely into the conversation when he asked Daniel when Matt would be able to see the kids.

"Did he ask you to ask me?" Daniel said, his voice sharp. He muted the bedroom TV, where he'd been watching a police procedural while drinking a glass of scotch.

"So what if he did? There's nothing underhanded about that," Derrick said with some exasperation. "You won't talk to him . . ."

Daniel was quiet. "If I felt it was the wrong thing to do," he finally told Derrick, "I'd really be struggling. But I know that it isn't. I feel good, Derrick. So angry sometimes I can hardly see, but weirdly good. I know the kids are suffering, but I think I'm doing right by them."

"'Doing right by them'? Are you sure? What must they think? I don't mean to pull my professional training on you, but—"

"Then don't," Daniel said. "Just don't."

There was a long pause. Then: "He feels used. And you can sort of see why."

The subtitles on the TV indicated that the detectives suspected the husband of the murdered socialite. "Maybe I did use him a little," Daniel conceded. "Sometimes I think I stayed with him because I couldn't imagine coming home with the kids alone."

Derrick paused, then said, "Really? I don't really buy that."

"What don't you buy?" Daniel asked, irritated; apparently he couldn't get anything right.

"You're saying that you didn't love him anymore at that point. But I think you did."

"You always think people are better than they really are," Daniel said. "I haven't felt anything for him for a while."

Derrick shot back, "You haven't felt much of anything, *period*, for a while. Including anger at the person who killed your brother. But Matt you can get angry with, Matt you can call a danger to your family."

Daniel groaned. "Did you call to harass me, Derrick?"

"No," Derrick said. "But I think you should let him see the kids."

"I'll think about it," Daniel said, willing to say anything at that point to get Derrick off the phone. He still needed to make the kids' lunches for tomorrow and take out the dog. He hung up and lay there for a minute, regretting having settled down with a drink in the first place before finishing his evening chores. He was tired of everybody being on his case. Derrick knew what Matt had done, and he was *still* giving him a hard time. He wished he had asked him what he would have done if *Brent* had barebacked—Derrick would have gone on a tirade about responsibility and consequences so furious it would have set Brent's hair afire. And *of course* he'd let the kids see Matt at some point soon; he wasn't a monster, he knew it was wrong to make him just vanish, as their parents had. But he couldn't bring himself to do it just yet.

THE LONGEST JANUARY HE had ever lived through passed into February, and Matt was learning to live alone again, without a partner and without kids. He handled his anger at Daniel for cutting Noam and Gal out of his life by spitefully luxuriating, when he awoke in the morning, in visions of Daniel having to wake them, dress them, feed them, and hustle them out of the house by himself, along with feeding and taking out the dog. He'd relearned the austere pleasures of making coffee for one, fishing clean laundry out of the basket when he was ready to wear it instead of folding it and putting it in drawers, sprawling on the queen-sized bed and watching HGTV at night and groaning over the idiots who rejected a home simply because they didn't like the color of the paint on the walls, downloading new music on his iPod for the first time in months. He revived a few friendships he'd been pursuing just when Joel and Ilana had been killed, which he hadn't had the time or energy to pursue after that; he drank martinis at dinner parties and slept a full eight hours a night. He ran and worked out at the gym, and got something of his old lean muscle back, although there remained a little too much paunch for comfort, a sign of getting older that he deplored. He aggressively pursued a few big jobs, and got a piece of one of them, with the promise of more. Derrick had been working for a while on setting up an LGBT version of Big Brothers Big Sisters, pairing queer and questioning high schoolers with queer adults in the Pioneer Valley, and Matt volunteered to be a big brother if it got off the ground.

It was exciting to revive his old self—fun, a good conversationalist, a sexual player. But he wasn't, of course, his old self; he had so much baggage now, he told people, he practically had to hire a porter to come with him everywhere. One night, he had a drink with Alex Connor, Northampton's one gay cop; he had a shaved blond head and an earring in one ear that he wore only when off duty, and his T-shirt stretched over his shoulders. Matt wasn't into the whole Aryan thing, the pale lashes, but he found the tension between Alex's sense of duty and his sense of irony appealing, and enjoyed Alex's stories about Northampton's seamy side. As he told Alex the story of his relationship with Daniel and the last year, Alex reacted with a series of "Whoa's," and he felt uncomfortable about how glamorously tragic it made him seem; he found himself underplaying things and omitting others, like the custody fight with the Holocaust-survivor grandparents. At the end of the story, he said, "So he just couldn't deal with a partner; he had to scapegoat somebody in the end, and it was me." He didn't like the way he sounded when he said that, either; if he'd been Alex, listening to him, he'd wonder what bad behavior of Matt's own he was leaving untold.

"Did you like being a parent?" Alex asked.

Matt thought. "I did. I didn't think I would, but I did."

"Do you feel like"—Alex's voice lowered dramatically, a little sardonically—"you never knew what it meant to love, till then?"

Matt looked at him sharply. "Of course not," he said. "That's bullshit. What did those people spend their lives doing before kids, jerking off?" As he spoke, he knew that he was overstating his objection to that cliché, out of worry that he was being mocked. Certainly he'd been willing to give up a whole lot for Gal and Noam, and sometimes he'd be walking down the street with them and know—just calmly know— that if a car swerved toward them, he'd fling his body between it and them. But somehow, that didn't feel like noble parental self-sacrifice, it just felt like the right thing to do. And would he have done any of this if he hadn't loved Daniel with his whole heart—if he hadn't longed to soothe that deep, deep grief?

"What's next for you?" Alex asked, his eyes traveling in a friendly manner over Matt's face and body.

"Not sure," Matt said. "I'm thinking about returning to New York."

Through a friend of Val's, he put down a deposit for a three-month-long sublet in the West Village, thinking he would go back and give living there a trial run before actually moving there. But the closer the time got to the beginning of the sublet, the less New York seemed to shimmer with promise, and he began to wonder whether, at this point, its wonder and excitement were just the mechanical fantasy of a queer living in the boondocks. He found himself getting lethargic each time he was supposed to be packing, and even if it was a total long shot, he felt he had to stick around in case he got to see Gal and Noam. Then his Jetta broke down and needed a new transmission, and for three days he obsessed over whether to continue investing in it—it had ninety-four thousand miles on it—or buy a new car. Either way, it was going to cost a fortune—and if he gave up his sublet, he'd lose his $1,700 security deposit as well.

What was wrong with him? He felt lazy and boring; it felt like an unconscious unwillingness to truly part from Daniel, and he dreaded being the pathetic ex-without-a-clue. He worried that the kids were just an excuse. He'd left New York four years ago because he couldn't take the scene anymore, because he was afraid of the drugs and the self-destruction, because he knew the answer to the game of Who's the Hottest Man in the Room?, and it didn't gratify him anymore. Did he fear that, at thirty-two, with just that infinitesimal thickening, he might not be in the game anymore? And even if he was, he didn't know yet whether he had HIV, and would have to conduct a sex life full of honest confessions and intense precautions with men he didn't even yet know, which wearied him just thinking about it. He had clumsily extricated himself from Alex Connor's muscular arms after their drink for that very reason.

He decided, finally, to stay in Northampton through the summer and consider going back to New York in the fall. It was money down the drain, but you couldn't push this kind of thing. And the truth was, he kind of loved Northampton. Unwillingly, and with a tremendous sense of self-irony, but he did: He'd turned into a nature-loving, dog-loving, hiking New Englander who knows the best local ponds and lakes to swim in, who gorges on farm-stand corn and berries in the summer, and gets his woodpile ready for winter so he can sit in the woodstove's warmth and watch the flames flicker behind the door. Not to mention his love of the cafés crowded with academics writing on their laptops or grading papers, the fantastic bookstores, the organic this and fair-trade that, the fiery debates in local newspapers about the Fourth of July or the Pride parade, or the whole development versus conservation problem. And the lesbians! Could he live without the lesbians now? His tenderness for them was no less deep for its comical condescension. How could you not love the jocks who returned from summer vacations at P-town and the Hamptons and Ogunquit with deep tans and new girl-friends; the buzz-cut butches with their husky laughs; the lesbian moms who were gamely supportive of their daughters who insisted on wearing nothing but tutus and tiaras and pink pink pink?

He didn't see Gal and Noam anywhere around town; it figured that in a small town where you saw everybody all the time, he wouldn't see the people he was actually dying to see. He kept himself from driving past Gal's school and Noam's day care, and past Daniel's house, and he didn't ask their mutual friends about them either because asking would have made him feel too pathetic. But he heard this and that from Val and Adam, Brent and Derrick, and Cam. That the kids missed him. That Daniel was still making plans to take them to Israel for the year anniversary. That he wouldn't keep Matt from seeing them forever. He couldn't, Matt thought. Surely he couldn't.

CHAPTER 18

"WHERE AM I going to sleep?" Gal asked.

It was early March, and they were in the car on the way to the Newark airport, a four-hour drive to begin their trip to Israel. Noam, strapped into his car seat next to Gal, was sucking his pacifier and clutching his doggie and two wool hats. Over the past few weeks he'd begun saying a few words other than *yeah* and *no*. His newest word was *doggie.* "What's your doggie's name?" people would ask, and he would reply, "Doggie." His second word was *more,* which he uttered with a huge astonished veer upward, in imitation of the few times they'd teased him about wanting even more of something.

"In your old bed, I guess," Daniel said to Gal. "And I could put Noam's crib into the little guest room if you want, so you can have your own room."

"Uh-huh," Gal murmured, thinking about that. "I think maybe he should sleep in the same room as me, because it's a new place for him."

"Okay," Daniel said. Lately, since Noam's cheek injury, she'd been solicitous to him, running to get his passy when he cried and wedging it into his mouth till he sucked; the other day Daniel had come into their bedroom to read a story and found them sitting on Gal's bed, holding hands.

"Where are *you* going to sleep?" Gal asked.

Daniel paused. "I thought I'd sleep in your parents' old room."

"No," she said. "I don't think that's a good idea."

She said it in her most carefully reasoning tone.

"Really?" he asked.

"Because what if I have a bad dream and I get up and go into their room? I'll think I'm going to Ema and Abba but then they won't be there, and then I'll feel even worse."

Daniel was quiet. Over the past few weeks she'd been full of anxious questions about their visit. Were they staying with her grandparents? Would she sleep over at Leora's house all by herself? Would they lock the doors when they were in the house? Suddenly she couldn't remember the Hebrew word for *Popsicle*, or for *sidewalk*, and her face flooded with relief when he reminded her.

"Why don't we play it by ear," he said.

His mind had been going over the vital things he'd packed or zipped into his inside winter coat pocket: wallet, passports, tickets, the kids' legal papers, the keys to the apartment in Jerusalem. His stomach and throat were tight, and for a few days, it had been hard to get food down. When he thought about opening the door to Joel and Ilana's apartment, he wondered what on earth he'd been thinking when he'd agreed with his father to keep it for a while. He imagined how stale and dusty the apartment would be, how half-vacated, how they'd keep coming across pieces of baby gear or freezer-burned food, every object haunted. He couldn't, for the life of him, remember whether they'd gotten rid of Joel and Ilana's clothes.

Gal gazed out the window at bare trees and dirty snow. Her brother's eyes were falling shut and then opening again. She'd wanted to go back so badly, to see Leora and her classmates and her grandparents, to be home. But as the time had approached, she'd had trouble falling asleep at night, as her mind spun with anxious conjecture. What if she got killed by terrorists? Or didn't remember how to say things? Or missed her parents even more? And Noam, too. The scar under his eye, which no longer needed a bandage, was healing slowly—you couldn't see the stitch marks anymore, but it hadn't yet turned white, either. It made him look fragile and damaged, and Gal dreaded everybody asking what had happened to his cheek, and finding out that she had been the one who hurt him.

She'd wanted to tell Daniel she wasn't going to go, but the thought of being separated from him frightened her. And what about her grandparents? She knew that their looking forward to her visits was what kept them alive, her grandfather had told her that. Daniel had tried to talk to her about the trip, asking her how she felt about going back, and she'd looked at him with door stoppers in her throat, words bumping against hard rubber. He sat next to her, wearing a T-shirt fraying around the collar, his hand warm on her leg. He told her that it was going to be hard, and sad, but also fun to see Leora and Shai and Ruti and her other friends.

"You know what the important thing is?" he asked Gal.

She looked in his face, which was serious and sweet. She knew the right answer was something like "That we all love each other."

"The important thing is that we'll all be together," he said.

"Is Matt coming, too?" she asked.

He sighed. "No, Gal. You know he's not."

She stirred and tried, with a deep breath, to disperse the bad feeling sifting through her like dust motes turning in a shaft of sun; she hadn't asked the question to be fresh or mean.

"But Yossi and Rafi are," Daniel reminded her. Yossi had been talking for a while about taking the family to Israel to visit his aging parents in Petach Tikva, and a few weeks ago, he had decided to go alone with Rafi. He planned it so they and Daniel and the kids could fly back and forth together, and so he and Rafi could come to the memorial. The news had flooded Gal with relief; she had the vague and scary sense of the family dwindling, failing, like the feeble trickle from a faucet after the water runs out.

"Is Rafi going to sleep over?" she asked now, her voice rising over the din of the car. "Where will he sleep?"

"I don't know yet, Gal-Gal. If he does, it'll just be for one night, and we'll figure it out."

"Why isn't Anat coming?"

"She's staying home with Ezra and Udi, remember? Because they have school and practices they didn't want to miss."

"Does she have to go to the lab?" Rafi's mother, Anat, who was doing a postdoc in physics, was famous for spending ungodly hours in the lab; Gal knew the Israeli Sign Language sign for *lab*.

"Yes," Daniel said.

When they arrived at the gate three hours later, flushed and hassled from parking and the shuttle bus and the long security line, Yossi and Rafi were already there. The lounge area wasn't even open yet; it was barricaded off till the security officers could arrive. They wandered around looking for a place nearby to settle and dump their stuff, Noam slumped in his stroller with his passy listless in his mouth; he'd been up three times in the night, and both he and Daniel were haggard. Gal and Rafi examined electronics and iPod accessories and sunglasses and inflatable neck pillows, prodded repeatedly by Yossi and Daniel to move along and keep within eyeshot. In the newspaper store, as the men bought magazines and chewing gum, they fingered the travel-sized items—toothpaste and collapsible toothbrushes, tiny bottles of shampoo and ibuprofen and moisturizer and hand sanitizer, miniature sets of Scrabble and chess. Each time Rafi went with his parents to the supermarket, he begged them for one trial-sized item, and in his room he had a bin of products in deliciously tiny containers that he and Gal loved to plunge their hands into, removing individual items to examine and caress.

On the flight, Gal and Yossi switched seats so she could sit next to Rafi, and she watched movies with a headset while Rafi worked tiny travel puzzles and a Game Boy with his thumbs. He sat slumped with his heels on the seat, tucked under his butt, and sometimes he'd gaze at the screen on the seat back in front of her, blinking with sleepy absorption, and she wondered, as she often did when they watched TV together—the sound turned up and the English subtitles making her eyes scramble all over the screen—how much he could understand. She took off her own headset and just watched the pictures, to see if she could follow the story, and he looked sideways at her, his lips curling up in a smile, then fished out his own headset from the seat pocket. He mimed putting them on and turning up the volume, and arranged his face into an expression of sage contemplation, and she laughed; he was showing her that he could hear if he put those on. He'd gotten a haircut for Israel, which made him look older, less elfin.

It was thrilling to choose and examine and eat their own dinner without the help of a parent. Yossi came by and poked his head in, but they yelled at him to go away till he slunk off, hands raised in surrender. They found the little packets of salt and pepper, the tiny tubs of margarine for their rolls—and they agreed with great pleasure that the meal was disgusting except for the carrot cake.

THEY PARTED FROM YOSSI and Rafi at the Pelephone booth outside of customs, where Daniel needed to stop and rent a cell phone. When Yossi lifted Gal and hugged her, she wrapped her legs around his back and laid her head on his shoulder. She felt his back vibrate as he murmured in her ear, and then he looked in her face and rubbed his beard stubble on her cheek, making her swat at him. "We'll see you next week at the memorial," he said. He put her down and bent to kiss Noam's head. Rafi waggled his fingers good-bye and slipped something into her coat pocket; when she took it out, she found it was a trial-sized tube of Jergens Ultra Healing moisturizer. She watched them walk off with a throb of unease.

The sound of native Hebrew jingled in her ears, and her brain rearranged itself with a smart click, like a metal washer onto a magnet. After he'd signed for the phone, Daniel put his wallet back in his pocket and ushered them away from the line, gesturing for Gal to wheel Noam in the little folding stroller while he wheeled the cart with the suitcases. He stopped, peered at the phone in his palm, and dialed Yaakov's cell phone. "Yaakov?" he said loudly. "It's Daniel!" He listened for a while, and Gal heard a torrent of noisy, distorted male speech come from the phone on his ear. Sabba, she realized with alarm, wasn't at the airport. Daniel kept trying to cut in and tell him it was no problem, they'd take a *sherut*. "Don't worry," he said. "Yaakov. Yaakov. Don't worry. Okay, *le'hitraot*. See you soon."

"Okay, guys," he told the kids. "Sabba isn't going to make it—he got a flat tire. So we're taking a *sherut*. C'mon. Gal, you push your brother, okay?"

"Did he get into an accident?" Gal asked as he herded her out the doors and into the crowd. Would Daniel know how to get them to Jerusalem, and remember that he had to pay with shekels, not dollars?

"No, no," he said. "He got a flat tire when the car was parked in front of the house."

"Are we still going to see him?" She was hurrying with the stroller to keep up with him.

"What?"

"Are we still going to see him? Wait for me!"

"Of course!"

The air smelled of exhaust and cigarette smoke, the high whine of idling planes punctuated by quick blasts of car horns and brake squeals. People were holding up signs, exclaiming, hugging. Taxi drivers approached and solicited his business in English, and Daniel waved them off till he saw a Shemesh van. *"Yerushalayim?"* he asked the driver, and when he nodded, Daniel wheeled the bags to the back, supervised their getting lifted into the trunk, and lifted Gal's backpack off her back so she could get in. He tossed it in after her, lifted Noam out of his stroller and struggled to collapse it with one hand, sweating in his winter coat, remembering the woman in the security line who'd said, "I'd help you with that, but I don't have a degree in advanced engineering."

He handed the folded stroller to the driver to stow away, lifted Noam into the van, and sat him next to Gal in the middle row, then climbed in beside him. The van vibrated loudly. In the back sat a religious couple with two little girls wearing sweatshirts over dresses. Daniel unzipped his coat and squirmed it off, feeling his shirt stick to his back and a trickle of sweat on his temple. "Whoosh," he sighed. "One more little drive and we're there."

They were the last ones in the van; the driver got in and pulled away. Now that Daniel was settled and had caught his breath, he remembered sitting in a van with his parents and Matt a year ago, the one that had taken them to the morgue, and for a moment something of the old shock came over him. When he could breathe again, he was glad to be alone, without his parents to manage and ward off, without reporters in his face. He put his arm around Noam and scooted him in closer.

He dozed, and was awoken when the van lurched into low gear as they began to ascend. It was warm in the van, and one of the little girls behind him was kicking at his seat; just when he was about to turn around, she'd stop, and then when he settled down, she'd kick again. He looked down at Gal, who was nodding and dozing with her head resting on the window. A scent memory of the morgue floated past him, and he concentrated on it for a second, trying to make it comprehensible, before letting it go in revulsion. The swing of the van through curves and the slash of sunlight in and out of his field of vision began to nauseate him. He closed his eyes, and when he opened them again, it was dark, the sun blocked by the massive wall of the cemetery where his brother was buried. Tears sprang to his eyes. His brother—*brother*—never had a word pierced his heart so sharply. A silent cry rushed through his chest and head.

Matt!

The slip was startling—although, he quickly reminded himself, it certainly wasn't the first time he'd called Joel "Matt," or vice versa. After all, hadn't Joel been his first beloved, the model for all future beloveds? He rubbed his eyes before the tears could fall, and shrugged off the soreness and longing in his heart.

THE APARTMENT WAS CHILLY and dark, the blinds on the porch making a hollow shuddering sound in the wind. They entered, sniffing and twitching. There was a faint smell of cleaning chemicals; Malka had had her housekeeper clean it.

Daniel dumped his bags in the hall and helped Gal off with her backpack. He turned on all the lights within reach, and flipped on the boiler switch next to the bathroom. He wheeled Noam into the kitchen and opened the refrigerator, peering in as if it would offer him the key to an important mystery. It was empty except for some condiments in the door—mustard, mayonnaise, capers—and had been wiped out by someone who'd done a half-assed job; tiny crumbs lined the edges of the vegetable drawers, and there was an intractable juice syrup spot with tiny shreds of paper towel fuzzed around its edges.

Gal went automatically to her after-school destination, the snack drawer, sliding it open and finding a few loose Bamba and pretzel pieces and crumbs in the corners. She put a piece of Bamba in her mouth but when she bit down on it, it felt like biting into a sponge and she spat it into her hand. She looked around for the garbage, or a paper towel, then held her hand with the tooth-marked yellow paste out to Daniel, and he wrinkled his nose and brought her by the wrist to the sink. The faucet coughed loudly twice before water came out and washed it off.

She wandered into the living room; there were the blue couch and the leather lounge chair around the pocked octagonal wood coffee table that she had jumped off of thousands of times—first, as a little kid, onto the couch, landing on her knees, and then, later, with a big thud onto the floor, making her parents scold her about disturbing the downstairs neighbors. There, on a shelf under the TV, were the DVDs: *The Sound of Music*, Uzi Chitman, *The Little Mermaid*. The TV had a light film of dust over its face. She put her finger to it to draw her name, and was nipped by an electric shock. Her heartbeat sped up, then slowed down. An unnatural quiet saturated the house; she wanted to speak into the silence but couldn't coax the sound out of her throat.

She walked down the hall to her room, studiously avoiding looking into her parents' room ahead of her. Her room was dim and stripped: just her bed and Noam's crib, no sheets or pillowcases, comforters uncovered and folded; no toys. With only its thin mattress, the crib looked like a tiny jail cell. The pictures were up, though, and in the middle of the floor, the rug with the frog. Sunlight bled through the blinds' closed slats. She sat down on her bed, then curled up around the cold, bare pillow and put her thumb in her mouth. She was chilled. She thought she could fall asleep.

She heard Daniel's footsteps and felt his shadow come over her. "Your grandparents are on their way," he said. "When they get here I'll go to the *makolet* and get some food into this house." He stood there for a few more moments; she could hear him breathing and then scratching his cheek stubble. "Okay," he said.

A minute later there was a knock on the door, light and peppy. Gal sat up, and from Daniel's delighted greeting she registered that it wasn't her grandparents. She came out of her bedroom to see who was there, slowed shyly. There stood Leora, wearing glasses!, and holding a plastic-wrapped plate with cookies and candy. And her mother, Gabrielle, in flowing bell-bottoms, a flowered blouse, and silver trinkets at her neck and wrists. "Welcome back!" Gabrielle cried as she and Daniel embraced. She caught sight of Gal over his shoulder. "Kookie, are you shy?" she said, her voice suffused with amused tenderness.

Gal blushed and trotted over, let herself be lifted and squeezed, her face tickled by Gabrielle's hair, her nostrils by her scent, which was like cucumbers. Gabrielle set her down and beamed at her. "You've gotten so big! How many teeth have you lost?" She peered into Gal's mouth, which was opened for inspection, and said "Psssh!" with an impressed expression. She caught sight of Noam sitting on the living room rug and crouched beside him. "Do you remember me? *Oy vey*, what happened to your poor cheek?" He reached out his hand and touched her face. "Num-num," she growled, pretending to gnaw on his hand. "Where's Matt? What, he didn't come?"

"Hi," Gal was saying to Leora, a little shy because Leora looked older and more serious with glasses on.

"Here's a Purim *mana*," Leora said, and thrust it at her with a smile.

IT WAS PURIM, AND the little-girl Queen Esthers in their pretty dresses were out in force. As were the teenagers with their faces minimally, wittily painted, and the men in drag, one of whom waited on Daniel in the coffee shop the next morning when the kids were at their grandparents'—a miniskirt encasing his slender hips, his breasts askew, his Adam's apple a-bobbing. That evening, Malka and Yaakov took the kids to shul for the reading of the book of Esther, and Daniel spent that time at home unpacking and cleaning up, then pouring himself a scotch and looking all over the house, fruitlessly, for a Bible, so he could reread Esther himself. He finally gave up and turned on his computer to check for wireless coverage, not very hopeful, although as the chord and the white apple greeted him, he marveled at how the sight of his own computer booting up could help him feel just a little more at home. And the wireless was working! Either his father had continued paying for Internet, or Netvision had forgotten to turn it off.

He read, sipping scotch. Vashti, the first queen, a feminist hero, who refused to dance for the king and his court. Then Esther, and her shadowy, ambiguous uncle/counselor/friend Mordechai. And at the end of the story, massacre. That surprised him, even though he'd read it before. Skimming along a chain of Google pages, he found a commentary from Elie Wiesel:

> I confess I never did understand this part of the Book of Esther. After
> all, the catastrophe was averted; the massacre did not take
> place. Why then this call for bloodshed? Five hundred men were
> slain in Shushan in one day and three hundred the next. Seventy-five
> thousand persons lost their lives elsewhere. . . . Is this why we are

told to get drunk and forget? To erase the boundaries between reality and fantasy—and think that it all happened only in a dream?

Daniel wondered how much of the story Gal was understanding, and he wished Matt was there to appreciate and deplore with him the way things hadn't changed in this latest version of Jewish nationhood, where disproportionate revenge remained such a central tactic. The scotch was beginning to warm him and soften the edges of his vigilant consciousness, and for a minute or two he allowed himself to miss Matt, to feel how much he picked up the slack, both parentally and emotionally. Who else would understand by a mere glance how Daniel felt reading the book of Esther? Without Matt to carry the indignation over the Occupation for the two of them, he now had to carry it himself. Along with ironic, queeny commentary about all aesthetic affronts. It was exhausting. Sure, Matt might snort a little too vociferously, jump to judgment a little too quickly and without sufficient nuance, but if he was being fair about it, shouldn't Daniel acknowledge that you really couldn't ask anybody always to have the most exact and perfect moral touch?

That thought came and then receded, too complex to hold on to in the vague glow of his buzz, but it left him feeling lonely. His eyes skirted the kitchen where he sat, the essential foods—coffee, crackers, cereal, two cans of cracked Syrian olives, two ripening avocados, the crunchy oily treat called "eastern cookies" that Gal loved, a few bars of Elite chocolate—that he'd lined neatly on the counter instead of actually putting into a cabinet, and the apartment's cold provisional half-emptiness made him feel provisional and half-empty, too. He thought he might write Derrick an email, and got up to pour himself another scotch beforehand. He sat and logged on, and found emails from work, from the producer of Joel's old show asking when the memorial would be and inviting him to the studio to look at the new editing room they'd dedicated to Joel's memory, and from an old friend of Daniel's from Oberlin who had married an Israeli man and moved to Jerusalem.

Debra Frankel had been a smart, spiky presence around the edges of his social circle at college, and he had seen her at his ten-year reunion, where they'd ended up in line together at a sandwich shop, joking about her impression of him back then as an aloof aesthete and his impression of her as someone who might eat him alive. It turned out that since the Peace Train bombing she'd been keeping track of him, which kind of touched him but also made him think, *You couldn't send a card?* He wrote to Joel's producer to set up a time, and left Debra's email for another day when he was less tired and vulnerable, more sober.

He heard the moan of the elevator door and a bustle and a knock. When he opened the door Gal burst in, excitedly spinning her noise-maker, which made a hideous noise indeed. "I saw a person throwing up on the sidewalk, and Savta said he was drunk!" she said. "And every time they said the word *Haman*, everybody made all this noise!"

"Awesome," Daniel said mildly, smiling at Malka, who'd come in with her as Yaakov wrestled the stroller, with a sleeping Noam, out of the elevator.

Gal pirouetted on the point of her sneaker, and Malka shushed her as Daniel stooped to unbuckle Noam's straps, picked him up and put him on his shoulder, and took him to his crib, where he dumped him as gracefully as he could, then leaned over to take off his shoes with stealthy fingers. Malka came in and looked over his shoulder. "Did you change him?" Daniel whispered.

"Yes, right before we put him in the car." She kissed her fingers and touched them softly to the baby's cheek.

They went back into the hallway, where Yaakov was standing with his hands in his pocket, watching Gal twirl. "Because that's what happens when you drink too much," she was saying. "Does beer make you throw up? Does wine make you throw up? Does . . . whiskey make you throw up?"

"Everything can make you throw up if you drink too much of it," Yaakov said.

"Even Coke?"

"No, no, just alcohol."

"Oh." She stopped moving and staggered over to her grandfather, collapsed against his legs. "Dizzy!" She laughed.

The three adults stood with indulgent smiles in the austere hallway, patches and holes here and there in the white walls where they'd taken down pictures to bring to Daniel's house or to the grandparents'. They were more relaxed on their home turf, Daniel thought, and Matt's absence probably helped as well.

Gal was still chirping when he helped her get into pajamas and brush her teeth. The women had had to sit separately from the men, she told him, but when you thought about it, on Purim, how would you even know? "Maybe a woman would dress up as a man so she could sit in the front of the *bet knesset!*" she said with a spray of toothpaste. "Maybe there was a man sitting back there with us, and we just couldn't tell! Wouldn't that be funny, Dani?"

"Funny," he said. He hadn't seen her so cheerful and relaxed in ages.

She spat into the sink and studied the string of saliva and toothpaste with interest, then swiped her mouth hard with her pajama sleeve. What a little savage, Daniel thought. He could just see her whirling that noisemaker in shul, eyes bright and teeth bared.

DURING THE DAYS WHEN the children were at their grandparents', Daniel spent the mornings working from home, corresponding with his staff via email. In the afternoons he took long walks, out from their neighborhood, past the playgrounds and the newer, smoother-hewn buildings of Yefe Nof. The almond trees were just starting to blossom, and from hillside lots he caught the scents of sage and rosemary just as they vanished. Above him, from apartment balconies, came the sounds of swishing mops and the thuds of women beating carpets. In the Jerusalem Forest, the paths were knobby and spongy from pine needles, and the treetops shifted against the swift-moving clouds.

He took Gal and Noam to dinner at Gabrielle and Moti's house, staying past the kids' bedtimes as they played Hearts, the adults sipping a sweet aperitif, Leora and Gal solemn with importance to be playing with the grown-ups, growling and slapping Moti away as he tried to coach them. He went to the *Israel Today* studio, where editors and soundpeople racing from one room to another with headphones on and clipboards in their hands lurched to a stop, clutched their hearts, and grasped his hand, asked him about the children before looking at their watches with alarm and rushing off. Rotem, Joel's old producer, ushered him into the new editing room with its state-of-the-art console, its plush, ergonomic chairs, and a small gleaming plaque on the door, dedicating it to Joel's memory. He was introduced to Joel's replacement, Mark Weitzman, a broad-faced, telegenic fellow who'd been a reporter for the *Hartford Courant* before making *aliyah*, who gripped Daniel's shoulder and said rather theatrically that he could only hope to live up to Joel's example as a journalist and as a human being.

He contacted Debra Frankel and she invited him over to her Gilo apartment for coffee. Her study was lined with titles in English, Hebrew, and Arabic; policy papers were heaped and scattered chaotically across her desk. She gave him thick Turkish coffee with cardamom whose grounds he tongued off his palate, and they were interrupted several times by excitable, brown-skinned sons wearing soccer clothes. Debra worked for a nonprofit that worked on fair labor rights for the large migrant population that had come to Israel in recent years. When Daniel told her he worked as the editor of a college alumni magazine, she said, "Huh!" And then: "You know, I always imagined you'd do something bigger than that. You were such a good writer. Remember *Rags and Bones?*" That had been the name of a campus literary magazine, not the official one, but the more edgy one he and some of his friends had launched. "I always went straight to your stories first. Remember the one where the grandfather is buying a boy his first expensive violin?" Debra was smiling and musing, coffee glass suspended in her hand. "They're all on display in cases in this shop where you have to have an appointment to get in, and the boy is trying them out. Your description of the differences in tone quality was so amazing. I've never looked at violins the same way since. And I remember thinking I'd kill to be able to write like that."

"Thanks," Daniel said, remembering that story, remembering how in the fiction-writing workshop he was taking, the professor had loved that part too, but pressed him to create a stronger conflict. She'd told the class that being conflict-averse might be a workable life strategy for some of them, but that it would not help them in fiction; and he'd sat there for the rest of the class wondering if he was conflict-averse. He was shocked and flattered that Debra remembered the story all these years later. And at the same time, a little irritated: Who was she to comment on his life?

As he was leaving, Debra said, "If you wanted to come work for us, I could probably make that happen." The editor of their newsletter and promotional materials had just left for another job. He thought about that on the bus ride home as he wedged past women with babushkas and men with briefcases and soldiers with traces of acne, whose weapons were propped against their thighs, and dropped hard into a seat in the back. When a pregnant woman approached, the handles of her straining shopping bag digging into white, puffy fingers, he stood to offer her his seat and leaned against a pole. He didn't know whether the job offer was serious, or just impulsive: he thought their Oberlin connection might have made Debra assume she knew more about him than she really did, and want to help him more than she was actually able. Surely there were people who worked in the nonprofit world who were more qualified than he was.

One chilly afternoon, when the sun started to glint through after a rainy morning, he walked into town to see the Peace Train Café. He'd been putting it off for days, but had decided by this point that he'd regret not going more than he dreaded going. It was rebuilt now, a slender Ethiopian guard with a rifle and a yellow vest at the door, the memorial plaque screwed into the stone facing. He stepped around a man in a white oxford, *tzitziot* dangling from his pants and a cell phone plastered to his ear, and suddenly remembered a moment with Joel from his last visit before Joel died: They'd gone to the hospital to visit a friend of Joel's who'd just had a baby, and because it was after hours—Joel had had to work late—they exited through the emergency room. There they saw a man, bloodied, clothes shredded, being rushed into the ER on a stretcher by the EMTs, one trotting alongside him holding his wrapped arm and an IV bag, another leaning over him pumping his chest, the doors sliding open with pneumatic alacrity, the ambulance light whirling in the dark. And the patient was talking on his cell phone. They'd marched out into the parking lot, turned toward each other, and died laughing.

He approached the plaque, found Joel's and Ilana's names on the white, dappled marble, ran his fingers over the elegant etched Hebrew letters. He didn't go inside; he didn't want to see the reconstructed, bustling space, the shiny state-of-the-art espresso machines. Instead he walked over to the café he'd gone to with Matt the time they visited the bombed-out site a year ago. He ordered a cappuccino and took it outside onto the flagstone terrace, wiped the wetness off an iron chair with a fistful of napkins, and sat in that viny, cultivated space, chilly and a little weepy and thinking the whole time that he ought to go sit inside. The coffee's warm foam brushed his lips, and he thought about how they'd sat at that table over there, Matt gazing moistly into his face. He remembered the clench in his stomach and shoulders, the cramp in his very soul. For some reason, it was so much easier to *feel* now. This whole crappy, horrific year, his insides had felt like a carnival, all garish lights and noise, whirling, grotesquery, nausea. Now the carnival had left town, the sawdust had been wetted and raked, and the wind blew clean and sharp through the abandoned stables and arenas.

It made him wonder whether he should just take the kids and move to Israel. He was surprised at how much he felt okay about being here, around Joel's friends and even Ilana's parents. The sheer beauty of the city was a source of constant pleasure. Matt had been the major impediment before now. A flood of memory came rushing at him—the two of them sitting on the floor, Matt convincing him to go back to the States to honor Ilana's wishes. The rawness of his eyes and nostrils from crying, the chasm that had broken open in him at the prospect of leaving Joel behind, Matt's panicky face and his fingers brushing Daniel's cheek, their hands clutching. It had seemed at that moment that he was being forced to choose between Joel and Matt.

He noticed that the sweat had dried on his back, and that he was shivering. He drained his coffee and brought the cup inside, and when he went back onto the street, he felt too tired to walk home and hailed a cab instead.

That night, the kids sleeping and the house quiet, he lay in bed, warm under the covers, his nose cold from the night air coming through the cracked-open window. He heard a car door shut and an engine sputter to life. The idea of moving the kids back to Israel was taking root in him. He thought of Noam, drowsy on Gabrielle's shoulder as she absently brushed her cheek against his hair. He was picking up some Hebrew—*sheli*, mine; *od pa'am*, again. Was it Daniel's imagination that he was learning it more quickly than English? And he thought about Gal hopping up and down with plans and ideas like a regular kid. Why couldn't he just stay here, where they clearly thrived, and where he could magically make an elderly couple happy? If four people—four devastated people—could be made happier by his moving to Israel, wasn't it his obligation to do so?

He wasn't forgetting Ilana's wish that they be taken away from Israel. But maybe, he thought, his thoughts moving gently and clearly, Ilana hadn't made the best decision; maybe her background had made her more punitive toward her parents than wise about her kids' futures. And he didn't have control over the whole geopolitical nightmare here. He didn't. What he had control over was one small piece of the world, four people, and he could make their lives better. That seemed incontrovertible.

He should stay: the thought jolted him awake, and he remained awake for much of the night, thinking. They would return to the U.S. so he could quit his job and discharge his obligations there, and put his house on the market. His mind spun around a thousand details: the furniture, much of which was Matt's, what his boss and colleagues would say, Gal's school. His parents: he was scared to tell them. He wished he had someone besides Debra to talk to about it all. He didn't want to raise hopes when the prospect of moving was so daunting, or to be persuaded out of it, which he thought he might be if he talked to Derrick. He would miss Derrick! The thought came with a stab.

He rose the next morning exhausted, and over the next few days he went about his business imagining that he lived in this city, in this apartment. He went to the offices of Debra Frankel's nonprofit and applied for a job, and over coffee they talked about the politics of migrant labor in a country with many thousands of unemployed and immobilized Palestinians. He asked her if she didn't think the migrants were like scab labor. Her position was: perhaps, but they're here, and if they're here, I can help protect their basic rights. And that felt right to him, or right enough.

THE AIR COOLED GAL'S clammy hand as Daniel released it to open his backpack for the soldier at the entrance to the Machane Yehuda market. It was an early Friday afternoon, three hours or so before the start of Shabbat, and a fog of bad mood, of sadness churning into anger, hung over her. Daniel had just picked her up at Leora's house. The soldier returned Daniel's backpack and Daniel zipped it up and slung it over his shoulder.

As they stepped into the market, the sun was abruptly cut off and they were engulfed by a wave of color and noise. She used to come there with Abba on Friday afternoons, and before coming back, she hadn't been able to remember those trips anymore. She just knew they'd taken them, because the story was told so often, and because she'd been quizzed on it. *What did he buy you there, Gal-Gal, do you remember? Half a falafel. And we'd split a can of Coke.* But now, taking in the market smell of cigarette smoke and citrus and roasted nuts and spices, she remembered again. Ahead of her, legs shuffled impatiently behind other legs

and swinging plastic shopping baskets; to the sides were stalls with colorful and bountiful displays of fruits and vegetables, nuts, candy, pre-
sided over by brusque brown-skinned men who threw bags of produce
onto scales and held out their fingers, cupped and upside down, waiting
to drop change into customers' hands. She remembered holding her
father's hand as he steered them through the crowd, as she held Daniel's
now; she felt the combative jostle of shoppers and the small dirty boys
on errands running against the tide; the taste of grapes came to her
lips, and she remembered taking them out of the bag in Abba's shopping basket—one, two, three off the stems without him noticing—and
feeling the dry, dusty unwashed outsides with her tongue and then the
sweet spurt of juice. For a moment she was back in her old life, with
her father. She always looked forward to going, but the feeling of being
overwhelmed and a little scared when she was actually there was familiar to her, too. There were times when they didn't go to the *shuk* at all,
because the Arabs put bombs there that killed people.

That wash of complicated sense memory came over her now as irritation, and she began to lag behind, causing Daniel to pull her a little
harder. "Ow!" she yelled. "Stop pulling so hard!"

He stopped and turned, causing a woman wearing a head scarf to
bump into him and give him an exasperated stare. "Sorry," he said.
"Sorry, Gal-Gal."

Her face was so stricken and so vulnerable he asked her if she
wanted him to pick her up.

"I'm not a baby," she said stoutly.

"Oh, honey, I know that," Daniel said. When he left her at Leora's,
she was being yanked by Leora down the hall to her bedroom. When
he returned, they were eating a snack of crackers and avocado at the
kitchen table with Gabrielle. Gal was sitting barefoot and cross-legged
on her chair, talking loudly with a mouthful of crumbs and green mush.
Leora was trying to talk over her, one admonishing finger held aloft,
and Gabrielle, her elbow on the table, her chin resting in her hand, was
listening to them gabble with a lazy, amused expression on her face.

"Can't you just stay here forever?" she said teasingly to Daniel. "I'm just crazy about this little girl."

Gal looked expectantly at him, then her expression corrected itself self-consciously as she realized it was just idle love-talk on Gabrielle's part. She'd been struck hard by Gabrielle's affection, Daniel saw, and he'd stepped toward her and laid his hand gently on her hair, wanting to tell her that they *could* stay there forever, they could, but knowing it wasn't the time. She moved it away, and turned slightly to block him from her sight. He felt a surge of empathy for her.

"I'll tell you what," he'd said. "Why don't you stay here for another hour, and I'll come back and get you on my way to the *shuk*."

"Okay," she'd said blithely.

He'd found a kiosk that sold newspapers, and sat in a nearby park reading for an hour before returning to pick her up, with a promise she could come back the next day. She was shut down and unresponsive in the car. He was conscious that he'd been sensitive toward her, and that she hadn't thanked him or even acknowledged that he'd been nice. *That, my friend*, he told himself, *is parenthood.*

"C'mon," he said now. "Let's buy some vegetables for dinner and then we'll go have falafel."

She allowed herself to be led again, looking straight ahead and down at blue jeans, women's calves encased in nylons, thick ankles emerging from pumps and sneakers, sprigs of greens fanning from plastic bags, squashed fruit smears and discarded peels on the cobblestones. She thought about Leora, who was taking a martial arts course, and who had shown her some moves, inexpertly trying in slow motion to wrestle her mother to the ground as Gabrielle laughed and mock gagged and complained facetiously, and finally collapsed gently onto the floor. Gal twitched at the sound of a man speaking Arabic nearby, looked up into his face; he was intently explaining something to someone, his thumb and forefingers pinched and jabbing the air for emphasis. She tripped on something, righted herself.

They passed a candy store that was one of the prettiest sights she'd

ever seen, more candy than you could even imagine in brightly colored wrappers, stacked, fanned, bunched, and binned. She stopped and
gazed into the little stall, pulling her fingers out of Daniel's hand gradually, experimentally. She waited for him to grab her hand again, but
when she looked for him he was at the next stall, picking out change
from his palm as a man tossed a plastic bag of carrots on a scale. She
took a few steps in the other direction, self-conscious under the gaze
of the candy stall proprietor. Would it scare Daniel if he couldn't find
her for a minute? The moment she thought that, the impulse to scare
him—not entirely conscious, just fizzing at the edges of her mind—
intensified.

And then, so quickly it bewildered her, she'd drawn away, and
couldn't see or hear him anywhere. She thought she heard him call her
name, but when she turned in that direction a different man was calling something else. She tried to retrace her steps back to the vegetable
stand where she'd seen him buying carrots, but found herself at a different vegetable stand with a woman in charge. She opened her mouth to
call his name, but felt too self-conscious to call attention to herself, and
closed it again.

Just then she noticed a cardboard box, unattended at the side of a
stall, its top flaps loosely folded in on one another. Her attention worked
it over for a long minute. She was supposed to report an unattended
package or bag; it had been drilled into her so often, she had to retrain
herself at the Jackson Street School not to go to the teacher about every
backpack she saw lying in some random place. But it occurred to her
now that she didn't know who she was supposed to report it to. She
looked for a soldier, but none passed by. She looked at the faces of the
people around her—stern and engrossed as they examined fruit, held
out money, felt fabric in their fingers—and panic seeped through her
body. She turned and began to walk away, then broke into a run, her
sneakers pounding the stones. It wasn't hard to dodge people; to antici-
pate the curbs and gaps in the sidewalk. She picked up speed, and as she
ran she felt an echo, a shadow, a hot presence at her heels: her parents,

running hard, being led by her to safety. She headed for brighter light, where the covered market ended and the street began, and when she reached it, she stopped, making people cry out "Little girl!" and lurch around her to avoid knocking her over. She looked behind her. She waited, panting. She went over to a wall and sat down on the ground, catching her breath, and waited some more. Her heartbeat roared in her ears.

There was no explosion. No panic, no screaming, no glass or limbs flying through the air, no spray of blood. No burning smell, no smoke, no sirens, no Ema and Abba lying dead. She cautiously let relief trickle though her, but with it barged in a loneliness so powerful she started to cry. "*Ema!*" she whimpered.

She sat there for a minute or two, exhausted, until a shadow passed over her. A big man in a dirty white apron was kneeling down in front of her. "I saw you running!" he said. "Are you lost?"

"Yes," she whispered.

"Did you lose your *ema*?"

"Yes," she said.

"Come with me," he said, holding out his hand, "and we'll find her."

She hesitated, too embarrassed to set him straight.

"Your *ema* probably told you not to go off with strangers," the man said. "But I'm no stranger. I'm Chezzi, and everybody knows me." He took her hand and walked her back into the market to a fish stall, where he gestured to a small battered chair beside the counter. "I'm just going to sit you right there," he said, "where everybody can see you."

He spoke with strong gutturals like Abba's friend Avram, the Hebrew of a Sephardic Israeli, and the words bounced in Gal's ears like a jeep on a rutted road. She saw the chair and thought it would be okay to sit in it, especially since nobody around her seemed frightened or upset. The smell of fish was overpowering. People were jostling in front of the counter, their eyes on the moist silver heaps of fish on display, shouting, "Give me a kilo of this!" and "Give me a kilo of that!" Behind her, a teenage boy wearing bunny ears and pink lipstick was hacking at a salmon on a slippery counter. Heaping a pile of fish on a scale, the fish man turned his head and yelled at him, "Stop stop stop! Smoothly! You're not cutting down a tree!" He muttered a few words to himself. "Come here and work the counter for a second. I have to take care of this little girl. C'mon, can't you see there's a line?"

The teenager tossed down the knife and moved to the counter, muttering, "Okay, okay!"

"What's your name, *motek*?" the fish man asked, taking a cell phone from his apron pocket and dialing.

"Gal."

"Gal! Isn't that a boy's name? Gal what?"

Gal shrugged anxiously. "Gal Rosen."

"What?"

"Rosen."

"I thought Gal was a boy's name," he said again, his ear pressed to the phone. "*Allo!*" he said. He talked with great volume and excitement for a minute or so, then cried, "Yes! He called! Tell him to come to Chezzi's fish counter—just ask anyone—okay. And to keep a closer eye on his niece!" He looked at Gal, nodding, still listening. "Okay. Okay."

He ended the call and said, "Your uncle is looking for you. He's terrified! He's coming to get you." He studied her, hands on his hips. "Do you want to learn how to fillet a fish?"

He put an apron loop over her head and wrapped the cloth several times around her body, tied it tight. "Come," he said, and positioned her in front of him before the counter; her nose was level with the salmon's belly, so he told her to wait a second and went to get the chair so she could stand on it. She stepped up. The fish was huge and shiny, and Gal looked down into its dead, rimmed eye.

"He's already taken out the guts and scaled it," the fish man said, and then muttered, "And that's all he'll be doing in the future." He gestured toward a pail with glop quivering in it and opened the fish at the slit with his thumbs to show clean, pink meat.

"Now, the first thing, your knife must be very sharp. Do you hear

me? Very sharp. And you must wet it with water"—he shook some
water over it from a liter Coke bottle with its label half peeled off—"so
that it doesn't catch on the meat. You never saw at it, like that *ahabal*
over there, because that rips the flesh. Look at this!" He tsked, gesturing
toward a small jagged part at the beginning of the cut. "What you do is,
you make a nice, long movement."

She watched him finish the cut behind the fin, down to the backbone. "See?" he said. "Now you cut along the backbone. You should be
able to feel the knife sliding along it."

His knife hand slid gracefully halfway down the length of the fish's
body. Gal stood between his arms, looking at the bones on the under-
side of the fish's head, which was now only half attached. She felt a
great, debilitating wave of fatigue wash over her. "You try," the fish man
said. He took her hand and closed it around the knife handle, then put
his own large and damp one over hers, and together they moved the
knife the rest of the way down the fish, to the tail. It made Gal queasy,
the gleaming pink flesh and the white-white bones.

"Wait, you didn't tell me you've done this before!"

"I never did!"

"What! Did you hear that?" he bellowed jovially to the people in
line at the counter. "This little girl is lying to my face!" He removed
the fillet and turned the fish over, and just when Gal was ready for the
teasing and the fish filleting to be over, she heard Daniel call her name.

His face was pale as he lifted her off the chair and held her so tightly
her ribs hurt. He was saying "Thank you, thank you, thank you" in
Hebrew to the fish man. He was babbling about how Gal didn't know
his cell phone number, and asking her whether she knew her Jerusalem
address. "I thought I'd lost you!" he was saying. "I was so scared!"

She could feel his hands clutching her, the warm dampness of his
shirt, his pounding heart. A sense of cold triumph filled her. But when
he finally put her down, holding her away from him by the shoulders to
examine whether she was okay, it was pity she felt, and embarrassment.
She suddenly wanted to drag him away, so the onlookers, who were

crowding around with jovial commentary, wouldn't see his naked, haunted face.

IT TOOK DANIEL A few days to recover, for the sensation of racing through the market, hot with panic, to dissipate into ordinary memory. *I can't spare her*: that was the thought that had pounded at his mind as he called for Gal, first tentatively and then with a scream that made people's heads whip around. And then, starting to run: *Ilana's going to kill me*—which now, in retrospect, he was able to laugh about. When he finally had Gal in his grasp, it felt as though he couldn't get her close enough to him, even as he was crushing her to his chest.

In the meantime, he had to put up with Gal compulsively telling everyone she knew the story of how he'd lost her in the *shuk*, which included flourishes like "If the fish man hadn't found me, I might still be lost today, or kidnapped!" and "I was so scared I thought I was going to die!" In her telling, Chezzi was the crafty, streetwise hero and Daniel the incompetent idiot, and that irritated Daniel to no end, although he went secretly to the *shuk* a few days later to bring Chezzi an expensive bottle of wine, which the fishmonger accepted with a blush and an "It's not necessary" before setting it carefully on the ground beside his lunch bag. He also had to put up with Yaakov taking him aside and reminding him that Gal was just a little girl, and he had to be careful when he took her into crowds. Clearly he and Malka had had a talk about the best way to handle this. "Malka and I were very surprised and disappointed to hear this," Yaakov admonished, shaking his head gravely. "You of all people should know that Jerusalem can be a very dangerous place."

At bedtime, Daniel arranged Gal's blanket and stuffed monkey around her chin, the way she liked them, sat at the edge of the bed and brushed the hair off her face with his palm. "You know I would have found you no matter what," he said. "With Chezzi, without Chezzi, I would have flown like Superman throughout that *shuk* till I found you."

"You didn't look very much like Superman when you found me," she told him.

He gave her a look. What a tough little stinker she was. Being on the other end of the sharp, speculative gaze she was leveling at him was daunting, and she was only seven. On the rare occasion he'd imagined the kids he might have one day, he'd never imagined one like this. Then again, he thought, leaning down to brush her temple with his lips, was *anyone* able to imagine their kid, the one that actually came to exist in the world?

Shabbat passed and the new week began, along with the playing-hooky feeling they got when the bus stops crowded once again with people heading to work. He'd borrowed Malka and Yaakov's car, and ferried the children to their house, to Leora's, to Gal's friend Ruti's. One evening he took Gal's hand and led her into her parents' bedroom, which she'd been phobic about even looking into for the week they'd been there. "What are you afraid of?" he'd asked, and she'd said, "Everything."

"It's mostly my stuff now," he told her.

"But does it smell like them?" she asked, yanking her hand away when he reached for her.

"I don't think it does anymore," he said. "Do you want me to go in and give it one more sniff?"

"I'm gonna hold my nose," she said, and she held it the entire time they were in there—held it sitting at the edge of the bed, peeking into the bathroom, and turning the TV on and off.

"This is where you used to come late at night and early in the morning, right?" he said gently, standing at the door. He didn't want to press it, but he did want to acknowledge it. "And when you were sick or scared."

"Yeah," she said in a small, nasal voice.

"Gal, you're making me laugh sitting there holding your nose."

"Don't!" she said reproachfully.

MALKA HAD TOLD HIM that she wanted to take him somewhere; she wouldn't say where, but they'd arranged to go on Tuesday morning. It was all very hush-hush; when they left, leaving the kids with Yaakov, she didn't even tell Yaakov where they were going. Daniel drove her car on the honking, bleating, chaotic Jerusalem streets, buses barreling by them in the bus lane and snorting huge blasts of exhaust, obeying her directions and stealing the occasional glance at her face. "Right here," she finally said.

"Har Herzl?" He slowed the car, looked at the gate, and pulled into visitor parking. They got out into the cool dry air and slammed the car doors shut.

"Come," she said.

She led him out of the parking lot and into the cool, spacious rock tunnel that served as the entrance to the national military cemetery, and he felt the chill of flagstones untouched by sun. He remembered visiting this place during his junior year abroad, when the Jerusalem memorial sites had affected him deeply, conjuring images of young Jewish warriors, men like himself, only called by history to be more selfless and valiant, and forming, astonishingly, the best army in the world. He'd wonder how he would have fared as a soldier during the early days of the state, and feel privileged and soft, and decide that he really couldn't know, because as an Israeli soldier he just wouldn't have been the same person he was back then. Then he'd wonder if that was just the easy way out.

He didn't feel that way anymore. Now the old romance seemed just that, romance. For one, he'd been a gay man for years now, and he understood how that vague shame over being soft came uncomfortably close to shame about being gay. For another, well, there'd been a lot of water under the bridge in his relationship to the State of Israel, and its idealized self-image. He prepared himself for some kind of lesson from Malka in national sacrifice, or national pride. It was a nice day, and he didn't have anywhere else to be; he could indulge her, he thought, especially since she'd been easy and kind since they'd arrived.

They emerged into a large sunny plaza and stepped up to the cemetery map. The areas were coded by number, and by places or wars in which the soldiers were killed: "Road to Jerusalem," "Yom Kippur," "Mount Castel." Then Malka led him into the cemetery. They walked among beautifully tended stone graves that resembled coffin-shaped raised gardens, with plaques on the headstones and small rocks placed by mourners here and there on the headstones or the edges of the grave. It was quiet here; through breaks in the pines along the edges of the hill, Jerusalem glinted, bright and dusty. Malka pointed toward a crane in the distance of the cemetery. "I wanted to show you this," she said.

Daniel followed her, his gaze lingering on the details of this grave and that, skipping over the Hebrew dates to find the dates he could recognize, reading the names of men who were born in South Africa, Poland, Germany, and died in battles he'd never heard of. Walking quietly with Malka, who wore slacks and a sweater and sneakers he'd brought her from the U.S., and large sunglasses that gave her the look of an aging incognito movie star, he felt more comfortable with her than he ever had before. After a few minutes he heard the ping of chisel on stone, multiple pings, then hollow hammering, and soon they came to a large space surrounded by a crane, a flatbed truck, several vans, and men at work. On a white stone wall was written, in iron Hebrew letters, *Monument to the Memory of the Victims of Terrorism*. There was a large rectangular stone sculpture standing on its end, with a hole with wavy sides carved into it; a flight of stairs led down to a plaza surrounded by stone walls on which bronze plaques with engraved names had begun to be mounted.

"Wow," he said. He studied the rectangle, and said, "So that's supposed to be a wall with a hole blown into it?"

"Ah," she said. "I hadn't thought of that."

"You know, stylized."

"Maybe."

"Do you think we can go down inside?"

Malka looked around at the workers. "I don't think so," she said. "It's not supposed to open for a few weeks, on Memorial Day."

He was quiet, then it occurred to him to ask, "Are Joel's and Ilana's names on one of those plaques?"

She nodded, and told him that she'd gone onto a website through which the National Insurance Institute was tracking names, and corroborated their information.

Men were calling out to one another, and two of them were consulting a map laid out on the bed of a truck. Daniel went up to a few of the plaques that were already hung and peered at them, but they were all dated much earlier. He looked around for a place to sit, and finally just stepped up alongside Malka and put his arm gently around her shoulders. They stood there for a few moments, and then she stepped out of his arm and gave his hand a squeeze before letting it go. "There's been a lot of controversy about this memorial," she said.

"Really?" Daniel said. "Why?"

"This is a military cemetery," she said. "The victims of terrorist attacks are civilians, not heroes. So the families of young men killed in war believe that it's unfair. The victims of terror are also going to be honored on Memorial Day from now on, and they don't like that either."

Daniel thought about that. "I guess I can see that," he said. "Their sons and brothers died fighting, while ours were—"

"Sitting in cafeterias and coffee shops," Malka said.

They turned to walk back. "How do *you* feel about it?" Daniel asked.

She shrugged. "I'm used to it. It reminds me of survivors of the Holocaust."

He tried to make the link in his mind.

"We are everything they don't want to be," she said, her face weary and bitter. "Victims. Weaklings. Everything this country does is supposed to be in our name, but really, they despise us."

He'd always wondered about that, but he was shocked that Malka thought it. "Do you think they despise victims of terrorism?" he asked.

She was quiet, then she gestured toward the military graves they were passing. "The message of this cemetery is: This is what we did to protect you. The message of the new memorial is: We can't protect you. How is anybody supposed to tolerate that?"

Whoa, he thought.

She sighed. *"Ain ma la'asot,"* she said, "there's nothing to do about it."

He glanced at her. Her mouth had tightened; she'd reverted back into banality, drawn back that tantalizingly sharp and trenchant part of herself. They turned back to the parking lot; she was no longer looking at him, and he thrust his hands in his pockets. He wondered if he'd ever see that part of her again.

JOEL'S PRODUCER, ROTEM, HAD wanted to have lunch with him, but her schedule didn't open up till the day before the memorial. She was a middle-aged woman with fancy glasses and sleek black hair that fell to her shoulders; she came from a famous military family, and projected an aura of cool authority. Joel—who called her *ha-mefakedet,* Commander—had told Daniel more than once that he would have looked like a total clown on camera without her supervision. Now, at a small, crowded café nestled among boutiques in a square near the TV station, Daniel watched her drench her salad with the dressing she'd asked for on the side, and this little war between discipline and appetite made him remember her husband, whom he'd met once at a dinner party at Joel's. What was his name again? He remembered that he was voluble and balding with ginger tufts of hair that sprang out from above his ears, and had a ready laugh that gobbled into a snort.

When Rotem had put down the small dressing cup, she leaned on her elbows and looked warmly into his face. "So," she said.

"So," he smiled, looking her over, assessing her as a possible friend.

"I was wondering if you'd like to be on our show."

He'd been about to take a bite out of a fancy little sandwich with prosciutto and goat cheese and esoteric greens, but now he lowered it to his plate. "For the year anniversary," Rotem explained. "We're planning a short retrospective, showing clips from some of the more famous shows Joel did. And we thought it might be interesting, and touching, to follow that up with an interview with you in the studio."

Daniel rubbed his chin with his hand. "I don't think so, Rotem," he said. "I just—I honestly don't know how I'd talk about my life." His relation to the terrorist attack, he said, was clearly unbelievable or repugnant to most people. And after some hesitation, knowing that Joel had probably already told her, he told her that he was gay, with that old familiar feeling of making a big deal out of nothing.

Rotem looked at him shrewdly, the journalist in her sizing him up. "So you think nobody's ever reacted to the death of a family member from terror the way you have? That your life is beyond the pale of what Israelis can hear, because you're gay and left-wing?"

"No," he said, feeling heat rise into his face, hearing in her questions the implication that he was emotionally fragile, self-congratulatory in his politics. Or else—the thought moved swiftly through him—she was just Israeli, and would be totally shocked to hear that her straightforward questions had given offense. "But look, I was already burned once for an interview I did in the U.S., and that was for a teeny local paper in Northampton." He told her about what he'd said in the interview, and the hate mail that ensued. "The *nicest* comment I got was that I was a self-hating Jew," he said. "But it was more like I was a faggot who wanted to be fucked by terrorists." He spat the word *faggot* in English, because Hebrew didn't have, as far as he was aware, a slur quite as juicy and potent.

"Idiots," Rotem said with a grimace. "Idiots. I'm sorry."

He sat back, mostly mollified, and picked up his sandwich, bit into the crunchy end of the baguette. He realized that with Rotem he was speaking in his straight register, his hands still, his voice compressed into a shorter range of notes; and as soon as he realized that, he realized that he'd been speaking like that since arriving in Israel, and that a strange fatigue was coming over him. Rotem was stabbing lettuce, peppers, chickpeas onto her fork with quick precision.

"Did you know," Daniel said, "that Ilana wanted the kids taken out of the country if anything happened to her and Joel? She was a daughter of Holocaust survivors." Rotem nodded. "She told me, if anything happens to us, get them out of here. I can't imagine an interview where I wasn't asked why I was raising them in the U.S. How could I explain that on Israeli TV?"

"That's a thought-provoking feature story," Rotem said.

"But I don't want to provide a thought-provoking feature story," he said heatedly. "If I did the interview, it would be to honor them, not to make people scrutinize their choices."

He saw that that displeased and disappointed her, and they were quiet for a few minutes, eating. The waiter came by to ask if everything was satisfactory. Daniel wondered how much he needed, or wanted, to tell Rotem, whom he was experiencing as something of a shark—"a thought-provoking feature story!"—and strangely, as something of a confessor. She'd been close to his brother, and that meant something to him. Finally, he ventured, "And I've broken up with my partner. So now the kids are being raised by a single parent on top of everything else."

She looked up from her food with interest, clearly lifted out of her brooding about the show. "So what, you're worried about looking like a failure on Israeli TV?"

"Yes," he said. "When gay people break up, it just goes to show that their relationships aren't lasting and legitimate."

"But marriages break up after a family member dies in a terrorist incident all the time," she said. "It's very common."

He sat back in his chair with a rush of feeling. It made total sense, but it stunned him, too, stunned and moved him to think that after the attack, he and Matt had been fighting against the odds. Why, he wondered, hadn't anybody told him that before? It might have helped!

"What's his name?" she asked.

"Matt," Daniel said. "Matthew Greene. He's younger than I am. He's handsome—I don't know why I said that, it doesn't really matter—and funny, and he took on the kids with enthusiasm, against every expectation I had."

"So what was the problem?"

His eyes fluttered closed and he shook his head. What *was* the problem? "He did something that broke my trust," he told Rotem, and the words sounded grandiose and unconvincing.

Rotem studied his face for a few minutes, and then wiped her mouth and set her crumpled napkin on top of the salad remnants on her plate. "Well, tell me you'll at least think about doing the show," she said. "Mark is a wonderful interviewer. And it would mean a lot to people to see Joel's face again."

A laugh sprung out of him. "You do realize that I'm not Joel, right?" he said drolly.

"I do," she said.

He'd hurt her feelings, he saw. He felt bad about that, although there was the slightest flicker of satisfaction that he had that power.

An awkward silence followed, then they both spoke at once. "Which shows were the famous ones?" Daniel asked, just as Rotem was bursting out with "It's just so amazing, how much you look, and sound, alike!"

"Oh, quite a few," she said, sitting back. "The profile of Amos Oz, where Joel got him to sing with him. The one about the security barrier. He interviewed the construction workers who were building it. There are parodies of it all over the place all the time." She laughed. "A columnist in *Ha'aretz* compared it to the gravedigger scene in *Hamlet*."

She put her finger up for the waiter, and when he came over she ordered an espresso, and Daniel said he'd have one, too. Another silence opened up the air. Then Daniel spoke. "You miss him," he said.

"I do," Rotem said, her eyes glistening.

"I do, too," he said, but he was thinking something else. *It would mean a lot to people to see Joel's face again.* What would Joel have said about that comment? Daniel imagined viewers from all over the country seeing him on their televisions, gasping, recovering, gabbling to their spouses about how fooled they'd been. Twinsism, of course, that's what Joel would have called it. Because how was it different from one of them sitting in on the other's exam? And then a thought followed that sank and spread into his chest. He was staying in Israel, sleeping in his brother's bed, raising his children in his house, taking on Joel's friends as his own. How was *that* different?

They parted outside in the windy square, Rotem's hair whipping across her face. "*Ad machar,*" they said. Until tomorrow. Daniel watched her walk back toward the station, hitching her purse higher on her shoulder. He walked to the bus stop and stood under the Plexiglas shelter with the cleaning women going home for the day. The wind battering its sides made his thoughts whirl like debris caught up in it. People stood and crowded toward the curb as the bus approached. He shouldered his way forward, snaking his arm around several bodies and clasping the cool bar to hoist himself in.

He could stay here and be Joel, fulfill the life Joel had been robbed of. But as he handed the driver his *cartisia*, saw the strong blunt fingers curled around the hole punch, he remembered that time so many years ago when he'd been staying in Joel's house, when stealing out of bed at night and hurrying out into the Jerusalem darkness to find men like himself had been his heart's desire.

THE UNVEILING HAD BEEN held at the *shloshim*, thirty days after the burial, but they'd decided to hold a service at the twelve-month anniversary as well, now that they could all come together without a custody battle to divide them. They stood on the outcropping of rock looking over the city, whose colors were muted under cloudy skies, the stone chalky and pale, the conifers dark gray-green, listening to the rabbi praying. Daniel held Noam on his hip, *kipot* on both their heads; lately, Noam had taken to putting his arm around Daniel's neck when he held him that way, which Daniel found totally heartbreaking. He counted around seventy people clustered about the headstones, which stated the dates of Joel's and Ilana's births and deaths in Hebrew and English, their love of their children, the love of their children for them. Their colleagues were there, standing with hands behind their backs and heads bowed, including the teachers and school administrators Daniel had come to know and Joel's coworkers too, Mark, Rotem and her husband, and the others.

The warm wind whipped at their hair and the women's skirts. Daniel's eye kept being drawn to movement in the distance, and he realized that part of him thought Matt might magically appear, surprise them as he had a year ago, the day before they loaded up their ark and sailed to Northampton. But when he looked up, it would just be a tree branch, or once, a solitary mourner approaching someone else's grave. Across from him, Gal stood next to Leora and Rafi, who had a *kipa* pinned to his hair and the spaced-out look he got when undirected speech was going on around him. Looking at them, Daniel saw that Gal did have friends, that among these children she didn't count as awkward or inappropriate at all, and that gladdened him. *I'm doing my best with them*, he silently told his brother and sister-in-law. *I really am.* He also vowed to do better.

Noam shifted on his hip and pointed to the headstones, let out an interested, tuneful cluck that made the people around them smile. "Ema and Abba," Daniel whispered into his ear. He'd been thinking about Rotem's assertion that it was common for couples to break up after they lost a child to a terrorist attack. Thinking that terrorism had broken him and Matt up, not a sex act at a party. Standing there half-listening to the rabbi's singsong, he thought about the blast of rage with which he'd cast Matt out, and felt shaken for a moment by the residue of that commotion. He handed Noam to Yaakov and stood for a second with his hands on his knees, like a winded runner. Who was he kidding? Matt wasn't dangerous. A fool maybe, for wantonly flirting with danger in a world that held plenty of horrors even if you just sat home in your chair all day and read a book. But he wasn't the cause of danger in the world, or at least not more than most people were. Daniel himself had almost lost Gal.

People looked at him with kind, inquiring looks that made his face grow hot. He closed his eyes and felt the pulses beating in his eyelids.

He straightened and let out a shaky sigh. The rabbi had finished praying and they recited the mourner's kaddish, Daniel and a few others reading it off a sheet of paper they'd been handed. Malka and Yaakov, he noticed without surprise, knew it by heart. He took Noam back from his grandfather and settled him into his stroller. As mourners started to wind through the rows of headstones to the cemetery exit, Daniel waited for Gal and put his hand on her head. "Come here for one second," he said in Hebrew. He steered her toward the headstones, and kneeled.

"What now?" she asked, kneeling.

He kissed his fingers and touched the cool granite of first Ilana's headstone, then Joel's. Gal solemnly kissed her own fingers, and touched each of her parents' graves.

THE RECEPTION AT THEIR apartment brought back many of the same people who'd come to the *shiva*, but to Daniel it felt sweeter and quieter, as if the explosion itself had finally stopped echoing and been folded into the air. His parents weren't there, for one; they'd intended to come but had been detained in the U.S. by the death and funeral of their old friend Lou Fried. Lydia didn't even give Daniel a hard time about it, or make him reassure her that she was making the right choice; she just said, wearily, with rare understatement, "It's been a hard year." And Matt wasn't there, of course. For a moment Daniel imagined him coming through the door, remembered how when Matt breezed into a room he seemed to change the very climate—to crisp and freshen the air there.

He let Gal take the other kids into her room, and when he looked in on them, the girls were practicing cartwheels in their jumpers and tights while Noam sat on Rafi's lap. He was slapping Rafi's *kipa* on his own head and tilting it so that it would slide off, then craning his neck to look at Rafi with an antic, expectant expression, and Rafi was saying dutifully, "That's funny." When he got back to the living room, someone was telling a long story about how Joel had gained the trust of his

Israeli crew when his predecessor, whom they'd loved, had been fired, and another did an imitation of an exasperated Ilana going off first on negligent parents and then on overinvolved ones, with a mixture of rudeness and comedy that was so spot-on, tears ran down their faces from laughter. As he wiped his eyes, Daniel felt a soft hand on his forearm; it was Malka's.

After everybody had left, stopping and turning at the door to take Daniel's hands in theirs and make him promise to keep in touch, Daniel sat with Gal and Noam in the living room, too tired to clean up all the empty glasses, the plates with blocks of half-eaten cheese surrounded by cracker crumbs, the bowls with dip crusting at the edges, the *bourekas* plate just flakes and oil. He'd turned on the TV to a cartoon. He closed his eyes and smiled again thinking of Ilana's friend's imitation of her, felt laughter pushing at his throat. His thoughts began to drift, curling pleasantly around Matt. He didn't resist them; it was as if all the Joel-love in the room had opened the spring of love in his heart, which then splashed noisily, refreshingly, over Matt as well.

"Noam!" Gal said in a high, bright voice.

Daniel looked over and caught his breath: Noam was on his feet, walking shakily over to him with a look Daniel could only describe as merry. He stumbled and fell against Daniel's legs, and Daniel picked him up and kissed him noisily on his plump, flushed cheek, saying, "Good job, buddy!" He looked at Gal and held up his hand for a high five; she gave it a resounding smack.

He shook out his stinging hand, smiling. "When we get back," he said, "I think we should see Matt."

She looked quickly at him, her face wavering with incredulity.

"Okay?" he asked.

She broke into a faint smile. "Okay," she said.

III

O N A WARM evening in early April, Matt hauled out the gas grill his landlords kept in their tiny shed and opened the lid to see what kind of shape it was in, nodded approvingly when he saw that they'd cleaned it before storing it. He didn't know how much gas was left in the tank, but hoped there was enough to cook a piece of fish, which was marinating in the kitchen. He lit the grill and stepped through the screen door from the patio into the kitchen, just in time to hear the doorbell ring. He went to answer the door, prepared to be irritated at anyone standing there with a clipboard in his hands.

It was Daniel, standing there alone with his hands in his pockets and his shoulders hunched. He was wearing a jacket and tie, evidently on his way home late from work; Matt wondered who was home with the kids. He had a grave expression that softened when he greeted Matt. "Hi," he said.

"Hi." Matt stood in front of the door, regarding him coolly as his heart buzzed. He wondered whether he should turn off the grill.

"Can I come in?"

Matt stood aside so he could enter.

Daniel came into the living room and looked around approvingly at the simple couches, the prints, the muted grays, beiges, and blacks of the room. "This is nice," he said.

Matt took this in with an acerbic little cocktail of feelings. Wasn't this ironic—Daniel's praise of the house he'd had to rent because he'd been kicked out of his own?

"Can I sit down?" Daniel asked, gesturing toward the couch. Matt nodded but remained standing himself. He worried that he was looking like a prick. He didn't mean to be one. It was just that he was pretty sure Daniel had come over to invite him to see the kids, but still, he felt he needed to guard against surprises. His whole perception of Daniel felt different; to his eyes, Daniel's seriousness now had a ruthless tinge to it, and his gentle kindness seemed like an attempt to mask that.

Daniel sat, leaning forward with his elbows on his knees, looking earnestly at him. "Matt," he said. It took some time, as he stammered out an apology and told him he loved him, for it to register to Matt that he wanted him back. It felt so unreal hearing the words he'd despaired of ever hearing, that Matt couldn't even revel in his own vindication. He sank into a chair, shocked, as Daniel talked.

He'd done a lot of thinking, Daniel said, about how badly he'd treated him. "I just didn't let you in at all," Daniel said. "I was grieving, Matt, and I didn't know how to let you help me."

Never had Matt wished more to be the kind of cool customer that could wait him out and make him squirm than when he began blurting, "I wanted to be part of it! I wanted to share responsibility. I wanted some freaking *credit* for being a partner in parenting. It was like you refused to let us go through it together! Was that the kind of love you wanted?"

"No, I didn't want *any* love!" Daniel said.

"Why not?"

"I . . ." Daniel paused, and put his hand to his forehead as if checking for a fever. "I just felt unworthy of it, and it felt like a huge pressure."

Matt sat, stumped. "That's just so . . . wrong," he said.

Daniel laughed, a sight so unexpectedly ravishing that Matt had to look away. "But I'm trying to say that now, I—I recognize you. Recognize what you were going through during this whole year."

"And what was I going through?"

Daniel paused, thinking. "You were someone thrust into this impossible situation, surrounded by grieving people, trying to help us," he said. "You threw out there all your generosity and intelligence and love and ingenuity, and you kept doing it even though we often threw it all back in your face."

Matt felt his face twitch, once, twice, and then tears stung his eyes.

"If we can manage to find our way back to each other," Daniel said, "I promise I'll try to make things different. Better."

That was all Matt could handle for a first conversation. "I just need some time alone," he said. He stood stiffly in Daniel's good-bye hug, like a straight man worried that the gay man hugging him might get the wrong idea. He closed the door behind him and watched from the window as Daniel, whistling, got into his car. *Wasn't he a merry fellow,* he thought. He went back into the kitchen, remembered that the grill was still on, went and turned it off. Then he called Brent and announced, "He wants me back."

"Shut up!" Brent shouted.

At his urging, Matt went over to brood. Daniel had said the exact words he'd always wanted him to say, he told Brent, who sat there with such a pink and rosy expression Matt expected him at any moment to break into song. But it wasn't that easy! It was one thing to be apologized to and acknowledged, and another to get back those feelings.

"You don't feel it anymore?" Brent asked, crestfallen. "If you don't feel it—"

"And now, if I don't go back, it's going to be *my* fault that the kids have to shuttle back and forth between us," Matt fumed.

Brent laughed before realizing he was serious. They were standing in the kitchen, leaning on the small island, Matt popping pretzels into his mouth and chewing furiously. On cutting boards arrayed around him were neatly chopped vegetables ready to be cooked. He looked at his watch. "Am I keeping you from dinner? Do you have a beer?"

"Nah, Derrick called and said he's going to be late." Brent went to the refrigerator to get him a beer. Matt opened it and took a long swig, set it down on the counter. "What should I do?" he asked. "I don't want to go back to him just because I'd feel guilty *not* going back."

"No," Brent agreed. "That can't be the only reason. Do you love him?"

Matt was quiet for a few minutes. "I've just spent the past two and a half months learning how to *stop* loving him."

"I have an idea," Brent said. "Let's make a list of things you love about him, and things you don't love about him."

They pulled up the bar stools and sat down with a pad of paper, and spent the next half hour drinking and brainstorming. Brent told him that when he and Derrick had hit ten years together, they'd stopped playing the Three Things I Love About You game, and started playing Three Things I Hate About You instead, which caused a small explosion of beer from Matt's mouth. When Matt was done with his list, he pushed the paper so it was between him and Brent and placed his palms on the table. "Okay," he said, "that should cover it."

LOVE ABOUT DANIEL:

Yummy Jewish looks

Smells delicious at almost every time of day

Can be sweet sweet sweet

Beautiful singing voice, can imitate k.d. lang imitating Elvis

Has been through hell ("That's not technically a thing you love
    about him," Brent pointed out.)

Thinks I'm hilarious

A good kind of quietness, until recent events

Smart enough for me

Conscientious about his kids

Good politics

DON'T LOVE ABOUT DANIEL:

Treated me like shit
Threw me out like trash
Judgmental, condescending prick
Craves the approval of straight people
Stiff and humorless at times
His parents!

They sat quietly and read, till Brent sat back and crossed his ankle over his knee. One of the cats had jumped onto the counter and was rubbing against Matt's pencil. "Dude," Brent said, "you should totally get back together."

"Really?" Matt said, looking at his lists again. "Where do you get that? 'Threw me out like trash' didn't impress you?"

"It did," Brent said, "but 'smells delicious'—you can't buy that kind of pheromonal compatibility, especially after so many years."

"Hmph," Matt said.

"You know, you don't have to decide right now. You could just go on a date with him."

"I don't know," Matt said. Something else was pushing at him, making him uneasy, and he cautiously let it enter his conscious mind. The thought of being back in that house with the kids full-time: it was daunting. In the months that had passed, his memory of the house, and everything that had happened in it, had gradually darkened, till it seemed like a dream that has the power to frighten even when its details have been forgotten. He was glad he would see Gal and Noam again—he missed them—but there lingered in him a strange hesitancy, even reluctance.

"Honestly, I don't know if I want kids," he told Brent with a challenging, defensive look. "Do you think I'm a terrible person?"

Irony and impatience flickered over Brent's face; Matt saw it and realized, his face growing hot, that whenever he asked that, he was being a needy pain in the ass. He made a silent vow never to ask it again.

Brent was sliding the salt and pepper shakers back and forth along the counter. Something dawned on him, and his hands stilled. "You know what I think?" he said. "I think that when they first came to live with you, it happened so fast and was such a crisis that you just took them in and didn't question it. Because let's face it, you really didn't have a choice. But now you do have a choice. Now it's not the heat of the moment anymore. And maybe you're absorbing only now the kinds of losses that come with kids. Honestly, I was surprised you didn't complain more at the time. You just—presto!—became Mr. Dad."

Matt listened, registering his own hunger to be praised, his relief to be back in Brent's good graces.

"Frankly, it creeped me out a little," Brent said.

"Shut up."

Brent laughed. "No, it was beautiful. Don't roll your eyes, I'm serious." He stood and rubbed his hands together. "Look," he said. "It's just one date." For him, it was settled.

"When's Derrick getting home?" Matt asked.

"Why? So you can deliberate all over again, and hope he'll guide you to a different conclusion? You know he won't."

Matt closed his eyes and groaned.

THEY MET AT THE bar at Spoleto. Daniel's parents were visiting, so a babysitter was not a problem. Daniel had dressed up a little, Matt noticed, which was sweet; and he was wearing a leather and silver bracelet Matt had bought him as a birthday present some years ago. His voice, which had become unpleasantly flat since Joel died, had regained—what was it?—musicality; something Matt had perceived without it quite reaching his conscious mind when Daniel had come over a few days ago. And his gaze had recovered some of its old searching, teasing quality. Warmth. *I remember this man*, Matt mused. He ordered a vodka tonic and Daniel ordered a glass of wine.

"You seem better," Matt said.

"Do I?" Daniel asked eagerly. "I feel better. I feel like I'm finally . . ." He paused as his voice broke. "Mourning." He laughed self-consciously as he coughed back the tears. "See? Better," he joked. "But seriously, it's so much better than that horror show I went through all year. Now I just miss my brother and Ilana, and I feel that, and cry for them, and feel my heart breaking."

Matt looked at him, thinking: Upside: more alive, and therefore handsomer; downside: still crying all the time. He wondered if he could just sit still and listen, or whether his mind would rush to assess everything Daniel said in pros and cons.

"It's a little disconcerting for Gal and Noam," Daniel said, "but I think it's better than an atmosphere of dread and guilt. Oh—I don't think I told you: I've enrolled Gal in karate. She starts next week. She's just— I think she's trying to figure out how much power she does and doesn't have in the world. Horseback riding has been great, but I thought that an activity that had controlled violence in it might help her."

"I don't know why we didn't think of that earlier," Matt said.

"I know."

They were quiet for a few minutes, sipping their drinks and looking down at the bar, Matt swirling his forefinger on the ring his drink had formed on a cocktail napkin. "Your parents must be thrilled I'm not there," he said.

Daniel hesitated. "I'm not gonna lie," he said, and they laughed. "I know we promised not to, but I had to tell them we'd broken up, because I really needed some help."

"What did your mom say?" Matt asked.

"I told her I didn't want her to comment, ever," Daniel said, and his eyes glinted in a way that told Matt she had commented anyway. "She said she was sorry I had to go through this alone."

Matt narrowed his eyes. "What did you tell her about why we broke up?" he asked.

Daniel took a sip of wine, and set his glass down carefully.

"I might get sick, you know," Matt blurted. And then, challenging him: "I might get sick. We don't know—it's still three months before a test result will be at all reliable."

"Don't you think I've been doing the math?" Daniel asked.

"And have you thought about what your response will be if I end up positive?"

"I've tried," Daniel said, his face coloring. "But I can't be sure."

"So there's a possibility you'll think it's my own damn fault, and with all you've gone through, you can't take on one more hard thing," Matt said, surprised at his own hard tone. "Or that you can't put the kids through another possible loss, and if it's between me and them . . ."

"Please don't set this up as a you versus them thing, Matt. That's really unfair, and really . . . unhelpful."

They were quiet, stunned that things had blown up so quickly, regretting being in such a public space, where people brushed against the backs of their chairs on the way to their tables and murmured, "Hey, how's it going." Matt didn't even know what he wanted Daniel to say; he'd just hurtled forward, needing to slam against this wall to see if it would hold. Finally, Daniel leaned forward and burst out quietly, "What do you want me to say? That I'll never think that we could have avoided this? Not even let it broach my thoughts for one millisecond? That I'll feel fine about having to put safety precautions into place, and about the prospect of you slowly dying in our house?"

"No!" Matt lied. "How about that you'll be really sad—and take care of me!"

Daniel sat back with an irritated sigh. "For Christ's sake, doesn't that go without saying?"

"No! It could use a little saying," Matt said. "I'm the guy who got kicked out."

Daniel shook his head wearily. He was willing to take his licks, he was; but Matt's need for him to say it aloud was insulting. As if he was such a monster he'd let him die alone! He took his wallet out of his pocket, consulted the check, and tossed his credit card on the table.

How had it happened that Daniel was dismissing *him*? Matt reached into his pocket and withdrew a crumpled ten, which he lay on the bar and smoothed out with his hands.

"You don't have to," Daniel said.

Matt shrugged, sardonic.

They walked silently through the downtown, hands in their jacket pockets, past a lot of couples out on a warm night and a line at the movie theater. They passed a few places where each of them could have turned off to his own house, both of them wondering what would happen when they parted, and when they reached the last possible point, they stopped. *Tell him you'd take care of him and cherish him to the end*, Daniel thought, *that's what he wants to hear.* But somehow, the words stuck in his craw. Instead, he said, "What's next?"

"I don't know," Matt said.

"I love you," Daniel said. "I didn't want this to end with a fight."

"Neither did I," Matt said. He was tired, his mind gummed-up.

They said their good-byes quietly, and when Matt got home, he knew it was over. Luckily, he hadn't let his hopes get too high. He dropped down on the couch with the dog and buried his face in her neck, and she snuffled and sighed, and he fell asleep there.

The doorbell sounded first in his dreams, and when he surfaced, chilled, his eyes searching out the light of the one lit lamp, he felt a spasm of primitive fear at the unexpected late-night phone call or knock at the door. He rose and went to the door, turned on the porch light, and peered out. Daniel stood there in his leather jacket.

When he opened the door for him, Daniel grabbed him by the belt and pulled him to him, slipped his hand between his legs, and cupped him hard. Matt let himself be led up to the bedroom and pushed onto the bed, let Daniel open his belt and fly, pull down his pants, kneel over him with his knee between Matt's legs, and kiss him roughly. "Turn over," he said, reaching for his own belt, and Matt obeyed, kicking his pants off his ankles. He heard Daniel pull his own pants down, then the rip of a condom wrapper and the small snap of his putting it on.

"In the drawer," Matt said, and he heard it open and Daniel's hand scurrying inside in search of the lube.

Daniel entered him awkwardly, rested there. He was still wearing his shirt and jacket and shoes. "Is this what you wanted?" he grunted.

Matt's eyes were closed, his ass burning like hell. As Daniel fucked him, his mind groped for the oblivion he craved, but he couldn't let go of the awareness that Daniel was playing a role. After all these years, he thought, it would take a prodigious act of imagination he probably wasn't capable of to get into this rough-trade fantasy. That ship had so sailed! Where to get the pleasure from, then? From the sheer brutality of the thrust? From gratitude that Daniel was still trying? From the danger Daniel was half-facing? From the idea that Daniel was angry, and punishing him?

It felt okay, it just didn't blow his mind. It wasn't really what he wanted. He rested, his cheek pressed into the mattress, and waited for Daniel to finish. After he did, Daniel eased out of him, both of them wincing, and flopped down next to him, on his back. His face was flushed. It was a large bed on a low wood platform, with a wood headboard; its sheets, blanket, and bedspread were various lovely shades of white. They lay there breathing and sweating. "This is an awesome bed," Daniel said.

"Other people's beds are always more comfortable than your own," Matt said. "I don't know why." He lifted the covers and they got undressed and crawled under. Daniel turned away and scooted gently backward so that Matt was spooning him. They fell asleep that way, and Matt awoke a few hours later with his face mashed into Daniel's hair. The windows were open and it was chilly on his bare shoulders, and he could hear the wind rustling in the tender new leaves of the trees. The only light came in from down the hall at the top of the stairs, and the room was dusky and soft. He lay there for a few minutes, taking in the smells of Daniel's shampoo, his breath, lubricant, and semen, Daniel's sweat or maybe his own. He was thirsty. He pulled away gently and wiped the tickle from his nose. Daniel stirred, then slipped around and was in his arms so quickly it shocked him. Daniel kissed his neck and face and mouth, Matt's hair in his fists; he was moaning, making a sound so private and full of need it was almost hard to hear. Matt felt his tears on his face, heard him say his name, over and over.

"Okay, okay," he said. "Okay." Until Daniel became still in his arms. Then Matt gently pushed him onto his back and kneeled over him, licking and sucking his nipples, his ribs, his stomach, his thighs, and his balls, and he had barely taken him into his mouth when Daniel came with a cry of surprise and pleasure. Matt straightened and wiped his mouth. "It's like making love to a teenager!" he said, which made Daniel laugh—and it was, and *that* was hot, giving pleasure to someone who had forgotten that such pleasure was to be had, who came quickly and hard even when Matt tried to calm him down and draw it out.

He made love to him on and off, and they slept in between. Once, he reached for him and Daniel said, "Ow, enough. I can't anymore," but then he could and did, and they fell back on the bed, hot and sticky, and laughed.

As morning broke, Daniel dreamed about a hike he'd taken in the hills outside Jerusalem with some religious friends, one Shabbat his junior year abroad. They'd taken along the two small, indispensable books for religious hikers, an Old Testament and a botany pocket guide, picked figs from trees and wild grapes from the vine, and when they stopped to drink and rest, one of them had read verses from one of the Samuels, and showed how the events had probably happened right in that very place. A sense of peaceful joy had filled Daniel at the beauty of the rugged stony hills, the comfortable power of his body in vigorous exercise, the ease of giving himself over to his companions' knowledge of where they were going, the feeling that there was no truer Israeli experience he could possibly have. The feeling of this being so much truer and purer than his stifling upbringing.

Later that afternoon they'd entered an Arab village, and an elderly man in a *keffiye* had greeted them as they passed his house, inviting them to stop and rest. They'd sat cross-legged with him on the stone patio in front of his house as his wife brought out a tray with warm pita, tomatoes, and tiny cups of harsh coffee, and while they hadn't been able to understand each other very well, Daniel's companions vigorously affirmed what the old man said as they stood to leave, in Arabic words that were close to the Hebrew: that Isaac and Ishmael were brothers.

It had been a beautiful, beautiful day, and he hadn't thought about it for ages.

He awoke into the faint light to see Matt lying on his back, his head resting on his hands, elbows akimbo, his eyes open, thinking. "I had a dream," Daniel told him. "More a memory, I can't tell if I was awake or not."

"What about?"

Daniel told him about it, tears pressing painfully at his face but not breaking. "Why does it make me want to cry? I have no idea. When I think about it now, I have no idea where we were, on whose land, or what town we entered. It must have been right before the First Intifada. That encounter with the Arab man could never happen now."

"Was Joel there?"

"No," said Daniel, "and I was probably really happy that I was having a more authentic experience than he was right then."

Matt smiled.

"I was such a different person," Daniel said. "So naïve." He paused, blinking up at the ceiling, then turned and looked at Matt. "Do I have to be all ironic about that experience now?"

Matt gazed at him and touched his face. "I'm afraid so, honey," he said.

Daniel was quiet for a while, then asked, "Where does the beauty go?"

Matt thought for a few moments, then slid his arms around Daniel's chest. "Right here," he said, kissing his shoulder. "Right here," he said, laying his palm on Daniel's back. "Where I can feel your heart beating."

Daniel buried his head in Matt's chest, moved and shy. "And then we weren't in Israel anymore, we were in Japan," he said, his voice muffled. "And my mother was there."

Matt laughed.

DANIEL SPENT THE NEXT four nights at Matt's, taking advantage of his parents' presence. The first night, he'd just slipped out and slipped back home at five A.M., and was in the shower before anybody woke up. But after that, he thought he ought to put someone in charge.

His father was asleep, but his mother was in the living room watching TV in her pajamas. She was nodding off, but her head snapped up when he sat down beside her. "Hi, honey," she said. "I've taken a sleeping pill." She took his cold hand in her two warm ones, and chafed it between them.

He perched beside her on the arm of the couch and watched the documentary for a few minutes. They were crazy little critters, meerkats; a laugh bubbled out of him when they rose on their hind legs to do sentry duty, the camera capturing their little heads popping up from behind sand dunes, their quick and alert little faces. They were led by a fierce and ruthless alpha female.

At the commercial, he stood. "Listen, Mom, I'm going over to Matt's for the night. So if the kids wake up—tell them I'm visiting him. I guess."

"Are you sure you won't be getting their hopes up?" Lydia asked. "If you don't end up getting back together, I mean?"

"Mom," Daniel said.

"I know you think I'm saying that because I hope you don't get back together," she interrupted. "But I'm not."

"Really?" he asked, with a penetrating look.

"I'm not an idiot, Daniel," she said. "I can tell when you're happy and when you're not."

"Oh," he said. "In that case—" He gave her a smooch on the cheek. "I'll have my cell phone on me."

He straightened, and then she spoke again, quiet but steady, her head resting against the back of the sofa. "Your brother is looking down on you, Daniel. He's so proud of you, and so grateful that you're here to care for his children."

He turned to look at her, surprised tears springing into his eyes.

THE NIGHTS HAD THE otherworldly feel of first-in-love. The moment Matt let him in the door, they were kissing. They had long, leisurely sex punctuated by surprises that made them laugh; they raided the kitchen, watched TV in bed with their bare legs entwined, eating a bowl of ice cream or drinking a scotch, had sex again. The old dog lay on the rug at the foot of the bed, snorting and farting, and the night deepened until day broke in soft shades of gray.

After Daniel left in the morning, unshaven and wearing the clothes he'd come in, Matt would get coffee brewing and get in the shower. He moved through his day languidly, his body airy and sated, finding himself jerking awake at the computer screen. He had no interest in food. At odd moments he'd find something unpleasant come over him, a flicker of rancor which, the moment he recognized it, was followed by despair, and he'd wonder for a second where it came from. Then he'd remember what Daniel had done, how he'd used Matt's very queerness, and the tenuous status it gave him in the family and the house, against him. Maybe, he'd think, the Daniel who was coming nightly to his bed— open, avid, loving—was the real Daniel, and that other, closed-off, brutal one an aberration. But it was one thing to have broken up with Matt, and quite another to take advantage of his legal vulnerability as a queer partner, to be the type of person who would do that. He just didn't know how to forgive that. He didn't know whether Daniel even registered that he'd done it.

He quizzed Brent and Derrick about it, and they insisted that Daniel *did* realize what he'd done. But it wasn't until the last night of Daniel's parents' visit, the last night they could carry on their affair in this strange, inviting house, that Daniel said something. They were in the kitchen, Matt making a sandwich because he'd hardly eaten that day, Daniel poking around in the fascinating cupboards of strangers and disapproving of the fact that the kitchen hadn't been updated since the '70s. It had pale green linoleum counters and a grubby wooden spice rack above the stove, crammed with spices bought at Asian specialty stores. "It's the only part of the house that isn't lovely," he said.

"I know," Matt said.

"How do you feel about moving back in and rejoining our family?" Daniel asked.

Matt's head whipped around. "Talk about your non sequiturs!" he said.

"I couldn't figure out how to work my way toward it more gradually."

Matt put his knife down and turned toward him, studied his face. They'd been so intertwined for the past week, pulling back and looking at each other felt solemn and intimate. Daniel was tense, his blinking deliberate, his teeth gnawing at the inside of his lip.

"I—" Matt said, and cleared his throat. "The thing is, it's hard for me to let go of what you did to me. The whole thing about my having no legal rights."

Daniel nodded. "I know," he said. "I wish I hadn't done it. I could have done it so differently."

He studied Daniel, wondering if that admission was enough for him. Finally, he said, "How can I be sure you won't do it again?"

Daniel scratched his cheek in mock ponder. "If only there were an institution designed to support couples who have vowed to stay together, and to legally protect them," he said.

Matt laughed, taken aback. "Seriously?"

Daniel shrugged, his eyes growing playful and warm. "It's going to be legal in Massachusetts in"—he looked at his watch—"three weeks."

"Okay, I really don't know how to think about that," Matt said with a small laugh. He turned back around and stared at the turkey and cheese sandwich he'd made, picked it up and took an enormous bite out of it. Then he hiked himself up on the counter and chewed.

"Well, give it some thought," Daniel said. "I know we haven't been very keen on the idea of marriage, but it's a way—it's my way—of helping you feel protected."

Matt took another bite, contemplated Daniel as he chewed. "What a lame proposal," he said.

"I know," Daniel said with a laugh that was more air than noise. "But I mean it. I want you to come back, and I want you to feel safe in our family."

"Okay," Matt said.

"Is that one of those robotic, compliant Gal *okays*?"

Matt scratched his chin. "I sort of understand now what she means by it!" he said. "It's like, 'Okay, I hear you and I get what you mean, but I have to go sit in my room by myself for a while now.'"

"I want you to be happy," Daniel said, coming up to the counter and standing between Matt's knees, resting his hands on Matt's thighs. "I want you to be psyched." His face crinkled into a mischievousness so rare and enchanting, Matt almost died of love right on the spot. "When Daddy comes home, it's a happy sound," Daniel sang, his voice husky. "Daddy!"

Matt laughed and touched Daniel's cheek. "I *am* psyched," he said. "I am. Let me just think about it."

MATT SAT IN THE car outside the Jackson Street School, waiting for the kids to start coming out. In the front of the low, long brick building stood a line of idling school buses, but Gal had been told to look for his car instead. It was a mild day, and he had the driver's-side window open and his sunglasses on. The trees still sent their bare spindles into the sky, but in front and side yards the forsythia was in bloom, the bushes that only days ago had looked like messy, snarled balls of wire now bursting with yellow flowers.

It had taken a week for Matt to even take seriously the idea of marriage. It felt like such a cliché!—as though Daniel was a cheating husband who'd gone out and bought him a fur coat or a Lamborghini so he'd forgive him. He'd just never aspired to marriage; the very idea seemed like a turnoff, like joining a church or moving to the Midwest. And he'd always worried, since the push for gay marriage in Massachusetts began, that the right to marry would become the expectation to marry, which would create two classes of gay people: the good ones who were normal and committed and monogamous, and the queers and deviants.

One day, he ran into his lawyer on the street, who told him that as far as he was concerned, the best thing about gay marriage was going to be gay divorce. "Meaning?" Matt said.

"Meaning that before, gays and lesbians in Massachusetts could screw each other financially, or in terms of custody, when we broke up. And believe me, we did! But now we're going to be subject to the same divorce laws as straight people."

"Right," Matt said, and that made an impression, especially the vision of legions of Massachusetts queers being screwed just as he had been. He had no illusions that gay people were more ethical in love than straight people, but thinking of his attorney routinely going to court on behalf of stay-at-home partners bilked out of alimony, or non-bio-moms having their kids taken away, gave him a slightly different vision of queer Northampton than he'd had, and bolstered the ironic stance he took toward the married state.

"But didn't he mean it as an argument *for* getting married?" Brent asked him, as Matt enlarged upon his critique with cutting pleasure.

"Oh," Matt said with comic deflation. "Right."

The school door opened and the first kids stepped outside, then a few clusters, some lining up for the buses, some taking off and racing for their parents' cars. And there was Gal, coming out by herself. She was wearing her parka, unzipped, and it looked as if Daniel hadn't taken her for a haircut since they'd broken up. He watched as she scanned for his car and then found it; he opened his eyes and mouth wide in a happy surprised expression, and she grinned and ran over. She opened the back door and swung her backpack off her shoulders, heaving it into the seat in front of her. "Mordechai, you're back!" she said. She climbed in and threw her arms around his neck from behind. "Did Uncle Dani let you come back?"

Matt tried to retain his dignity in the midst of the choke hold and the slightly demeaning question. "Uncle Dani and I agreed that you guys should come over for a sleepover," he said. They'd planned at first to have him reunite with the kids at dinner at Daniel's, but after a few days' thought, he'd realized he just wasn't ready yet to go over there, to resume his role in the family, with all the expectations that would raise in everybody. So they'd settled on telling Gal that they were a couple again, but that Matt was staying in his own house because he'd committed to taking care of the dog.

"Phew," she said, plopping herself back onto the seat. "TGIF. So you have a dog over there, right?"

He glanced, smiling at the American slang, into the rearview mirror. "I do. I mean, I'm taking care of her for these people."

He swung by and picked up Noam at Colleen's, where he was shocked to see him just get up, thank you very much, and run over to him, a faint, rakish scar on his right cheek. He picked him up—he was heavier!—and squeezed him, said "Kiss?" and was rewarded with Noam's patented air-kiss, a flat-lipped *pop*. "Do you know you're coming over to my house?" Matt asked him.

"We've been talking about it all day," Colleen said. "Daniel said he'll come by with their stuff after work."

"What happened here?" he asked, smoothing the scar with his thumb.

"There was an incident with a toy tent pole," she said.

He brought them back to his house and let them explore as he went into the kitchen to find them a snack. Gal ran upstairs and then came back down. "Are we sleeping here?" she asked, leaning against the doorway.

"Yep," he said, handing her a granola bar. "It's a sleepover, remember? Just us." He and Daniel had realized just yesterday that he was assuming that Daniel would sleep over, and Daniel was assuming he wouldn't; it was only when Daniel said, with slow, comic, burning intensity, "It would be my first night without kids for, like, a year," that Matt had laughed and agreed to take them by himself.

"What's that?" Gal said, pointing to a Buddha on a little altar on the fireplace mantel across the living room.

"That's the Buddha. He's a religious figure. He's supposed to be very wise."

She looked doubtfully at its secret, serene expression. "I think he's weird," she said. "There's one upstairs, too."

He couldn't really settle in with them till Daniel had come and gone; for reasons he couldn't pinpoint, he'd been nervous about it all day. When the doorbell rang, something went off in his chest, like a wind burst sending dust and candy wrappers flying. Daniel was wearing work clothes, a jacket and a loosened tie, and had in his hands and at his feet what seemed like an inordinate number of suitcases and stuffed paper bags. Molly caught sight of him and barked, and hustled to the door looking very in charge to make up for not having heard him ring the bell. She sniffed him with a wheezy harrumph, her stumpy tail quivering in greeting. Gal called from the kitchen door, "Who's that? You're not supposed to be here!" Daniel took just a few steps into the house, and stayed just long enough to show Matt the dose of Noam's antibiotics for his ear infection.

Matt brought the suitcases and paper bags into the house as Daniel kissed the kids good-bye and said have fun and reminded them that he would pick them up tomorrow morning. Matt set bibs and bottles and medicine on the shelf above the kitchen sink, and hauled the Pack 'n Play up to the TV room down the hall from his bedroom. The room was furnished with a futon couch facing a small television, a woven oval rug, and bookcases with novels and biographies and rows of Lonely Planet guides. He popped up the frame's locking sides and pressed the center down, put the mattress in and pushed in the corners.

He'd planned to have Gal sleep on the futon next to her brother; he'd found some double-bed sheets for it in the linen closet and washed them to get out the dust smell. But she wanted to sleep in the tiny third bedroom with the whitewashed paneled walls and the curtains with a leaf pattern in fall colors. There was a very old bed in it, a relic, sized for a child but so tall Gal had to run across the carpet and leap onto it. Matt scratched his head. "If you fall out of that thing, you *know* who's going to get in trouble."

"You!" she shouted.

"Right you are," he said.

He'd ordered pizza, and he ran downstairs when the doorbell rang, telling Gal to keep an eye on her brother. Noam was walking, and he wasn't a baby anymore. It was as though, Matt discovered over the course of the evening, becoming ambulatory had released a whole new personality; the placid chubby baby had become a worker bee, a mover of furniture, a carrier of things back and forth. After feeding the dog, Matt watched Noam squat, diapered butt brushing the floor, and carefully pour the remaining kibbles into a Tupperware container. "Not for eating, Noam," Matt said, but he realized as Noam poured them carefully back into the dog bowl, that far from eating them, Noam was more likely to perform a Montessori activity with them. He could say *my* and *mine*, and had developed a very impressive screech to enforce those categories. He said *ee-eye-ee-eye-oh* and knew what a cow says and what a bird says, and when Matt sang "The babies on the bus go—" he made obnoxious whining noises. "That's how he says *wah wah wah*," Gal explained.

After dinner, he bathed Noam in the claw-foot tub and brought him into the bedroom, dug his fingers under the flap of the box of diapers he'd bought, and pried it open. Then he opened the suitcase Daniel had brought, and found it entirely filled with diapers. He diapered Noam and set him on the floor as he looked for pajamas, finding them in a different suitcase. "Here ya go, buddy," he said. Holding the pants at the waist, close to the floor, with his thumbs and forefingers, he waited for Noam to step into them. From down there, a curl of pain winding along his lower back, his view was chubby little legs scuttling back and forth. Finally, he grabbed him. He was sweating when Gal came in the room, asking, "Can we get a dog for this house?"

Matt said, "Honey, we have a dog."

"I mean a real dog," she said.

He sat on the futon couch with a child on each side, reading *Night-Night, Little Pookie*, shouting, in unison with Gal, when little Pookie is asked whether he wants to wear the pajamas with the cars or the ones with the stars: "Stars *and* cars!" Daniel had also sent over an alphabet book illustrated with animals. Noam pointed to the bird under *B* and said, "Pitty teet-teet."

Matt laughed, and looked at Gal, amazed. "What did he say? A pretty tweet-tweet?"

It took Noam a long time to fall asleep; first he sang to himself for a while—if it could be called singing, Matt thought; it was actually more of a drone—and then he cried a vexed, overstimulated cry. Matt kept the hall light on, and after racing upstairs three times, plopped himself down on the hall floor. After a few minutes, he heard the quick, quiet thumping of Gal coming up the stairs in bare feet, saw her peek around the corner at the top. She'd taken off her sweater and socks. He put a finger to his lips and motioned his head toward Noam's room.

She tiptoed up to him and sat down on the floor beside him, cross-legged, and he laid a hand on her knee. "How's it going?" he whispered.

"Good," she said.

"Hey, how was Israel?" he murmured.

"That was a long time ago," she said, twisting and untwisting the fringe of the runner that ran the length of the hall.

"Was it good to see everybody?"

She nodded, and Matt tried to think of a better question, one that would draw her out. When she started school, he'd found that asking "Did anybody cry today?" could sometimes elicit a juicy story.

"What was the best part and what was the worst part?" he asked.

There was a cry from Noam, and they were quiet, ears straining, till they heard him start sucking his passy again. Gal gazed up at the ceiling and frowned. "A real head-scratcher, huh," Matt said.

"What?"

"A head-scratcher. That's a hard question you have to think about a lot."

"The best part," she said slowly, her voice going thoughtfully high on *best*, "was definitely playing with Leora. And seeing Sabba and Savta." She added this last in a rush, nodding and gesturing as if to say that it went without saying, which is why she hadn't mentioned it first.

"And the worst thing?"

She shrugged. She didn't have words for the soreness and longing, the feeling of being home-but-not-home, the wild fear of being lost, the fleeting sense of triumph and the loneliness that had overwhelmed her when she crumpled to the sidewalk, her throat opening and closing like the gills of a salmon yanked into the air. Matt peeked down at her without moving his head, saw her hands lying limp in her lap. "Noam's asleep," he said quietly. "Should we get into pajamas and read a story?"

After he'd read to her, she lay on the high, narrow, strange bed trying to sleep. She'd asked to sleep in this room, but now she felt that had been a mistake; she felt like a dead child laid out in a coffin. And she couldn't stop casting her eyes anxiously at the shadows cast by a street-light into the room, imagining Buddhas emerging from the window, hordes of them marching in with their secret smiles, with beards and jumpsuits; they'd become, in her hectic mind, a mash-up of Buddhas and the Keebler Elves on her cookie packages.

At around four in the morning, she awoke with a cry. Matt awoke, adrenaline coursing through him, and ran into her room, saying, "What? What? What?" He lifted her by the armpits till she was sitting.

"I want to go home," she said. "This house is weird. I don't like it."

"I thought you liked this bedroom," Matt said.

"I thought we were going to Dani's," she said, staring at him vacantly; he wondered if she was fully awake. "Dani said that you were going to bring us to our own house."

"No, he told you you were coming to *my* house," Matt said.

"No," she insisted. "He didn't."

He was totally perplexed. "So why do you think he was dropping off all that stuff?"

She shrugged with confused misery.

"Why didn't you say anything? Like when I made you dinner and unpacked your pajamas and put you to bed?"

"I don't know."

He thought, *This is a bad idea; she doesn't know if we're really together or not, and we'd better give her a clearer message soon.* They sat there looking at each other in the dim room, a cone of light cast across the floor by the hall light through the half-open door. The old Gal, he knew, would have screamed at him the moment they'd pulled up at his house, refused to get out of the car. She wasn't a little beast anymore, he realized; she was growing up, and the sharp edges were wearing down as age and grief rubbed at them with patient, chastening hands. Even her crying had a different, less outraged tenor: it seemed to express surprise that the world had even more pain in store for her, when she'd thought she couldn't be surprised anymore. It saddened him. Maybe it was just developmental, he thought, and this is how she would have turned out anyway. Maybe it was a good thing, a better way of being for the long haul. Maybe she'd turn back into a beast when she hit twelve.

He ran his hands over his arms, chilled in his undershirt and boxer shorts. "Do you think you can go back to sleep?" he asked.

"Can I sleep with you?"

He thought of the knees and elbows that would pound him as she slept her strenuous sleep. "Okay," he sighed. He helped her down and gathered her pillow and stuffed monkey, ushered her down the hall with his hand on her back. As they got into bed, Gal paused on her knees and peered at the big Japanese painting. "I wonder what that's a painting of," she said, fully awake and intrigued.

"Oh no you don't," he said sternly, switching off the bedside table lamp. "No chitchat."

They lay still for a while, till she flounced onto her side with a groan. "Sleep, Gal," Matt said.

"I can't," she said. "I'm scared."

"What could you possibly be scared of? I'm right here, next to you."

"I'm still scared," she said in Hebrew.

"What are you scared of? Should we make a list?"

There was a pause. Then she said, "That Dani will be mad at me. That I'll try to be good but be bad by accident. That robbers or bears will come into the house. That Noam's scar will never go away. How many is that?"

"Four." He understood her perfectly, but replied in English, thinking that for this conversation, they might each need their full linguistic capacity.

"That I'll never see you again," she said.

He took her arm and gave it a little shake. "I'm right here! And I'm not going anywhere."

"You know what else I'm scared of?" she asked. She didn't sound spooked anymore; she was warming to her theme, getting late-night philosophical. This could be a long night, Matt told himself. "That I'll be at a scary movie and I won't be able to run out of there before the scary parts happen, and even after I'm in the lobby, I'll still hear the sounds, and even if I go into the bathroom, I'll still hear the sounds."

"Yikes," said Matt, remembering his similar fears around the time *The Shining* came out. "What about falling off a horse?"

"*Pshh*. I'm not scared of that." He smiled in the darkness at the dismissive pride in her voice. "But I'm scared my body will get ripped up, and it will hurt so bad."

"That *is* scary."

"Don't tell Dani."

"Why not?"

"Just don't."

His mind swirled around this, fighting the fatigue that was thickening it, like cornstarch. Which part was important to keep from Daniel? He wondered whether he should ask, and then he did. "Is he mad at you a lot?"

She thought about it for a while. Actually, he wasn't anymore; he was different since Israel. He touched her sometimes—her hair, her cheek—and his face would come alive again, like something kissed in a fairy tale. "Not really," she said.

She was on her side, facing him, fists at her chin, her eyes slowly blinking. "Gal," Matt said sleepily, "you're scared that something bad will happen, but what's really scary is that something bad *already* happened."

"But bad things can still happen."

"They can," he conceded, as the thought of HIV pushed darkly into his mind. "But I'm pretty sure it'll never be as bad as that. That's like a once-in-a-lifetime bad thing."

"How do you know?"

"I just do."

"Sabba and Savta had *two* bad things happen to them."

He couldn't argue with that.

Gal said, mournfully, "I think they must be the unluckiest people in the whole world."

He was on the verge of sleep, but through the dim gleam of his consciousness he felt he couldn't let the conversation end that way. He'd be letting Ilana down if he let her daughter carry the weight of her grandparents' unfathomable suffering, or, God forbid, compare their suffering to her own, and find herself wanting. But he couldn't think of anything reassuring to say. So he turned her gently away from him and pulled her by the hips, wrapped his arms around her as she squirmed backward and settled into his chest. Thinking about his own health, trying to reassure himself with the thought that even if he got HIV, people lived for a long time with it these days, kept him awake long after Gal had fallen asleep.

IN THE END, IT was Gal who helped Matt warm to the idea of getting married. "Wow!" she said, her eyes alight, her mouth stretched into a comic rictus of glee, when he and Daniel told her. "Wow! That's all I have to say: Wow!" She told everybody she knew, "Wow! That's all I could think of when they told me!" She was so thrilled by the prospect, he decided that if he had the capacity to make her feel safe and happy, he owed it to her. And seeing a wedding through her eyes—the dignity, solemnity, and joy of it, the knitting together of their family—the tendrils of Matt's imagination began to wind around the idea. He imagined a justice of the peace or a clergyperson saying, "By the authority invested in me by the Commonwealth of Massachusetts . . ." and got a little goose-bumpy. He hadn't moved back home yet; he was sleeping at Daniel's but was still responsible for Molly for another few months, so he'd left most of his clothes and his computer at his own place, and spent the days there, the windows open to the May breeze, after the kids went to day care and school. It suited him. He knew he'd have to move all the way back soon, take up his place as a full-time partner and dad. But sometimes, sitting at a desk in the pretty book-lined study, he wished that this was how he'd gotten involved with the Rosens in the first place: enjoying outings with the kids, gaining their confidence and affection over time, urgently making out with Daniel outside the front door before they tore themselves apart and he went home to his own, quiet refuge.

THEY MET FOR LUNCH on a summery Tuesday, at a café halfway between Northampton and Amherst; they sat outside on the same side of the table, crowding into the shade of the umbrella. Daniel was trying to tell Matt about this upsetting thing he'd read in the materials he got from B'Tselem, the Israeli human rights organization, while Matt was examining the inside of his sandwich to make sure they'd put Dijon mustard on it, as he'd requested, instead of honey mustard, which he hated. "Are you listening to me?" Daniel said. He clunked his shoulder against Matt's.

"Stop, I am," Matt said.

"There's this new Israeli law," he said. "Actually, I think it might be an extension of an old law."

A shadow fell across the table, and they looked up to see Yossi, his face bright and benign, standing over them. His hair, which had grown out since Matt had last seen him, was disheveled, his T-shirt dark with sweat. He had a gym bag slung over his shoulder and a cup of coffee with a lid on it in his hand. Matt's heart popped with surprise and revived anger, the inevitable ribbon of attraction tied around the whole messy package.

"I was just getting my coffee," Yossi said. "I understand that mazal tovs are in order!"

Daniel stood and they hugged, while Matt remained seated, watching their hands clap each other's backs in the way of straight men while Yossi held out his coffee cup so it wouldn't spill. He didn't know how he was supposed to greet Yossi, who had clearly decided he wasn't worth remaining friends with after the breakup; he refused to stand and hug him. But he was conscious of sitting there, slumped and sullen, like a big baby.

"I'm very happy for you," Yossi said in Hebrew, beaming at them. "I, for one, support gay marriage a hundred percent."

"Great!" Matt said, and felt Daniel give him a sharp look. A sparrow landed a few feet away, and he broke off a tiny piece of bread and tossed it in its direction, onto the stone terrace ground, then watched as the bird bustled over, seized it in its beak, and flew off. Yossi and Daniel were making a plan for a Rafi drop-off later that afternoon after school, looking at their watches. *Metzuyan,* Daniel said. Excellent.

When Yossi had left, Daniel sat back down and took a bite out of his sandwich. Matt sensed his gaze on him, and turned. "What?"

Daniel raised an eyebrow.

"How about a little loyalty?" Matt asked heatedly. "You know he dumped me as a friend, right? And still, you're nice to him."

Daniel flushed and blinked as he took in Matt's anger. He swallowed his food. "I'm sorry. It's just—he's really been there for me and the kids. Coming to Israel for the memorial—"

"Well, he wasn't there for me," Matt said flatly. "Do you care at all about that?"

"I do, Matt." Daniel leaned over and slipped his arm around Matt's waist, nuzzled his cheek. "I do. But maybe you're madder at me than you are at him? Maybe *I'm* the one who wasn't there for you?"

Matt sat stiffly, accepting his embrace and kiss, half mollified. "He's always been a condescending prick with me. He's not like that with you."

"No," Daniel said.

"Like I'd lost sleep over his support of gay marriage! Give me a break."

Daniel laughed, and they ate in silence for a while, Matt fretting over the various slights he'd experienced from Yossi. They weren't exactly slights, he thought—they didn't even rise to that level; it was as if Yossi didn't take him seriously enough to slight him. As soon as he thought that, he wondered if it was true—or whether it was just his own insecurity that made him feel like a less substantial person than Yossi.

"This Israeli law I was telling you about?" Daniel was saying. "Get this: The law states that if a Palestinian living in Jerusalem marries someone from the West Bank, they can't live legally together in either place. In either place! Can you believe it?" He was looking at Matt, waiting to see the information register on his face. "And did you know that if a Palestinian kid lives with one of its parents in Jerusalem, that kid has to leave Jerusalem when it turns eighteen and go live on the West Bank?"

"What? Why?" Matt turned his head in Daniel's direction, bewildered; it sounded nonsensical, and he thought that maybe he'd missed the initial sentences while he was brooding about Yossi, the ones that explained what the hell Daniel was talking about.

"Why? They always say it's for security reasons. But this is about demographics. About keeping the Jew-to-Arab ratio in Jerusalem stable." Daniel had read about the law quickly, when the materials from B'Tselem had first had arrived, and then more slowly and carefully; but it was so convoluted and had so many poisonous ramifications, it had taken him a while to even understand it. He'd read the testimonials from Palestinians about standing outside in line all night at the Interior

Ministry with their infants and documents, only to be told they were missing a document, or to return in three months, or that their claims were denied, or that the ministry was closing early so clerks could get home for an approaching Jewish holiday. It had made him think how pathetic and subhuman a long weary line of humans always looked, like refugees or convicts with their wooden bowls, waiting for their portion of rice. It made him think that a big strategy of the Occupation was to flood the brain space of Palestinians with the countless cryptic details of petty bureaucracy. And it made him think, irately: *Sorry, Joel, but how is that not like apartheid?*

"I just don't know what to do with this information," he told Matt now, irate all over again. "Seriously. What am I supposed to do with it? Just be glad that I get to get married, and to hell with everybody else?"

"I don't have the slightest idea what you're supposed to do with that information." Matt couldn't say it, but he was secretly glad that Daniel also had complicated feelings about getting married. It made him feel less alone with it.

Daniel took the straw out of his iced tea, sucked on it, and laid it on the table. "I called the Bereaved Families Forum," he said.

Matt turned sharply and looked at him. "Seriously? When? What did they say?"

"The guy's going to call me back on Tuesday."

"Good for you, honey! I'm glad."

Daniel shrugged. "Yeah, they probably don't let American Jews join—it's a group for Israelis and Palestinians—but maybe, if not, they can suggest another group."

"I'm glad," Matt said.

He'd disarmed him, Daniel knew; Matt had been wanting him to join an activist group for a while now. Even if they did let him join, which he doubted, he didn't know what kind of role he'd have, and what kind of travel that might entail. He didn't know if it was the right way to enter the fray. But a yearning had overtaken him, to connect in a human way with Palestinian people. Maybe the impulse was silly or naïve. It was hard to explain, even to Matt. But his fate was tied so intimately to people he'd never met in the flesh—unless you counted that hot, shocking moment when flesh was blown off of bodies. Unless you counted his brief handshake with that Palestinian man, Ibrahim, at the Smith College panel, who'd been too busy or distracted to focus on him. Or maybe he hadn't been. Maybe, it occurred to Daniel as he diffusely took in the heat of the afternoon, the murmur of people's conversations around him, he'd needed so much from Ibrahim at that moment—so much that he couldn't even name—that no response could have lived up to his hopes.

Matt ran his hand gently over Daniel's, and Daniel turned over his palm and entwined his fingers with his. He appreciated how lucky he was to have Matt in the flesh, not to be kept apart from him by a sinkhole of military and legal space. He squeezed Matt's hand hard, to feel him, because it was hard sometimes to feel Matt's presence even when he was right there. Hard to be there for him, when sometimes the dead and the dispossessed felt more real than the man breathing right beside him.

And yet, Matt—Matt had been there for him. He'd been an ark to him and to the kids, carrying them out of dark, catastrophic waters. Solid, durable, sensual, he'd carried them through.

THE UNCLES WERE GETTING married. They said that men could marry each other now, and they weren't teasing her, it was really true. Gal sat aboard Caesar, swaying easily with his walk, while Matt watched, forearms resting on the ring's railing and chin propped on his folded hands. She was waiting for permission to canter and feeling the cool air encase her bare arms; right before she went in, she'd stripped down to her T-shirt and tossed her sweatshirt to Matt. It was hard to wait, because cantering was the most thrilling thing she'd ever done in her entire life. Her heels were down and straight, her thighs pressed easily into the saddle, the reins looped around her soft, able hands. She remembered being at weddings in Israel, running around with other kids in huge, brilliant banquet halls, round tables with white tablecloths as far as her eye could see, flower arrangements and dishes of hummus and olives and wine bottles and glasses of water placed on them, the grown-ups talking in loud voices over the deafening music. Dancing with her father, straddling his hip, while he held her hand straight out in front of them and put on a pompous dancing-master face. The memory moved through her with a languorous ache, like a pearl falling through honey. She gathered in her reins to raise Caesar's head and grazed him with her heels, gathering him, keeping her eye on Briana, who was the teacher today, and who was reminding them to pull the rein near the railing and nudge the horse with that heel. She didn't need to hear that instruction again. She was ready. Her body was light and airy, a knitted baby blanket, a round crystal glass with water shimmering inside.

"Okay," Briana said, and Gal broke into a canter.

CHAPTER 20

B EHIND A DOZEN other couples and a crowd of kids, Daniel, Matt, Gal, and Noam stood in line at the Northampton courthouse, waiting for a marriage license on the first day they would be issued to gay couples in the United States. Some courthouses in Cambridge and Provincetown, Matt knew, had opened at midnight to let their gay citizens be the very first in the U.S. to receive marriage certificates. Despite that gall to his competitive spirit, he took in with pleasure the sun warming his shoulders, the feel of Gal's hand resting in his, the sheer gorgeousness of the blue spring sky, doubly precious because they'd earned it by slogging through the grueling, grueling winter. Lesbian couples stood in front and in back of them, wearing their pretty dresses, their suits, whatever counted for them as finery. He himself was sporting bright blue shoes and a fedora. A butch passed by them, scanning for someone in line and muttering to herself; she was wearing a cowboy dress shirt with pearl buttons tucked into black jeans. Matt whispered, "Check out Farmer Brown over there."

Daniel slapped his arm. *"It's her wedding day,"* he admonished.

Around them, people milled and called out to each other. "Tying the knot?" "Taking the plunge?" "Making an honest homo out of him?" They laughed at the idea that those everyday expressions could have anything to do with them. A small Asian-American girl passed by on her father's shoulders, playing the "Wedding March" on a child-sized violin. Several people circulated in caterers' clothes—black pants, white dress shirt—proffering trays of canapés, business cards stacked prettily around the trays' edges. Matt watched them, a smile pulling at his lips at their entrepreneurial spirit.

History had come down and tapped them on the shoulder, and it was hard to know what to feel in the moment. Marriage wouldn't have been Matt's fight, but now it had happened, and that was pretty remarkable. He was proud to live in Massachusetts, USA; other than that, he drew something of a blank. Maybe, he thought, you could only feel these moments in retrospect. He remembered the day that *Lawrence v. Texas*, the Supreme Court case that had overturned Texas's sodomy law, had come down, the Court's majority writing that *Bowers v. Hardwick*—to gay people, an infamously repulsive decision—had been misguided and wrong. He and Daniel had happened to be at Derrick and Brent's for dinner, and they'd all lifted their wineglasses and looked at one another with bemusement, at a loss for the right words, the right emotions, until Brent piped up, "To sodomy!" and they'd all laughed and touched glasses.

The line inched forward. Noam, who was wearing a T-shirt with a bow tie and tuxedo front silk-screened on it, and whose stroller's handlebars had been bedecked with a small rainbow flag, said, "Out! Out!" and Matt unbuckled him, lifted him out, and set him down. "This is taking forever," he said to Daniel. "I'm going to take a walk with him. C'mon, Shorty." Matt let Noam lead him around, a tiny hand clasping his pointer finger. People smiled at the sight of the tall, graceful gay man with the toddler chugging along at his side. They walked to the edges of the crowd and Matt stood watching while Noam stooped to pick up and examine some gravel pebbles at the edges of the parking lot.

"Hey," he heard behind him. It was Brent, smiling, wearing jeans and a blue T-shirt with the big yellow equals sign on the front, a baseball cap to protect his head where his hair was thinning. "We found Daniel in line, and he said you guys had gone for a walk."

"Change your mind?" Matt grinned.

"No," he said. "We just came to join the celebration." He and Derrick had decided not to get married. "It's not for us," Derrick had said in tactful nonjudgment. "At least not right now." They'd been together for fifteen years, since freshman year in college, with only an experimental break when Brent had gone abroad to Paris his junior year.

Now Brent looked into his friend's face with an expression both sweet and keen, and slid his arm around his shoulder.

"I've been thinking about Ilana and Joel today," Matt said.

Brent nodded.

"I think they'd be happy. They trusted us. They trusted us together." He stepped forward abruptly. "No, honey, that's yucky," he said to Noam, before Noam's fingers could close over a cigarette butt on the ground.

"Dass yucky," Noam repeated. He turned to Brent. "Dass yucky," he said solemnly.

"Yes it is," Brent said. "And let me commend you on your good talking!"

"It turns out I wasn't so trustworthy," Matt said. "I don't know why. Well, I do know why. I didn't want to have to spend the rest of my life worrying about being safe. Or something."

Brent was quiet, his thoughts playing across his face.

"It feels good to say fuck you to the universe!" Matt said. He scanned the courthouse, the peaceable crowd, the cars passing by with supportive beeps, the serene blue sky, and he and Brent laughed, struck at the same time by how very benign the universe was looking at that moment. "Seriously, though," he said. "That's what this marriage is, too. A leap of faith. Like: We're not going to wait to climb this mountain till they've put up guardrails and signage along all the cliff faces. We're not! Because we want to climb."

Noam came over to Matt and gave him a handful of stones and street sand left over from the winter plows. "What am I supposed to do with this?" Matt asked, looking at the dirty pile in his hand.

"Take home," Noam replied.

Matt looked at him, sighed, and emptied it into the pocket of his clean, pressed pants. "Nothing," he said to Brent, "and I mean *nothing*, makes me feel like a parent more than holding out my hand so they can spill or gag or spit disgusting shit into it." He rubbed his hands together to clean them off and picked Noam up, raked his bangs back from his forehead with his fingers. "You're a good friend," he said to Brent. "I'm sorry I haven't been a very present one lately."

Brent waved his hand and shook his head, his face pinking with little blots of emotion. "It's okay—"

"It's not okay," Matt said, and Brent clasped his shoulder hard.

When they got back to the line, Daniel and Gal had gotten almost to the courthouse door, and Daniel was anxiously looking around for him. Gal was watching as a little boy on the verge of a tantrum was alternately diverted and scolded by his moms, who were worried their impending moment would be ruined by a screaming toddler. A middle-aged lesbian couple in a suit and a dress were emerging from the courthouse's other door, and raising their clasped hands in the air as reporters took photos of them; there was a wave of applause, then it became rhythmic, and people began to chant, "Thank you! Thank you!" Matt cocked his ear toward a woman next to him. "Goodridge," she told him. "One of the couples who filed the lawsuit."

Then Daniel was holding the door open for him, peering into the paneled, crowded hallways in front of them, and then they'd stepped inside. Standing around tables and sitting on benches against the walls, couples were bent over forms, writing. Four clerks behind the long counter were handing out forms, gesturing and talking, collecting money. Daniel and Matt took theirs from a middle-aged woman with curly hair, big glasses, and a face pink from the humid warmth of bodies, who said in a voice whose hassled quality was just barely covered by mirth, "Good luck finding a place to sit down!"

Daniel, who attributed his ability to slice through lines and crowds to the years he'd spent getting on buses in Israel, disappeared for a second, and when Matt found him, he'd slipped onto the corner of a bench and was patting it in an invitation to sit next to him. Matt sat, excused himself to the woman he was making shift over, and smoothed the form over his thigh; they sat and wrote, knees touching. Addresses, parents' names, city of birth. There was a burst of joyful noise, and they looked up—it was two of the Jewish lesbians; their rabbi had arrived, and was singing a *shehechianu*. Gal and Noam had disappeared down the hall, and just as Matt turned to ask Daniel where they were, they returned, Gal holding a hunk of cake on a paper plate, both of their mouths covered with frosting; in a room down the hall, the city of Northampton was celebrating the right of its gay and lesbian citizens to marry with a wedding cake. "Give me a bite," Daniel said, leaning forward chin-first. He leveled a stern look at Gal when the plastic forkful she offered had just cake on it, no frosting, and she rolled her eyes and stabbed the fork into a gooey heap of white frosting, held it out to him. He grunted with approval, eyes glinting, and took it in his mouth. Matt turned back to his form with a smile.

Their own wedding would be a tiny one at home, a few weeks, or maybe a month from now. They were still debating whether to have a justice of the peace or a rabbi preside. For Daniel, the main appeal of a Jewish wedding was the chance to break the glass at the end, to symbolize the shattering of their lives when Joel and Ilana died, and the continued shattering of Palestinian lives. But he was still trying to figure out whether he'd be satisfied with the one Jewish custom at the end of a secular service. They were also still thinking about whether to invite Malka and Yaakov, along with their parents and their best friends. Or whether to invite anybody but the kids and Yo-yo. They were trying to have a wedding and dodge the idea of a wedding.

"Here we go," Daniel murmured, his lips grazing Matt's ear. He laid his forefinger on the signature line, and signed.

ACKNOWLEDGMENTS

For various forms of vital and enlivening support, I am grateful to the National Endowment for the Arts, the Corporation of Yaddo, the MacDowell Colony, and the Dean of Faculty's office at Amherst College. Warm thanks to Ellen Geiger and David Highfill for their faith in the book, and for shepherding it through multiple revisions, each better than the last.

In Jerusalem, the David family—Paula, Uri, Maya, and Tamar—took loving care of me during my research trips, accompanying me to the sites of café bombings, watching sad documentaries with me, introducing me to various professionals, cooking delicious food. Gila Parizian and Ruth Matot talked with me about the various aspects of the work social workers do when there is a terrorist attack in Jerusalem; I thank them for their generosity with their time, and for their emotional energy.

Anston Bosman, Edmund Campos, Stephanie Grant, and the Sánchez-Eppler family made crucial interventions in the novel at various points, and I thank them and my colleagues in the English Department at Amherst College for their enthusiastic and challenging engagement with it. Alexander Chee, Amity Gaige, Daniel Hall, Amelie Hastie, Catherine Newman, Andrew Parker, Paul Statt, Susan Stinson, and Elizabeth Young provided encouragement, advice, and support; I cherish their collegiality and friendship. Amy Kaplan's friendship is one of my greatest pleasures, and her thoughtfulness and erudition about Israel/Palestine made her an essential interlocutor.

Elizabeth Garland is my first and last reader. I thank her for the rigor and conviction with which she approaches my work and for buoying me, always, with her outsized faith in my abilities. Abigail and Claire were born when I was midway through writing; they slowed the process down, but they also provided loads of new material, which is, of course, what having children is all about. I love them all dearly.

This book is dedicated to my mother, brother, and sister. We moved to Israel in 1976, and the consequences of that move continue to reverberate in our lives even though three of us have been back in the U.S. for decades. Thank you, Tony and Paula, for being my companions through our Israeli experiment and its aftermath, for the openness and humanity of your political views, for your equanimity about my plundering aspects of our lives for fiction, and for your love.

My mother died while this book was in proofs. She had already read it several times; it was on a topic dear to her heart, as her relation to Israel/Palestine had undergone a sea change late in her life. She read my work with wonder and appreciation. I love you, Mom, and I'll miss you.

About the book

Read on

P.S.

Insights,
Interviews
& More . . .

My Mother's Israel
An Essay by Judith Frank about Writing *All I Love and Know*

FIVE YEARS AFTER our father's death, when my sister Paula and I were seventeen and my brother Tony fourteen, my mother moved us to Israel. It was an unlikely move for a family like ours: we were secular Jews living in the Chicago suburbs—my siblings and I third-generation Americans—we had no relatives in Israel, and other than a trip my parents took there shortly after the Six-Day War, Israel had never played a big part in our lives. None of us but our mother wanted to move. My brother had no choice but to go; he was only fourteen. Nearly eighteen, my sister and I could have gone on to college in the United States, as had been our plan. But our father had committed suicide, after years of depression, when we were only twelve, and his death had frightened us, taught us the bitter lesson that loving us was not enough to tether anyone to this earth. We weren't ready to be so drastically separated from our remaining parent. We left the States with a sense of dread.

I'm writing this seven months after my mother's death. She struggled with health problems for much of her life, but had such a powerful life force that for months after her death, my siblings and I would hang out on the phone mumbling stupidly, "I can't believe she actually died." She died shortly before *All I Love and Know* was published, having read two drafts of it, having bragged about it to every Jew in the greater Chicago area. She would have loved the physical book, which is uncommonly gorgeous, and the reviews and responses. My own deep gratification about the publication of the novel I worked on for so many years has been laced with grief that she is not here to see it.

My siblings and I have our theories about what made the idea of *aliyah*—the Hebrew word for moving to Israel, literally, "rising"— so compelling and urgent for our mother. After five years of mourning the death of her husband, not to mention the years trying to keep a profoundly depressed man alive, she understandably needed to get away—from her grief, her parents, the community she and our father had lived in together. But I think there were other elements to her thinking, conscious or not. I think there might have been something there of the fantasy about Israel as a cure for the enervating effects of the Diaspora—the hope that, like the emaciated and victimized postwar European Jews who in Israel became robust tillers of the earth, my siblings and I, damaged by our father's death, would somehow be transformed. I also wonder, now that I'm at the age where many of my peers have young adult children who flit uneasily and sometimes obnoxiously in that space between dependence on their parents and leaving the nest, whether my mother had decided that having been left widowed with three grieving children at thirty-five, it was *her* turn to fledge. I was furious even then that at this moment when most American children move into the first stages of independence from home, my mother had decided to preempt us by leaving home instead, leaving more audaciously than we could even imagine, as if our dreams of a residential college were puny and uninspired. It felt like a huge ethical violation.

Israel was a time of depression for me, especially in the first years. I was a verbal kid with a highly developed sense of humor, coming from a place where I was deeply rooted and had many friends, now living in a culture where I didn't know a soul and didn't speak the language. I spent a year feeling literally struck dumb. I felt it to be a metaphysical dumbness, I felt I simply had nothing to say. Maybe I was dead like my father, I thought. Much later, I would explore that strange, deadened mourning state in my first novel, *Crybaby Butch*; indeed, mourning continued to preoccupy me in *All I Love and Know*. Only later would I think, Well geez, I didn't know the language! I was mourning my father, but I was also going through culture shock, a shock I could only fully register once it had abated.

I spent the first year with a group of young Americans in a Jewish Agency program in which we studied Hebrew and then became volunteers at a kibbutz in the Galilee. I hated the people in my group, I can now say definitively; but back then I was simply baffled and cowed by them. These decades later I can't get a handle on who they were, exactly. I think I must have been the youngest, and I think that at least some of them must have been sent to Israel by parents who hoped that a military society would shape them up. There was a worldly jadedness about the group, a kind of grossness that passed as humor, that depressed me. We volunteers lived on the edges of the kibbutz in primitive little shacks. Even forty years later, I can conjure the feeling of being a stranger on the margins of a community, and my intense loneliness and shame that it wasn't easier to make friends.

But I also have vivid, pleasurable sense memories from that time. We gathered in kibbutz-issued work clothes at chilly daybreak, where we were warmed by hot, sweet, milky coffee from canisters as the apple-picking trucks idled. Lined on benches on the beds of the trucks, we clattered on dirt roads and dipped below the fog line into the glistening, dewy apple orchards. Each apple picker drove a "michelson," a cherry picker, using the controls to swing ▶

My Mother's Israel *(continued)*

herself or himself into the branches of an apple tree. We were supposed to pick quickly and carefully. I remember lowering my load of apples with a crank, as slowly and gently as possible, into the large crates at the end of rows, and eating apples so gloriously crisp and flavorful they made me an apple snob for the rest of my life, the family member who leaves the soft or bland apples in the bowl for others to soldier their way through. I remember break time, when the American boys tossed bruised apples into the air like baseballs, and smashed them with sticks used as bats.

All the while I was learning Hebrew as though it would be my salvation. After apple season was over I got a job assisting in a children's house for seven-year-olds. Back then kibbutz children were still raised communally, eating, sleeping, and going to school under the care of a *metapelet*, a caretaker, in a house for their age group, visiting their parents during certain hours of the afternoon. It was there, conversing on a daily basis with children, that my Hebrew really got going. I remember their comical frustration at the limitations of my understanding; it was rejuvenating to be treated like a person worthy of frustration and teasing and instruction. Their parents started taking an interest in me, bringing me just a little closer into the life of the kibbutz. The other thing I remember from the children's house is changing thirteen comforter covers every Thursday, which makes me, to this day, as opinionated about how to put on a comforter cover as I am about apples.

When the program ended I went to university. There I was on slightly surer footing; I had always thrived in school. I studied English literature and made some friends, including an Israeli roommate, Rivka, who was to become my closest friend. Rivka was religious, a bright, pragmatic soul. I'd ask, "Can I scratch my back with a milk fork?" and she'd say "As long as you don't break the skin." I'd say, "I don't think I could ever be religious, because I don't believe in God," and she'd say, "Oh Judy, in Judaism the last thing you need to become religious is to believe in God." She loved language, and under her warm, engaged tutelage my Hebrew refined. We would sit talking in the bare, slummy dorm room we shared—in those days, at least, Israeli dorms were extremely rudimentary, as the country is small enough for most students to go home over weekends—eating bread and butter, olives, clementines, soft-boiled eggs out of the shell. I remember those foods, and Israeli folk dancing, which I loved, and working very hard at learning the lyrics to Israeli songs. That last effort made it into *All I Love and Know*, where I made Daniel the guitarist I've always wished I was, and had him learning chords on his guitar and poring over his Hebrew-English dictionary to learn the words.

As you can tell, visceral, sensory Israel stays with me still, almost forty years later: the feel of the language on my tongue, palate, and throat; the light and smells and food. And anyone who's lived in Jerusalem remembers in their very bones the slap of sandals on stone, pale pink light off the Jerusalem buildings, cool mountain air at night, the bark and cough and blasts of exhaust from Egged buses, the sight of people scurrying home carrying challot and cakes for Shabbat. When my brother fought in the Lebanon war, my family endured that quintessential Israeli experience—the one David Grossman's protagonist Ora famously flees to avoid in his devastating *To the End of the Land*—of dreading the unexpected ring of the doorbell. ("It's me, it's me!" people quickly called out at the door, over intercoms, so we wouldn't think they were the army notifiers.)

After six years in Israel, I came back to the United States for graduate school, going into the PhD program in English at Cornell. It was there that I made the intense friendships many Americans make in college, and I caught up on other things American kids learn in college, too, like feminism. I encountered gay people for the first time, which was a revelation. These days you can meet young gay people who lived in isolation in small towns all over the United States, and who nonetheless came out at fourteen and fifteen. They have the Internet, sure, but even so, their powerful senses of self are pretty remarkable. For me, it took seeing a vision of thriving gay life to be able to let myself know that I was gay, and to venture out of the closet.

In graduate school, I also started realizing there was a critique of Israel I hadn't had much access to. I can't quite specify how I slowly came to distrust the received narratives about Israel and the Palestinians, except to say that reading feminist and queer theory created in me the disposition to distrust *many* kinds of received narratives. I tried to express the connection between these things in *All I Love and Know*, in the flashback to Joel's Israeli wedding, where Daniel remembers feeling marginal and unseen because he is gay: "And his increasingly keen awareness of the way oppression operated by making certain things invisible to the eye—things like his own emotional life—began to bleed into distaste and anger about the things he himself couldn't see because Israel made them invisible."

My reading taught me that these things Daniel can't see, by which he means Palestinian life, are invisible by design; Israeli roads and architecture are designed to make big swaths of Jerusalem invisible to a Jewish person in a car or on a bus. I found it stunning that while I knew Israel so intimately in some ways, my geopolitical education couldn't begin until I'd left; for like many Diaspora Jews, I'd grown up with the idea that unless I lived in Israel, I couldn't understand it well enough to judge its policies. Writing *All I Love and Know* was partly a way to explore the question of what you can see from close up, and what you can see from far away. Matt, for example, has had a lifelong critique of the Israeli occupation, but talking to his beloved Shoshi, the social worker in charge of guiding the family through identifying Joel's body, challenges his perceptions: "But her struggle to help grieving and traumatized people . . . pressed upon his worldview and scrambled it a little." And Daniel has a painful argument with his parents about his brother Joel's failure as a television reporter to probe deeply enough into the injustices of the occupation and the treatment of Israeli Arabs, in which they call him arrogant for thinking he can know more about the situation than his brother did. ▶

My Mother's Israel (continued)

Roughly a decade later, my mother, who had had a thriving career in Jerusalem as a social worker and a university lecturer, started going through the same process. My sister Paula, who met and married an Israeli man, ended up the only one of us who stayed. My mother and brother returned, one by one, to the Chicago area in the nineties, and in the last decade or so of her life, my mother belonged to Jewish Reconstructionist Congregation in Evanston, Illinois. An expert in early childhood development, she worked as a consultant for the synagogue's nursery school; for several years, baffled and alienated the entire time by the mysterious language of management and bureaucracy, she served on the JRC board. JRC was the center of her social and professional life. She also befriended JRC's rabbi, Brant Rosen. While my siblings and I initially joked that Brant was "the good son," her relationship with him came to take on the intense and combative character of many of her close relationships. And it was with Brant, who is an activist for justice for Palestinians, that my mother's own geopolitical education about Israel took root.

A turning point came for her in 2010, when Rabbi Brant took a delegation of JRC members to the West Bank and East Jerusalem, where they met Palestinian activists and did homestays at Palestinian refugee camps. My mother's health was poor at the time, and she made the trip in a wheelchair, but the experience was transformative for her. Upon their return, she, Brant, and another member of the delegation were interviewed on *Worldview*, on WBEZ, Chicago Public Radio. The podcast of that interview is the place where I can go to hear my mother's voice again. She says of the years she lived in Israel, "The whole time I lived there I paid no attention to the fact that there was an issue here. . . . If I ever had a conversation with a Palestinian it was to buy something. And when I came back I . . . slowly became more aware. I'm very upset with myself. I felt that I had to go back to see what's going on." The families she met were warm and loving, she said. "These people were so like Jews! . . . They could have been my family." She also said something that the radio host described as "eye-popping": "When one country is oppressed and occupied by another, there's only one side to the story, and that's the story of the oppressed. I'm not wiping out any history, I just think that in order to be able to talk about this history, you have to have people who are free to talk about it with you."

My mother died on a bitterly cold day in February 2014. That winter was a particularly hard one in Chicago; as I flew back and forth during her last months, Lake Michigan, I could see from the air, was almost frozen over, lunar and sublime. The roof of my mother's house had such enormous ice dams, we had to have roofers come out so we could wrench open the front door for the shiva, and as we watched chunks of ice and snow sail down I kept thinking that ice had covered her house because her soul had left it. Brant officiated at her funeral—as I write I can conjure him standing before me, gently tearing the black mourning ribbon on my jacket—and his friendship to me and my siblings is something we'll never forget; we felt so lucky to have a rabbi who knew and got our mother, who both loved her and was as irreverent about her as we were.

Three months later, we sold our mother's house, and experienced that new wave of loss, the loss of the family gathering place. Six months later, during the Israeli attack on Gaza, Brant Rosen resigned as rabbi of JRC, feeling that his activism was putting untenable pressures on both him and the congregation. He had never been my rabbi, but his departure felt like yet another loss of home.

For months after she died, my siblings and I were grateful and relieved that our mother had died the death she'd wished for. She wasn't in pain; she didn't linger in dementia or disability; the bodily indignities she suffered were grueling, but manageable. In her last months she was even able to achieve a measure of the tranquility that had eluded her until then. Because she was a chronically ill person, we'd been anxious for a long time about how our mother would die. And now we knew. And now that the ending has occurred, I can look back and see the entire shape of her life. I do so with a novelist's eye, searching out event, causality, proportion, irony. It's an amazing story. My mother was galling and formidable and difficult. She was also astonishingly perceptive and open-minded and capable of change. I will never write her story as it occurred, because I'm a novelist, not a biographer or a memoirist. But of course she's in all of my stories, including this one. ◠◡

The podcast of the interview with Marjorie Frank, Brant Rosen, and Michael Deheeger: http://www.wbez.org/episode-segments/evanston-rabbi-takes -congregation-west-bank-and-east-jerusalem

Questions for Discussion

1. The first forty-five pages of *All I Love and Know* are narrated from Matt's point of view. Why might Frank have chosen him as the initial point-of-view character in this novel? How does Matt's outsider status— as a young gay man, as a non-Jew, as "the goyfriend"—put him in an awkward or advantageous position as Daniel's partner in this crisis? What about as a parent to Noam and Gal?

2. In what ways is *All I Love and Know* about the experience of being a twin? What does being a twin mean to Daniel, and how does it affect his thinking about rebuilding his life after Joel's death? We're told that he and Joel "invented the semifacetious idea of *twinsism*: the act of stereotyping or fetishizing twins." What does that running joke tell us about their feelings about twinship?

3. *All I Love and Know* can be read as a novel about parenting and being parented: as these gay men become sudden parents, they are thrust into contact with their own parents and confront their feelings about being their parents' children. What are the aspects of parenting that the novel asks you to think about? What do you think Daniel and Matt's relative strengths are as parents to Gal and Noam?

4. Matt moved to Northampton after his best friend Jay died of AIDS. How does Jay's death change the way he handles this new crisis? How does this AIDS story relate to the central narrative of terrorism and trauma? What is at stake in the fight Matt and Daniel have over the relative "innocence" of Jay's and Joel's deaths?

5. Why do you think Frank decided to make Malka and Yaakov Holocaust survivors?

What does their experience add to the novel's story of survival? At the military cemetery, Malka surprises Daniel by comparing victims of terror to Holocaust survivors and claims that Israelis despise them both. What is the connection, in her mind? Does her bitterness make you think differently about her?

6. Israel is very important to many American Jews, and it appeals to the Rosen sons in different ways. What does Israeli culture have to offer Daniel and Joel as young men from an affluent Jewish-American family?

7. In a central event of the novel, talking to a reporter, Daniel says of the terrorist who killed his brother, ". . . I can understand trying to violently place yourself within the Israelis' field of vision, in a way they can't ignore. I don't condone it, but I do understand it." He receives hate mail in response, and wonders whether he has "breached an important code of conduct, or failed at some response crucial to the common human enterprise." What do you make of Daniel's response to the terrorist attack? Is he doing something wrong? Does the novel make you think any differently about terrorism?

8. Daniel has a left-of-center position about the Israeli occupation. From what kinds of sources does he get his information? What factors from his personal life contribute to the way he feels about Israel's policies? And conversely, how does his political position impact or impede his mourning process? What do you think the novel is trying to say about the tension between the personal and the political?

9. Daniel grieves throughout the novel, sometimes in alienating ways. He believes Matt and his friends are pressuring him for "grieving wrong," and feels they're trying to push him into therapy. Matt believes that Daniel has become "frozen" and "different." What are the factors that have made Daniel's process especially grueling? How did you respond to the ways in which he becomes "frozen"?

10. Does Gal get lost accidentally or on purpose in the Jerusalem *shuk*? What kind of internal drama is being enacted as she races away from the suspicious box, feeling her parents at her heels? What kind of figure is Chezzi the fishmonger? What does this frightening event express about Gal's relationship with Daniel?

11. The idea of gay marriage comes up in this story, and it takes one character some time to warm to the idea. In this era of victory for marriage equality in many U.S. states, why do you think some gay and lesbian people might be ambivalent about getting married?

What I Was Reading While I Was Writing *All I Love and Know*

Children of the Holocaust:
Conversations with Sons and Daughters
of Survivors
by Helen Epstein

Hearing the stories of children of Holocaust survivors helped me imagine the silences that structured the lives of Ilana and her parents.

Independence Park:
The Lives of Gay Men in Israel
by Amir Fink and Jacob Press

Ethnography is one of the most useful ways I learn to imagine how people experience their lives.

To the End of the Land
by David Grossman

This is a searing novel about loss, war, and parenting, by one of Israel's best writers and its moral conscience.

My Happiness Bears No Relation to Happiness:
A Poet's life in the Palestinian Century
by Adina Hoffman

I learned a lot about Palestinian village life from this biography, which also has an unforgettable description of the arrival of Israeli forces in 1948, and the expulsion of a community from its village.

Losing a Parent to Death in the Early Years:
Guidelines for the Treatment of Traumatic
Bereavement in Infancy and Early Childhood
by Alicia F. Lieberman

This book, by a leading expert in early childhood trauma, helped me grasp the experience of Gal and Noam.

Palestine Inside Out:
An Everyday Occupation
by Saree Makdisi

This book taught me about the banal, everyday hurdles that Palestinian people experience as they try to navigate the bureaucracy of the occupation.

A Tale of Love and Darkness
by Amos Oz

Anyone attempting to write well about Jerusalem should read Oz's enchanting description of his childhood there during the 1940s and 1950s.

The Question of Zion
by Jacqueline Rose

I learned from this book that there was a dissenting strand of Zionism that warned from the start about the ethics and possible consequences of displacing the Arab population in Palestine.

Wrestling in the Daylight:
A Rabbi's Path to Palestinian Solidarity
by Brant Rosen

This is a collection of blog posts by a peace activist and former rabbi at a Jewish Reconstructionist Congregation in Evanston, Illinois; I went often to the blog for incisive writing on everything from checkpoints to biblical *parashot*.

The Counterlife
by Philip Roth

Roth's novel is a noisy, engaging, and provocative meditation on Israel and American Jewish masculinity.

The Lemon Tree:
An Arab, a Jew, and the Heart of the Middle East
by Sandy Tolan

A story about what happens when a young Palestinian man returns to the house his family had lived in before their expulsion in 1948, and the fraught, unlikely friendship he strikes up ▶

What I Was Reading While I Was Writing
All I Love and Know (continued)

with the nineteen-year-old Israeli college
student whose family has lived there since.

Hollow Land:
Israel's Architecture of Occupation
by Eyal Weizman

It's from this book, by an Israeli professor of
architecture, that I took the material about
Jerusalem stone that appears in a conversation at
the shiva for Joel and Ilana. ❧

Discover great authors,
exclusive offers, and more
at hc.com.